Cambridge studies in sociology 10

THE BLUE-COATED WORKER

A sociological study of police unionism

This series is published under the auspices of the Committee of Management of the Department of Applied Economics, University of Cambridge

EDITORS

R. M. Blackburn, Senior Research Officer, Department of Applied Economics, Cambridge University

John H. Goldthorpe, Official Fellow of Nuffield College, Oxford University

ADVISORY COMMITTEE

J. A. Banks, Professor of Sociology, Leicester University

A. Giddens, University Lecturer in Sociology and Fellow and Director of Studies in Social Sciences, King's College, Cambridge University

J. C. Mitchell, Official Fellow of Nuffield College, Oxford University

K. Prandy, Senior Research Officer in Applied Economics and Fellow and Director of Studies in Social Sciences, Fitzwilliam College, Cambridge University

Cambridge studies in sociology

1 *The affluent worker: industrial attitudes and behaviour* by John H. Goldthorpe, David Lockwood, Frank Bechhofer and Jennifer Platt

2 *The affluent worker: political attitudes and behaviour* by John H. Goldthorpe, David Lockwood, Frank Bechhofer and Jennifer Platt

3 *The affluent worker in the class structure* by John H. Goldthorpe, David Lockwood, Frank Bechhofer and Jennifer Platt

4 *Men in mid-career: a study of British managers and technical specialists* by Cyril Sofer

5 *Family structure in nineteenth-century Lancashire* by Michael Anderson

6 *Workers on the move: the sociology of relocation* by Michael Mann

7 *The aristocracy of labor* by Gavin Mackenzie

8 *Elites and power in British society* edited by Philip Stanworth and Anthony Giddens

9 *In search of the new working class: automation and social integration with the capitalist enterprise* by Duncan Gallie

Cambridge papers in sociology

1 *Size of industrial organisation and worker behaviour* by Geoffrey K. Ingham

2 *Workers' attitudes and technology* by D. Wedderburn and R. Crompton

3 *Perceptions of work: variations within a factory* by H. Beynon and R. M. Blackburn

4 *Community and occupation: an explanation of work-leisure relationships* by Graeme Salaman

5 *Fertility and deprivation: a study of differential fertility amongst working-class families in Aberdeen* by Janet Askham

THE BLUE-COATED WORKER

A sociological study of police unionism

ROBERT REINER

Lecturer in Sociology, University of Bristol

CAMBRIDGE UNIVERSITY PRESS

CAMBRIDGE

LONDON · NEW YORK · MELBOURNE

Published by the Syndics of the Cambridge University Press
The Pitt Building, Trumpington Street, Cambridge CB2 1RP
Bentley House, 200 Euston Road, London NW1 2DB
32 East 57th Street, New York, NY 10022, USA
296 Beaconsfield Parade, Middle Park, Melbourne 3206, Australia

© Cambridge University Press 1978

First published 1978

Printed in Great Britain by
Western Printing Services Ltd, Bristol

Library of Congress cataloguing in publication data
Reiner, Robert, 1946–
The blue-coated worker.
(Cambridge studies in sociology; 10)
Bibliography: p.
Includes index.
1. Trade unions – Police – Great Britain. 2. Police
– Great Britain – Attitudes. 3. Police – Great Britain.
I. Title
HV8195.A2R44   331.88'11'36320941   77–85695
ISBN 0 521 21889 6 Hardback
ISBN 0 521 29482 7 Paperback

In memory of my mother, and with love
to my father and Miki

Contents

Preface ix

Acknowledgements xi

PART ONE: INTRODUCTION AND HISTORICAL
BACKGROUND

1 Introduction to the study of police unionism   3
   Arguments about police unionism   3
   Methodology of the research   9
   Outline of the book   17

2 The history and structure of the Police Federation   19
   The history of the Police Federation   19
   The structure of the Police Federation   49
   Summary   53

PART TWO: POLICE ATTITUDES TO UNIONISM

3 Policemen's evaluation of the Federation   57

4 Evaluation of specific Federation activities   65
   Pay negotiations   65
   Conditions of service   68
   Influencing the public image of the police   73
   Communications within the police force   74
   Influencing legislation   76
   The welfare of policemen   81
   Efficiency of the force   82
   Assisting in cases of discipline charges   88
   Summary   92

5 Policemen's desire for unionism   94

6 The goals and institutionalisation of representation   114

Contents

7 The Federationists and the men   123

8 Attitudes to unionism outside the force   138

PART THREE: THE POLICE AS AN OCCUPATION

9 The background and initial orientation of policemen   149

Who are the police?   149

Reasons for joining the police force   157

10 Orientation to work   168

Satisfaction with police work   171

Relationships between the ranks   184

Personal aspirations and the promotion system   194

Police professionalisation   202

Police work and private life   208

The nature of the police role   213

11 Police and outside society   219

12 Understanding police unionism: a typology   228

PART FOUR: CONCLUSIONS

13 Conclusions and implications of the study   257

POSTSCRIPT AND APPENDIXES

Postscript: The Scarborough 'Events' 24–6 May 1977   273

Appendix 1: The introductory letter   277

Appendix 2: The interview schedule: questionnaire on police attitudes towards the Federation   278

Appendix 3: The prohibited questions   283

Bibliography   284

Index   289

Preface

The police occupy a contradictory position in the class structure. Their role in maintaining a particular economic and political system normally encourages a conservative social ideology, but at the same time they are wage-earners, and subjected to a regime of discipline and control in which they have little say. This has driven the police in most Western countries to create organisations of a union-like character to represent their interests. The way that these contradictions manifest themselves in the consciousness of policemen is the focus of this book. It is largely based on an intensive survey of police attitudes to work and unionism, carried out in 1973–4. But it is a central argument that 'attitudes' are not a fixed entity to be discovered by social research. Consciousness relates to specific historical situations and must be understood in relation to these. A sensitivity to the contradictions and tensions expressed in thought means that changes can be understood as a response to new circumstances, perceived through the spectacles of existing orientations. The historical development of police unionisation in Britain is traced in order to locate the research in its proper context, and subsequent events are outlined. Police representative organisation is currently in a considerable state of flux, but an understanding of the road to the present situation is necessary to make any sense of future changes.

Robert Reiner,
Bristol University, May 1977

Acknowledgements

Professor Michael Banton supervised the Ph.D. thesis on which this book is based, and without his efforts it would never have got off the ground. My colleagues, Dr Miriam David (my wife), and Theo Nichols painstakingly read and commented on the script. My friends Dalbir Singh, Dorothy Hahn, Allen Maunders, Vernon Reynolds, Phil Stanworth, Chris Husbands, Geoff and Sandy Millerson and all the other Bristol sociologists provided stimulating conversation and ideas at various points. Professors Martin Albrow and Derek McClintock, who examined my thesis, made many valuable suggestions on editing it for publication, as did John Goldthorpe. I am most indebted to all the above for their invaluable help. My late mother, who sadly passed away during the final stages of the fieldwork, provided constant encouragement and inspiration. My father and sister were always supportive when the going got rough (all the time). The S.S.R.C. provided a grant towards the cost of transcription. The officials of the local Federation branch board were of enormous help, in particular Fred Durbin, Arthur Canning, Ernie Watts, Pete Roberts and Bob Brown. I must profusely thank all the respondents for their warm co-operation. Susan Allen-Mills and Elizabeth Wetton of the Cambridge University Press were most helpful in advising on editing and preparing the manuscript. Last but not least, Mrs Doris Macey has my gratitude for the speed and efficiency with which she has typed the work.

PART ONE

Introduction and historical background

I

Introduction to the study of police unionism

Arguments about police unionism

This study explores policemen's attitudes to work and, more particularly, towards trade union representation. It is related to two traditions of sociological research. One is the emerging area of the sociology of the police. At the same time, as a study of work attitudes and trade union attachment, it bears upon the sociology of work and occupations. This particular meeting point of interests has never previously been given serious attention. Studies of the police have hitherto, perhaps understandably, concentrated primarily on problematics of a broadly criminological kind. The growing sociological attention paid to the police in recent years has various sources, but it has been motivated mainly by a concern about the *output* of police work.

One stimulus was that redirection of focus in research and theorising on crime and deviance which became fashionable in the 1960s, and can rather loosely be referred to as the 'labelling' perspective. (Characteristic examples would be Becker 1963 and Lemert 1967.) This concentrated attention on the process of social control, but surprisingly generated little empirical work on the police. (Taylor *et al.* 1973: chapter 5 provides a useful critique.) Another source of interest has been the implications of the fact that policemen do not automatically translate enacted law into enforcement operations, but exercise considerable discretion. (The way in which this has inspired research is elaborated in Lambert 1969 and Cain 1973: 14.) A civil libertarian concern about police deviation from the model of due process of law suggested by democratic theory has motivated research, especially in the U.S.A. Westley's pioneering study in the late 1940s, for example, was especially concerned with the phenomenon of police 'brutality' (Westley 1970). Skolnick's major work was directed at understanding the pressures on policemen to violate legal restrictions on how they collected evidence and apprehended deviants (Skolnick 1966). With the emergence of collective protest in the 1960s, involving frequent instances of confrontation between police and demonstrators in the civil rights, student and anti-war movements, much attention was paid to the problems of police control of crowds (Skolnick 1969). In Britain there have been valuable sociological analyses of the nature and determinants of the police role (Banton 1964; Cain 1973). But none has examined the character of the policeman's economic and employment situation, nor the manner in which he attempts to pursue his interests as a worker together with his colleagues.

The collective organisation of policemen to advance their interests as employees is becoming of great importance. The economic and social tensions of recent years have made policemen increasingly militant, in both Britain and the United States. Militancy has been aimed at influencing not only pay but also social policies affecting the work situation. This highlights a gap in the previous police literature, namely an analysis of the policeman from the perspective of his situation as an employee, which generates pressures that can conflict with the demands of his role as a law enforcer and upholder of the social order.

This perspective raises issues of a kind normally considered within the sociology of work and industry, although students of occupations and unions have tended to overlook the policeman. It can be suggested that this is due to certain paradoxes of the policeman's market and social situation. In many respects the policeman is subject to the same pressures towards unionisation as other white-collar workers. He is a salaried employee in a bureaucratically structured organisation, with an interest in defending his economic rewards, status and work conditions. White-collar workers have been traditionally noted for their comparative recalcitrance to trade union organisation, and the sources of this have been much discussed. There have also been analyses of the recent growth in white-collar unionisation and militancy (for example, Lockwood 1958; R. M. Blackburn 1967; Prandy 1965; Bain *et al.* 1973). Various factors tend to separate policemen from the trade union movement to an even greater extent than is the case with white-collar workers in general. These give his collective organisation a peculiar character, which will be analysed in subsequent chapters. The determinants of the policeman's economic situation are to an extent diametrically opposed to those for other workers. This is because, when governments attempt to implement policies of wage restraint against union opposition, the police assume a peculiar importance due to their role in situations of industrial conflict. Thus they will have to be treated as a most 'special case' in pay negotiations. Furthermore, their work situation, in particular when it involves confrontations with trade unionists at pickets, inclines them towards a conservative world-view and a sense of alienation from the labour movement. This conflicts with pressure towards forms of collective organisation of a more or less unionate nature, deriving from their *own* concerns as employees.

This central tension in police work has largely escaped attention. Many studies have shown how the policeman enforces laws, maintains order, and provides various services. But they have ignored the fact that he is at the same time an employee, seeking to earn a living, and concerned with the conditions in which he does this. It is true that policemen are, compared to many other workers, relatively non-instrumental in their attitudes to work. But while he may be *comparatively* less concerned about extrinsic rewards, the policeman is still worried about his standard of living and goes to work to earn a wage. *All* work is at some level instrumentally motivated, even if the primacy of financial or other considerations in choosing a job may vary.

Furthermore, the social origins of policemen are mainly working-class. This might be expected *a priori* to incline them to sympathise with the labour movement. (Drawing policemen from working-class backgrounds was an explicit policy in the establishment of 'professional' police forces, designed to remove the task of controlling dissent from the middle and upper classes themselves, and hence deflecting popular resentment. See Silver 1967: 12.)

When they have experienced pressure on their economic and other interests, policemen have (in all liberal–democratic societies) developed collective means of defence, in the form of police unionism. At the same time, these organisational efforts have met considerable resistance. The view that the police force is a unique work organisation, in which unionism is completely inappropriate, has often been put forward. Trade unions for the police have been legally prohibited to a greater extent than for any other occupation, excluding the military.

This is usually justified in terms of the supposedly disastrous consequences to the public of police industrial action. For example, an article in the F.B.I. Law Enforcement Bulletin (1967) declared: 'They have no right to strike. Policemen are and must remain separated from the rest of us by an obligation that's bigger than all our grievances...Because they alone stand guard at the upstairs door of Hell.'

Certainly, as the Liverpool police strike of 1919 described in chapter 2 (and various North American incidents such as the strikes in Boston, 1919, and Montreal, 1969, discussed in Burpo 1971: 3–4, 13–14, 79–80) illustrate, such occurrences *can* result in considerable damage to people and property. But other work stoppages by policemen, for example, the London strikes of 1918–19 described in chapter 2 (as well as some American ones such as Detroit, 1967, and Vallejo, California, 1969, and other cases recounted in Bopp 1971: section III), seem to have passed off with no apparent harm. The consequences of industrial action by policemen appear to depend on various attendant circumstances, such as the character of the population policed, the timing of the action, the preparedness of the authorities, and the availability of suitable alternative forces as replacements. The horrific results predicted by opponents of police unionisation are by no means the usual pattern. On the other hand, strikes by firemen, ambulance-drivers, power-workers, doctors or other medical workers could result in as much destruction of life and property. Nonetheless, no other civilian occupation has been subject to so complete an outlawing of union activity. It seems that opposition to police unionism derives more from a military model of the appropriate form of police organisation than concern about public safety.

Different conceptions of the police role, derived from conflicting theories of the nature of law and society, imply different reactions to the issue of police unionism. Conservative, liberal and radical positions on the police can be distinguished, with varying stances on the appropriate form of representation of policemen's interests. (For an account of these perspectives on law and its enforcement see Taylor *et al.* 1975: 20–8.)

The *conservative* perspective regards a military model as the most suitable for the police. This is hardly surprising in view of the 'war against crime' imagery utilised by conservatives. The police are to be organised in a strict hierarchy of authority in which subordinate ranks are expected to execute dutifully and unquestioningly the decisions and instructions of their superiors. This is especially important on those occasions when the police act in a quasi-military capacity as a tightly co-ordinated body, such as in crowd control situations. It is also vital in ordinary patrol work, especially because of the relatively autonomous and unobserved (by organisational supervisors) position of the policeman out on the street. Inculcating strict notions of obedience to orders, by drill and discipline within the stations, is a means of ensuring that the constable will carry out his duties in the prescribed fashion when not under immediate supervision. Even more important, a crucial aspect of the police contribution to maintaining order is their *example*. Policemen in uniform patrolling the street are a symbol of authority, and it is essential that their internal organisation and general demeanour reflect the desired pattern for society as a whole, a smoothly operating, hierarchically structured system of co-operating units. Within this perspective, independent organisation by rank-and-file policemen, and certainly industrial action, is uniquely heinous, not so much because of any immediate consequences for public safety, but because it is a contradiction of the basic function and principle of the police force. If the keepers of order do not keep their own house in order, this undermines their role in the most fundamental way. A police withdrawal of labour is not a strike but a mutiny. It must be absolutely ruled out. The police, like the military, cannot have the rights of other citizens. It is essential that they subordinate their own interests and inclinations to the demands and decisions of their superiors. Of course, the wise commanding officer will be most concerned about the morale, and hence welfare, of his troops. He will seek to be informed of their feelings and needs. But this cannot be forced on him by collective organisation by the men. The proper channel for the communication of views is the established chain of command. Those at the bottom must obey and implement the decisions of those at the top, who in return will attempt to safeguard their men's welfare, in so far as compatible with the exigencies of the work (I.A.C.P. 1958: 3; Chapman 1962: 40). Thus, from the conservative perspective, a tightly disciplined, militaristic police force is the best, both in terms of efficiency in the field and as a model of order for society. Policemen generally share a conservative perspective, and such views about the internal organisation of police forces are echoed by many policemen themselves, as subsequent chapters will show.

From a *liberal* social perspective, police unionism is regarded with ambivalence. Some liberal writers have seen unionism as a civil right not to be denied policemen. Others have regarded it as a potential source of 'democratisation' of police forces. The view that union membership is a civil right from which policemen ought not be excluded is a clear premise of the most comprehensive study of American police unionism (Juris & Feuille 1973: xii).

The most explicit advocate of police unionism as a source of democratisation of police forces is Berkley. He compares the organisation of European and American police forces to discover why the former approximate more closely to his ideal of the 'democratic policeman...wielding an influence born of ability and humanity rather than of weapons and power' (1969: 212). One source of this, he argues, is the greater degree of institutionalisation of police unionism in Europe (46–7).

Berkley attempts to substantiate the point by reviewing the operation of European police unions. He documents the links between many of these and Social Democratic movements. He also seeks to show that they have tended to support liberal penal and social policies. The implication is that the 'radical right' stance of grass-roots American police associations derives from their lack of institutionalisation.

While his argument may have some validity in relation to Scandinavia, he considerably oversimplifies matters with regard to Britain. His information on the Federation seems to come from one or two leading officials noted for their liberal views. As the discussion in chapter 7 on the activists will indicate, Federation work does seem to attract men with trade union sympathies and, in this respect at least, more liberal leanings than most members (though the ambiguities of this liberalism will be shown). But whatever their private principles, representatives have endeavoured to put forward the illiberal views of members on such issues as capital punishment. The Federation has recently initiated a 'law and order' campaign to reverse what it describes as a liberal trend in penal policy and society. Thus in recent years, the Federation, like American police associations, has *not* been a force for democratisation in Berkley's sense.

This illustrates the reasons for the ambivalence in liberal opinion about police unionism. Many liberals have been dismayed by the current attitudes and activities of rank-and-file policemen and their representatives in the U.S.A. and Britain. Skolnick, for example, is clearly disturbed by the political implications of police association attempts to influence policy in a right-wing direction. He documents the growing militancy and politicisation of a 'radical-right' kind in the police, building upon the framework of representative associations founded for 'bread-and-butter' pursuits (Skolnick 1969: 268–92). He argues that the police must abide by the tradition of non-involvement in politics and accept limits on their rights. Their function is to carry out policies enunciated by their commanders, but ultimately deriving from the will of the people as expressed in the legislature. The role of the police in a democratic society places special limits on police activism. To Skolnick, the crucial issue is a reassertion of civilian control and a curbing of police power. This is anathema to most rank-and-file policemen and their representatives, as he documents in his account of police opposition to Civilian Review Boards. In Skolnick's view police union activity is a threat to democratic society.

Radical thought has not paid much attention to the issue of internal police organisation. Some socialist writers have argued that the legally enforced separation of the police force from the labour movement is a factor ensuring the conservative tendencies of policemen and their hostility to trade unions, manifested, it is alleged, in their handling of industrial disputes and political protests. In the next chapter it will be seen that, during the development of police unionism before 1919, some elements in the trade unions and Labour Party placed much store by the possibilities of incorporating the police in the labour movement. Later socialists have also seen the prohibition of police unionism as a device for guaranteeing police support of the status quo (Bowes 1966: 231; Cliff 1975: 102; *Labour Research* 1975: 31; Bunyan 1976: 35, 68–9).

Some argue that the 'objectively' working-class position of policemen, expressed in unionism, offers some leverage for change within police forces. A recent radical analysis of the American police stresses

the contradictory nature of policing under capitalism. Although the police are. . . a repressive institution that operates to contain the poor and the powerless, they are also themselves exploited, not only by miserable working conditions and social isolation but also as instruments of laws and policies which they neither control nor benefit from. The police protect private property but do not own it; as guardians of the peace, they defend government policies of imperialism and racism but do not derive any significant profit from them; and in their repression of popular movements, the police legitimise a political order, which they did not create. Control of the police, therefore, should take into account their dual role as both victimisers and victims, and we should examine possibilities for organising police resentment into political action. (Centre for Research on Criminal Justice 1975:144)

However, after reviewing the recent resurgence of police unionism out of the doldrums of previous decades, it stresses the right-wing character of its politicisation. 'If anything, police organisations have strengthened right-wing and para-military tendencies within police departments' (146). Therefore the prospects are 'uncertain. . .we should not underestimate the problems and setbacks. . .But the potential for progressive organising should not be completely discounted' (147–8).

The concern of the present research was to explore the views of rank-and-file policemen themselves on these issues. The previously cited discussions of the appropriate form of representation of policemen's interests have taken place in almost complete ignorance of the feelings of the men themselves. The focus of this study is an exploration of what might be called the 'trade union consciousness' of policemen. I am not using the term in its vulgar Marxist sense, which regards it as a form of 'false consciousness' (see Hyman 1971; Mann 1973). I adopt the stance recommended by Lockwood in his study of the class consciousness of the clerk.

To study the class consciousness of the clerk is to study the factors affecting his sense of identification with, or alienation from, the working class. More precisely, such a study should aim at an understanding of the relationship of the black-coated worker to the trade union movement, the main vehicle of working-class consciousness. . . If then we are to make an empirical investigation of the class consciousness of the black-coated worker it is best to postpone judgement on the question of 'false' class consciousness. . . (Lockwood 1958: 13–15).

In the same way, this study of the trade union consciousness of the 'blue-coated worker' is concerned to discover the actual consciousness of policemen, and relate this to their situation as a way of making sense of it, rather than seeing it as 'false' by some *a priori* criterion. The previously cited radical analyses of the policeman imply that because he is divorced from ownership and control of the means of production and, as a result, forced to sell his labour power to earn a living, he is objectively 'proletarian'. Potentially, therefore, he is part of the labour movement, but in so far as he does not identify or organise with it, he is 'falsely conscious'. This position is rejected here. The aim is to explore the extent to which policemen feel they need and wish to have trade union representation to protect and advance their interests. This can vary both between individuals, and in the degree to which the person wants an organisation which is more or less 'unionate'. (For the definition of this term see R. M. Blackburn 1967: 18.) This will be related to the men's conception of the police force as a work organisation, their orientation to work and its part in their lives and how they see the police role in society.

Methodology of the research

This study has been guided by Weber's tenet that understanding has to be both 'causally adequate' and 'adequate at the level of meaning' (Weber 1964: 99–100). Attempting to reconcile these two criteria led me to reject various possible approaches. One strategy would have been to use a precoded, fixed-choice questionnaire on a large sample of policemen. This could have generated a set of precise statistical relationships between various attitudes to unionism and other aspects of the policeman's work. But this would not establish that the relationships were sociologically meaningful. It would have yielded no insight into the process by which any relationship is generated, or the way that the men interpreted the world.

However, to have been solely concerned with the exploration of the consciousness of a group of individuals would have meant losing sight of the requirement of 'causal adequacy'. The deepest insight into the complex views of some men could have been obtained by intensive interviewing, or better yet, working with them as a participant-observer. But I would have had no means of knowing how those men who were concentrated upon related to the general pattern for all policemen, or any means of testing the insights gained into their subjective world-views.

I therefore decided to try and optimise the balance between range of coverage and statistical generalisation, on the one hand, and gaining insight into the policemen's own subjective view of the world, on the other. I tried to achieve this by drawing a representative sample of a police force, and interviewing them in a way that would combine some standardisation of questions to permit comparison, but also allow men to express their reasoning as completely as possible, so that one knew what the categories meant to *them*. This was combined with a more intensive study of the Federation activists themselves.

My initial contact with the Federation was in 1970 with the then chairman of the Joint Central Committee, and with the local Branch office in a provincial city force. The study was concentrated in one large city. I would argue that for various reasons the picture given would be fairly typical of other city forces. Firstly, the demographic material corresponds with other research in city forces (e.g. Cain 1973); secondly, whenever questions were asked which were comparable to the national *Man-Management Survey*, the results are in line with theirs for city forces (Home Office: 1970); and thirdly, representatives from other forces have claimed that the conclusions are similar to what they would expect. However, it is likely that the situation in county forces, or the Metropolitan, which have a somewhat different structure and setting, would be different. This would make a useful subject for further study. It was generally believed that city force activists were more militant and pro-union in their outlook than either county men or the national officials.

In 1971 the local Federationists arranged for me to do twelve pilot interviews. On the basis of this I constructed a final questionnaire, and submitted this to the Chief Constable with a request to interview a repre-. sentative sample of the men. He in turn sent it to the police department in the Home Office for their advice on the matter. In April 1972 I attended an interview at the Home Office. Present were two senior Home Office officials, a Scotland Yard Assistant-Commissioner, and the local Chief Constable. There was some concern expressed about the confidentiality of the results, and the danger of some of them being irresponsibly broadcast by the press. It would be unpleasant to read a headline saying 'x% of the force want the right to strike'. It was also pointed out that, as the Home Office was absolutely opposed to granting the Federation any of the powers of an ordinary trade union, there was no practical policy purpose in asking the men for their attitudes. In the Home Office view, the Federation was perfectly adequate, so they were not interested in the study. However, there was no objection in principle, apart from the practical problem of the loss of police time involved in men being interviewed during duty-hours. Eventually the Chief Constable allowed me to do a survey of not more than about 150 men.

While there was no objection to the survey in general, the raising of questions about political attitudes, or about perceptions of the class structure, was completely ruled out. It was felt this would challenge the traditional notion that the British police were outside any form of politics. With regard to the questions on class structure it was believed that 'the ordinary man is a bit dim sometimes – he wouldn't see the point'. Final consent to the research was withheld pending the views of the national Federation, and my deleting the questions to which opposition was made. I saw the Joint Central Committee secretary on 21 April 1972, to obtain his permission, which was forthcoming. The questionnaire was then revised, omitting the political and class questions, and resubmitted to the Home Office. (The questionnaire is shown in Appendix 2. The prohibited questions are given in Appendix 3.)

On 22 August 1972 I obtained written permission from the Home Office to proceed with the revised questionnaire. It was reiterated that the political and class perception questions were, '*not* acceptable, for the reasons we have discussed, and this view is shared by the Police Federation, and, we understand, by the local Branch Board. This sheet should not therefore form part of the research project.' It was stressed that 'the co-operation of individual police officers in this project is on a purely voluntary basis, and no doubt you will ensure that all officers are made aware of this'. It was also pointed out that 'the availability of police officers for interviewing' was at the Chief Constable's discretion.

I spent September 1972 in the force Research and Planning Department drawing up the sample. The sampling frame used was a list of the whole force, arranged by rank and division. It provided details of their age and length of service, as well as dates of promotions in the case of supervisors. The list was not random, but neither did it follow any clear system, such as alphabetical order. Within each division and rank the men were ordered by their police numbers. This was not a systematic ordering.

Men were continuously moving in and out of positions because of retirement, promotion, transfer and recruiting. Men who joined a division were allocated a number that had been vacated. After many years of this the ordering was quite unsystematic. There seemed to be no bunching of men of similar ages or lengths of service at any points.

At that time there were 1112 officers in the federated ranks of the force. These broke down in terms of age, division and rank as in Table 1.1.

TABLE 1.1. *Distribution of federated ranks by age, division and rank*

	19–39		40+	
	Uniform	C.I.D.	Uniform	C.I.D.
	%	%	%	%
Constables	607 (55)	47 (4)	173 (15)	28 (2.5)
Sergeants	66 (6)	11 (1)	76 (7)	27 (2.5)
Inspectors	11 (1)	3 (0.3)	41 (4)	21 (2)

(The percentages in brackets are the proportions of the total in each category.)

I aimed to take a sample that would total one-fifth of the federated ranks. I anticipated considerable refusal of individuals to co-operate, in view of the reticence of policemen to outside investigation which many previous studies had indicated. I thought that aiming for a sample of one-fifth (222) would probably ensure a final response of around 150, the size the Chief Constable had agreed to spare. I stratified the sample by age, rank, and uniform versus C.I.D. work, to ensure that it corresponded in these features to the force as a whole. Within each cell, I chose one in every five names randomly, using a table of random numbers. The numbers selected in each category are shown in Table 1.2.

TABLE 1.2. *Sample selected, by age, division and rank*

	19–39		40+	
	Uniform	C.I.D.	Uniform	C.I.D.
Constables	121	10	33	5
Sergeants	13	3	14	5
Inspectors	3	1	10	4

As anticipated, the final sample contacted fell short of that selected, and totalled 168 (an overall response of 76%). There were two sources of failure to interview. Firstly, a substantial number refused to be interviewed when initially approached. (This was by means of a letter sent out by the Research Department on my behalf, reproduced in Appendix 1.) This was the main source of non-response, accounting for 70% of it.

Given the stipulation that interviews were to be voluntary, I was not permitted to follow up this initial letter. Secondly, for a variety of reasons, men who had originally agreed to be interviewed could not be contacted. Sometimes this was because they were no longer in the force, because of resignation, prolonged courses elsewhere, serious sickness or death, by the time I came to interview in their division. On other occasions people did not turn up for appointments. In these cases I attempted to arrange several appointments, and only gave up if the person failed to appear on three successive occasions. The main source of non-response, as mentioned, was initial refusal to be interviewed. This was highly concentrated among the policewomen (and hence the apparently sexist reference to my sample as 'the men' is almost literally accurate, there being only five women), and the constables who worked on court-duty (none of whom consented). The actual sample interviewed was distributed as in Table 1.3.

TABLE 1.3. *Sample interviewed, by age, division and rank*

	19–39		*40+*	
	Uniform	C.I.D.	Uniform	C.I.D.
Constables	77	6	26	3
Sergeants	12	4*	12	5
Inspectors	5*	2*	12*	4

The numbers with asterisks all represent cells where the final number is greater, by one or two, than in the sample selected. These are accounted for by promotions and transfers into these categories which had occurred between the time the sample was taken and the interviews actually held. (The men are analysed in terms of position at the time of interview. There are six cases of this kind altogether.) The category which falls furthest short of the number selected is that of young, 'uniformed' constables. The two heaviest sources of non-response mentioned above occur in this cell.

It is contended that the sample is representative of the operational policemen. The non-response is fairly large, but for the reasons given, little could be done to reduce it. (A clue as to the reasons for refusal was provided by a uniformed sergeant I passed in the corridor one afternoon. He told me he was one of the people who had refused to be interviewed. He said the police had always been suspicious of the media. I replied that I had nothing to do with the media. He said he realised that, but by media he meant any outsiders. The police had always been suspicious of talking to outsiders.) With the exceptions specified (policewomen and the court department), non-response was fairly evenly spread. The numbers in several cells are too small for separate statistical analysis. These could have been increased somewhat by taking a larger sampling fraction in some cells and then weighting down for the total figures, but it will be noted that in most of these categories the *total* numbers are too small for meaningful analysis, so that even taking the whole population in these cells would not have helped matters much. This would have been at the expense of the proportions in other cells, given the restrictions imposed on overall size. I did not feel that the number of ordinary constables could be safely reduced if a representative selection of these was to be made, because of the heterogeneity of this group. The small numbers in some categories therefore had to be accepted, and analysis could usually be only in terms of differences between ranks, and sometimes sets of divisions in global terms like 'specialist' and 'non-specialist', occasionally with age or length of service held constant. Chi-squared tests were calculated, and all relationships discussed are significant at the 5% level, unless otherwise stated. (The typical pattern was that the constable/inspector difference was significant. While sergeants were almost invariably in between these ranks on most issues, they were often too close to one or the other for that difference to be significant.)

I began interviewing in January 1973 and completed the field work in December. Men were interviewed at the stations they were attached to. The interviews were tape-recorded and lasted from a minimum of forty-five minutes to a maximum of four hours. The average time was one and a half to two hours.

I was keen to use tapes for various reasons. Firstly, I wished to preserve as much detail as possible of the men's reasoning as it informed their replies, so that the meaning *they* attached to responses could be ascertained. Secondly, though this is debatable, the taping allowed for greater *rapport* once the discussion had got under way. There was frequently initial resistance to being taped, which I overcame by saying I would be prepared to switch off at any point if requested. This never occurred. On one occasion, with a detective sergeant, I was unsuccessful in persuading him and had to record the interview by pen. In my initial discussions with the activists I had experimented with various recording methods. Usually I tried to recall what had occurred, without any record being kept at the time. This, of course, meant a considerable loss of material. When I attempted to take notes with a pen in these discussions, the conversation immediately became punctuated with the injunction: 'Now this is strictly off the record', even in the case of apparently insignificant items. In the pilot interviews I had also felt that the constantly visible taking of notes was off-putting and prevented deeper discussion of any item. With taping, however, after a few minutes of hesitation, discussion ran smoothly and the recording device did not seem inhibiting.

That this is so is supported by the fact that in almost every case the men made statements which would have been most embarrassing to them, and possibly even grounds for a discipline charge, had they been reported to their supervisors. Nor were the men unaware of this, and the controversial nature of some of the items. Many expressed anxiety about the confidentiality of the interviews, and the possibly damaging nature of their replies. Typical examples of comments made after the interviews were:

I hope it's confidential...I'm a little surprised to find you've been allowed to ask these questions. Have you signed the Official Secrets Act, because anything to do with the internal organisation of the force is an official secret? You can't really be communicative about it.   (C.I.D. constable)

Oh my gosh! I've said things on that tape I would get hung for!

(Uniform constable)

If you publish the truth about the job, they'll never let you. The Home Office would never like people to read what the job is like. If you say the truth, you'll never get permission to publish it.   (Uniform constable)

These questions were a bit controversial weren't they? ... But I've been looking forward to talking to you. I've heard from some of the lads you're not a student type. So I've felt free to say anything... If only people realised exactly – you know, if I sat down and wrote exactly what the police force did, there'd be one or two things would happen. They'd refuse to publish it on the grounds that it was fiction, the publishers, and the people reading it would just not believe what goes on.   (Uniform sergeant)

In fact, it seemed to me that if 'the lads' did not see me as exactly a 'student type', they did nonetheless regard me as closely connected with students. An almost obligatory remark after I'd finished was: 'Now that you've asked me what you want, there's something I'd like to ask you... Why are students so anti-police?' At any rate, I was generally seen as an outsider, and unconnected with the police hierarchy.

The one exception to this was in a station within D division where my work unfortunately coincided with a Home Office survey being conducted concurrently on another topic. Several of the respondents here told me that it was rumoured I was a 'Home-Office spy', but of course *they* didn't believe it. The rumour didn't have a noticeable effect on the responses in this division. The more usual view of me seemed to be summed up by the desk sergeant at another station, who greeted my arrival in the mornings with a cheery: 'Hello! Here comes Mr Social Survey himself!' I could not quite shake off the 'student' image, despite taking care to have regular barbering and to wear a sober, grey suit. In spite of these precautions, references to my 'long hair' were frequent. But in some ways the 'outsider' image was an advantage. Many men seemed to treat the interviews with gusto, and to regard me as a potential saviour who would reveal to the world the injustices rife within the force, or put over the police point of view to an uncomprehending public:

When you get it finished, I hope you get it published. I reckon it's about time someone put a real, comprehensive report on, because we need someone to voice our opinions for us really, and the Federation's not always able to do it, to be our spokesman.   (Uniform constable – one of the ones who mentioned the 'Home Office spy' rumour to me)

I really want to protest about the conditions, and the way we're treated, by our superiors, and people outside. . .I hope our little chat this afternoon's taught you to see the other side of it now.   (Uniform constable)

I wonder, being a little bit selfish, whether this can help us in any way. It's no use going to the Branch Board or the Chief Constable, because they're not democratic at all. I wonder if anything you report would help us, through the Home Office, or whether the powers that be in the force will cover things up. What we actually feel – not what we *should* feel, what we actually feel. . .there's a lot of unrest in the police force. I hope it gets published and stirs things up.
(Mounted police constable)

Many men seemed glad of the opportunity to be heard, which surprised me in view of the problems of gaining access in the first place, and the initial non-response. Some had experience of being respondents on previous surveys of policemen conducted with closed questions. They preferred the opportunity to explain their views in detail, and questioned whether any valid interpretation could be placed on their response to predetermined items.

These forms were introduced with a view to getting the idea of an average policeman's working day. This form was divided up into various types of duty, foot patrol, car patrol, this type of thing. And you had to put a tick for every hour of a particular type of duty, say cycle patrol 2 to 3, one tick. Whereas in actual fact you might be stopped by somebody in that hour and asked directions, or you might get sent to tell somebody their parents had died, or their child had been involved in a road accident. But this just wasn't catered for on the form. Until eventually you finished up on the chart with a load of ticks that didn't really bear any relation to the day's duty that had been done. . .I don't think you can get anything by asking straight questions off a piece of paper.
(Traffic constable)

In fact, the fixed choice parts of the interviews I conducted attracted similar criticisms, as these sarcastic remarks illustrate:

Do you get a blonde secretary if you get this right?
It's like the *News of the World* contest.
I never win on these card games.

Analysis of the material, apart from the pre-coded replies to some questions, was a laborious and lengthy process. I read each transcript, developing a set of categories to classify the issues which the men had raised. I then constructed a card-index of quotes to illustrate the meaning attached to the answers. I had also recorded an account of my initial impressions of each man immediately following each interview, together with any incidents that had occurred. This informed my attempt to place the man in terms of the typology developed in chapter 12. As explained there, this was done on the basis of the interview as a whole, rather than a precise operation in terms of specific responses to certain questions, though these were the foundation.

I would argue that there are two major pitfalls that attempts to understand and explain attitudes through interview or questionnaire can fall into. The first is excessive *idealism*. Ideas are explained in terms of other ideas expressed by the respondent. This attributes too great an element of rationality to the process by which ideas are developed. It is the danger of any typification of world-views, like the one given in chapter 12. It must always be recognised that the coherence of such portraits is a result of the deliberate construction of an ideal-type, and actual thought deviates more or less from that standard of internal rationality. The opposing danger is that of excessive *materialism*. Ideas are correlated with structural positions, say attitudes to unionism with rank. The danger here is to regard the ideas as straightforward emanations of material factors, to interpret correlation as causation. In either case, the complex process of social interaction in which ideas develop is reduced to a simpler relationship, either one of logic or a simple reflection of material circumstances.

The problem is that interviews (even in a longitudinal study) cannot trace the process of social interaction in which ideas develop, as men with various initial orientations to a situation encounter circumstances and other actors that have the power to frustrate or satisfy these expectations. All that can be done is to reconstruct a plausible account of how present ideas, and their relationship to other ideas and to material factors, *could* have developed. This account can be supported, but never conclusively tested, by statistical relationships and insight gained from the statements made by the actors. Thus no account can be considered final.

Outline of the book

The next chapter will review the origins and development of police unionism in Britain. This will provide a guide to the historical background and immediate social context in terms of which the interview material has to be understood. This chapter will also describe the formal organisation of the Police Federation and its negotiating machinery, in order to introduce the institutions to which the men are responding.

Part Two concentrates on the men's subjective evaluation of the formal structure, and their ideas about changes in it. Chapter 3 will consider their overall assessments of the Federation as a representative organisation. In chapter 4 this global evaluation will be broken down in an examination of their assessments of eight specific areas of Federation activity. Having considered their attitudes towards the existing representative system, we shall examine in chapter 5 the question of how alternative types of organisation with different powers of action are viewed. Chapter 6 will consider the extent to which the men feel they should be involved in decision-making through the Federation, and how this and other activities should be institutionalised. The preceding chapters looked at the men's views on the *structure* of representation. Their attitudes towards the Federationists, the men who represent them, will be considered in chapter 7. The perspectives and characteristics of these representatives in relation to the men they represent will also be looked at. The final chapter in Part Two, chapter 8, will discuss the men's feelings about outside trade unionism, in relation to their experience of it, as well as to their views on their own representation.

Part Three will examine the characteristics of the police as an occupation, and in particular the men's orientation to their work. The purpose will be to illuminate and help understand their views on unionism as described in the previous part. Chapter 9 will look at the backgrounds of policemen, their social origins, previous experiences, modes of entry, and motivations for joining. These will be related to subsequent progress in the force, and attitudes to unionism. Chapter 10 will examine their current orientation to work, in terms of six aspects, and their relationship to attitudes to unionism: (a) satisfaction with the work; (b) conceptions of the relationships between the ranks in the force, especially as these are reflected in supervision and discipline; (c) personal career aspirations and assessments of the promotion system; (d) attitudes towards police 'professionalisation'; (e) the relationship between work and non-work life; (f) views on the nature and purpose of the job. The general social philosophy of policemen, their conception and analysis of the problems in society which they face, will be the subject of chapter 11. These chapters will all seek to characterise the distinctiveness of the police orientation to work, and suggest some of its sources, though the distribution of varying attitudes will also be indicated. Chapter 12 will emphasise not the general features of the police outlook and its contrast with others, but rather the structured variations *within* it. This will be in terms of developing a typology of different perspectives policemen have on work, and their sources in the career structure of the force and men's progress in it.

Finally, in Part Four, chapter 13 will review the results of the previous chapters. The implications of these findings for the future of police representation are also discussed.

2

The history and structure of the Police Federation

The history of the Police Federation

This history can be divided into four periods: (a) the origins of police unionism in the 1870s until the establishment of the Police Federation in 1919; (b) 1919 until the changes after the Second World War; (c) 1950 until the late 1960s when the Federation began to become more active in wider policy issues; and (d) the recent developments in the 1970s, which constitute the immediate background to the research.

The origins of the Federation

The Federation was a consciously fashioned government device to smash the independent Police Union which had developed during the First World War. The struggle over the Union, and the subsequent evolution of the powers of the Federation, can be understood in terms of two opposed factors. On the one hand, the authorities, and usually most of the men, believed that the police constituted a special case in terms of the inappropriateness of union representation. On the other hand, economic and social circumstances repeatedly challenged that belief. The establishment and evolution of negotiating machinery was not the result of government reflection that this was desirable on *a priori* grounds, even if that is the implication of the wording of legislation after the event. Concessions have been forced on governments in the face of situations where they were the only means of averting more widespread disaffection.

The origins of the demand for the 'right to confer', as it was usually put at the time, go back to the last three decades of the nineteenth century. The first recorded instance of collective action by policemen occurred in the Metropolitan Police in 1872. Dissatisfied with pay and conditions, 179 men at Bow Street station refused to turn out for duty on 16 November. The protest only lasted a few hours. It resulted in improvements in pay and other conditions of service. The men who refused to work were all suspended from duty, but eventually reinstated with the exception of the instigators. Similar events occurred in 1890 at Bow Street. Again the action was successful in so far as it led to a rectification of some grievances, but unsuccessful in that the leaders were dismissed from the force.

Neither event led to the establishment of more permanent machinery for the presentation of grievances (Reynolds & Judge 1968: 202–25).

The demand for negotiating and consultative machinery was first explicitly formulated by John Kempster in 1893, when he founded the *Police Review*. This journal, still published weekly, was intended to discuss police matters from the point of view of the rank and file. It aimed to be the mouthpiece of the ordinary policeman, otherwise denied a say. Over the years, with the development of the Federation (and in the last decade its own journal), the *Review* has lost this function, and become increasingly establishment oriented. But at the time of its inception it was intended to publicise police grievances, and to press for the granting of the 'right to confer'. Kempster was, however, quite opposed to the idea of a union with powers of industrial action. What he envisaged was an organisation more or less along the lines of the Federation as it was ultimately established. In 1894, Kempster set up the Police and Citizens' Friendly Association to propagate his views.

More directly related to the formation of police representative machinery were the activities of John Syme in the years immediately preceding the First World War. Syme was an ex-inspector in the Metropolitan Police, who had been dismissed in 1910. He, and many others, saw his treatment as victimisation, but he could find no channels of redress. He began a long personal campaign to clear his name of the charge of insubordination. As the years went by this became increasingly frantic and bizarre, with Syme threatening the Home Secretary, Prime Minister, and finally even the King.

The more exotic later episodes of Syme's saga are only of passing interest here. But his case is important in two ways. Firstly, it illustrates one of the major sources of policemen's disgruntlement in the years around the First World War. This was the arbitrary and at times almost tyrannical power of senior police officers, coupled with the absence of adequate channels of appeal in discipline cases. Secondly, the early part of Syme's personal campaign against 'injustice' in the Metropolitan Police involved the formation of the Police Union. In 1913 Syme and some of his sympathisers founded the John Syme League, with the aim of pressing for the establishment of a trade union in the police force. Later that year, the Metropolitan Police Union was founded, with Syme as secretary. It soon established a branch for provincial members, and in 1914 became The National Union of Police and Prison Officers, and started publishing a journal to air police grievances. Membership was secret and the Union met in a clandestine way. This was necessitated by the Union's illegal status and the vigour of official opposition. Policemen discovered to be members were suspended. This did not succeed in deterring the formation or development of the Police Union.

Against the view of Syme and others that justice for the policeman necessitated a union, Kempster continued to argue for a different form of representative body, without full union powers. The Home Office, the Metropolitan Commissioner, and the Chief Constables opposed even this more modest proposal. Police authorities in this period tended to favour a militaristic organisation of their forces, with strict discipline, and to regard any action by subordinates as a mutiny. (See the views of the then Commissioner of the City of London Police Force. Nott-Bower 1926: 283.)

Despite official condemnation, the Union survived during the war years. Attachment to the Union in its early days was determined by disgruntlement over discipline and conditions of service as well as pay. It is hard to generalise about police pay in this period, as it was not until 1919 that a standard national rate was established. Before that, police pay varied quite considerably between forces. This was itself the source of some dissatisfaction. The trend in the pre-war years seems to have been a slow erosion of the real value of policeman's pay, despite money rises. In the 1890s they had achieved a standard roughly comparable to skilled workers, a considerable improvement from the general parity with agricultural labourers which had prevailed during the course of the century. But in the 1900s the cost of living rose more rapidly than police incomes, and by the war the policeman's pay was approximately that of most unskilled labourers (Martin & Wilson 1969: 14–21). In addition, there was discontent over various aspects of conditions of service, such as the lack of rest-days. The operation of the disciplinary structure was often seen as oppressive, as the Syme case illustrated. All these particular grievances suggested to many the need for the police to have some form of representative machinery to safeguard their interests. During the war, with the rapid inflation that ensued, these pressures mounted considerably.

As police membership of the Union grew during the war years, control passed out of the hands of Syme, whose concern was primarily his personal vendetta against the Home Office. In 1917 a controlling executive of policemen from London was elected. The new leadership attempted to gain recognition for itself by vain efforts to present an image of 'responsibility', for example by the adoption of rules precluding strike action. The Home Secretary, oblivious to the disaffection of the men, remained adamant in his opposition. Police militancy was further stimulated by disciplinary action against Union members.

The Union was gradually forging links with the labour movement. The relationship was always somewhat brittle because of the mutual hostility bred in the pre-war years by police involvement in the control of strikes. But the Union's leaders were all sympathetic to the labour movement, and the latter on the whole was favourably inclined to the 'democratisation' of the police force. Jack Hayes, a leader of the Police Union, and for many years a Labour M.P. after his dismissal from the force, wrote: 'We state emphatically that the only solution. . .is the democratisation of the Police Force, the full and complete recognition of the Union and the closer linking up of the Police with organised labour' (Picton-Davies 1973: 81). The Union became affiliated to the Labour Party, the T.U.C., and many local Trade Councils. The 1919 Labour Party Conference passed a resolution supporting the Union's struggle to survive. At various times during 1917 and 1918 the T.U.C. sent delegations to the Home Secretary seeking recognition of the Union. These efforts were unavailing. If anything the association with organised labour stiffened official resistance.

The immediate stimulus for the 1918 strike was the dismissal, on 27 August, of a leading Union member, Constable Thiel. The Union submitted its previously formulated demands for a pay increase and union recognition, plus the reinstatement of Thiel, accompanied by an ultimatum that if these were not met they would suspend the rules prohibiting strike action. Even at this point the authorities seemed unaware of the gravity of the situation. On 28 August, the day before the ultimatum was to expire, the Metropolitan superintendents reported that everything was all right in the force. The extent to which the authorities were caught by surprise is illustrated by the fact that the Home Secretary, his Permanent Under-Secretary, and the Commissioners of the Metropolitan and City of London forces were all on holiday on the day the ultimatum expired (Reynolds & Judge 1968: 6). The Union's deadline was ignored, and the strike began at midnight on 29 August. By the next day, the strike was virtually total among both the Metropolitan and City of London forces. Lloyd-George and the government were extremely alarmed by events. General Smuts, veteran of the Boer War, was appointed to try and negotiate a settlement.

The government's fears were largely based on the association between the police and the labour movement. They thought that this might be the prelude to a general strike that could assume a revolutionary character. In the official view, the police union movement was instigated more by other labour organisations than the grievances of policemen themselves. It was feared that the strike had been deliberately timed so that, if the authorities failed to get the men back before the T.U.C. Conference on 2 September, it could suspend its agenda, demand recognition of the Union, and if necessary, call a general strike of all workers, including the police. In the background was the alarm engendered by the Russian Revolution of the previous October. Some years later, Lloyd-George commented: 'This country was nearer to Bolshevism that day than at any time since' (Reynolds & Judge 1968: 70). This apocalyptic analysis was shared by sections of the press and public. The *Star* newspaper described the links between the Police Union and organised labour as a plan 'in the last resort. . .to consummate finally the wreck of modern civilisation'. 'It was seriously suggested that the Kaiser's gold might be backing the Police

Union...*The Morning Post* was already speculating on the "German-sounding" names of Thiel (the Boer War veteran and ex-Guardsman) and Zollner (the City of London policeman who was on the Union executive and, as a Grenadier, had served in the war)' (Reynolds & Judge 1968: 70).

In the event these fears about the awful consequences of a police strike were not realised. 'The strike of 1918 seems to have taken the underworld by surprise' (Picton-Davies 1973: 178). There was no discernible consequence in terms of crime or public disorder. In the words of *The Times*, the strike would have 'a lasting place in the social annals of the country for the proof it afforded of the people's ingrained respect for law and order' (2 September 1918).

Given its analysis of the situation, the government determined that it was imperative to get the men back to work at once, but at the same time to avoid recognising the Union. It was felt this could be achieved by an offer of pay, and some means of redressing grievances in future. Smuts's first attempts to negotiate a settlement came to nothing because he refused to meet the men as a deputation from the Union, as distinct from the force. Finally, on 31 August, the executive of the Union met with Lloyd-George and the Home Secretary, and a settlement was achieved. This involved substantial concessions by the government. The financial gains to the police were considerable, Thiel was reinstated, and a promise made that an authorised representative organisation would be established. The manner in which this last point was made by the Prime Minister contained the seeds of future dispute. Lloyd-George had made a statement to the effect that the Union could not be sanctioned during the war, but men could continue to belong to it. Consideration would be given to the question of representation in peace time. The Union negotiators took this to imply a promise of future recognition, and this was the message they conveyed to a mass meeting of policemen on Tower Hill that afternoon. The government for their part felt that no firm commitment had been given. As no records were kept of the talk between the Union executive and Lloyd-George, both sides continued to offer conflicting accounts of what had occurred.

For the moment it was clear that the Union had won a considerable victory and the men returned to work that evening. The London awards were soon followed by pay increases in several provincial forces, even though none had gone on strike. In the aftermath of the strike there was a large rise in Union membership. From 10 000 in August it rose to 50 000 in November, and represented approximately five-sixths of the policemen in the country (Allen 1958: 136).

The ensuing months saw a struggle for recognition develop between the Union leadership and the newly appointed Commissioner of the Metropolitan Police, General Macready. He had a reputation not only as a martinet but also as a strike-breaker. He had commanded the troops at the notorious 'battle' of Tonypandy in 1910, as well as several similar incidents. In the event he was able to out-manoeuvre and smash the Police Union.

Soon after the strike, the promise of representative machinery was implemented. A Representative Board was established in the Metropolitan Police, on the basis of annual election by ballot among all policemen below the rank of chief inspector. The Union itself was not recognised, but an agreement was reached that policemen could belong to it on the condition that it did not in any way undermine force discipline, and refrained from striking.

The leaders of the Union set out to try and control the Representative Board. They made all the Board's executive committee *ex-officio* members of the Police Union's executive. While the Union attempted to gain control of the Board, Macready initiated a strategy to weaken their power. He made elaborate, secret arrangements to minimise the effects of any future strike, for example, by planning for the army to take over police stations if necessary. He also realised that the constitution of the Board strengthened the Union's hand by basing elections on the whole force irrespective of rank. The Union activists were heavily concentrated among the constables, and most of the men elected to the Board held that rank. Macready drew up an alternative representative scheme, based on separate boards for constables, sergeants, inspectors and superintendents. The Home Secretary accepted this proposal. This strategy of divide and rule was taken over later in the constitution of the Federation.

Undaunted, the Union initiated a campaign aimed at recognition, a further pay rise, and the reinstatement of some men that it claimed had been victimised. The government, for its part, set up the Desborough Committee to inquire into 'the method of recruitment for, the conditions of service of, and the rates of pay, pensions and allowances of the Police Forces in England, Wales and Scotland'.

In the meantime, the relationship between Macready and the Metropolitan Representative Board deteriorated further. In March 1919 the government declared its decision not to recognise the Union, and Macready ordered all his men to leave it on threat of dismissal.

The Union reacted to this pressure by changing the rule prohibiting strike action to one permitting it if two-thirds of the membership supported it in a ballot. One Metropolitan constable, Spackman, was dismissed for Union activity and his reinstatement became a major issue. Deprived of formal channels of representation, the Union organised mass meetings, and made plans for direct action. It organised a ballot of members, asking them whether they would support strike action over the issues of Union recognition, Spackman's reinstatement, a pay rise and the 'total abolition of military control of the police'. They were expected to reply only 'yes' or 'no' to this rather complex and varied set of demands.

In an attempt to head off support for the strike, the Home Secretary announced that a substantial, back-dated pay rise would be offered. Macready issued Orders making it clear that any men who struck would be automatically dismissed with no hope of reinstatement. Despite this, the ballot showed a majority in favour of strike action. The Union did not organise a strike, however, probably because it realised that the promised pay rise would have weakened support in the meantime. Its hand was soon forced by the government proposal to introduce a Bill into the Commons which, in line with Desborough's recommendations, would establish the Police Federation and make membership in the Union illegal. There were some protests from Labour M.P.s and trade unionists at the prospect of the destruction of a union. The proposed Federation was regarded by them as contrary to the principles of trade unionism because it was not independent of control by employers.

Within the police force itself there was a decline in support for the Union, largely because the government granted a lump-sum of £10 immediately in anticipation of the Desborough recommendations. The Union was forced to fight desperately for survival. After two repeated failures to gain an audience with Lloyd-George, it reluctantly called a strike. The response of members was slow and small. Ultimately, only 1156 Metropolitan policemen (out of a total of 18 200) responded. Only 58 out of 970 City of London policemen joined the strike. As one striker remarked: 'It's marvellous what a £10 note will do' (Reynolds & Judge 1968: 151). As in 1918, little crime or violence resulted in London.

The story was somewhat different in the provinces. In most forces, there was no response to the strike call. In Birmingham, 119 out of 1320 policemen came out. In Liverpool, however, the strike had substantial proportions. Over half the force struck (905 constables and 49 sergeants). This resulted in an outbreak of violence and looting lasting several days and eventually quelled only by the calling in of troops. The strike also spread to the Birkenhead and Bootle forces. The experience on Merseyside lent substance to the widely expressed fears about the awesome consequences of police strikes. All the strikers were dismissed, and despite a thirty-year campaign on their behalf by the Union (which remained in existence with a membership of the sacked men), supported to some extent by the Labour Party and T.U.C., not one was ever reinstated. The strike was thus a completely abortive attempt to save the Union and the Federation was established as an official substitute.

The Federation between the wars

The Federation was clearly instituted as part of the official campaign to destroy an independent union movement, by providing some measure of the 'right to confer'. It was successful in achieving this because ultimately most of the men *did* accept the legitimacy of the existing system. Their grievances had not stimulated more than passing support for the view that the most effective, if not the only, means of defending their interests was the Union. The discontent was contained by satisfying the men's immediate needs and providing a fairly token system of representation.

That the Federation, as established in 1919, was intended as a control device, rather than a truly effective means of representing the men's interests, is apparent from an examination of the limited structure which was set up. The dismissed strikers dubbed it 'the goose club' to emphasise its incapacity to do anything but march in step with the authorities.

As originally constituted, the Federation was not even a body with any clear negotiating function. The 1919 Police Act established a Police Council which was a 'round-table' organisation consisting of superintendents, chief officers and police authority representatives, as well as Federation officials. It was a body with advisory and consultative functions, rather than machinery for collective bargaining. The Desborough Committee had explicitly rejected the introduction into the police force of an institution along the lines of the Whitley Councils, then being set up in the public service generally. These had two distinct parts, a 'staff side' and an 'employers' side'. Desborough considered this inappropriate to the police force, which was seen as based on a consensus of interests and basic outlook. The non-negotiating nature of the Federation is stressed in its 1919 terms of reference, 'to consider and bring to the notice of police authorities and the Secretary of State all matters affecting their welfare and efficiency other than questions of discipline and promotion affecting individuals'. This latter exclusion is of great significance, as much of the impetus for the development of the Union had been concern about individual cases of 'victimisation'.

The government concern that the Federation should act as a means of containing police dissatisfaction is further brought out by other aspects of its early constitution, most of which remain in force. It has already been pointed out that Macready's experience of the Representative Board, elected by a constituency including all the men, was that it was captured by the constables, the most numerous and militant rank. His amended voting system, in which each rank elected a separate board of representatives, was carried over into the Federation. Constables, sergeants and inspectors separately elect branch boards in every force, with each rank in each division having one representative. The separate boards also work together as a Joint Branch Board, which in fact conducts most business. Joint Branch Boards send delegates to Annual Conference, in relation to the size of the forces they represent, and this body elects the national Committees for each rank, which together function as the Joint Central Committee. The important point about these arrangements is that on all the *joint* bodies (which both at local and national level are the most active), each rank has an equal number of representatives, despite the far greater number of men in the rank of constable. This can be seen as a device for preventing domination of the boards by the more militant constables.

The Police Act of 1919 tightly restricted the means which the Federation might use in representing the men. Any form of industrial action was prohibited and made punishable by sanctions. So was affiliation, or even association, with outside bodies. Membership of trade unions was forbidden. At local level no machinery was set up to provide for consultation with either chief officers or police authorities.

Few resources were made available for doing what *was* permitted. All policemen were automatically members, but the Federation was forbidden to raise money from them. It was entirely dependent on a small Home Office grant. Officials had to work in their own time, and none were full-time. The Federation thus seems to have been designed as a fairly ineffectual organisation, starved of resources and shackled in action. This was reflected in its performance in the inter-war years. It was generally unsuccessful in most of its endeavours.

The position in the years after its inception is thus summed up by its official historian:

It could hardly be termed a lusty infant... All traces of militancy had been exorcised by the dismissal of every police striker. Moderation and responsibility were the new watchwords. No more strikes, threats, ultimatums, demonstrations in Trafalgar Square or abusive letters to chief officers. The Federation had 'the honour to be, Sir, your obedient servant'. (Judge 1968:10)

Chief officers and police authorities were generally hostile to the Federation. Most local councils resented the fact that because the Desborough Committee had recommended the fixing of a national rate of pay for all forces, they now had to give their men the same high wages awarded to London constables. In the twenties and thirties a battle developed over the maintenance of the absolute level of the Desborough award. As the economic situation deteriorated, pressure built up to reduce police pay in line with cuts elsewhere. The rising level of unemployment undermined the police bargaining position. The police force, with security of tenure and relatively high wages, was a desired occupation and applicants greatly outnumbered vacancies. In these two decades of deflation the police remained well-off in real terms, despite a series of pay-cuts. Their earnings were considerably higher than most manual and lower-level non-manual workers. In these circumstances, it is not surprising that the Federation was unable to resist the series of cuts which began with the 'Geddes Axe' of 1921.

The Federation's manifest lack of power as, in effect, a company union, meant that it had little support. In the late 1920s it became hard to find anyone to take on the arduous position of secretary to the Joint

Central Committee, a job which had to be combined with full-time police work. In the end the Home Secretary was prevailed upon to make the office a full-time one. All other officials continued to function on a spare-time basis, and the funds granted remained niggardly. At local level matters were even worse, and there was extensive 'victimisation' of Federation representatives (Judge 1968: 25).

The only official channel available for the presentation of Federation views was the Police Council. During the inter-war period, the Federation was consistently unable to have its views adopted against the opposition of the police authority representatives, sometimes supported by the chief officers on financial issues, and invariably on discipline matters. (The record of discussions of the Police Council in this period has been analysed in Picton-Davies 1973: 167.)

During the 1930s the position of the Federation was undermined even more. This was partly the result of the economic situation. The Depression made the police force an even more desirable occupation than in the twenties.

The advent of a new Commissioner of the Metropolitan Police further threatened the Federation. Lord Trenchard, with lifelong service in the armed forces, took a particularly autocratic approach to his job. He had concern for the welfare of his men, but it was that of a benevolent paternalist. He could see no reason for an official representative organisation, a body that the R.A.F. (of which he had been Marshal for eleven years) managed to do without.

Trenchard set out to break what little power the Federation had in its stronghold, the Metropolitan. He reduced the permitted number of meetings of branch boards. The Federation had held a widely publicised series of open meetings, packed with protesting policemen, to fight the wage cuts of 1931. He persuaded the Home Secretary that these were seriously detrimental to discipline, and reflected the lingering vestiges of the 'Bolshevism' which had produced the 1918–19 strikes. Accordingly the Federation was banned from holding such meetings. Trenchard proceeded to reorganise the force in accordance with his ideas. In his view discipline and morale were low and the quality of senior officers appalling. He clashed with the Federation over the establishment of the Hendon Police College, intended to provide opportunities for rapid promotion for especially able constables, and also for direct entry into senior posts. It was the first of a series of attempts, continuing in the post-war period, to boost the number of well-educated men who join the force and provide highly qualified senior commanders. The Federation has always been suspicious of such schemes, partly for good trade-union reasons of protecting the promotion prospects of existing members. In its weakened state in the 1930s its bitter resentment of Trenchard's plans was completely ineffectual.

During the Second World War, as during the First, inflation rapidly eroded the real value of police pay and its relationship to outside earnings. The police force was no longer a highly desired occupation, able to choose from numerous applicants. At the same time, the war imposed considerable extra duties on the police. The Federation repeatedly presented the men's grievances to Morrison, the Home Secretary.

Morrison took the same approach as Lloyd George before him. The government was not prepared to consider extending negotiating machinery in wartime. He further took the view that the role of the Joint Central Committee was not to convey the men's feelings to him, but to explain the official position to the men and thus keep them in order.

The end of the war allowed policemen to vote with their feet. There was a mass exodus into better paid outside work. This achieved what argument had never done, a reformulation of the representative machinery.

The Federation since the Second World War

The main theme of the post-war development of the Federation is its evolution into a fully-fledged negotiating body. It is increasingly accepted as the spokesman for the lower ranks, to be consulted and have a say on all issues concerning the police. But the Federation remains far less independent than most trade unions and is still shackled in terms of powers of action. The official historian goes too far when he writes: 'In spite of its restrictive constitution, the Federation has arrived as a full partner with authority' (Reynolds & Judge 1968: 239). At most it could be described as a rather junior partner.

The basic condition of its growth in organisation and influence was the altered position of the police force in the full-employment, inflationary labour market. While police pay has generally maintained its relationship to outside industry, the ratio was no longer one in which police wages were much greater than the national average. There were several periods when it lagged behind inflation. In the post-war economy a comparison with outside wages was no longer as accurate a guide to the true position of police pay. The earnings of workers in outside industry tended to outstrip their basic wages, because of the availability of overtime, as well as the other phenomena usually summarised as 'wage-drift'. Nor were the security and welfare advantages of police work as impressive as they had been before the advent of full-employment and the welfare state. Although the actual size of police forces has grown considerably since the war, they have faced an endemic shortage in relation to authorised establishments, due to problems of recruitment and premature wastage (Martin & Wilson 1969: 83–90).

The persistent manpower problem was undoubtedly the major factor which stimulated the growth of Federation power and influence. The most important changes took place soon after the war, due to a dramatic loss of police manpower. Between 1939 and 1949, total police strength fell from 63 980 to 60 190, while the population rose from 41½m. to nearly 44m. (Martin & Wilson 1969: 47). The morale of those who remained was low, in view of the failure of police pay to keep pace with rapid inflation.

The situation forced the government to set up another committee to investigate police pay and conditions, under the chairmanship of Lord Oaksey. The short-run gains greatly disappointed most policemen. Oaksey refused to follow the example of Desborough in 1919, and give the police any great pay advantage compared to the industrial average. This was partly because the government's first pay 'freeze' coincided with the committee's meetings in 1948–9. Oaksey also attached great importance to the allowances and other 'hidden' benefits of police work, especially the pension.

While the immediate gains from Oaksey proved disappointing to the Federation, the committee also proposed improvements in its status and power. Essentially the recommendations involved the establishment of proper negotiating machinery, recourse to arbitration in cases of disagreement, and the institution of independent funds.

A new Police Council for Great Britain was established, divided into an Official Side consisting of the Home Office and the police authorities, and a Staff Side including representatives of the Federation, the Superintendents' Association, and the Association of Chief Police Officers. (Police Advisory Boards were also set up, with similar constitution and functions to the old Police Council.) In the event of failure to reach agreement, there was recourse to arbitration, by a special tribunal, with three independent members chosen by the government.

The Federation was allowed to supplement the Home Office grant by a voluntary subscription. The uses to which funds could be put were limited. They could not, for example, be used for supporting political candidates, contributing to trade unions or other outside bodies, or paying for the defence of members in civil, criminal or disciplinary proceedings (with certain narrowly defined exceptions). Despite its strictly voluntary nature, almost all policemen have paid their contributions. (In the force studied, for example, only two men opted out). Oaksey insisted on the principle that the Federation could not be entirely financially independent (Home Office 1949 para. 348: 72).

The Report rejected the suggestion by the Constables' Central Committee that a 'free association" should replace the Federation. Oaksey felt this would 'introduce a disruptive influence into the service' (para. 344: 71).

A representative organisation in a disciplined body of men, and especially one with the prime responsibility for law and order, must be prepared to accept certain limitations. For example, it is common ground that the police 'trade union', whatever form it takes, must not become affiliated with other trade unions and cannot be free to call on its members to strike or to commit any other breach of discipline. To express this in more general terms, the police trade union's activities must be so conducted as not to impair in any way the authority of senior officers or the confidence of the community.   (para. 343:70)

In other words, while Oaksey recommended some considerable advances in the Federation's status as a bargaining body with proper negotiation machinery, its power was still to be considerably restricted by comparison with outside trade unions.

There is no doubt that these changes have transformed the Federation into an organisation of some substance compared to its pre-war weakness. But the only 'weapon' in negotiation remained the pressure of external economic circumstances. Its new status as a body with negotiating rights and some independent funds did allow it the chance to capitalise on these circumstances, whereas in the pre-war period discontent was often allowed to fester for long periods without redress.

One use to which the funds were put was the employment of a Parliamentary Consultant and Adviser. James Callaghan was the first man to hold this post, from its establishment in 1955 until his entry into government in 1964. The Federation also quickly made use of the possibility of arbitration. In 1955 a pay dispute was referred to arbitration, and Callaghan presented the case for the Staff Side. The arbitration award of £30 on the starting rate went well beyond the official side's final offer of £5. However, two subsequent awards, in 1957 and 1958, revealed to the Federation the limits of the arbitration machinery. While they felt they received more as a result of it than would otherwise be the case, a dispute of principle was becoming apparent between the Federation and the tribunal. The Federation wanted pay to be set at a sufficiently generous level to ensure satisfactory recruitment and curb wastage, which they felt meant a return to the pre-war lead in police pay over the national average. The arbitration tribunal was only prepared to maintain the post-war parity, and was also sensitive to the needs of Government economic policy aimed at controlling inflation. In the second half of the 1950s controversy over a special London rate of pay dominated Federation meetings. Dispute between the provinces and the Metropolitan became increasingly acrimonious. By 1959, it seemed possible that the Metropolitan might apply formally to the Home Secretary to be recognised as a separate Federation. The dispute was never resolved, but merely submerged by the clamour developing about the general level of pay, which heralded the 1960 Royal Commission on the Police.

The Commission was not appointed primarily to deal with pay, and it it unlikely that this problem alone would have called it into being. It arose out of growing concern with the relationship between police and public, highlighted by some well-publicised incidents. These also raised the issue of the accountability of the police, and the relationship between chief officers, police authorities, and parliament. It was these matters, rather than the problem of pay, which stimulated the appointment of the Commission, chaired by Sir Henry Willink. The Federation was able to persuade the Commission to turn its attention first to the problem of pay, and discuss this as an urgent issue, producing an interim report that year.

This greatly pleased the Federation, but annoyed the government and local authorities. Not only did the Commission award virtually the whole of Callaghan's claim for the '£1000 per year policeman', it went beyond its brief of reviewing the 'broad principles' governing pay, to suggest a formula. It justified this by referring to the Federation case stressing the diminution of the strength of the force in contrast to the rapid increases in recorded crime rates and the demands placed on the police (para. 62).

Willink attempted to develop a formula which would achieve 'the maintenance of an efficient police service fully up to strength and based on conditions recognised by the police themselves and by the public as fair and reasonable' (para. 201). This was based on wages in a list of eighteen occupations, but added more because of the policeman's inability to take outside work (a supplement of 45%), 'the constable's duties and responsibilities, his way of life, his knowledge and professional skill, and his physical and personal attributes' (a supplement of 25% of the previous two factors), and then deducting a small amount to take account of rent allowance or free housing (para. 178–9).

The recommended pay scale (£695–£910 for constables) was introduced immediately. The result was reflected in the recruitment figures. A net loss of manpower of 372 in provincial forces in 1960 was converted into a net gain of 2409 in 1961 (Martin & Wilson 1969: 85). But the police authorities and government refused to accept the formula itself. In 1962, the Police Council did sign an agreement providing for biennial reviews of pay to maintain the level then holding in relation to the wage index, and having regard to the general economic state of the country. Since then the Federation has continuously struggled, albeit unsuccessfully, to maintain the real value of the Willink award. As inflation grew faster, the biennial review came to restrict keeping up with the outside world. The comparison with the *wage* index also became more limiting as increases in earnings outstripped rises in basic pay. Negotiations were increasingly hampered by the attempts of successive governments to introduce policies of wage restraint. Against this the Federation has (until the last few years) had the 'weapons' of manpower shortages, and the need to maintain morale in the context of worsening problems facing the police.

The most notable change in the Federation since the mid-1960s has been its increasing attention to more fundamental questions of force policy and indeed to general problems of society as well. For the first forty-five years of its existence the statutory terms of reference 'all matters affecting welfare and efficiency' had been interpreted mainly as implying that, in pressing its claims for 'welfare', the Federation ought also to regard the requirements of 'efficiency', i.e. it was to act 'responsibly'. Now, however, the Federation began to assert its views on matters directly affecting the 'efficiency' of police forces. In 1965 a document called *The Problem* was launched by the Federation at a Press conference to support its pay claim. This was intended to show that 'owing to manpower difficulties, the police forces of Great Britain are in grave danger of losing the fight against crime'. Although the recruitment situation had continued to be buoyant during the early sixties, premature wastage was beginning to mount alarmingly, reflecting a serious loss of experienced men. The manifesto argued not only for pay rises to cope with this, but also for better equipment and new, less dictatorial, approaches in management. The authorities were furious at this Federation initiative. The Press gave it a welcoming reception. This was of no avail, as the arbitration tribunal accepted the Official Side's offer on the 1965 pay claim in view of the pay norm of 3–3½% imposed by the government.

The advent of Roy Jenkins to the Home Office in 1966 gave the Federation some hope that they would do better in future. He demonstrated that he accepted their desire for greater involvement in policy by establishing three working parties drawn from the Police Advisory Board to consider *Manpower, Equipment and Efficiency*. These working parties had Federation representatives on them, and indicated the advances made by it towards recognition as the legitimate spokesman for policemen on wider issues than pay and conditions. Jenkins further showed his commitment to the police by pressing for them to be exempt from the pay freeze introduced by the July measures of 1966. This had come shortly before the police pay review of that year, and caused 'a powerful protest', in which the Federation was united with the Official Side. Pressure was so effective that, not for the last time in the years to come, the police were made a special case. Their pay rise was delayed only for six months, not for the full year of the freeze.

The fruits of the working parties appointed by Jenkins appeared in 1967. Their Report was acclaimed by the *Federation Newsletter* as 'the chance of a lifetime'. It was seen as 'mainly a product of the initiative taken by the Federation in 1965'. The proposals included a new system of policing, the Unit Beat, involving the introduction of modern equipment, notably personal radios and panda cars. New management methods were also advocated. 'Those who are talking about a "revolution" in the police are quite right...the working parties have pointed the way to modernisation and to a status for the constable never achieved in the past' (*Federation Newsletter*, January 1967: 3).

The relationship between the Federation and the Labour government took a distinct turn for the worse after 1968, paradoxically after Callaghan, the erstwhile champion of the police, became Home Secretary. A series of clashes developed between him and his former employers, beginning with his acceptance, without consultation, of limitations on police recruiting, as part of the economy measures introduced by the government in 1968.

The Federation in the 1970s

By 1970 discontent in the police force had reached considerable proportions. The pay negotiations of that year were accompanied by a great deal of anxiety and acrimony amongst the members. They felt that the problems of policing had intensified considerably and that this ought to be reflected in pay. The late 1960s and the 1970s show mounting police concern about what they perceived as a trend to lawlessness, disorder and increasing violence, manifest not only in rising rates of crime but also in growing problems of crowd control arising out of political demonstrations, industrial militancy, and the spread of terrorist tactics. Concern with these social issues pervades Federation meetings, documents and actions in the 1970s. Anxiety about these problems interpenetrates with bread-and-butter issues. Pay demands come to be seen as morally justified by the danger and difficulty, as well as crucial social importance, of police work. In addition, the 'demonstration effect' of growing industrial and political militancy has tended to erode commitment to institutionalised and established channels of negotiation, most clearly since 1975.

These developments have been anticipated by events in American police forces in the 1960s. Police unionism in the U.S.A. originated in a variety of fraternal and benefit associations formed during the period 1890–1915. The economic consequences of the First World War which stimulated the Police Union here also worsened the position of American policemen, and there was a movement towards unionisation of many of these fraternal organisations in the period 1917–19. This movement was destroyed by the violent Boston police strike of 1919. The result was not institutionalised representation as in England, but a virtual taboo on police organisation.

In the last decade the situation has changed dramatically. Police associations have mushroomed, often trying militant tactics of various kinds: strikes, go-slows, 'blue flu' (a concerted move by policemen to simultaneously report sick). These have not only been used in support of material demands, but also to put pressure on government to implement policies favoured by the police (Skolnick 1969; Capune 1971; Burpo 1971; Bopp 1971; Gammage & Sachs 1972; Juris & Feuille 1973; Halpern 1974; Ruchelman 1974; Levi 1977). The new militancy of 'blue power' organisations was attributable to economic grievances, resentment at the efforts of liberal politicians and the courts to criticise and control police actions, and the 'demonstration effect' of the Civil Rights, anti-war and student movements.

Economic and social pressures in Britain have produced similar results. Police pay negotiations have been surrounded by considerable tension in 1970 and 1975–7. Sandwiched between was a period in which the police seemed to receive favourable treatment, the years when the Heath government was attempting to control the trade union movement by the Industrial Relations Act. There has also been mounting feeling amongst policemen that a change in penal and social policy was required to cope with the trend towards 'lawlessness' which they perceived. A most significant departure for the Federation recently has been its emergence on the political arena in a public campaign to press for 'law and order' policies.

The 1970 pay negotiations were conducted against a background of bad feeling amongst policemen. *Police* declared in its first editorial of the 1970s: 'The morale of the police service today is lower than it has been for many years past...We start 1970 with a solemn warning. Unless something positive is done quickly, the police service will be facing a crisis within a few months' (*Police* January 1970: 3). An interim award granted at the end of February did little to ease the tensions. The Federation resorted to unorthodox tactics. Members were urged to write to their local M.P.s. This was frowned on by the Home Office. 'Some of our recent tactics have been causing raised eyebrows in the Home Office...Our sins can be loosely described under the general heading of "ungentlemanly conduct" ...Admit it, chaps, you've been writing to your M.P.s haven't you?' (*Police* December 1970: 3). In reply to a leader in *The Times* supporting the Official Side, the Federation took out a large advertisement urging its case (7 December 1970). There was much discussion about the possibility of industrial action. The Federation Conference (19–21 May) debated several motions seeking the right to strike, and other powers, though these were rejected. Speakers pleaded for 'weapons to fight a bloody-minded Home Office' (Edited Proceedings: 18). The Joint Central Committee opposed the demand for union powers. It swayed the opinion of delegates by arguing: 'Now I don't see a red under every bed. Not every bed [laughter]. But you will agree with me that there have been sustained attacks, from what we euphemistically call political extremists, to undermine the police service...Isn't this [granting the Federation union powers] just what those who would like to see anarchy in this country would dearly love to achieve?' [Applause] (Edited Proceedings: 16–17).

Despite the Conference defeat, discussions about the possibility of police industrial action continued. After negotiations at the Police Council, Federation spokesmen were interviewed on TV about the possibility of such action (B.B.C. News, 30 November 1970). I.T.V. ran a *This Week* special recalling the events of 1918–19, and outlining the current discontent. In January 1971, after the advent of a Conservative government had failed to produce satisfactory improvements in the Official Side's offer, a humorous article on a possible attack of 'blue flu' appeared in *Police* ('The Great Police Sick-In', *Police*, January 1971: 17). 'The mysterious virus which attacked almost all Britain's 100 000 police officers so suddenly. . .appeared to disappear with equally startling swiftness when it was announced that there was likely to be a "substantial" offer on police pay.'

After prolonged and tough negotiations, agreement was finally reached on 25 February 1971 on an award which *Police* described as 'a significant achievement'. They had 'gained all this against the discouraging background of economic difficulties and industrial unrest. . .Leaders of several unions. . .were astonished at the contrast between the police award and the "final" offers made by the employers to such groups as the postal workers and teachers' (*Police*, March 1971: 3). This heralded a period of nearly four years during which the police were treated comparatively favourably in pay negotiations. Many policemen attributed this to the need to preserve police manpower and morale during the Heath government's struggle with the trade union movement. This is the background to the research reported on in later chapters, and is clearly reflected in the men's attitudes.

An example of the favourable treatment accorded the police is the interim award in December 1971. This was 'negotiated. . .in record time . . .Those of us who remember the many occasions when we have had to fight the Official Side for every last penny will have been pleasantly surprised at the ready response. . .and the speed with which a settlement was reached' (*Police*, January 1972: 3). One prominent Joint Central Committee official intimated to me that the Federation had reached an understanding with the Conservative leaders before the 1970 election. In return for giving Callaghan a rough ride in his appearance as Home Secretary at the Annual Conference (which was believed to be damaging to Labour's prospects), the police would receive sympathetic attention in pay negotiations. Whatever the truth of this conspiracy theory, the police certainly did enjoy a series of awards which 'pleasantly surprised' both Federation negotiators and members.

One such rise was achieved shortly before interviewing for the present research began. 'The sudden and altogether unexpected agreement on a 15% pay increase, reached on 31 October at the Police Council, has been well received throughout the service. Perhaps the dominant reaction of our members has been relief that the settlement was made a few days before the Government imposed its freeze on all increases in incomes' (*Police*, December 1972: 3). The reasons for this special treatment were not hard to find.

For more than a year, they have held the line. They have been sworn at, spat at, kicked, thumped, injured. They have faced hundreds, and at times thousands, of enraged men 'demonstrating' against Government and employers during industrial disputes... They have guarded property and run the gauntlet of abuse to protect the rights of others to work. They are, of course, the police.

(*Police*, November 1972:4)

In 1972 the struggle over the Industrial Relations Act, and the Heath attempt to curb trade union power and advance his counter-inflationary strategy, were at their height. It was the year of the miners' strike which included the confrontation at Saltley, as well as numerous other clashes between police and pickets. 1973, the year in which interviewing for this study was carried out, saw active preparations by the government to strengthen police ability to cope with similar conflicts, in anticipation of future disputes.

Despite favourable treatment, concern remained about police manpower in relation to official establishments. On 9 December 1974 the House of Commons held an unprecedented three-hour debate on the police. It was rare indeed for such a debate to take place without being occasioned by a specific alarming incident. The stimulus for the debate was concern about what was regarded as an acute shortage of police to deal with the growth of severe problems of lawlessness and disorder. (Ten days before this debate the House had passed the Prevention of Terrorism Act, to which frequent reference was made. The immediately preceding debate had been on the topic of juvenile crime.) Rising crime was contrasted with the shortage of policemen, measured in terms of numbers actually employed relative to authorised establishments, and an actual loss of strength in the Metropolitan Police. It must be noted that these 'shortages' of police manpower are in relation to officially estimated needs. In absolute terms the number of police in Britain increased by a quarter (from 90 000 to 112 400) between 1963 and 1973. But authorised establishments, i.e. the number deemed necessary by Chief Constables and the Home Office, rose by a third. The 'shortage' is thus not an absolute one, but socially defined.

Anxiety was especially acute about the shortage of men in the Metropolitan Police. Concern in government circles was so great that in 1973 the Federation Annual Conference had been prevailed upon to abandon the principle of a national rate of pay, and agree to an increased London allowance. This was not agreed to without much argument and heart-searching by the representatives of provincial forces. As in the 1950s, this issue for a time threatened Federation unity (*Police*, February 1975).

Both sides of the House agreed that the police must be an exception to the financial stringency affecting all other aspects of government expenditure. (This has, in fact, affected all police forces in recent years. Many have experienced economy drives, and much internal controversy about the distribution of cuts.) The House seemed united on the principle that the police were the most special of special cases. Sir Keith Joseph, not normally noted for his profligacy with the public purse, noted:

The British tax payer has to pay a large amount in taxes. . .for many things of which he disapproves. . . But there is I believe one element of the tax system which the tax payer would pay readily – those taxes to increase the strength and effectiveness of the police forces. That is the sort of taxation which the British tax payer thoroughly understands (*Hansard*, vol. 882, 6–12 December 1964:104)

Roy Jenkins, as Home Secretary, agreed with this priority. He referred to recent pay agreements which gave 'a substantial increase to all ranks'. He pledged the government to finance any further increases in expenditure which might be necessary to alleviate the manpower shortage.

The role of the Federation was analysed during the debate. Its present constitution and behaviour were attacked from opposing sides.

Jonathan Aitken (Conservative) attacked the Federation's opposition to an increase in the Special Constabulary, which he saw as a suitable device for boosting police strength. The proposal was blocked by what he called 'the shop-steward level of the police forces'. He referred to the November 1974 issue of *Police*, in which some cartoons had depicted 'special constables as geriatric half-wits'. He charged that the Federation acted in a sectional, small minded way to impede changes which were necessary for efficiency in the modern world, in order to preserve the narrow interests of its members. The Federation's attitude is 'prejudiced and antiquated clap trap that has no place in Britain in 1974. . .We cannot regard the police force as a closed shop. . .The Federation is in danger of behaving like dinosaurs in an I.R.A. world.' The Federation had too much of the perspective and power of a trade union, and police efficiency required the curbing of this.

Tom Litterick (Labour) put forward a diametrically opposed view. In order to ensure conditions which would attract sufficient numbers of policemen, they 'should be accorded the rights of freedom of association and freedom of representation enjoyed by everybody else'. In addition to the economic argument, there were other reasons for allowing the police a trade union. 'If we make the mistake of creating the police as a recognisable separate group, we create the danger of alienation between the community and the police.' It was a fundamental right of the police, like other workers, to have union representation. 'Policemen are workers, like everyone else who works for a salary or a wage. . .But are deprived of the right of freedom of action which is enjoyed by trade union members in this country.' The restrictions on police organisation dated from the situation in 1919 when 'the frightened politicians thought that the Russians were coming'. But 'policemen are highly responsible people. . . They should be deemed officially by the State to be sufficiently responsible to choose their own trade union.' At present they were treated in a patronising, paternalistic way. They were told: 'You can have any association you like – so long as it is the Police Federation.' In short, Mr Litterick argued: 'A free society can afford to give its policemen equal rights.' This view was not shared by the House. The general opinion seemed more in agreement with the sentiments expressed by Michael Mates (Conservative): 'It would be a sad day if bodies that are able to carry out their work in society on the basis of their inbred discipline, loyalty and *esprit de corps* were to have all that eroded.'

In the first half of the 1970s the police were in a strong bargaining position because of the high 'demand' for their services in the face of concern about crime and disorder, while the 'supply' of policemen was unfavourable. Anxiety about police manpower and morale were the 'weapons' used by the Federation in gaining pay rises. In the last few years, however, the rapid increase in unemployment has altered the situation considerably. Recruitment rose dramatically in 1974, and wastage fell compared to previous years. This was despite the erosion of the real value of police pay by rapid inflation. It was also in spite of the growing strain on policemen caused by continued under-manning in relation to increased work-loads. (See, for example, a *Sunday Telegraph* article on 8 June 1975, which described the record numbers of police officers 'cracking up' under the stress of overwork.) The buoyant manpower situation, despite the relative deterioration of pay and conditions, undercut the traditional Federation argument for better pay to cope with shortages. Unemployment drove men into the service.

The 1975 pay negotiations were accompanied by even more tension than those in 1970. The Home Secretary, Roy Jenkins's, speech to the Annual Federation Conference faced a stormy reception. He was heckled with cries of 'rubbish' and general expressions of dissent, to a degree which made him declare: 'You must not make me think I'm dealing with the International Marxists'. The delegates' animosity was occasioned by considerable anxiety about the impending pay offer, due to be announced on 4 June 1975, five days later. On the first day of the Conference there was much discussion of alternative ways of bringing pressure to bear on the authorities. Various suggestions for demonstrating the strength of feeling were aired at the constables' session. One delegate urged a walk-out. Another suggested they should 'give him the cold shoulder, the calm, the quiet and ignore him' because 'he will come prepared to smarm us. Let us show our disrespect by not standing, and remaining silent.' Both ideas were rejected, but are testimony to Conference's militant mood.

Conference also decided to suspend standing orders and debate a resolution urging a referendum of all members to decide whether or not the police should have the right to strike. This resolution had already been rejected by the Conference Arrangements Committee, which draws up the agenda, on the ground that a similar motion had been discussed and defeated in 1974, as well as at some earlier Conferences. Nonetheless, some delegates' mood was such that they forced a debate on the rejected motion. It was considered on 30 May, but defeated.

The Federation believed that rises of between 42% and 65% were justified in the light of the recommendations made by the Report of the Police Council Working Party on Pay, published in March 1975. The pay award of 20–30% announced on 4 June fell far short of the Federation's claim. To rub salt into the wound, superintendents were awarded between 35% and 38%. The official response of the Federation was reluctant acquiescence. The chairman said: 'This will be accepted by our members but without any great enthusiasm.' The unofficial response of members was more bitter. On 5 June, 200 members of the North Tyne branch decided to withhold their voluntary subscriptions. In succeeding months, however, opinion among the men came to accept that the award was the best that could be hoped for in the worsening economic situation, and in the absence of bargaining power. The J.C.C. chairman, Les Male, told members: 'The last pay settlement was, contrary to some opinions, far better than we had hoped for and certainly higher than almost all other awards during the last twelve months' (*Police*, November 1975: 12). Nonetheless it continued the erosion of the policeman's relative pay from the pre-war 'golden age'. 'In 1939, a constable was appointed at 112% of average manual workers' earnings. In 1960, this was 97%, and in 1974 it was 96%. The constable, on maximum pay, in 1939 was getting 163% of manual workers' earnings. In 1960 he was getting 158% and in 1974 it was 143%' (*Police*, July 1975: 3).

The 1976 pay negotiations were attended by considerable acrimony, making the issue of police unionism front-page news for the first time since 1919. The immediate trigger was a dispute between the Official and Staff Sides on the Police Council concerning the interpretation of the 1975 award, its relationship to the pay policy agreed to between the government and T.U.C., and the implications for the police rise due in September 1976. The Official Side's position was that the September 1975 award included the £6 maximum rise under the first phase of the 'Social Contract', and had indeed been granted to the police under a special transitional arrangement allowing it to be paid after the start of the policy. Thus the 1976 negotiations had to be within the 4½% limit of Phase Two. The Staff Side maintained that the 1976 award had reflected only the restructuring recommended by the 1975 Police Council Working Party, together with an element to compensate for inflation since 1974. Therefore the police had not yet received an award within Phase One and the 1976 rise should be within the £6 limit. The two sides proved unable to resolve this disagreement. The Staff Side were embittered by their inability to persuade the Official Side of the justice of their case and to present a demand to the government with the backing of the whole Council. They felt that negotiations in the Council were useless because the Official Side considered themselves bound by government pay policy, with no power to move outside it. The representatives of the Federation for England and Wales argued that this signified the impotence of the negotiating machinery. If the Official Side were merely acting in accordance with government policy, negotiations ought to be directly with the Home Secretary. Consequently, the English and Welsh representatives walked out of the Police Council in July, demanding direct negotiations with the government because they had lost faith in the established negotiating body. As an article justifying this move in *Police* declared: 'If the monkey's lost its teeth, talk to the organ grinder' (*Police*, August 1976: 10). The Scottish representatives remained on the Council, arguing that it was the only available negotiating forum. As a result of the walk-out the future of police negotiating machinery is uncertain. The issue has broadened beyond pay alone, with the Federation seeking a comprehensive review of the representative organisations.

The pay dispute has remained deadlocked. After the seamen's strike threat in September 1975 resulted in an award combining a package of fringe benefits plus a straight pay rise, the Federation's tactics altered. While still arguing that they had not received an award within Phase One, the Federation suggested a similar package including fringe benefits, such as additional annual leave, reduced pension contributions, and a standby duty allowance, as a way of achieving a satisfactory rise without breaching the pay policy. The government have rejected this solution as also constituting a violation of the norm, and making the police a special case. The Federation argue that they have been singled out as a special case by not receiving a Phase One award, and in being bound by a 'voluntary' agreement between government and T.U.C. while prohibited by law from affiliation to the latter.

The prolonged dispute has been accompanied by increasing evidence of rank-and-file bitterness. The Federation leadership have consistently maintained that they do not seek the right to strike or affiliation with the T.U.C. But, in addition to pursuing the pay claim by increasingly unorthodox tactics, they have begun to argue the case for a 'free association', the constitution of which would be determined by the members.

Throughout the autumn of 1976, at a series of open meetings, rank-and-file members called for militancy and strike action. At a meeting in South Wales on 22 September the national representatives were apparently dismayed by the strength of feeling expressed by the floor speakers ('Police in strike poll call', *Bristol Evening Post*, 23 September 1976). A meeting at Central Hall, Westminster, on 30 September attracted several thousand policemen from round the country to hear Federation secretary Joe Martucci. When he denied intending to seek the right to strike, he was shouted down.

Platform speakers were constantly interrupted by the noisy and unruly police audience in civilian dress who seemed to have stripped off decorum with their uniforms. There were storms of shouts, jeers and boos every time the Police Council...was mentioned. But every time the word 'strike' was heard, there were wild cheers and applause. When platform speakers urged their audience to lobby their M.P.'s there were groans and boos, and one shout rang out 'Mine's in gaol'.

(*The Times*, 1 October 1976)

Some more militant leaders of the Federation attended the T.U.C. Annual Conference in Brighton in September 1976 to talk to union leaders. In the words of one, 'we were well received and they had a lot of sympathy' ('Police campaign for right to strike', *Sunday Telegraph*, 26 September 1976). Clive Jenkins was reported to have drawn up a model constitution for a police and armed forces union, and discussed the possibility of links with A.S.T.M.S., and T.U.C. affiliation ('Police may claim the right to strike', *The Times*, 24 November 1976).

As Home Secretary Rees continued to reject the Federation's claims for a package deal, the campaign was stepped up, fuelled by rank-and-file discontent. On 16 December the Federation organised an unprecedented lobby of Parliament. The government's adamant stand was partly underpinned by buoyant recruitment due to growing unemployment. In 1976 the strength of the Metropolitan Police rose by 1010, the largest annual increase for thirty years. Policemen were unable to express their discontent by resigning and getting better-paid jobs. They were forced to seek remedies for their grievances as *policemen*. (By mid-1977, however, there were signs that wastage was beginning to rise again.) Many forces submitted resolutions for the May 1977 Federation Annual Conference seeking the right to strike, T.U.C. affiliation or a 'free association'. A series of referenda in provincial forces in early 1977 made it seem probable that for the first time such motions might be carried ('Police polls favour right to strike', *The Times*, 16 April 1977: 3). By the eve of Conference, thirty-one out of the forty-three forces in England and Wales had held referenda on the right to strike, and this had been supported by majorities ranging from 60% to 80%. In two polls the question of T.U.C. affiliation had also been raised, but rejected by a majority of about 2:1.

Conservative politicians have urged the government to treat the police as a special case, and condemned Labour for pursuing its pay policy in a way which threatened to push policemen towards unionisation. At a debate on 'law and order' at the Conservative Party Conference in October 1976, Mr Angus Maude described the Labour Government as 'extraordinarily silly', and urged it to settle the dispute by concessions to the police along the lines of the seamen's deal. 'The Government ought to say now that as soon as it can get off the hook of its pay policy and find a way to pacify its paymasters in the T.U.C. it will meet the just demands of the police.' As the dispute became increasingly acrimonious, and the pressure for the right to strike attracted publicity, other Conservatives added their voices to this argument. On the 23 February 1977 Conservative back-benchers heavily supported an early-day motion declaring: 'That this House, believing that an efficient and contented police force is in-dispensable to the maintenance of the Queen's Peace, calls on the Prime Minister to procure a speedy solution to the police pay dispute on the principles applied in the case of the seamen's pay settlement.' *The Daily Telegraph* argued in an editorial on 2 March that

Of all the many dangers which confront the country today none is plainer or more immediate than that presented by the growing demand of the police for the right to strike. . . . It is not only because the police have it in their power to plunge the country into instant anarchy by the withdrawal of their labour. . .it is also because. . .a police force with the right to participate in trade union activity automatically loses its political impartiality.

The Press was united in expressing alarm at the growing militancy of the police. Most newspapers supported the justice of the police claim, and urged the government to make them a special case. *The Guardian* and the *Sunday Times* were exceptions, describing the police pressure as 'blackmail'.

On the Labour left, however, voices were raised supporting the police right to unionisation. Mr Arthur Lewis, for example, requested the Home Secretary to amend the law so as to enable police forces to have the same trade union rights as every other type of civilian employee ('Review of police rights', *The Guardian*, 1 February 1977).

The government remained unprepared to change its bargaining posi-tion. Rees did suggest that there might be more pay forthcoming after the end of Phase Two. He also indicated that a review of the negotiating machinery was possible. In a Yorkshire TV interview following crucial talks with the Federation on 3 March, Rees advised the police to join the T.U.C. and 'learn how they negotiate'. (How the Federation could follow this advice when T.U.C. affiliation is forbidden by the 1919 and 1964 Police Acts was not explained.)

The 3 March meeting between the Home Secretary and the Federation appears to have been especially acrimonious. The Federation representa-tives were incensed by the fact that Rees told them to return to the Police Council, instead of dealing with substantial aspects of the claim. Callaghan met the Federation leaders on 7 March – the first time a Prime Minister had personally intervened in a police pay dispute since 1919. However, any hopes of obtaining greater satisfaction from their erstwhile parlia-mentary champion were dashed. Callaghan made it clear that the govern-ment would not increase its offer, and urged the Federation to return to the Police Council. He intimated that a more generous settlement would then be possible under Phase Three, starting in September 1977.

The Federation issued a statement declaring its affront at the treatment it had received:

Our meeting with the Prime Minister was friendly, but it produced no solution and no forward movement whatsoever. If anything, Government has tried to force us two steps backwards. These are: the scotching of all proposals for a fringe benefit settlement under Phase Two; and by demanding that the Federation return to the Police Council from which we and our Ulster colleagues have irreversibly withdrawn.

This is a black day for the police service and, we fear, for the country.

No member of the police service wants to take industrial action. Only a very few police officers want affiliation with outside bodies which could compromise political neutrality, but we are no longer prepared to be treated as unique.

It comes to taking risks and accepting restrictions that no other group of workers would tolerate on their civil rights, while not being treated as unique when it comes to pay and conditions... We are sick and tired of being pushed around and now we appeal responsibly and confidently to the public and to Parliament for support in our legitimate struggle.

James Jardine, the chairman, amplified this by commenting: 'If we can't be treated as a unique body of workers then we want to be treated as other workers and to have the 1974 Trade Union and Labour Relations Act applied to us.'

On 15 March, the Police Council reconvened with the staff side represented only by the Scottish Police Federation, the Superintendents' Association, and the Association of Chief Police Officers. Sir John Nightingale, Chief Constable of Essex and chairman of the Council, was authorised to attempt to break the deadlock by holding unofficial talks with the representatives for England and Wales.

In the meantime, the Federation continued its campaign to influence public opinion. On 21 March advertisements appeared in *The Times* and *Guardian* aiming to rebut official figures which had been released purporting to show that police pay was well above average. On the same day, some 600 policemen's wives from around the country demonstrated in London, under banners such as 'Lobby for my bobby'. A deputation met M.P.s afterwards. (This followed several months in which many letters had appeared in the Press from police wives describing their financial plight.)

The eventual outcome of these developments is uncertain. But the issue of police unionism seems to have been clearly laid on the political agenda, and to have become an important question in the consciousness of policemen. At the same time, the development of the dispute, especially the repeated declarations by the Federation leadership that they were not seeking the right to strike, indicates the considerable reluctance of policemen not only to engage in actual strike action but even to seek full union powers. The preferred position would seem to be one where the police receive special treatment in exchange for accepting their special status as a non-unionised body (an exchange which the Conservatives have explicitly been urging on the government). The polls revealing support for the right to strike suggest a growing awareness that only unionisation can guarantee power when the police bargaining position is weakened by a healthy recruitment situation or other factors. Whether this growth in trade union consciousness will continue, and result in any changes in the structure of the police negotiating machinery, has yet to be seen. But any pressure in that direction is limited by the contradictory position of the police in the class structure (Wright 1976: 40–1). On the one hand, their interests as salaried employees may, in certain conjunctures, push them to seek trade union powers as a means of defence, in the same way as other workers. Against this, however, is the normal role of the policeman, which tends to push him in a conservative direction. This contradiction is revealed in the nature of police discontent, and their desired solutions for their problems. Economic grievances highlight the policeman's situation as an employee who might be helped by trade unionism, as recent events indicate. But the extent of bitterness presently experienced by policemen derives not only from financial problems. It is also the result of an accumulated anger at social trends which are seen by the policemen as exacerbating the difficulties of his job. The policeman's analysis of his non-economic grievances, and how to remedy them, pushes him into political directions which alienate him from the labour movement.

   This is clearly seen in another important development of recent years, the emergence of the Federation as spokesman for the rank-and-file policeman on matters of penal and social policy. These issues probably have deeper salience in police consciousness than the economic grievances. As previously remarked, Roy Jenkins's response in 1967 to the pamphlet *The Problem,* and his inclusion of Federationists on the three working parties he set up in that year, heralded the new developments. Since then the Federation has been increasingly consulted at national level on legislation and proposed changes in penal and force policy. Throughout the 1970s there has been growing concern about crime (especially violent offences) and politically motivated disturbances. In 1970, the chairman began his speech to Conference with the statement 'We have been eyeball to eyeball with the fanatics, the lunatics and the hooligans' (Edited Proceedings: 31). In September 1970, *Police* drew attention to the institution of a 'Pig of the Month' contest in an 'underground' newspaper.

Should we be upset? Not at all. The pig has made a notable contribution to our national well-being over the centuries. As such, it has a great advantage over hippy squatters...whose concepts of sanitation are often far more primitive than its own... In America, they say P-I-G stands for Pride, Integrity and Guts.
(*Police,* September 1970: 6)

During the 1970s policemen grew increasingly frustrated by what they saw as too great an influence of anti-police elements on society, reflected in such tendencies as 'lenient' penal and sentencing policies, and the demand for independent review of complaints against the police. At the end of November 1975, in response to this feeling, the Federation launched an unprecedented campaign for 'law and order'. The general aim, as outlined to members in *Police*, was 'to harness the public's growing concern about the state of crime and public order in Britain into a programme for positive action' (*Police*, November 1975: 13–14). The more detailed list of specific objectives was to publicise:

(1) Concern about the growing *volume* of crime... (2) Anxiety about *violence*... (3) Concern about the effectiveness of existing criminal legislation... (4) The attitude of the courts at all levels towards the punishment of offenders... (5) The need for changes in criminal justice administration procedures... (6) The attitude of some people and some bodies in public life towards the rule of law, instancing the sympathy shown to law breakers whose crimes have allegedly 'political' overtones. The need for the 'silent majority' to assert itself in order that politicians and judges fully understand the true feelings of the public. (7) The need for public support for the police to be more positive.

The campaign was inspired by the success of pressure groups supporting liberalising reforms of the law. 'The pattern of recent years has seen the dominant influence of pressure groups, often representing a minority view, able to secure major changes in the law.' Examples were given: the abolition of capital punishment, homosexual law reform, changes in the law affecting children and young persons, abortion law reform, legislation for sexual equality, race relations, independent examination of complaints against the police etc. The police were to learn from these bodies, and seek to influence 'opinion-makers' in support of the 'rule of law'. The national campaign was to be backed up by local activity.

In response to this suggestion, Branch Boards urged the public to write to M.P.s and councillors supporting a reversal of 'soft' penal policies. Letters were sent to branches of trade unions, the C.B.I., and political parties around the country, seeking talks to discuss the problems of crime. The campaign was supported by various bodies, including the Superintendents' Association and some Chief Constables.

The campaign was condemned by many other sections of opinion. This was not only on the grounds of substance, but also because it seemed to signal a departure from the established Federation policy of non-involvement in politics. A group of twenty-five Labour M.P.s laid down a motion on 21 November 1975, regretting the campaign and the incipient political activity of the police. Magistrates and social workers defended themselves against allegations that they were over indulgent to criminals. In '*Socialist Workers* [sic], weekly comic of the far left...Beth Stone, of the National Union of Teachers, is warning us all about the sinister menace of one Les Male of the Police Federation, the organisation which is trying to get her Union to co-operate in its current campaign on the problems of crime

...."another attempt is to be made to twist and warp the minds of Britain's school-children"...What really upsets her is that our approach to the N.U.T. executive resulted in "only 3 members voting against". Against what?' (*Police*, March 1976: 6). Some policemen dissociated themselves from the political implications of the campaign and felt it might be counter-productive (Letter from Inspector G. Marsden, *The Times*, 6 April 1976). However, as chapter 11 will indicate, the campaign seems to meet a need long-felt by most policemen.

The Federation defended itself against these accusations, by arguing: 'What is "political" about crime? So far as we know, all responsible political parties are committed to the rule of laws enacted by elected Parliaments.' The Federation had a right to comment on legislation, all of which 'affected the working lives of police officers who might have strong views on it' (*Police*, December 1975: 3). In the same issue, the cover was a cartoon which attracted much comment in the Press. (This cover marked a considerable departure for *Police*. I have examined every issue since 1970, and this is the first one having any reference whatsoever to police involvement in law-enforcement. All the previous covers depict policemen in friendly contact with members of the public. Prominently featured are policemen with children, animals, old people, pretty girls or playing sports, frequently in an idyllic rural setting.) The cartoon showed a courtroom scene, in which all the legal functionaries, the jury and the accused were depicted as grotesquely deformed, while the lone policeman in the witness-box was drawn as a clean-cut, stalwart young man.

The Federation also gave much publicity to a public opinion survey it had commissioned, which, it claimed, 'reveals strong support for the Police Federation's views' (*Police*, March 1976: 18–19). The questions tended to be so ambiguously worded as to defy meaningful interpretation. For example, '82% of the sample either agreed or strongly agreed with the statement "too much is done for criminals and not enough for their victims"'. It is by no means clear that 'doing something' for 'criminals' precludes effective concern for the 'victim'. By the same token, the 82% may be concerned that more be done for 'victims', without wanting less to be done for 'criminals'. Many of the other questions similarly lumped together various issues, so that it is not clear to which one respondents are replying. Nonetheless, the Federation's conclusion was that 'support for action does indeed come from a moderate, and perhaps silent, majority'. The survey seemed to locate resistance to the campaign amongst 'younger people, those in the upper socio-economic groups and those with the highest level of educational attainment'. It therefore recommended that a special effort be made 'to address those *least* likely to provide support', e.g. university societies, '*as well* as those groups who might be more immediately in sympathy', e.g. Rotary clubs, Townswomen's Guilds. It was also found that there was widespread support for 'more liberal sexual attitudes'. Members were consequently urged to dissociate the campaign from any taint of a general attempt to impose moral standards.

> Be careful not to confuse acceptance of violence with 'declining standards of morality', particularly sexual morality.... The Federation would be in danger of alienating support...if it tried to equate support for public order with an overly conventional view of sexual or other personal morality. It would be right to stress the value of the family and family togetherness and a respect for conventional discipline as a support for combating crime but, for younger people, this does not entail what they might conceive of as a repressive attitude to freedom in personal behaviour.

The most recent step in the campaign was a seminar on *The Challenge of Crime* held in April 1976 at Cambridge, attended by 'politicians, church leaders, magistrates and trade unionists, leaders of voluntary bodies and members of the police service'. Among the main speakers were Justice Melford Stevenson and Enoch Powell, whose invitation was attacked by representatives of black people's organisations. (See 'Police assault bolsters claim of "racial bias"', *The Observer*, 18 April 1976.) This criticism is understandable in view of Powell's previous image with regard to race relations. This cannot have been improved by his speech itself, with its reference to 'the introduction of these alien wedges into the population of our cities' as a major source of the increase of violence represented by 'mugging'. (See his speech '"The Thing" that swept the world', *Police*, April 1976. 'The Thing' referred to in the title is the spread of political protest. 'It was the thing that started in Berkeley. It took various forms; university disorder; civil rights movements; anti-apartheid activities; race and immigration. The essence of "The Thing" is that violence is used in order to subjugate the will of the majority.' It would thus seem to be Powell's view that 'race and immigration' in themselves constitute elements of 'The Thing'.) Criticism of the Federation's invitation to Powell was attacked by the chairman, Leslie Male, as 'ill-conceived and totally misdirected...In a free society an organisation must be free to hold what meetings it wishes and invite which speakers it wants, without having to submit them to the Community Relations Commission for prior approval' ('Police leader rejects criticism over Powell', *Daily Telegraph*, 15 April 1976).

This campaign marks a significant departure for the Federation. Whatever its success, it is clearly the result of a careful consideration of pressure group tactics, and a judicious appraisal of strategy, informed by 'scientific' study of public opinion. It is the climax of ten years of change in which the Federation has sought to broaden its scope beyond the confines of a narrow, collective bargaining body, and a very tame one at that.

Later sections discuss members' attitudes to the Federation. It must be stressed that the interviews were conducted during 1973–4, an exceptionally favourable bargaining period for the police. The men's comments clearly reflect this. Since then the bargaining position has weakened, and attitudes have altered. Another major change is the 'law and order' campaign. This responds to long-felt frustration about these issues and may well affect members' assessment of the Federation. But consideration of the reasons underlying responses to the survey helps understand the new attitudes which develop as circumstances alter.

The structure of the Police Federation

The formal structure of the Federation will be reviewed to provide a setting for members' views. The description of a local branch is based on the city in which research was conducted, but all forces have a similar structure. (Since 1974, the force has been amalgamated with the surrounding counties. Policewomen are now incorporated into the other divisions.)

All policemen, up to and including the rank of chief inspector, are automatically members of the Federation, the statutory basis of which is the 1964 Police Act. Detailed regulations are given in *The Police Federation Regulations 1969*, No. 1787. While policemen cannot opt out of membership, they can refuse to contribute the weekly levy. But in fact hardly any exercise this option.

The city force in which the research was conducted was organised into two kinds of division. There were four territorial divisions, A, B, C, and D, responsible for patrolling the different areas into which the city was divided. Each had two sub-divisional stations. Command of each division was in the hands of a superintendent; a chief inspector headed most sub-divisional stations. A division was the largest, and included the central city area. The other territorial divisions covered the rest of the city. Each uniform division annually elected one representative in each rank to the Federation (with the exception that A division by virtue of its size elected two in each rank). Thus there were five representatives respectively for the ranks of constable, sergeant and inspector from the territorial divisions.

There were also four specialist divisions. E was the Administration, and included, apart from the Central Headquarters staff, the Mounted and Dog section, the Courts Department and Research and Planning. F was the Criminal Investigation Department. This was broadly subdivided into 'operational' detectives, who worked from each sub-divisional station (and some who were seconded to the Regional Crime Squad), and 'inside' technical support like fingerprint experts. G was the traffic division, which covered the city in powerful cars and motorcycles. (The Operations Room at headquarters was also organised under G division.) Before the advent of the panda system, traffic had been something of an elite, handling emergency calls, but the motorisation of routine patrol had meant a relative decline in the status of G division. (Direction of traffic in terms of point-duty was the responsibility of the territorial men.) W was the police-women's division. Each of the specialist divisions also elected one Federation representative per rank. (There were also some specialist departments like Vice and Special Services which were part of A division strength.) Altogether, therefore, there were nine constables', sergeants' and inspectors' representatives respectively. The important thing about this arrangement is that each rank in each division elects the *same* number of representatives despite the different numbers in each rank. The constables', sergeants' and inspectors' representatives constituted respectively the constables', sergeants' and inspectors' Branch Boards. These could meet separately if they wanted to discuss matters peculiar to one rank, but normally they met together as the Joint Branch Board. This elected officers who handled the day-to-day affairs. The secretary was a full-time post, and the chairman became one during the research period. All other officials and representatives were operational policemen, though they had limited time off to attend meetings. The Joint Branch Board was entitled to one quarterly meeting lasting one day, plus special extra ones at the Chief Constable's discretion. The constitution of the Branch Board is summarised in Figure 2.1.

FIGURE 2.1. *Organisation of the local Federation branch*

	Division	Constables	Sergeants	Inspectors
	A	2	2	2
Territorial	B	1	1	1
	C	1	1	1
	D	1	1	1
	E: Administration	1	1	1
Specialists	F: C.I.D.	1	1	1
	G: Traffic	1	1	1
	W: Policewoman	1	1	1
		9	9	9
		Constables' Board	Sergeants' Board	Inspectors' Board

27 members of Joint Branch Board

When it is noted that during 1973 there were 81 inspectors, 183 sergeants, and 873 constables it will be clear that the system of *equal* representation for each rank results in a swamping of the constables compared to their strength in the force. As the historical account indicated, this was instituted in 1919 as an explicit control device.

Each local Branch Board elects two delegates per rank to attend an Annual Central Conference. (There is also one additional delegate per every 500 men in the force establishment.) The Annual Conference lasts three days. On the first day the delegates of each rank meet separately, but on the next two days they meet together as the Joint Central Conference. This is customarily addressed by the Home Secretary. Each rank elects a Central Committee to handle its affairs during the year. For each rank this consists of two London members, plus one from each of the six regions into which the country is divided for policing, plus one police-woman, a total of nine. The Joint Central Committee can hold meetings of up to three days every two months as of right, plus extra ones at the discretion of the Home Secretary.

The national Federation institutions are summarised in Figure 2.2.

The Joint Central Committee employs some civilian staff at its Surbiton headquarters. Some of these are ex-policemen, such as the editor of the Federation magazine *Police*, Anthony Judge. It also employs a Parliamentary Consultant, who is always a member of the Opposition.

Figure 2.2. *Federation national organisation*

(a) Annual Central Conference			
Joint	(i)	Constables' Central Conference	⎫ for each: 2 delegates
Central	(ii)	Sergeants' Central Conference	⎬ per force (+ 1 per
Conference	(iii)	Inspectors' Central Conference	⎭ 500 establishment)
(b) Central Committees			
Joint	(i)	Constables' Central Committee	⎫
Central		(elected by *a* (i))	⎪ for each: 2 London
Committee	(ii)	Sergeants' Central Committee	⎬ members + 1 from
(27 members)		(elected by *a* (ii))	⎪ each of 6 regions
	(iii)	Inspectors' Central Committee	⎭ + 1 policewoman
		(elected by *a* (iii))	

The 1964 Police Act gave statutory footing to the negotiating machinery established in 1953, following the Oaksey Committee's recommendations. The main institution of this is the Police Council of Great Britain. This is divided into an Official Side and a Staff Side. The Official Side consists of representatives of the Home Office (5), the Scottish Home Department (1), the County Councils Association (7), the Association of Municipal Corporations (7), the Association of County Councils in Scotland (2), the Convention of Royal Burghs in Scotland (2), and the Association of Counties of Cities in Scotland (2), making a total of 26. The Staff Side consists of the Commissioner of the Metropolitan Police, 3 representatives of the Association of Chief Police Officers of England

and Wales (A.C.P.O.), 3 representatives of the Superintendents' Association of England and Wales, 9 members of the Police Federation for England and Wales, 2 representatives of the Chief Constables' (Scotland) Association, 1 member of the Association of Scottish Police Superintendents, 6 members of the Scottish Police Federation, and 2 extra members from the Superintendents' Associations and Police Federations of England and Wales and for Scotland, considered jointly. This makes a total of 27, of whom 6 are chief officers, 5 are superintendents, and sixteen represent the Federated ranks. (There are 5 constables, sergeants and inspectors respectively plus a policewoman.)

Matters affecting only one rank are handled by separate Panels of the Council. Panel A deals with questions concerning chief officers, B is for the superintendents, and C for the federated ranks. Panel C consists of 15 Official Side members and 16 Federation representatives. The Federation members are not in fact a majority, because on panels B and C, the Commissioner of the Metropolitan and three other chief officers selected by the Official Side, sit with the Official Side as advisers. It is on Panel C that pay and other negotiations for the federated ranks takes place. The number from the Official and Staff Sides are not crucially important, because all agreements must be arrived at by the concurrence of *both* sides. If agreement is not reached, either or both sides can refer the matter to arbitration. The arbitration tribunal consists of 3 members appointed by the Prime Minister, and its decisions are treated as though they were agreements by both sides of the council. (The future of this machinery has been called into question by the Federation walkout in July 1976.)

The 1964 Police Act also established the Police Advisory Boards (one for England and Wales, and one for Scotland). These replaced the previous Police Councils which had been set up in 1919. They are 'round-table' organisations, consisting of Federation representatives alongside those from the Chief Constables' and Superintendents' Associations, and representatives of the police authorities. Their function is not negotiation, but to *advise* the Home Secretary on 'general questions affecting the police'.

There are different sorts of 'police authority' for the various kinds of police forces in Britain. Under the 1964 Police Act, four types of forces were distinguished. The police authority for the Metropolitan force has been the Home Secretary ever since its foundation in 1829. The authority responsible for the City of London force is a standing committee of the Court of Common Council. Provincial forces are of two kinds, county forces and borough forces. The police authority of both varieties consists of two-thirds elected councillors and one-third local magistrates. In counties this body is called the Police Committee, in boroughs the Watch Committee. Until 1964 this difference in nomenclature corresponded to a difference in composition. Watch Committees were then made up entirely of elected councillors, and county police authorities were half made up of magistrates, half of councillors.

The Police Act of 1964 defines the general duty of the police authority as being 'to secure the maintenance of an adequate and efficient police force for the area' (section 4.1). The precise relationship, constitutionally and in practice, between police authority, Chief Constable and Home Office is a complex and much debated matter. The Police Act of 1964 seeks to clarify and rationalise the situation, but it can be argued that it has failed to do so (Marshall 1965: 87, 96–101). The sections relevant to the problem appear to be self-contradictory, as well as vague, at crucial points. Altogether, regarding the Act's definition of the roles of those in control of the police, 'the net effect. . .has probably been to strengthen the hands both of the Home Office and of Chief Constables at the expense of local authorities' (Marshall 1971: 3).

The establishment and rank structure of a force are determined by the police authority (subject to Home Office approval), and they are also responsible for the maintenance of buildings, equipment etc. The cost of the police force is paid 50% by local ratepayers, with central government providing the other half, subject to the Home Secretary being satisfied the force is efficient as determined by Her Majesty's Inspectors of Constabulary. This grant has never been withheld since the nineteenth century, though shortcomings are sometimes pointed out and pressure for improvements brought to bear (Critchley 1967: 309). The police authority appoint the Chief Constable, but the latter is then responsible for the deployment of men on a routine basis. He has the sole right of appointment, promotion and discipline of the men. The police authority is empowered to call for reports, but the Chief Constable may refuse if the Home Office supports him. (The Home Secretary can also call for reports from Chief Constables.) The police authority's power to dismiss the Chief Constable is subject to Home Office veto.

Various writers have suggested that the degree of local accountability of police forces has been further restricted with the growing size of police areas due to amalgamations. They have bemoaned this, and suggested possible remedies (Marshall 1971; Banton 1974). Marshall recommends the introduction of non-statutory watch committees, within the new police authorities, corresponding to the areas prior to amalgamation. Banton's proposal is for the police authorities to become 'peace committees', incorporating a wider range of interest-groups from the locality with a concern about law-enforcement, and also Federation representatives.

Summary

The Police Federation is now clearly recognised as a bargaining organisation for pay and conditions, and negotiating machinery has been established at central level. It is still prohibited, however, from involvement in *individual* cases of promotion and discipline. It has acquired some measure of independence with the ability to levy a voluntary contribution from members, though this can only be put to a limited range of uses. Any form of industrial action or 'incitement to disaffection' remains forbidden. Affiliation with the T.U.C. is also prohibited, though in 1972 the Federation was granted permission to 'associate' with outside bodies at the discretion of the Home Office. At local level its position is less institutionalised and more subject to the views of individual Chief Constables. The Federation can make representations, but has no *right* to regular consultation or access. Nor are they entitled to attend meetings of, or meet with, the police authority. The present situation has been summed up by a cartoon in *Police*, commenting on a newspaper report that policemen lead the list of occupational groups having vasectomy operations. The caption has a policeman saying: 'A vasectomy recipient is rather like the Police Federation...equipped with all the negotiating machinery... but without the power to strike.' (*Police*, February 1975: 9.) In the next Part we shall examine the members' reaction to this impotence.

PART TWO

Police attitudes to unionism

3
Policemen's evaluation of the Federation

Previous research findings

The only existing material on policemen's perception of the Federation is contained in a Home Office Police Research and Development Branch study, *The Man-Management Survey*, which has never been published. This was carried out in 1969, and was based on a national sample. The results are of some interest, but because of the limited nature of the questions and the analysis, do not explain how the men react to their restricted situation, and the reasons for variation.

The following conclusions can be drawn from the study. Firstly, policemen in most forces seem to be satisfied that the Federation is doing as much as it can, although this satisfaction is greater with the local branch than the national body, and among men in county and borough forces than in city forces. Secondly, despite this, most men, especially those in city forces, feel that insufficient notice is taken of the Federation at national level. A majority in county and borough forces feel that sufficient notice is taken of the Federation at local level, but this feeling is only shared by a minority of city policemen. Thirdly, the main area in which the men dissatisfied with Federation activity feel it could do more at national level is pay. With regard to local activity no one issue stands out. Finally, the main explanation given by those who feel insufficient attention is paid to the Federation is that it has insufficient power, specifically to take industrial action. This is especially felt by city policemen. Some feel that anti-Federation, or anti-police, attitudes held by the authorities are also important.

There are several questions left unanswered by these findings. What, if any, changes would be desired by the men, especially the dissatisfied ones? Satisfaction with Federation efforts *within the limits of its powers* seems to be combined with lack of satisfaction by many with the results of its activity. Does this mean that there would be support for a change in Federation powers? The survey only considered variations between types of forces. While these are of importance, and show some interesting patterns, what is neglected is variation *within* forces. The sample includes not only the federated ranks, but also ranks above that. It would be interesting to know if similar results hold when only the federated ranks (i.e. up to and including chief inspector) are included, and what, if any, variations there are *within* the federated ranks (i.e. between constables, sergeants and inspectors). Vertical differences, i.e. differences between specialisms, also have to be examined. Also, the reasons for varying attitudes to the Federation are not sought. How do these relate to different orientations to work? How can one account for acceptance or rejection of the existing forms of representation?

It is these questions I hoped to illuminate by a more detailed and deeper analysis of opinion within one force. These results also help explain some of the patterns of variations found in the national research just referred to.

The present study

The findings of this study are not usually comparable in quantitative terms with the national one. The questions were not identical. (The reason for this is that the Home Office survey is an internal, unpublished enquiry, and only came to my attention after the research was under way.) Furthermore, the nature of the samples was different. The national one included superintendents, whereas the present one was confined to the federated ranks. Nonetheless, the range and pattern of answers to similar questions was much the same as those found for city forces in the national survey. This would support the view that the present research gives some insight into the opinions that would be held by city policemen in general.

Policemen in this sample were asked whether or not they felt that the Federation was, on the whole, an adequate representative body for them. Overall, 52% felt that the Federation was adequate taken as it stood, 44% thought it was not, with 4% don't knows. As in the national survey, a majority is satisfied with the Federation, although there is considerable disagreement.

This general statement concerning Federation adequacy tells us very little. It is necessary to explore the location of different attitudes within the force, and the reasons offered, as well as the direction in which change would be desired. Satisfaction with the Federation varied clearly with rank, as Table 3.1 shows.

The level of satisfaction with the Federation among constables is much lower than among inspectors, with sergeants falling in between. More constables (49%) are in fact dissatisfied with the Federation than are satisfied (46%). The overall picture of satisfaction outweighing dissatisfaction is due to the inclusion of inspectors, who are prediminantly satisfied, and sergeants, who also tend to be.

Contrary to what might be supposed, the job a policeman does in the force, holding rank constant, does not seem to affect his degree of satisfaction with the Federation, as tapped by this question. *A priori* it could be expected that specialist divisions would have different feelings about the Federation. They have special conditions of service, and might be presumed to have somewhat different conceptions of the nature of the job. But in fact, holding rank constant, specialist and ordinary territorial divisions seem similar in their judgement of overall Federation adequacy. (The numbers in each specialism when rank is held constant are too small for separate numerical comparison.) Later sections will show that there are indeed differences in the way specialist and non-specialist divisions view the Federation, though these are not apparent in this general question.

TABLE 3.1. *Satisfaction with the Federation, by rank*

	Constables %	Sergeants %	Inspectors %
Federation inadequate	49	45	22
Federation adequate	46	52	78
Don't know	5	3	0
Total	100	100	100
	N = 112	N = 33	N = 23

Before examining these, however, it is useful to look at the reasoning behind the judgements of Federation adequacy so far considered. This will reveal something of the variation in attitudes to the Federation which underlie similar global assessments of its adequacy.

The first point to be made is that analysis of the reasons offered for the overall judgements shows that the variations in these did not reflect different perceptions of the *actual* power of the Federation. It was generally held that the Federation was a pretty powerless body, and any successes it achieved were largely due to factors beyond its control. The difference between those who nonetheless judged it as adequate and those who did not was over the question of the form of representation the police ought or needed to have.

The men came up with a number of colourful metaphors to describe the weakness of the Federation's position. This perception of powerlessness was common to the men, whether they deemed the Federation adequate or not. The following quotes from uniformed constables are typical of the general attitude.

It's a toothless dog really. They can kick up a noise and fuss about everything, but when all's said and done, any decision is going to be by the Home Office anyway.

They're a toothless tiger. In the last analysis, if the government says jump they jump.

Despite this perception of the powerlessness of the Federation, 52% of the men felt it was an adequate body. The reasons for this could be classified into three categories.

The reasons for seeing the Federation as adequate

(a) 64% of the men who were content with the Federation believed that a powerful representative body was not necessary to ensure the satisfaction of policemen's interests. The position of the police in society was so crucial that, under the circumstances they had experienced, the police were likely to do well even without union powers. They were in what might be called an expanding industry. On the one hand the need for police protection was increasing due to rising crime rates in general and the threat of social and political unrest, while on the other hand police forces continued to face severe manpower problems. As we have seen in chapter 2, the interviewing took place in a period which was most propitious for the encouragement of this perspective. It was the time between the two miners' strikes during which the Heath government was trying to prepare the ground for an impending confrontation with the union movement. There was also growing concern about political violence of other kinds, the increasing number of demonstrations and the rise of terrorism, first with the Angry Brigade incidents and then with the extension of I.R.A. activities to England. Many policemen felt that a Tory government was more likely to respond to such challenges by strengthening the police. But it was also believed that the police were vital to society regardless of which party was in power. The view that political and social trends were giving the police considerable bargaining power – and thus that union power was not necessary for them – was reflected in the comments of many of the men who felt the Federation was adequate, despite its lack of muscle.

We had a fairly substantial pay rise two days before the freeze went on. Well, you're not going to say that was paid solely on the justification the Federation might have put forward. It was really to secure police support in times that might be a bit difficult, with militant trade unions. It wasn't the Federation who secured us the pay rise, it was the political temperature and the scene at that time.   (C.I.D. inspector)

Up in the Home Office they tend to look after us really. You know what I mean? They know we're important and are trying to enforce the law, and they haven't got to make it too difficult. They've got to try and play along with us. I mean, industrial disputes are in the future, aren't they, so they've got to try and keep us happy.   (Uniform sergeant)

We've got one great factor in our favour. When the government decides that there's going to be some sort of clamp-down like the latest freeze, there's going to be trouble on the industrial front. They have to keep the police a little bit sweet, which is the only reason we got our 15% before it came to trouble.

(Traffic constable)

The above quotes illustrate the view, mentioned by two-thirds of the men who were contented with the Federation, that stronger powers of negotiation were not necessary for the police force, because they were so important to government that they had reasonable success without industrial action. This position is clearly informed by events shortly before and during the period of interviewing.

Just over half the men who argued that the vital social role of the police gave them adequate leverage in negotiations even without industrial sanctions, considered this to be especially true when a Tory government was in office.

We have higher pay rises when the Conservatives are in power than when a Labour government is in power. We're the protection for the people in power, everywhere they go, so they've got to keep us slightly sweet. (Uniform constable)
I feel with the Conservative government you can get almost anything you want. The Angry Brigade achieved more in one night than the Federation did in fifty years, when they blew up Robert Carr's front door. . .
The Conservative government relies more on the police for its protection than a Labour government. The Labour government would put down their foot instantly, sort of, they were the bosses. But it seems that with the Conservative government they get virtually what they asked for. . .
[I pointed out that Unit Beat policing and other reforms had been introduced by Labour.]
Yes, but not necessarily by a Labour government. It was introduced by Roy Jenkins. He's a strong person, and he doesn't toe the party line. Really he isn't one hundred per cent Labour. (Uniform constable)

At the time of interviewing, the general feeling was that social and political circumstances favoured the police. This situation could not be expected to last, of course. But while the Conservatives were thought to be more responsive to police wishes than Labour, the police were felt to be vital to any government, and this would give them a basis of power independent of Federation strength. Altogether, an analysis which sees the Federation as largely irrelevant to the determination of police pay, and which locates the determinants of this in wider social and political processes, would tend to divert attention away from concern with the strength of the Federation itself, even if the outcome was not as satisfactory to the police as at the time of interviewing. This perspective helps to explain why some of the men felt the Federation to be adequate despite its lack of independent power as a negotiating body. The police were seen as having a sufficiently powerful position to obtain satisfactory treatment regardless of any powers of industrial action. They might do better under a Conservative government than a Labour government because of the centrality of law and order to the political philosophy of the former. But the power of the police was seen as stemming not only from a particular political perspective, but from its structural position in society, which made its morale and manpower of crucial importance to any government.

(b) Another argument was developed by some of the men who felt that, although the Federation was lacking in power, it nonetheless was adequate as a representative body. They regarded the crucial determinants of policemen's welfare as being the psychological disposition of the authorities and the Federation representatives. They had a personality theory of power which made the *structure* of the Federation largely irrelevant. The outcome of bargaining depended on the individual skill and determination of the respective spokesmen for either side. This was argued by 19% of those who felt the Federation was adequate.

A lot of this business of demanding rights and granting rights, it doesn't matter. It depends on the personalities and the willingness of the two parties to work together, no matter what rights and aids you give them. (C.I.D. inspector)
Rights of access and other powers are useless. If the chief is down on the Federation you're on a loser. He can sit there with cotton wool in his ears.
(C.I.D. constable)

To these men the Federation was adequate despite its lack of muscle because the outcome of negotiations was seen as dependent on factors of individual personality – goodwill and skill – rather than a balance of power arising out of any considerations of structure.

The above two analyses share the common feature that they see the question of Federation power as irrelevant to policemen's welfare. This is seen as dependent on other factors – in the first analysis, the structural position of the police in society, and in the second, the individual personalities of negotiators and authorities.

(c) The third reason why the Federation might be deemed adequate despite its lack of sanctions is the *moral* undesirability of such weapons in a body like the police. For principled considerations policemen have to eschew a powerful representative body. This is not incompatible with either of the above views. It may be the case that they are also seen not to *need* more power, for one of the two previous reasons. But even if it was felt that in the absence of power the police might be exploited, and that greater Federation sanctions could benefit *policemen*, many still saw this as undesirable to society. Forty-five per cent who thought the Federation was adequate gave principled objections to a more powerful police organisation.

It was feared that a more powerful police representative organisation might harm the public. Industrial action by the police would be dangerous because they perform emergency services and are responsible for public order. Efficient police work was considered by many to require a strictly hierarchical organisation and to preclude granting more influence to lower ranks. Some felt that an intrinsic moral obligation to forgo union power stemmed from the police oath of office.

The Federation can't have too much power because you've got to have discipline – a nasty word these days. But there comes a time in the force when action is needed. Whether it's a fight in the street, a couple of rebels, a man in premises, somebody's got to do something. And somebody's got to say 'Well, I want that done'. Decisions have got to be made. And I feel that if the sergeant said: 'Well, Joe Brown, 47A, you do so and so', and Joe Brown said 'I won't because my union wouldn't like it', you'll have no effective police force. (C.I.D. inspector)

We're adequately represented. Talk of union powers is lawyer talk. I like it as it is, a gentleman's agreement. We could go out and do the militant thing, we can shout if we've got an axe to grind. But there's a right way and a wrong way. I'm loyal to the Crown. We could get the likes of Clive Jenkins to shout the odds and ride roughshod over someone else's personality and feelings, but the poor Home Secretary would get shot down for it. It's wrong. (Uniform constable)

So the 52% who felt that the Federation was an adequate representative body on the whole, despite its lack of powers, justified this by an analysis of the determination of policemen's pay and conditions which made the Federation largely irrelevant (because the crucial factors were either wider structural pressures or individual psychology), and/or by the argument that such powers would anyway be undesirable in the police for moral and principled reasons, regardless of the sectional interest of policemen.

The reasons for seeing the Federation as inadequate

The 45% of the men who felt the Federation was inadequate took the view that, in the absence of stronger powers, situations were likely to arise where policemen did not get a fair deal. Because of the possibility of adverse social and political circumstances, or unfavourably inclined authorities, the Federation needed the safeguard of independent sanctions. Moral indignation and personal concern about inadequate consideration of policemen's welfare overrode any potential inhibitions about giving the Federation more power because of the public good. How far particular policemen were prepared to go in the direction of granting the Federation greater powers of industrial action varied. This will be considered later. These justifications for viewing the present Federation position as basically inadequate are illustrated below:

They don't have enough power with the Official Side. If the Official Side say no to something there's no further means of pressure. We've got to go away like a little naughty schoolboy. I should like to see them able to do more than what they are now when they can be pushed off by some Fascist Whitehall minion that says no. (Uniform constable)

I've been brought up in a family that owned a business, so I had the attitude you get as much work out of a man as you can possibly get and pay him as little as possible. I've been quite anti-union. But one gradually mellows. I've come round to the attitude: 'Look after No. 1'. From that point of view, the Federation isn't strong enough. It hasn't got the teeth to get immediate redress to any grievance. The moral responsibility of people seems to have left them. Teachers come out on strike, doctors were threatening to. I don't see why the policeman should be any different. Students sit in – they prevented the students who want to work from studying. Why should I be different? (Traffic constable)

Opinion within the police force is divided as to the overall adequacy of the Federation as a representative body. There is a general recognition that the Federation is an organisation lacking any real sanctions in negotiations and hence with little independent power, although while 52% of the men find this acceptable, 45% do not. Satisfaction with the Federation as a representative body is directly related to rank.

4
Evaluation of specific Federation activities

The Federation performs a variety of services for policemen. How these are each evaluated helps explain policemen's overall view of the Federation, and to situate this in a more concrete context.

The assessment of Federation activities was based on eight separate aspects of its work. These were pay negotiations, conditions of service, influencing the public image of the police, communications within the force, influencing legislation, the welfare of policemen, the efficiency of the force, and helping in individual cases of discipline. The evaluation of these is shown in Table 4.1.

Pay negotiations

These are handled by the Federation nationally. Table 4.1 shows that half the men felt the Federation was quite effective in this respect, with slightly more of the rest saying it was very effective than not at all. This partly reflects the general feeling that the police pay situation was reasonably satisfactory at that time.

During most of 1973, the constable's *minimum* basic pay was £1251 per annum. This was 75% of the average *earnings* of all male workers then, £1673. The constable's *maximum* (after seventeen years) was £2061 per annum, which was 123% of average earnings of all male workers. However, the *earnings* of policemen are considerably more than basic pay when their various allowances and overtime are included. An earnings survey carried out by the Police Council in May, 1974 showed that on average basic pay constituted only 76% of the gross earnings of uniformed constables in England and Wales.

Seventy-three per cent thought the level of pay was quite good compared to standards outside, with another 14% saying it was very good, and only 11% not good at all. Most men felt some sense of grievance about pay, and frustration about the Federation's lack of power in this respect. The immediate situation at the time of the study was generally recognised as comparatively favourable. But even then many felt that the level of pay was not commensurate with what they thought was a proper recompense for the special characteristics of police work.

As noted already, the power of the Federation was not regarded as an important determinant of police pay. Rather pay was seen as dependent largely on factors beyond their control, notably the political and social climate which underlay the *demand* for police, together with outside economic circumstances which affected the *supply* of policemen. Given these conditions, the Federation could be more or less effective in pressing home the case for pay rises, influencing public opinion to support them and determining the timing of increases. This was seen by many as the major, if not only, role of the Federation. As one uniform P.C. put it, 'If I was earning £50 a week, there'd be no need for a Police Federation.'

TABLE 4.1. *Evaluation of Federation performance in specific areas of work*

Aspect of Federation Work	Very effective %	Quite effective %	Not effective %	Don't know %
Pay negotiations	28	49.4	21.4	1.2
Conditions of service	30.4	48.8	19.6	1.2
Influencing the public image of the police	7.7	19.6	69.6	3
Communications within the force	30.4	44.6	29.2	0.6
Influencing legislation	10.1	36.3	47.6	6
Welfare of policemen	50.6	38.1	7.7	3.6
Efficiency of the force	13.7	33.9	47.6	4.8
Helping on cases of discipline	82.7	10.1	4.8	2.4

Base: N = 168

Given the importance of overtime and allowances as a component of earnings, it is crucial for the Federation to ensure that the men get their due. This is a matter of continuous watchfulness and struggle by *local* representatives.

An example was the achievement of payment for overtime in September 1972. Until then policemen could only accumulate time-off in lieu. The change was regarded as a significant Federation success. But it was also felt that it made little difference in practice. Supervisors were encouraged, it was believed, to arrange work schedules in such a way as to minimise the need for overtime, whereas when this was unpaid there had been little concern to avoid making the men work long hours.

The extent to which the authorities were seen as concerned to minimise the men's gain is illustrated by the following example. When overtime was unpaid, a constable might be expected to perform extra hours of duty in order to maintain 'continuity of evidence'. But this principle ceased to be of such importance once it had to be paid for.

We now have the option if we do overtime of payment or time-off. Prior to that regulation coming in, if a man had, for example, a breathalyser on nights – all the procedure is gone through, and the man gives blood. Two specimens are given to the prisoner and two specimens are retained for laboratory analysis by the policeman, the arresting officer. That arresting officer has to always retain those samples in his possession and take them up to the Forensic Science Laboratory for analysis and hand them direct to one of the chemists there, against signature. This was, they said, continuity of evidence. The arresting officer on nights may not have gone off duty until 3, 4 or 5 in the morning, but he had to get up in the morning to take those up to the Laboratory.

Now a man has a choice of payment or time-off. Well, that ceased straight away, it's no longer necessary now, and there's a chief superintendent's instruction on it. He can continue his tour of duty till 6 in the morning and hand those samples to an early turn officer who'll take them up for him. That was entirely consequent on that regulation of a man having the option for payment, because it would cost them money, and they don't want that. It's not a question of being cynical, it's a question of being realistic.

This was a good piece of work achieved by the Federation, but it's now down to the local forces and authorities to make sure they don't get as much as they did previously. Although they'll never admit it naturally, there's no doubt in my mind and most policemen's mind, that the local authorities say to the chief: 'We've got payment for overtime for your chaps now, you keep it down'. And the chief says keep it down, so you keep it down, and this is it.   (Uniform sergeant)

Thus even when the Federation have negotiated an improvement in pay, they cannot guarantee that the men will necessarily benefit. They may merely have transferred conflict to another level at which it must be taken up anew. But the Federation and the men are not powerless in the face of the authorities, even though the sanctions available are weak. Initial gains must be supplemented by struggle to ensure the fruits.

We've had a recent argument over weekends. In this force at the moment, only on Friday and Saturday nights, they want more men until 2 o'clock in the morning. They asked for volunteers to do 6–2 evenings instead of 2–10. And they didn't get any. So the inspector was then told he had to detail three men. I must point out that the three men detailed were young in service, and they didn't like to say a lot. Anyway, we kicked and complained on behalf of those down the shift, that if they want extra men on Friday and Saturday evenings they should pay. The inspector agreed with us. He's put on a report and I've found out since that it's been sanctioned that four men will be paid from 10 p.m. to 2 a.m. They only ride around in the Land Rover, but there again we've won something.
(Uniform constable)

An important part of police earnings are the allowances. The most important was rent allowance, but there were also others, e.g. boot and shoe, removal and detective duty allowance. Basic rates are set by central negotiation, but a crucial question is the application to individual cases, which depends on local watchfulness and skills.

Conditions of service

Policemen considered five issues under 'conditions of service': (a) the physical environment of work; (b) the quality of supervision; (c) their side of the wage/effort bargain; (d) facilities for work; and (e) restrictions on out-of-work life.

To a certain extent each of these, but especially (d), implicitly raised issues about job control, the prerogatives of supervisors and subordinates. A hard distinction between 'instrumental' concerns about pay and conditions and 'ideological' demands for participation in control cannot be maintained.

Just under half see the Federation as moderately successful in relation to conditions, with nearly a third seeing it as very effective, and a fifth feeling it was not at all effective (Table 4.1).

(a) *The physical environment of work.* Work environments varied with the task performed. Outside work was obviously seasonally variable. More than half (55%) felt that working conditions could not be compared to most jobs. Nearly a third (31%) felt that conditions were bad by outside standards, and only 13% felt they were good. Conditions were viewed as largely beyond the control not only of the Federation but also of the senior ranks. But there was disgruntlement about the Federation's failure to remove *avoidable* discomforts.

Some, especially detectives, felt that concern with detailed conditions was petty. They took pride in putting up with rough conditions. (This is paralleled in other occupations with an aura of 'masculinity', as studies of, for example, miners or deep-sea fishermen have shown.)

The Federation haven't done a lot you knew. These little things really. They throw them back in your face, and you think, lick their boots, you know, thank you ever so much. They're giving us Halibut Liver Oil tablets, instead of 6 bob, we're getting them for 3 bob, thank you.   (Mounted constable)
Like many C.I.D. when you're involved in doing the job, you're less worried about the rights and wrongs of it... Bloody trivial stuff!
(Regional Crime Squad inspector)

However most *were* worried about physical conditions.

It was diabolical... A squalid little filthy dining-room, which was a recreation room as well. So you had the table-tennis balls landing in your breakfast, things like this, quite literally. We all got on well, so there was no violence. But it should never have been.

[Question: 'How far do you feel the change in conditions was influenced by the Federation?']

I'd say, very little... The station they've closed was erected in 1834, and the gents' was in a disgusting condition. It got to the point where the only way we could get something done about it was for a P.C. to go directly to the Public

Health and complain. And they came down and said 'Well if you don't do something about it there's going to be trouble'. Well, you know, the Federation, they weren't too bothered about it.   (Uniform constable)

Most felt the Federation was *reasonably* successful in obtaining improvements.

Certain concessions they've got the ordinary beat man, such as full-length individual lockers, whereby a man can come to work in civilian clothes and change into uniform here. He needn't be the butt of all sorts of comments which are given just to goad a policeman, on the bus if he's got to sit there in uniform, with his tongue in his cheek, or wearing a part-uniform with a civvy mac showing a blue shirt and a black tie, and probably a pair of size 10 boots, you see? They did that for us.   (Uniform constable)

(b) *Quality of supervision.* The severity of discipline had declined in recent years. The militaristic style had been replaced by a 'man-management' approach. About two-thirds approved the change, but the others saw it as a deterioration of standards.

Most thought the Federation had played a part in encouraging the movement towards less strictly disciplinarian man-management.

We had to do point duty just outside here so that when the chief superintendent went to dinner, he could go easily and not have to wait in traffic jams. And everybody used to create hell about that. We used to say, you know, it's a bit of a cheek making one of the lads go out and do three-quarters of an hour point duty so that the chief superintendent could go home for dinner! What about all the other traffic points! Something was supposed to be done about that by the Federation.   (Uniform constable)

The Federation's contribution to ensuring satisfactory treatment by supervisors was limited.

They have this officer's mess, and occasionally there were dinners and things, a superintendents' dinner or whatever. It was the practice, it still is the practice in fact, to use cadets as waiters. And this was a practice to which I objected strongly personally, and to which a number of cadets objected to me, as I was the constables' representative then. So naturally I pursued the matter, and it was taken to the Chief eventually. What happened is that the cadets were confronted by the training officer. A direct confrontation, which was wrong. I was a little incensed on it. They were asked what their objections were, and the answer to the Branch Board resolution which went forward eventually, was that far from objecting to it, the cadets enjoyed it because they had a free meal! And of course the ground was completely taken from under my feet. But I still feel the same way; that if I had a son who was a police cadet and he came home and told me he'd been waiting at table, I'd be rather annoyed as a parent.   (C.I.D. inspector)

In cases of alleged victimisation the Federation is often inadequate.

Take for instance if a chappie comes along to A. [Branch Board secretary] and says that, you know, he's having a saddle on his back. You know what I mean? He's being overworked. A. makes a few enquiries. Then when he's on the phone to the chief inspector, he'll say 'Sir, we've had a complaint, Sir, from P.C.

so-and-so. And it appears that he feels he's being victimised, Sir'. 'Oh, yes. Well, this has been this and that and the other', you know? That's how I view it – it always ends up whereby the cooling of the situation is achieved.

Like, well, I came here with a complaint. . .some form of victimisation. . .I was on point duty, and quite unknown to me I stopped the Assistant Chief Constable on the corner. I stuck my hand up, you know? And I didn't know it was him. . . There was a lull in the traffic and he must have thought he was going to go, because he peeped his horn, and went like that [Gesture]. . .I turned round and completely ignored him, you know, I thought he was a member of the public – it shouldn't make any difference anyhow – and I thought well bugger him. And he said, when he came along I wasn't on point duty, I was staring in the window of the Alliance Building Society, and all this crap. Anyway, he in effect called me a liar. So I come over here [headquarters] and after receiving a bollocking – you've got to receive one – I come over here [Federation Office] and talk about it. 'Well, who was he saying f--- to?' So this attitude, 'Don't let's make a mountain out of a molehill'. . . No, I haven't actually got punished, but there's a principle in the thing, being called a bloody liar. Not that I've got many principles, but that's one of them. . .I don't like being called a liar.
(Uniform constable)

In these cases where supervisors use their power in what is seen as an unwarranted way, and the Federation is incapable of taking action, the result is usually bitterness. In some instances the men have been able to resort to unofficial tactics of their own.

When I was at T. Station six years ago, the inspector in charge there shut the back door so that blokes couldn't sneak in round the back, as he put it. And my suggestion to the Federation rep. was that they put a stop to this due to the fact that a fire regulation was being broken, and things like that. Anyway, we achieved more by getting a little job done on the side, you know... We had 2 tons of manure dumped in the front garden for the inspector, and well, he got the message, you know. And so the door was opened.   (Uniform constable)

A minority felt that far from the Federation having a useful role to play in improving 'human relations' it contributed to a deterioration in discipline. The Federation ought to seek a return to old standards, rather than further precipitate a disastrous decline. This view was especially prevalent among the C.I.D.

When I first started you had the parades. Now the Federation have stopped that... It's a result of pressure brought by the Federation that it's stopped. Therefore you get blokes who go out on patrol now, they're not so fully aware of what's gone on as they were. They're entrusted to make themselves aware (by reading reports), but I don't think policemen are any different from any other worker. If you trust a bloke to do his job, one day he's going to be called and he won't bloody do it. If he's made to do it that's different – after all, you're being paid to do the job. I'm the same. I mean, if someone says to me 'There's a bloke, find out what's going on' – if I know who's wanted, what's been nicked, I'll do it. But sometimes in the morning I might come on and I've had a few drinks the night before and I think 'Oh bugger that!' You see, people are like this. . .but you're being paid to do your job so you should do it every day. The police is a disciplined force and you've got to accept somebody's got to give the orders and somebody's got to obey them.   (C.I.D. constable)

The Federation is credited by most with having contributed to a more humane relationship between ranks, and continuing to ensure decent supervisory behaviour. But there are cases, especially allegations of victimisation, in which it has not made much headway. In such instances the men either have to accept the brickbats or fight back with unofficial and illicit tactics.

(c) *The wage/effort bargain.* How far has the Federation succeeded in reducing the length of the working week, increasing periods of leave, and ensuring reasonable shifts? Most felt that the Federation had been effective here, but that shifts still left much to be desired. Built-in constraints on flexibility limited the Federation's achievements. It was impossible to plan for unforeseen contingencies and develop rigid rules which would suit everyone. The Federation's role was not only to negotiate national rights, but also to develop smooth relationships with local supervisors. This ensured co-operation in optimising the balance between the needs of different men and the exigencies of service operations.

(d) *Facilities for work.* A grievance about the 'tools of the trade' *implicitly* raises the question of job-control – the respective prerogatives of 'management' and 'men'. The Federation is not seen as effective here.

The public don't realise the conditions what you've got to work in. You see, the other week, they were told that there was going to be trouble at the Rovers' grounds. They had five policemen there! It's stupid! Well, they literally had a running battle as they came out. You see, the Federation should say 'Alright, if they know they're going to have trouble at some place, we'll have about forty or fifty policemen there!' They should then back it.   (Uniform constable)

The biggest laugh going now is the cars. You're now limited on mileage. It's like giving somebody a job to do, they don't do the job properly because you don't give them the proper tools, and then you moan at them. They're supposed to do a panda system here, but what happens? The Corporation, they say to the Chief Constable: 'You're using too much petrol'. So the Chief comes and says you're limited to a mileage. How can you do it? So here is somewhere the Federation should say 'Well, if you *want* us to do the job, *let* us do it!' The Federation, as far as I'm concerned, is just a farce.   (Uniform constable)

These issues encroach on what, from the other side, are seen as the prerogatives of management, the existing power associated with rank. The Federation was not regarded as successful in helping the men acquire what they saw as proper facilities for carrying out the job.

(e) *Restrictions on out-of-work life.* Stipulations about the 'private' behaviour of policemen and their families are written into regulations

(Police Federation 1965). Some are explicit, e.g. 'A constable shall not take any active part in politics', 'The place at which a constable resides shall be subject to the approval of the Chief Constable'. These are bones of contention. Furthermore, the Chief Constable has the prerogative of imposing other restrictions if they are 'designed to secure the proper exercise of the functions of a constable'. This vague formulation generates arguments about what constitutes 'proper exercise'.

There is widespread dissatisfaction with the encroachment on 'private' life. The Federation is not credited with much success or power in alleviating this.

The discipline code is rather out of date, and they've done nothing about that... You can't be a policeman and go about untidy or you won't command respect when you're in uniform. But how you command that respect, is not for any piece of paper to say do it this way... They've got to be allowed a degree of freedom or they *can't* command any respect. You know, you get a student walking down the road – I'm saying a student, because that's the easiest one to pick on. He looks at us and says 'he's indoctrinated, he's got a tie and collar on!' Personally I like wearing ties and collars, but I don't like this attitude of 'you *will* wear a tie and look smart because you're a policeman'. You can't have no rules and regulations because then you'll always have the one individual who's going to go silly, start injecting himself with heroin, smoking pot and everything. But I'd like to see a little bit more freedom to what you can say and what you can do.

(Uniform constable)

Especially resented were those restrictions which extended to the families of policemen.

A memo came out from the Chief Constable's office recently, with regard to road accidents. Words to the effect of: whenever a police officer, or his wife or immediate family, or a civilian employee, is involved in a road accident, the implication being on or off-duty, the accident book will be submitted through the divisional chief superintendent, with the recommendation made, and be forwarded to the Assistant Chief Constable. There's immediately a big outcry from the Federation blokes and from the troops. And we [the Federation] are there to represent the interest of the troops, so we think, well we've obviously got something here... A policeman involved in an accident is always well investigated, better than a member of the general public. This we accept as reasonable, we're quite prepared to accept the policeman part of the memo. We're also prepared to accept the civilian employee bit. We were even prepared to go along with the implication that it applied on or off-duty. But we did draw the line at our wives and immediate family! We couldn't for the life of us see why if, for example, my wife drives my car and has a bang, and the police are called and find out she's my wife, and I'm a policeman, why the accident book has to come down to the A.C.C. He doesn't see accidents involving two members of the general public, so why should he see one involving a member of the public and my wife? Ridiculous to our way of thinking! Well, Fred and Arthur [officials of the Federation] go to see the Chief, and Fred says 'I have to notify you that my brother fell off a camel in the Arabian Desert!', which the Chief apparently didn't find at all funny. I mean it's hilarious – it really suited my sense of humour! It was ridiculous, because there was no boundary to the rule. The Chief came and addressed us at a meeting and tried to palm us off with some story that it was nothing to worry about and we were all up in arms over nothing. Well the Board discussed it, and it was unanimous. We thought the Chief had brought in a load of rubbish and we still wanted it changed. So they're now cutting out the words 'wives and immediate family'. (Traffic sergeant)

The predominant view is that the Federation is moderately successful in defending and advancing conditions of service. Success in some areas is contrasted with failure in others. While on the whole its efforts are appreciated, the ultimate determinants of conditions seem largely beyond its control because of lack of sanctions.

Influencing the public image of the police

Policemen are very anxious about their standing with the public, which they see diminishing. 'Public opinion', as described in surveys, does not confirm this fear (Royal Commission on the Police 1962; Belson 1975). There are various ways in which the apparent contradiction can be resolved. There may be a gap between what people say in the context of an interview, and the way they respond to policemen in the frequently uncomfortable situations of real interaction. The standing of the police with those they do their policing 'for' will be very different from those who are policed 'against', but the latter may be crucially important in shaping the constable's perception of 'public' attitudes.

The majority sees the Federation as not at all successful in this respect (Table 4.1). A substantial body does not see the Federation as the appropriate vehicle for public relations. Senior officers are seen by many as having more of the social polish and intellectual graces to convey a favourable image of the police.

A minority does see Federation efforts to put across the police point-of-view as effective, though not necessarily frequent enough. There is appreciation of Federation activity on behalf of individual policemen who were attacked by the media.

When the Federation go on TV it does do good. Particularly, what's his name? The chairman of the J.C.C. . . . . Reg Gale. He goes on battling with M.P.'s or do-gooders, people like this. He's very good at holding his own and he gets a lot of sympathy. I've heard a lot of people say, after he's been on 'Ah, they were trying to run him into the ground but he won.' (Traffic inspector)

More commonly the Federation was held to be ineffective in this. The police image was thought to be influenced more by the appearance and actions of constables on the street than any public relations efforts by either the Federation or senior officers.

The public, they're being conned all along the line. A little bit of flannel here and there. There's no answer to this good relationship business. A person likes the police until such time as he gets reported for a parking offence. Then straight away all his opinions go. Straight away, you're bastards, that's the end of it. With this public image you're beating your head against a brick wall. When I was on the Area we used to go along to schools and give the children talks, tell them we're your friendly policeman etc. They accept it and then they get home and tell their Dad 'I've just had a talk from my friendly policeman.' And he turns round and says 'He wasn't so friendly. He's just booked me for parking down the town!' (Uniform constable)

Many see these efforts as actually counter-productive. This is partly because the Federation highlights conflicts and grievances within the force, which presents a detrimental impression of bickering or pettiness. It is also because Federationists are often seen as lacking the polish or style to be effective as spokesmen in the public eye. This role should rather be handled by senior officers who, it is believed, are able to make a good impression as responsible professionals, and to portray the police as a united, disciplined body. Sir Robert Mark is especially appreciated for his activities in this regard.

I'm not happy about the Federation acting as a representative or spokesman for the police service... You get Mr Gale as Chairman of the Federation. He sets himself up – not sets himself up, that's a bit unfair. He's invited as a spokesman for the Police Federation. I sometimes squirm a little bit when I see him on television... I'm not sure he presents a terribly good image. You get Pamplin [Federation J.C.C. Secretary] or what have you, get up on the goggle box and he'll be speaking as a Federationist rather than a policeman. I'm not worried about a man's accent. A bloke with a good old country accent, for example, a detective superintendent interviewed on a murder, makes his appeal – he's not an actor, he's a bloke who's doing his job. But the Federation shouldn't act as spokesman on police matters. (C.I.D. inspector)

Federation failure is also blamed on an anti-police bias perceived in the media. Policemen generally feel that the media select items or adopt perspectives which discredit the police. This is either because these have more news value from a 'sensationalist' point of view or because of personal anti-police values.

They don't project themselves, the Police Federation... People like Gale may be on TV expounding a theory on programmes like Frost on police brutality. But that's a load of rubbish, because they're as biased as hell. (Uniform constable)

In sum, then, the Federation is not seen as effective in conveying a good public image of the police. It is not seen as the most suitable vehicle for this, even in so far as there *is* some scope for efforts at public relations to succeed.

Communications within the police force

The Federation is seen as quite effective in keeping the men in touch with developments (Table 4.1). Locally, there were Federation bulletin-boards in all stations, and circulars and notices appeared regularly describing the state of negotiations, achievements gained and failures. There were also Open Meetings. In proportion to his personal zeal the divisional representative kept members in touch with events in the Federation world. Nationally, there is a monthly colour magazine, *Police*, periodic special circulars, and personal visits by national representatives or officers of the Federation. These, like the purely local meetings, are more or less well attended by the members according to the imminence of a new development about which they are concerned, like a pay rise.

The men often feel in the dark about the progress of negotiations and events they are anxious about. This is not entirely blamed on the Federation. The men realise that there is a quantity of information made available, and see their own 'apathy' in attending meetings and consulting documents as largely responsible for their ignorance. But they generally feel more could and should be done by the Federation to keep members informed, by putting out news regularly in eyecatching format. Personal communications are seen as most effective, but are usually too infrequent. This is because of limits inherent in the nature of the job itself, the outside, dispersed character of patrol-work and crime investigation. In uniform divisions the men are only assembled together at the start of the shift and then go their separate ways. In crime investigation they are scarcely ever gathered together as a body. Further, as there is only one representative per rank per division, the men will only work with him personally if they happen to be on the same shift and at the same sub-divisional station. Most of the men will seldom, if ever, have occasion to meet their representative in the course of their work. They are thus left dependent on their own efforts to track him down, or on his conscientiousness in keeping in touch.

The feeling that there was a lack of information was widely expressed.

We don't get any information in the service. Most of the stuff you learn in this force comes through to you up the drain-pipe, when they've whispered it somewhere and it's been overheard. So-and-so told me in the pub that such-and-such is going to happen. What about amalgamation? There's young chaps here now buying houses, their lives can suddenly be disrupted. Why the hell don't they tell us what's happening? There's rumours about disbanding D division but we know nothing about it. If the Federation don't know, they ought to find out. If the information is there they should demand to know in the interest of their men, and they should shit on somebody's bloody doorstep until such time as they find out.   (Uniform constable)

The Federation's point of view is that they do the best possible given limited resources. They partly blame members' apathy.

There's this general apathy, which isn't foreign to the police service. It's part of conservatism with a small C. It's a very thin line where apathy finishes and conservatism begins.   (Uniform constables' representative)

Some argue that this lack of interest is a sign of contentment. One inspector put it thus: 'If people aren't keen on the Federation it shows things can't be so bad. If things are diabolical you'd have more people shouting.' Most men justified their lack of involvement by the argument that the Federation's powerlessness made it useless as an agent of change, so there was no point in activity for it. Membership apathy and organisational powerlessness mutually reinforced each other.

The degree to which communication was experienced as inadequate was not uniform in the force. It varied with position in the division of labour; for example, those who worked on the same shift as a representative, found it less of a problem. Personality differences between representatives also had an influence. These variations were superimposed upon the general barriers to internal communication which stemmed from the fact that policemen are seldom assembled together in one place for work purposes. Contact with Federation representatives thus required either deliberate effort, or relied on chance meetings in corridor, canteen or car. These restrictions imposed by the work structure were widely recognised.

It's difficult to talk to them because the only time you really see them is outside when you're both attending a job. And you're not going to discuss Federation work right in the middle of a road accident. When you have your refreshment three-quarters of an hour, oh dear! [laughter]. Pitiful isn't it. You come in, you have your meal and you're usually straight on the snooker table, or get the cards out. You just don't talk about the Federation usually. The opportunity's not really there, as if we were two office people and had time together all day.
(Traffic constable)

The exigencies of the work limit the degree of personal contact and communication between representatives and men. Policemen in their work are spread out from each other in time (because of shifts) and space (because of the mobility in the job), so that one divisional representative, who is also a working officer, cannot meet them all. Thus the effectiveness of the Federation in internal communications is considerably limited by constraints derived from the nature of the job.

Influencing legislation

Assessment of the adequacy of the Federation in putting forward the police view on legislation raises two issues. Firstly, did it adequately convey the opinions of practitioners about the substantive *content* of legislation? Secondly, was it able to ensure that the police were given what they saw as the necessary *means* for effective law enforcement? As is seen from Table 4.1, nearly half the men felt that the Federation was not influential at all in this area, and only one in ten thought it was very effective. Over the last decade, the Federation has, in fact, been increasingly involved in commenting on many types of legislation, either at its own or the government's instigation. Those who are involved closely in

Federation work recognise that it has made great strides in recent years as a pressure-group, although the effects of this are not usually recognised by the men. The secretary of the local Branch Board informed me: 'We've been gaining considerable ground over the last few years, particularly since we've been in a position to employ a parliamentary adviser. The benefits he brings are probably only known to a small number of the police...we have on several occasions gone to Westminster to speak to our M.P. I believe Mr Maudling remarked that the police lobby in the House was probably the strongest in the country.'

However, from the point of view of the rank and file, the Federation seemed to remain relatively ineffective in this respect, although the recent 'law and order' campaign may alter this perception. Most of the men thought that police feeling was not sufficiently taken into account in drafting legislation. This doesn't mean that the police feel that they should have the power to determine the law. It was accepted that police *determination* of law would be incompatible with democracy. But the police feel that, as the body who actually implement legislation, their expert views on the feasibility, enforcement requirements and actual consequences of proposals ought to be given greater weight. The issue that was mentioned most regularly by the men was punishment, especially capital punishment. There was widespread resentment that the police view on capital punishment had been overridden by the power of what they saw as an unrepresentative and naive group of educated liberals, castigated as 'do-gooders'. The police were prevented from having the powers and back-up deemed necessary to carry out their allotted tasks. The latter were in themselves often unreasonable, especially without the necessary means. Furthermore, their lot was continually aggravated by the efforts of the liberals and 'do-gooders' to control police activity more closely, for example by introducing independent elements into the investigation of complaints against the police. The Federation seemed relatively powerless to halt this insidious process of erosion of police powers, and often the policeman had to resort to the one piece of legislation invariably available, the Ways and Means Act. (This was the phrase used to describe the plethora of devices available to circumvent the full rigours of the law.)

The view was widespread that the law was drafted by ivory-tower intellectuals, with no awareness of the real conditions of life in society, or the requirements of the enforcement situation. This was reflected in the peculiar language of legislation, as well as the numerous loopholes invariably included, which the practised eye of the practitioner could have predicted. The following is an example of this attitude that laws are expressed in a language remote from 'real life':

I don't think for one minute that the police are ever considered when they draft laws. They don't ever take into account the enforcing of them, or there wouldn't be so many loopholes. We've got to bear the brunt of everything. If someone makes a stupid law, we've got to enforce it. Take the language they tell us to write reports in. You never see anything, you always observe it! Back in the valleys, I arrested a man for rape once. He confessed and everything to what he had done, and I gave him a statement to sign saying he admitted to unlawful carnal knowledge of a female against her consent. And on reading this, he said 'Oh no! I never done none of that. None of that carnal knowledge business. I fucked her, yes. I raped her, yes. But I never had no carnal knowledge! I'm not signing that!' (C.I.D. constable)

The main complaint made about substantive legislation was that its manner of drafting seemed to reflect lack of concern for the practical problems of enforcement. Consultation with experienced 'professionals' could have avoided this in many cases.

Legislation should always go back to the grass-roots, where the thing's actually being done, before it's formulated. Road traffic law, for example, is very complicated. Some aspects are so complicated it would take a university professor, a superhuman, to be able to carry it round in his head. Like you're limited to the number of hours a driver can drive a heavy goods vehicle, which is in itself a good idea. But they specify so many exceptions. Well, the practical bloke out there, he can't carry it all – I know I can't. You can't go out there armed with hundreds of law-books, so it's unenforceable. We should be represented on it.
(Traffic sergeant)

If I thought the Federation had anything to do with legislation I'd be greatly surprised because there's so many loopholes in the law. You get these bods up there who're making the law, and they don't know how to put it into practice. They ought to come down here on the streets and do it, you know. Like the breathalyser for instance. It's all very well saying 'just blow into this and if it's over the line you come into the station'. But you meet up with people who've got medical certificates to say they're not strong enough to blow up the bag. Met one with bronchial pneumonia, something like that, and he couldn't blow up the bag in one go, he needed three goes, and he was stinking of alcohol, but that doesn't prove it. I was with the sergeant and he didn't know what to do either, so we let him go in the end... People run into houses and take drinks of beer and you're chasing after them trying to give a breath-test. If the police had a chance to have their views put forward in legislation they'd sort a lot of these problems out.
(Uniform constable)

When laws are made in this country no consideration is given to the police force who have to enforce them. People say 'If you get the police involved it becomes a police state.' This is bloody rubbish. This breathalyser law they brought in. Some bloody stupid bugger thought give them the bag and phew! Fill it up, this is ideal. But you go out on the streets and get blotto, absolutely paralytic drunk, you know? I come along as a policeman and form the opinion you're drunk, you plead not guilty, it's drunk and disorderly just the same. You put the same man behind the wheel of a car it's different, we need a breathalyser test. The reason being thus: the legislators, possibly people like yourself to a certain degree, lecturers, doctors, what have you – all the people involved in bringing legislation for our enforcement can't conceivably think that you or anybody else in that bracket would possibly be drunk and disorderly. An M.P. drunk and disorderly! Oh dear! But they could see themselves behind the wheel of a car. Oh yes! So what do they do? Make the law a little bit more complicated for the sake of the politicians. The powers that be ought to say to the police force, 'We would like to make the drunken driving laws more strict, how would you go about it?' And get somebody from the Police Federation, a couple of constables, together and say 'Right, you've got a fortnight chaps. Come up with something that would work and be accepted.' Then put it to the M.P.s who would debate it and put the seal on it. But at the moment the laws cause trouble and friction.

(Uniform constable)

In general the substantive laws were acceptable, but the influence of 'do-gooders', 'more concerned with the criminal than the victim', had so hedged round the powers of the policeman that they were unable to enforce the laws as intended. The Federation should press for more police powers of search and arrest.

When a law is made, M.P.s look at it from a layman's point of view, which tends to cloud their judgement sometimes. The fear is that if the police had more say it would get a police state. But we need more power. The circumstances that come to mind are let's say at 3 o'clock in the morning we see someone in peculiar circumstances but not really committing a crime. You're very nearly certain he's up to no good. You go up and ask him what his name is, and he tells you to piss off. Now, according to the letter of the law, there's nothing you can do. There could be powers for a policeman to do what he thinks fit. Perhaps not search him, that's infringing liberty to a certain extent, but at least a means of ascertaining who he is, where he's come from. It would serve the law-abiding citizens much better if we had these powers... The only persons you'd be oppressing are the law-breakers and speaking from a policeman's point of view it doesn't give a damn if we oppress law-breakers, because they're oppressors in their own right.

(Uniform constable)

Parliament might have greater regard to the difficulties of the police in enforcing the law. For instance, the power of arrest. To make the thing look less like a police state they limit it in some ways. If a man has an offensive weapon, say, in a public place, the police officer may arrest him if (a) he doesn't give his name and address satisfactorily etc. Now what bloody gobble do you think that is? Why don't they say reasonable suspicion of having committed offences? That would be enough, but they have to hedge it round with all this terminology to constrain the powers of the police. If they want policemen not to arrest somebody, why don't they say? It's no skin off my nose, or the man outside. He gets the same money every month. (C.I.D. inspector)

Instead of giving the police more powers to do the job properly, the government, under the influence of misguided liberal opinion, was proceeding to hedge them in further. The Federation was unable to prevent this.

Influence legislation? There have in the past been very sensible and sound solutions put up to the persons in charge which have done no good. For instance, a certain pamphlet came round once which explained to the public in full how they could complain about the police. Now I'm one of those individuals who believe in democracy, and once you start any form of Gestapo or anything I would be opposed. But these documents were very badly worded, and there were thousands of them to be given out to the public at random. Now this had gone up Federation level before they were issued, and they were told definitely such a pamphlet would not be issued. Then out of the blue, contrary to that, about a fortnight later they're put out. Well, what's the good of the Federation if these things are going to happen?   (C.I.D. constable)

The legislature had further weakened the position of the police by not providing sufficiently strong sanctions for apprehended offenders. Notable here as a *bête noire* was the issue of capital punishment, which had been abolished despite much police protestation in favour of retention.

The Federation interest in restoring capital punishment for all classes of murder not just policemen should be noticed. If there isn't capital punishment, at least life imprisonment should mean life imprisonment, incarcerated for the rest of his days. So if a man commits murder he knows he's there for the rest of his life. If he goes out, it's feet first.   (Uniform sergeant)

I've never really noticed any influence on legislation. They got as far saying 90% of the police are in favour of capital punishment. But even what the public think doesn't matter in that, it depends on the M.P.'s individual conscience or what his Party says. At present Robert Carr, the Home Secretary, takes some notice of the Federation as he's the first Home Secretary that ever had an attempt made on his life! But when Maudling got in as Home Secretary before him, they were all advocating law and order, this Conservative Party, and then did nothing.

(Uniform constable)

The basic cause of this unfortunate state of affairs was that the people who had the power to make laws were naive and out of touch with the conditions of life in society generally. They needed guidance from the 'professionals' who were in daily contact with the problems for which they were framing solutions.

The trouble is the Government think they're legislating for educated men with the same intellect as politicians. But the people here are animals, they're thick. How can M.P.s legislate for morons like that? Take family allowances. To reasonable blokes, like we are sort of thing, you don't think about having to rely on family allowances. These buggers do, these animals. They rely on it, love it. Getting money off the State for a quick jump, that's the way they see it. Means nothing to 'em. M.P.s are completely out of context altogether. They make these rules and regulations. They live in a different world. I mean, every meal these politicians have is a six-course one! . . .I've got a cousin who's an M.P., used to be Chairman of magistrates. He's a shit-ass, honestly. He spoke to me about certain things, you know. About the 'Job' and 'Society' and all the rest of it. He gave me a load of this, that and the other. I said: 'Eddy, I'm sorry, you're just talking from the back of your head!'   (Uniform constable)

So the majority of policemen did not feel that their influence on legislation was sufficient. They wanted more say on both substantive content to prevent the passing of unenforceable laws, and on procedural laws and punishment to ensure they had adequate means to perform their tasks. This they felt was justified by their particular expertise as the people actually cognisant of the conditions of law-enforcement. Politicians were seen as out-of-touch with the practical exigencies of implementing the legislation they created. Also, policemen had a moral right to a say as the burden of enforcement fell on them. This was not seen as a threat to democratic norms as they were only asking for more consultation and influence, not absolute power.

A minority was prepared to accept the more traditional theory of a strict separation between law-formulation, which was the task of Parliament, and law-enforcement, which was the function of the police. They were sensitive to the threat to existing notions of democracy entailed by giving the police a significant role in drafting legislation. Difficulties could arise, but had to be accepted as part of the job.

I don't think the police should be influential in legislation. The first thing that comes to mind is to allow policemen to run in everybody who's got long-hair! Well, really! We must tackle what comes within the area of our work, difficult, impossible, or not. It's not the views of the police that should create the laws in a democratic country like ours. It is the views of the people themselves.

(Administration inspector)

The more general view, however, was that the consultation of police opinion ought to take place far more than at present. As mentioned previously, the Federation has recently initiated a campaign to propagate these sort of views about legislation and penal policy to the public.

The welfare of policemen

The Police Federation attempts to cater for the welfare of policemen in a variety of ways. Indeed, this forms one part of its explicit terms of reference under the Police Act. 'Welfare' is hard to distinguish clearly from pay and conditions of service. The basic distinction I have adopted is that welfare refers to the benefits, in cash or kind, which the policeman receives from the force or the Federation, other than what is given in *direct* exchange for work done or as a regular allowance during working life. Some of the issues treated under this heading include benefits which are fairly closely related to basic pay in that they are negotiated by the same machinery and constitute significant aspects of the job's reward structure, e.g. the pension scheme, rates of sickness pay, etc. Also included are a variety of services and benefits provided by the Federation itself on a local basis. These include a special gift of £1 from every member of the force to the widow of any man killed on duty, hospital visits and help while sick, financial aid to policemen finding themselves in monetary difficulties and so on. It should be noted that some part of the Federation's role in this respect had been taken over in recent years by the institution of a specialised Welfare Officer for the Force. The policemen's assessment of the effectiveness of the Federation in the area of welfare is the most favourable of any item so far considered (Table 4.1). More than half the force sees it as very effective in this work, with a further third seeing it as quite effective. Only a small minority say it is not at all effective. The main significant factor qualifying the response of the men to this item was the view that some financial advantages of the job in previous periods, like the pension, had been comparatively eroded by the development of state provision for all workers.

There is widespread appreciation of Federation welfare activities at local level, as illustrated below:

Welfarewise you couldn't better this force, they look after their own. Like we had a chap unfortunate to have his leg amputated. A lot of forces would have slung him on the scrap-heap as he was a probationer, but they gave him an inside job.
(Uniform constable)

I know several instances where policemen, being human, have got themselves into financial trouble. They've bent over backwards to help. One case I can remember, the P.C.'s left the job now, and quite rightly so. He got up to his neck in debt, H.P. Nothing unlawful, but it's no good for a policeman to be in debt and being chased by all sorts of people writing letters to the Chief. They made him a cash grant of quite a considerable sum to clear his debts. It wasn't supposed to be paid back, just to get him on his feet again. It didn't work in his case, I don't think anything would have. But they're good at coming forward to help you. If I went to the Federation today and explained I was in debt or some financial trouble I just couldn't cope with, there's no doubt they'd help.
(Traffic constable)

As Table 4.1 indicated, while there was considerable commendation of the Federation's efforts in the welfare field, there was also a substantial body of opinion that more could be done. This partly took the form of discontent about the *level* of benefits. It was felt also that certain circumstances were not adequately catered for. The latter sentiment varied in a somewhat idiosyncratic way according to particular misadventures a policeman might have personally experienced which drew attention to gaps in provision.

However, despite some grumbles about inadequacy of welfare provision, either quantitatively or qualitatively, the overall feeling is that the Federation does a good job in this regard. It is one of the main sources of what support it enjoys.

Efficiency of the force

Advising on matters concerning efficiency is one of the two explicit terms of reference specified for the Federation by the Police Act. Measuring, or even defining, the 'efficiency' of the police is notoriously problematic. (See, for example, the discussions in Skolnick 1966: chapter 8; and Laurie 1972: chapter 11.)

As demonstrated by Table 4.1, nearly half the men considered it not at all effective in this regard, while a further third saw it as only quite effective. Only a few saw it as very effective. A crucial issue was the extent to which its brief to protect or advance the welfare of the men was seen as compatible, or conflicting, with its contribution to force efficiency.

This depended partly on how the Federation's potential influence on the efficiency of the force was envisaged. Some saw this as emerging from its contribution to the welfare of the men. The Federation helped efficiency indirectly by ensuring the morale of the men. Others conceived of the Federation as having a more direct part to play in efficiency. This was by putting forward the views of lower-rank personnel about what policy ought to be formulated and how it should be implemented. The opinions and knowledge of the men actually doing police work at 'ground-level' had a vital part in ensuring that policies and decisions were suitable. The extent, and manner, of this more direct participation in policy was debatable.

Both types of potential contribution were double-edged. The indirect effect of improving or maintaining morale *might* aid efficiency. But it might also be the case that under certain circumstances force efficiency required the men's welfare to be sacrificed. In the eyes of some the actual operation of the Federation was detrimental to the work process. It achieved gains which were at the expense of efficiency. Similarly, direct participation in policy-making *might* yield useful suggestions derived from the immediate concrete experience of the 'front-line troops'. But it might, on the other hand, produce a damaging dilution of decision-making authority. This could be either because less clear-cut decisions were arrived at, or because it undermined the power of the senior officers to issue orders which were not conducive to the men's welfare or ease of working. Participation in policy-formulation could contribute to efficiency, in other words, only if there was a consensual notion of what constituted 'efficiency'. If the values informing decisions were shared then the views of the lower ranks might suggest useful means of achieving these. But if there were conflicting values involved then participation would either confuse issues and prevent any coherent policies emerging, or actually result in decisions which were detrimental to efficiency, as conceived of by the senior ranks.

Most of those who felt that the Federation *did* aid the efficiency of the force saw this as the result of its welfare activities. The argument was the familiar 'human relations' one of the positive contribution of morale to efficiency. This was particularly stressed for police-work because of its individualistic character. Most police jobs involved only one or two men, enjoying considerable discretion, so that morale was particularly important. Like 'human relations' theory in industry, this conception rests on a consensual image of the force. It does not recognise any possible conflict between a managerial notion of efficiency and the interests of the men. They can both be maximised simultaneously.

Welfare and efficiency go together fairly evidently. You can't play the fiddle if you're sitting on a rusty nail. (Uniform constable)

The 48% who felt that the Federation played no part in efficiency argued that its achievements were detrimental to their conception of an efficient force. To some this did not matter. The Federation's primary role was to advance *members'* interests.

The Federation is basically 99% for welfare and 1% for efficiency. That's the concern of the officer-class. (Uniform constable)
If the public only knew, we're about the most inefficient organisation. If we were a private company we'd be bankrupt. Poulson would have nothing on us. But who's going to go along and say 'Look we're getting too much money and we're doing too little work?' That's not the Federation's job. (Uniform sergeant)

The Federation inhibited efficiency in cases where the men's interests conflicted with work requirements. Examples were standards of entry, and job security. The Federation has always tried to ensure all recruits equal treatment, and prevent special incentives being offered to a potential 'officer-class'. Some see such efforts as detrimental to efficiency, which would improve with better educated recruits.

I disagree with the official Federation policy and attitudes. They don't seem to appreciate the need to attract a wide spectrum of young men into the service. They seem content to let the more physical type of recruit into the job. We should endeavour to recruit from every strata of society. Mix them all together in the barrel and turn them out: university graduates, farm labourers, everybody. The way the efficiency of the force can be maintained is by ensuring a continuing stream of high quality recruits. I'm afraid the Federation don't always do a good job in fostering this. (C.I.D. inspector)

By protecting policemen's security of employment, the Federation has also weakened the sanctions which could be wielded to encourage efficiency. It has enabled a lot of unable or unwilling men who do little actual work (the 'uniform-carriers' or 'coat-hangers') to remain on the payroll.

We've got a policeman out here pushing brushes in a little short blue dust coat for £30 odd a week. A woman would do the job for 12 quid and do it better. They say he was in the Commandos, he's so nervous it's unbelievable. He goes round repeating himself. He's not a geriatric or anything, but there's nowhere you can funnel him, so they've got him cleaning... You get what we call uniform-carriers, the policeman that comes on duty and goes off duty and just picks his wages up. There was one in B division was so useless in the street they put him in the station, they thought he could at least answer queries. But he kept calling men back into the station to deal with jobs. In industry you'd say 'pick up your cards next week'. But there's so much security here you can't get rid of him unless he does something criminal. He's there till he retires. (Uniform sergeant)

Most of the Federationists explicitly rejected such views. Manifest efficiency was a source of support in negotiations. The enlightened Federationist would thus be as concerned as senior officers with the personal efficiency of the men. Obvious shirking, malingering and other symptoms of 'uniform-carrying' weakened Federation demands. Many representatives were keen to reduce the security of men who did not work properly. Some officials of the Federation who were renowned for their activism in pursuit of benefits for the men, and their criticism of the hierarchy, were also personally regarded as strict supervisors who would enforce the rules at least as tightly as the rest. They were not concerned to bend rules, but to change them (if they were deemed unfair or inappropriate). Men who obviously didn't carry their weight workwise were an impediment to pay and other demands. (For a parallel example in industry see Beynon 1973: 140.)

When I was a sergeant I was in a car one night with a representative, and we caught a policeman sleeping. And he really went for him! Afterwards I said 'you were a bit hard there!' He said: 'Because I belong to the Federation I want to see the job improve. I want the right man, and I don't want layabouts pulling us down.' I have known this with Federationists – it doesn't mean they're soft. If they're sergeants or inspectors and somebody's been irregular or misbehaving in a minor way, they won't say 'poor chap, it's because there's bad conditions'. I think they should be quite hard and say they're working for the Federation image. Why should they be tied down with layabouts. They want to prove to the authority they're one of a damn good team who deserve better conditions.

(Uniform inspector)

Federationists did not necessarily share the same notions of efficiency as senior officers. There might be conflicts over what constituted the most effective policy in which the various ranks had opposing opinions. But this is a different matter from the allegation that Federation aims or achievements hindered efficiency in some obvious or neutral sense such as featherbedding. Indeed some activists made the contrary accusation, that the Federation could contribute to efficiency by rooting out managerial malpractice!

To what extent did the Federation influence the efficiency of the force *directly* by offering suggestions for policy reflecting the views of lower-rank personnel? It was generally felt that the Federation did not at present perform a major role in this way. The extent of involvement of the Federation in decision-making varied between forces according to the personality and attitudes of the Chief Constable, and how he got on with the local Branch Board. It was acknowledged that the relationship in the force studied was relatively fortunate in this respect, and there was a fair amount of consultation and contact. This was contrasted with the more hostile stance taken by the Chief Constables of some county forces in the region which had acquired notoriety for this. But the local situation was not seen as ideal. Many men, especially among the representatives themselves, felt that there had been numerous occasions where policies had been implemented reflecting senior officers' interest or perspectives, but which the men did not see as the most efficient.

The Branch Board chairman argued that the Federation was prevented from doing as much as it wanted to for the efficiency of the force, because of senior officers' opposition.

We aren't as influential as we would be because in my own experience the official side don't want us to be. They don't regard efficiency as one of our tasks. Yet the Police Act quite clearly defines it as 'welfare and efficiency'. I remember on one occasion we were discussing something with the Chief, it was regarding the number of men required at a football ground to deal with the crowds and we were complaining that there weren't enough. And he said that he decided how many would be there and, you know, the usual waffle that we were in danger of impinging on his operational responsibility. And my reply to this was that I was there in the interest of the welfare of the members. If there were fifty there and seventy were needed, then that fifty were likely to get clobbered. I might have upset him if I'd asked for it on grounds of efficiency, and he isn't a bad sort of chap. But on this we obviously had him on one foot, and I've realised that if he starts to come back at us he's in a bit of a corner – this is my interpretation of his reaction. And of course it was rather noticeable that shortly afterwards the numbers at the ground increased so we achieved our object without falling out with him.

The way in which notions of efficiency can vary with rank is epitomised in the following case, as narrated by a Branch Board member who was a traffic sergeant. It also illustrates how their feeling about the Chief Constable's reluctance to allow them a full say on policy matters leads to self-censorship.

Our Chief was told he's got to cut down his expenditure, so as a result he brought out what can loosely be called an economy drive, cutting down on everything. We're no longer to be issued with biros, we've all got to have pencils instead, and this sort of rubbish. Anyway, the first we know is when it is brought out in orders that this is what you're going to do! No more than that! At our next Federation meeting it's brought up. And we didn't even think he should have agreed to it in the first place. But having agreed, we thought he should have asked the Federation for their views as to ways of economising. The result was that we formed a sub-committee to discuss ways of saving money which we thought were better than those they'd already put forward. We did a fair bit of homework on it. Now one of the things they've cut down is our mileage. We're now restricted to sixty-five miles in a tour of duty. This really is ridiculous – we're supposed to be a mobile traffic patrol. Now it might not sound very bad, particularly when the superintendent worked out that the average of all cars over a period was seventy-five miles in a tour of duty so it's only reduced by ten. But there are occasions when it's a right nuisance, there's no two ways about it. You drive round and suddenly find after four hours you've done sixty miles so for the next four hours you've got to do five miles. That's ridiculous. The average is meaningless. So much depends on the area of patrol you've got, is it city centre or motorway? So we discussed it fully, but the ways we could see of economising the amount saved would be negligible. Then somebody points out what would save a great deal of money, but we knew that it wouldn't be at all popular with the hierarchy. Each divisional commander has an official car. Mr G. has just got a brand new Morris 1800. I don't know how much it cost – haven't a clue. The only purpose they use these cars for is getting to and from work. We couldn't see for the life of us why they ever crept in! Alright, they've got some status – but we all use our own transport getting to work. They've all got their own cars as well. We found that was the only idea we could come back with that would save a fair bit of money and not effect operational work. But we thought it would be a little bit naughty, you know, saying 'we don't like the idea of your economy drive, we don't like your economies, and instead of all *you've* said *we* suggest you take all the superintendents' cars away'. It wouldn't go down at all well so in the end we said, let the sleeping dogs lie.

Sometimes, when the Federation didn't voice any protest because of the anticipated reaction of the senior ranks, the men themselves were able to take the task on.

There was regulations concerning panda cars that they were to do thirty miles each shift, which was farcical – that's four miles an hour! The Federation should have gone to the Chief and said so. They did the same in Glasgow when I was there, and a few of us – militants, shall we say – parked our cars after 10 miles and walked away from them, but still in our area. And we got calls to a job, we'd phone in and say 'fair enough, I'll go, but I'm so many miles away and it's going to take me ten minutes to walk there'. So after that it all stopped and we were back to, within reason, doing our miles per shift. I feel if the Federation had gone to the Chief and pointed out this was utter farcical, the force would be better, more efficient. But I don't see how you can run it on a shoestring budget. (Uniform constable)

There was an order recently about panda cars. They had to be checked before going out, water, oil etc. We explained to the rep. that by the time you do all this, check the pressures and so on, it would be say 20–25 past on the shift before any cars rolled. He just said, 'well that's what the orders say'. So one day we all started doing it as per the book, have the bonnet checked, wash your hands and everything. Our sergeant went spare because every car was still down the police station at 20 past 2, you know? So it went by the board. (Uniform constable)

The general view seems to be that the Federation is hardly effective in promoting force efficiency. In so far as it has an effect, it is mainly in-direct, via welfare and hence morale. But this connection is double-edged. A substantial minority see the Federation's concern for the members' interests as inimical to force efficiency. This charge is rebutted by men closer, or more sympathetic, to the Federation. They argue that the Federation *is* concerned about maintaining and encouraging personal efficiency of the men, because slackness, 'uniform-carrying', weaken its hand in negotiations. But the Federation is recognised as having little *direct* influence over policy in the interest of efficiency even in the force studied, where relationships with the Chief Constable were comparatively good. He was known to regard this as interfering with managerial pre-rogatives. This led to a degree of self-censorship by the Federation about suggestions which reflected conflict between the ranks about the means of achieving efficiency. The men were thus forced on occasions to take the law into their own hands.

Assisting in cases of discipline charges

This was the area of Federation activity which was overwhelmingly seen as the most successful. Table 4.1 shows that most felt the Federation was very effective in discipline cases. This is paradoxical because the Police Act explicitly excludes 'individual cases of promotion and discipline' from the Federation's purview. Yet this is now seen as the Federation's one outstanding area of success! Federation involvement in it has taken place because of the need of men facing discipline charges to have expert advice and assistance at hearings. According to the disciplinary regulations a policeman *is* entitled to consult a 'friend' in the police force about the case, and if he chooses, have this person as his representative at the hearing. This practice is enshrined in Regulation 8 (6) of *The Police (Discipline) Regulations 1965*, issued by the Home Office. The Federation has issued *A Handbook of Police Discipline* which offers guidance on the discipline procedure, including the choice of a 'friend'. It is made clear that the institution of the 'friend' provides a means for the Federation to help men in discipline cases.

In practice the Federation usually provides the 'friend' of the accused at a hearing, even though it cannot act officially as an organisation in these cases. Some representatives have become experts in this task. The success of their efforts is reflected in Table 4.1. It was well known to the men that if they were accused of a charge the first thing to do was to consult the Federation. Obviously they do not always succeed in getting him acquitted. But it was felt they do their best, and while the Federation was not capable of performing miracles, the man was at least ensured a fair and reasonable chance. Many men felt this gave them a degree of confidence and security in their work which the constant fear of complaints and other accusations would otherwise inhibit. The small number of dissentients who saw the Federation as ineffective in this area usually had some personal ill experience, justified or not. Among them (and some of the others), there was a demand for the right to employ professional legal representation in internal hearings. But the general opinion was that the Federation 'friends' were keen and competent in the task. Some even felt they might do better than professional lawyers because of their knowledge and experience of internal force matters. The appreciation accorded the Federation in this work reflects the tremendous apprehension and fear that the policemen have of disciplinary hearings, and of being subject to complaint. Despite all the outside criticism of lack of independent elements in the process of investigating or adjudicating complaints, the feeling amongst *policemen* was that the hearings are scrupulous in their examination of conduct and showed no favour to them. Some even thought that senior officers were tougher than external investigators would be, because of their concern to be seen as impartial. The Federation was looked on as a reliable ally which would do its best to help the defence of any man who convinced them he was not in fact a 'bent' copper. Indeed in the eyes of some, especially among the more senior officers, the Federation was too ardent and successful in this regard, and secured the dismissal of charges against men who deserved sanctioning, either for breaches of internal discipline regulations or more serious offences.

The Branch Board studied, like many others round the country, had several members who specialised in discipline cases, and this was as institutionalised a situation as was possible given the formal ban on such activities.

The general appreciation of this was reflected in the following comments:

The only time you ever use the Federation is when you're in the shit.
(Uniform constable)

Discipline charges – this is their prime use really. Because for a bloke who's on the fizz if you can get help from somebody who knows something about the procedure, not just from the bloke with the next locker who's been on the same charge the week before, it's a great help. Then you don't go to the hearing and make yourself look a pudding.   (Uniform constable)

They're experts at discipline charges. If you go up before the boss and he's given you a bollocking, asked you to make a statement and all that. Fred has told us to 'just keep your mouth shut and wait till I get there', you know. He's like a solicitor for the defence, which is fantastic, because the superintendents are like crafty lawyers. They ask you for a statement, and then they say 'Oh, that's fair enough. Now what really happened, off the record?' And then they serve papers on you!   (Uniform constable)

A friend of mine has been complained against on four occasions, and he has been defended by the Federation representative. The defence has been well put forward and he's been discharged on each account. This is one reason why I personally wouldn't be afraid to have a go. I'm confident of the ability of the Federation to put forward a fair defence, if it's justified. If I go out there and give someone a bunch of fives for no reason at all, then I expect to be charged criminally in court. But if you're out there and injure someone in your own defence, then the Federation is excellent, you couldn't wish for better.
(Uniform constable)

You have to apply a lot of self-discipline when you're on the street dealing with people who are really anti-police, and don't assist you in any way. As opposed to losing your temper and doing what you personally think and feel like doing. Sometimes of course you do get a little bit out of hand and express yourself! This is unfortunate, but then the Federation come in and they do a very good job of defending on discipline cases. They know the various wriggles to get round them.
(Uniform constable)

Thus there was widespread recognition of the Federation's ability to help in such cases. This functions to give policemen a measure of confidence in their work, which would otherwise be haunted by fear of complaints.

The role of the Federation in such cases can perhaps be best elucidated by some examples of help it has offered in particular instances:

I don't think you should see the superintendent when you've had a complaint served on you unless you've seen the Federation first. Some of these senior officers, you know, as soon as they've got a policeman on the end of a piece of string, that's it. They'll tie you in knots, there's no doubt about it. Don't get me wrong – I don't like bent policemen, and I'm not bent. But I don't like it when they try to squeeze everything out of you.

I mean, I've had a complaint, I must admit. I was firm with this bloke up in the underpass. He was playing the guitar, people were throwing money into his case there. I went up to him and said: 'Look, my son, you can't do that here. Move on, see?' So he was quite prepared to stop and put his guitar away and move on. Anyway, some idiot passer-by said: 'Well, they're enjoying it – the children.' I said 'I don't have to explain my actions to you. I said he's got to move, and he's got to move.' Anyway, they didn't enter into any more argument and the chappie went his way. I walked on round Broadmead and came back to the underpass about half an hour later. And he was back again playing his guitar. So I went over to him and said: 'Look, this is the second warning. I've told you once. If I find you a third time I'm arresting you under the Highways Act. Now, will you pack up?' He said: 'I'm not doing any harm.' I said: 'I know you're not doing any harm. I like the music. But you can see the position you're creating. These children are standing here and they're blocking the underpass. If I let you stay I shall have everybody in the underpass – it'll be completely blocked.' So he accepted the fact. I asked: 'Anyway, where do you come from?' 'Liverpool. I'm just travelling on down to Cornwall, and I thought I'd just stop off and rest a little bit. Thanks for not doing anything.' I said: 'Well, I could knock you off for begging or busking. Are you going to move on?' So he went. Anyway, the passer-by who butted in the first time sent a letter to the Chief Constable regarding my boorish attitude, and the way I went on at the chap. 'The officer said "What I say goes"' etc. At any rate, I was asked for a duty report. That means the Chief thinks there's no disciplinary action to be taken, but I must put on a report to say exactly what happened. Anyway, I saw the Federation rep. on our group. He said 'Well that's O.K. You can put a report on and if they try to serve papers, come and see me. Because they can't serve papers on you after a duty report.' So I did what he said, and a few days later I had to see the chief superintendent. He showed me the reply the Chief Constable sent to the chap. He put basically what was in my report, to the effect that I was in my right to tell this person to move on, and I did not have to tell this passer-by my reasons.

(Uniform constable)

In another case that actually came to a hearing the Federation were able to give helpful advice, even though the charge was upheld this time:

I've been on disciplinary. I came to see the Federation before I went and was told not to say anything. I was accused of failing to stop after an accident and they accused me of drinking. Well, I was with a female, and they wanted to know if she was driving. I did hit some parked vehicles, you see. And I left a note on this car as it was early in the morning, and went home. I'd been out drinking that night, I must admit. They came to the house, knocked on the door. I said: 'I was reversing down the road. When I went in the cars weren't there, but when I came out they were! [laughter]. And I just touched them, but I left a note.' They took the breathalyser in the house, which they're not allowed to do, as far as I was concerned. I may have been over the top, but they couldn't prove it. I took my mother as a witness, that as soon as I got home I had some more drink. They thought the woman might have been driving. The Federation gave me good advice, because I was young in service and might have opened my mouth to the superintendent completely. I was told to say the bare minimum. The super. wanted to knew who was in the car with me. He tried his hardest. I was accused of going out with another policeman's wife, a chief inspector's daughter, you name it, I was accused! But they never found out and they never will. But anyway, I was found guilty, and went upstairs and got reprimanded.

(Uniform constable)

While there is overwhelming satisfaction with the Federation and its efforts in connection with discipline cases, a small minority of men feel it is not effective enough. This is usually based on some individual bad experience. Probably the Federation is being blamed for failing to achieve the impossible, as in this case:

We had an incident two or three years ago where a policeman on the W. Rd had a notification of a stolen car in the city, it had been stolen a few minutes. He sees a car come up on the road, headlights going – he could just make out the shape of it, it was the same model, same colour. It was the early hours of the morning. He couldn't see the number because of the headlights. He got in the middle of the road. Thought he'd see him in the lights. Out there, beautiful, full uniform, full regalia, torch. And this bloke who was driving the car nearly knocked him for six! But he swerved to the right. And as he did, the policeman quick as a flash got his truncheon out and threw it straight through the windscreen. And this bloke – Lord, blooming hell!, you know. Bang! Straight into a tree! Anyway, it wasn't the stolen car. The policeman was taken to the civil court, charged with damage to the bloke's car, conduct beyond his police duties, and all this rubbish. The police force never even stood by him. The Federation defended him the best way they could, employed a solicitor, fair enough. He got to court, and after hearing the preliminary circumstances for about five minutes the judge adjourned for a ten minute recess. And the police authority settled out of court and paid this bloke's damages, loss of earnings, transport and the rest of it. Now, if that wasn't admitting the policeman was wrong! He was banged in front of the Chief Constable and got a reprimand. A fortnight later he resigned and is now in the Fire Brigade. That was his sentiments about the police service! (Uniform constable)

Another case of Federation failure to defend a man against a possible discipline charge is reported below:

When I first came here I was being shown around by this older policeman. He was a bit of a ladies' man, this lad. We got involved in this accident we came across – nothing serious. There was a couple of nurses in this car and, of course, he was chatting them up. He's supposed to be supervising me as a probationer! And I omitted to take the insurance number and certificate of the other driver. So we get back to the station, and the inspector looks at the book. 'Where's the insurance number?' 'Forgot to put it in.' 'Right, when you finish at 2 o'clock (this was about mid-day), you get on your bicycle and get to F. (where the nurses lived) and get that number. I want it on my desk before three o'clock, or you're on a charge!' It was my own time you see, I had to ride on a pushbike all the way. Lucky they were in! ... I went and saw the Federation about it. But they couldn't help me. 'Oh, well, Joe. You missed those numbers, you should do the job efficiently!' (Uniform sergeant)

Inspectors often criticise the Federation's record on discipline cases, because of their position on 'the other side'.

> I see this from both sides. I admire my colleagues in the Federation who are prepared to take on a 'toe-rag' and represent on his behalf. I admire them not for their integrity but for their gall! Because I'm damned if I would. I feel when a chap's hard done by it's extremely unlikely to reach the stage of a hearing. But when he's culpable and on a charge, then I've got very mixed feelings about trying to get them off!   (Uniform inspector)

Criticism came mainly from supervisors who had seen some cases from the 'prosecuting' side, and felt the Federation performance misplaced. Generally the men saw the Federation as the first port of call if in trouble, and they expected it to be of some help. This gave them confidence in doing their job.

Summary

The Federation's most highly valued activity was one which it cannot legitimately deal with as an organisation – helping individuals on discipline charges. The Federation was primarily thought of as the policemen's *legal-aid centre*, as the defence for policemen in trouble. This work was mainly carried out locally, and partly accounts for the better evaluation of the Federation at branch rather than national level.

It was less successful in its collective bargaining activities, pay, conditions and welfare. Welfare work was most praised, but here again it was local, *ad hoc* help which was applauded rather than national bargaining. Pay was influenced mainly by the demand for and supply of policemen, which varied according to the social and political climate. The same applied to expected levels of work input, allowances and benefits. Some aspects, like outdoor work, were outside its control. But on issues which were subject to local representation, like ensuring fair 'man-management', it was seen as more effective.

The other activities, influencing the public image and legislation, internal communications, and efficiency, were more the work of a 'professional association' than a quasi-union defending 'men' against 'bosses'. On all of these the Federation was viewed as ineffective. With respect to the public image of the police, Federation efforts were seen as largely useless. Public attitudes depended more on concrete experience, and the pervasive anti-police bias attributed to the media. Federation efforts were viewed as often counter-productive, relative to the superior ability of senior officers as public spokesmen. Its efforts at internal communication were seen as not entirely adequate and limited in impact by the prevailing apathy about Federation matters. Its attempts at influencing legislation were scarcely noticed, and when they were known about, e.g. the capital punishment issue, felt to be largely futile. The Federation was regarded as achieving very little for the efficiency of the force, even though this function is one half of its statutory terms of reference. What impact it did have was largely felt to be indirect, via its work for the men's welfare, and hence morale. Even this was dubiously regarded by many men, especially among the C.I.D. and more senior officers, who felt that many achievements which were in the interest of Federation members could be detrimental to the work of the force. In terms of direct contributions to efficiency through conveying the know-how and suggestions of operational policemen, the Federation was seen as playing a very circumscribed role. Representatives tended to feel that the senior officers would object to a larger role as an encroachment on managerial prerogatives. This led to an element of self-censorship. The issue was not just one of protocol about who had the right to articulate ideas about policy. Efficiency cannot be viewed neutrally or independently of the way specific decisions impinge on the interests of different groups. Ranks and sections conflict over what constitutes the most effective way of running the force, as the example of the economy drive illustrated.

5
Policemen's desire for unionism

A distinction has frequently been made between two forms of employee representation: trade unions and professional associations. (Blackburn 1967; Millerson 1964.) The difference between them is not absolute; they form a continuum. Organisations vary in being informed by a 'class' or 'status' ideology, readiness for militant action, and having wider interests than instrumental ones (Lockwood 1958: 137 and 194–8; Prandy 1965: 42–7; Blackburn 1967: 27).

Trade unions are said to hold a conflict image of the work organisation. Groups are differentiated in terms of material rewards, work situation, status, and power in the decision-making process. The only way subordinates can influence their position is by collective action, utilising what power they have through the organised withholding of labour. They may extend this to concerted political action together with other unions to further the shared interest of all workers. This is related to a 'traditional' working-class image of society, which identifies a fundamental conflict between two distinct and polarised classes (Lockwood 1966; Bulmer 1975).

Professional associations correspond to a consensus image of the work organisation. Internal status differences are regarded as due to individual variations in talent and effort. Personal advancement is up a promotion ladder based on agreed merit standards. The purpose of association is to improve the interests of the whole group by controlling certification, and developing the knowledge on which this rests. This is not in conflict with the interests of outsiders, because it ensures a high level of competence. This ideology and occupational strategy reflects a consensus view of society, held to be characteristic of non-manual workers.

This simplified version of the argument obviously requires much qualification. Different forms of representative body do not necessarily correspond to, or develop because of, particular conceptions of the social organisation of the work place. The growth of unions or professional associations has to be understood in terms of a variety of factors, including the attitudes and policies of management and government, the market conditions of the enterprise, and other constraints. The *character* of a representative body is not a simple result of the consciousness of the work force. It involves a more complex interplay of members' attitudes with the strategies of other groups. There is a dialectical relationship between the *ideas* of the participants and the material circumstances underlying their interests. Consciousness cannot be realistically regarded as corresponding in a clear-cut way to one of the crude images of society outlined above, and ideas do not simply reflect the influence of position in the enterprise or the larger society. Therefore the kind of representative body existing in an organisation cannot be taken as an index of either the image held by employees of social relationships at work, or *a fortiori* their class consciousness in a wider sense.

There were debates about these issues going on in the police force when the research began. The view that the police ought to be represented by a body more like an ordinary trade union was strongly argued by some activists in the Federation. There was also a body of opinion favouring a rather different strategy, replacing the Federation by a single professional association representing all ranks.

A professional association was supported by the view that *consensus* of interest between *all* ranks in the service made separate representation neither necessary nor desirable.

Separate representation of ranks is a pile of rubbish, because even the Chief Constable was a constable at one time. You see, everybody in the police service has come up the same way. Everybody's got to be a probationary constable at one time irrespective of what rank he attains later on. I feel that all ranks should be covered by the one body. (Uniform constable)

In industry it's a different matter because it's an employer and employee relationship. This isn't. You're virtually self-employed apart from the fact that... well, you take orders from people. But once you're out on the streets you're on your own. (Uniform constable)

Conversely, those rejecting a single association saw *conflict* of interest between ranks.

The Chief Constable wants us all to have...take hair as an example...wants us all to be smart, clean turned out little boys. And us at the bottom, we don't want it that way. It's still an 'us' and 'them' complex. If we are all in the same union so to speak, it would be very awkward. (Uniform constable)

The senior ranks get more money for doing an easier job. They're the fighting chairborne! (Uniform constable)

I would be totally against a single association. In fact, quite frankly, I don't think the Federation should have any rank above P.C. This job is a very cut-throat job. I would always be suspicious of the superintendent sat at the back. His mere presence would quiet a few chaps down from speaking at meetings.

(Uniform constable)

Forty-four per cent thought the Federation should be a single professional association, 43% were against, and there were 13% who didn't know. Support for a single association is related to position in the internal stratification system, as Table 5.1 shows. The table demonstrates that the idea is much more popular with inspectors than constables. (It is also more popular with sergeants than constables, but this difference is not statistically significant.)

TABLE 5.1. *Support for professional association instead of present Federation*

	Constables %	Sergeants %	Inspectors %
In favour of professional association	38	45	70
Against	46	42	26
Don't know	15	12	4
Total	100	100	100
Base	N = 112	N = 33	N = 23

A priori one would expect the nature of the job done, whether a police-man worked in the ordinary uniform branch or a specialist division, to have some effect on responses to this question. In fact it turns out to make some difference, but a statistically insignificant one. Fifty per cent of the specialists (N=54) as opposed to 41% of the uniform men (N=114) support the idea of a single association. When constables only are con-sidered, the difference remains but is still insignificant. Forty-four per cent of constables in specialist divisions (N=25) support the idea, while only 37% of uniform constables (N=87) do.

The term 'specialist' lumps together a motley collection of different jobs. However, the numbers within each are too small for comparison. The impression I got was that support for a single association was strongest in Administration and policewomen, intermediate in the C.I.D., and lowest in the traffic division, who were almost as opposed as the ordinary uniform men. The Administration and the policewomen could be expected to be more favourably inclined for the same reasons that clerical and women workers tend to be recalcitrant to unionism. One ardent policewomen's representative told me:

Women don't quite look at trade unions and strikes as men do. We're a bit different. I don't know whether we're more passive in nature, not the aggressive part of the human race. I know women have punch-ups and things sometimes, but we don't go off to fight wars like men do.

The C.I.D. were subject to cross-pressures. On the one hand, the nature of their work situation, and their orientations prior to becoming detectives, incline them to a 'professional' conception and an identification with senior rank personnel. On the other hand, distinctions between the C.I.D. and uniform men are strong. Thus while detectives may be less acutely aware of differences based on the dimension of rank, they are more sensitive to a gap between themselves and other divisions which would incline them against common representation.

Support for a single association was *not* consistently opposed to desire for a trade union. There were two axes of debate. The first was the drawing of lines of cleavage within the force. The second was the manner and powers of the representative organisation, whoever was in it. These were logically distinct issues, even if empirically related. The former was tapped by the professional association question, the latter by the trade union question.

The idea that the Federation should become more like a trade union was supported by 38%, and rejected by 57% (5% didn't know). Overall the idea is less popular than the single professional association, though neither has majority support. Desire for a union is related to rank, but in the opposite way from support for a professional association.

Table 5.2 shows that constables are more in favour of a trade union than are either sergeants or inspectors. (Sergeants are also more in favour than inspectors, but this difference is not statistically significant.) Specialist divisions are less likely to favour a trade union but again this difference is not statistically significant.

TABLE 5.2. *Support for making the Federation more like an ordinary trade union*

	Constables	Sergeants	Inspectors
	%	%	%
In favour of trade union	44	24	26
Against	52	64	74
Don't know	4	12	0
Total	100	100	100
	N = 112	N = 33	N = 23

The argument for a union was usually that policemen needed more power to avoid exploitation. 'To get anything nowadays you must have some leverage. Now, don't get me wrong, I'm not trying to be a right Red. But you must have some leverage' (uniform constable).

A few, mainly Federation activists, argued on the grounds of the intrinsic moral right to a union which they felt all workers had: 'Basically I feel that every working man, a person who has to work to live, should be in a union. I support it basically politically' (uniform constables' representative).

Opposition to a trade union reflected the considerations which led policemen to see the Federation as adequate. A trade union in the police force was either seen as unnecessary because the structural position of the police in society gave the Federation adequate power, or because person-alities rather than structures were seen as important. Unionism was also rejected on grounds of principle, whether or not it would be needed to ensure fair treatment for policemen themselves. This acceptance of the *status quo* was frequently backed up by references to the evils of unionism in general. (Many of the men who supported the idea of a police union were also suspicious or critical of outside unions.) This general anti-union feeling was a major reason for rejection of police unionism. A union was seen as a way of importing undesirable and alien political influences into the police.

I feel the Federation is an adequate form of representation, though I don't think it's an organisation with teeth. We certainly have nothing like the powers or the bite of a trade union. There's a very good case for maintaining it in its present form. I'm probably prejudiced in that I haven't any great respect for the trade union movement. Primarily I suppose because one hears so much about the left-wingers in it that one does tend to be put off. I admit there are a number of moderate union leaders who do a very good job. But I would not want to be subject to the discipline and kinds of carryings-on which the trade unions have.
(Traffic inspector)

A professional association and a trade union did not constitute anti-thetical forms of representation to the men. This is shown by cross-tabulation of the answers to the two questions, in Table 5.3.

TABLE 5.3. *Trade union and professional association support*

		Professional association		
		Against	For	Don't know
		%	%	%
Trade union	Against	19	28	10
	For	21	14	2
	Don't know	2	2	0.6

(Percentages are of total sample of 168.)

On the assumption, suggested by some of the literature, that the two forms are antithetical the cell containing 14% of the sample, i.e. those supporting both types of representation, ought to be empty. The reasons given by these men explains the apparent anomaly. They perceive a consensus between ranks *within* the force, but conflict with the civilian authorities. Thus they want a single association for all ranks, but this should have more of the character of a trade union than the existing Federation, so as to give more power to *all* policemen. The general point is that the unit of conflict or consensus must be clearly specified. The main lines of cleavage and interest-group formation can be perceived as occurring at various points in the force hierarchy, or the overriding conflict may be seen as being between the police as a whole and outside authorities, i.e. the Home Office and/or the Watch Committee. This latter view is illustrated by the following:

The Home Office is our lord and master. (C.I.D. inspector)
The Chief Constable is one of the boys in blue. But the Watch Committee are just our bosses. (Uniform constable)
We're bucking local authority and central government expenditure. Whereas if it was one complete police body, we could speak on all aspects that affect the police service... But a single police association would not be tolerated by government. They would be rather frightened of such a police body...it would be too powerful. (C.I.D. inspector)

There are four distinct perspectives, revealed by the combination of the two questions in Table 5.3.

(a) *Against both a trade union and professional association (19%)*

This implies a belief in the suitability of the present Federation organisation and approach. Specifically, it implies that the Federated ranks are seen as having distinctive interests from senior ranks which precludes representation by a single body i.e. there is conflict within the force in that sense. However, the present style of approach, involving negotiation without any powers of industrial action, is adequate, or at any rate must be accepted as the only feasible one in the police force. In this sense there is a belief in an ultimate consensus between the federated ranks, senior officers, and the Official Side, so that presentation of a reasonable case will prove sufficient to achieve a fair outcome. In this perspective, while groups in different structural positions have different interests, any problems derive, in the classic phrase, from a lack of communication. To resolve them, an exchange of views is adequate. In so far as this fails to occur, it is because the channels of communication are clogged up or non-existent, and not due to any structurally generated irreconcilable conflicts of interest.

This outlook can be illustrated by examining how the attitudes of one person holding it cohere into a specific viewpoint. An example is F., a 33-year-old detective constable with five years' service. D/C F. felt the Federation, as it stood, was an adequate body to look after the interests of policemen. 'As it is at the moment, I think it's the best we can expect for the police force.' His evaluation of particular activities was pretty near the norm for the force as a whole. The Federation was not at all effective in influencing pay negotiations, the public image of the police or legislation. It was quite helpful on conditions of service, and internal communications. He deemed it very successful at helping on discipline charges and providing welfare benefits. D/C F. didn't know about anything it did towards the efficiency of the force. But despite this relatively mediocre or even poor performance of the Federation, he was against having a union, on the moral grounds of the disastrous consequences to the public of a police strike, as well as generalised hostility to unionism.

A militant union is something I wouldn't want because I don't agree with the police being able to strike. We've got a duty to the public, to protect them from themselves, and their property... A lot of these unionists seem hell bent on causing as much destruction as they can to the country.

While a police union is rejected on these grounds, the idea of a single professional association is also ruled out because the ranks have different interests which conflict.

If we include everybody in one body, we'll get their problems added to ours. All the superintendents and chief inspectors, they're not going to have meetings with us because they're not getting any advancement for themselves... You've got the lower ranks, sergeants and below as the working force, and then you've got the people in the higher ranks, the superintendents.

So altogether the present Federation structure and style are the most suitable. A move in the direction of a single association is ruled out because the ranks have varying perspectives and interests. But a more unionate body is also precluded by the moral duties of policemen. There are adequate channels of communication between the Federation and the Chief Constable, and in turn the latter and the Watch Committee. 'They often meet each other, you know.' There are also adequate channels between the men and the Federation. 'We get a vote each year and select the person we want. You couldn't be more democratic than that.' Thus the conclusion is: 'I quite like the way it's run at the moment, we've got a good system here.'

(b) *For a single association, but against a union (28%)*

This is a more far-reaching consensus model than the previous one. There is not only an ultimate consensus in the sense that communication of interests between different sides in negotiation can lead to a mutually satisfactory outcome. There is also sufficient similarity of interests between ranks *within* the force as not to require representation by separate bodies. Not only are the Federation's powers of action adequate, but it would be improved by including all ranks rather than perpetuating the groundless notion of a conflict of interest. An example of this perspective is a 45-year-old chief inspector, subsequently promoted superintendent during the research period. (He was, incidentally, at one time a sergeants' representative on the Branch Board.)

Chief Inspector T. saw the Federation as an adequate body to represent the police. He ruled out any change in a unionate direction as harmful to the job. It was also unnecessary because the Federation did very well using its present resources of moral pressure. He had an unusually favourable evaluation of the Federation's influence. It was, he felt, very effective in pay negotiations, in communication of information internally, and in helping with discipline cases. It was also quite successful on conditions of service, in influencing the public image of the police, and in aiding the welfare and efficiency of the force. The only area in which he felt they were not influential was legislation. While viewing the present Federation performance as very good, he felt that a move in the direction of a single professional association would help it, as the ranks were very close in their interests and becoming more so. Indeed the signs were that more mutual co-ordination between the representative associations for different ranks was already occurring, and this was a pointer to the future.

I think they do the job adequately in their form at the moment. So I don't think there is any necessity for them to have the power that trade unions wield, and I think it would mar the job. It's a job which breeds a different state of mind to chaps who are employed outside, particularly where there's a trade union involved. For example, this isn't the sort of job where you can sort of shut up shop at 5 and leave it... The Federation have used the limited weapons available to them very well, pressurising M.P.s and so on. This is the right way to go about it. Bringing influence to bear rather than being bloody-minded... I've often thought this [a single association] was a good idea, and I think it's gradually happening. Over the last two or three years there's been much greater liaison between the Federation and the Superintendents' Association... I see every reason for them to work very close together, and I think it's happening. The objects of all are so closely entwined now.

The above two perspectives are both based on a consensus image in the sense that negotiation without sanctions is deemed adequate, or at any rate must be accepted for the police force. The difference between them is the extent of perceived conflict of interest according to rank, and how far this necessitates separate representation. The two perspectives outlined below both perceive a need for greater powers to be given the police representative body, but they differ in terms of the degree of conflict seen to exist within the force itself.

(c) *For both a single association and a unionate body* (*14%*)

As already outlined, this reflects the view that while *intra-force* differences between ranks are not so wide as to require separate representation, conflict between the force *as a whole* and the authorities require a unionate approach.

This position can be illustrated by the case of Constable P., a 25-year-old uniform man with three years' service. He felt that the Federation was not sufficiently powerful to look after policemen's interests.

They're trying to do as much as they can, but it just doesn't carry any weight behind it. It would help to have some big stick behind you if it was needed. Not like the unions now. They've gone a little bit too far. Between what the Federation is now and what the unions are now, a middle line is what I'd like.

This would improve the performance of the Federation, which he evaluated poorly. It was not at all effective on pay, public image or legislation, and only quite good on internal communication and legislation. He could not evaluate their work on conditions, but their welfare work and help with discipline cases was very successful. Despite his perception of the poverty of the Federation's performance and the need for greater sanctions, he was also in favour of a single body for all policemen. He felt all ranks were basically the same. There was no fundamental conflict between them even though he was worried about the degree of social distance and snobbishness maintained by some supervisors. But a single association would help break this down. Ultimately they were in the same boat, and shared common grievances.

A police force is a police force whether you're a constable like myself or a superintendent or Chief Constable. You're still working for the constabulary. It would get less of a gap between the P.C. and sergeant group, and the inspectors and above. They're sort of very cagey sometimes.

On the whole he evaluated every aspect of the job, including the supervision, as very good compared to outside work, apart from the pay which he was only quite satisfied with. But in this respect all ranks share a common interest. So the appropriate form of representation for the police would be a single association with greater powers of action than the present Federation.

(d) *For a union and against a professional association* (21%)

This implies the more complete conflict view that not only is a more unionate approach necessary in negotiations with the authorities, but this is needed also to represent the interests of the lower ranks against the senior ranks within the force. While on some issues the sharing of common interests is not precluded, there is conflict between ranks on most things.

Constable N provides an example of this outlook. He was uniform man of twenty-eight with nine years' service behind him. He felt the Federation was not adequate in its present form. 'I don't feel they can help me a great deal in any way. They just do the best they can at the present, not being a union. My view is they could do better if they were a union.' He saw the Federation as quite good on pay, communications, legislation and discipline. It was very good on welfare and conditions, but not effective at all in promoting force efficiency or a favourable police image. He felt that 'from a personal point of view as a policeman it would be a good thing to be with a trade union. I would approve of it in this day and age.' This he saw as valid for all workers, 'Unions are the only representation of the other side of the country, the 90% who own only 10% of the wealth. We're still demanding wages, and they're still turning out their huge profits.' But while he wanted the Federation to have more power, like other trade unions, he did not want it to extend to senior ranks.

> You've got to have separate bodies for separate ranks. They look after themselves. I mean, there are basic policemen, men who are used to a fair day's work – or night's work! They've got different things in their mind to people who are in offices, fairly ambitious men who're moving the wrong way in any case. They disregard entirely what the policeman does and thinks. They're not much better to us than the public. Superintendents and such have a different way of life completely. They're not policemen as policemen. They're doing the job for different reasons, and different things affect them to what it does a policeman.

So in his view a common association was not appropriate because the ranks were divided by different interests, and the lower ones needed protection against the others. The organisation representing them should be a stronger one with more of the powers of an ordinary trade union.

Thus policemen's perspectives on the nature of the social relationships between groups within the force, and between these and the authorities, cannot be comprehended within a simple conflict/consensus dichotomy. Rather, there are two separate issues involved which must be distinguished: (i) which are the most important sources of differentiation of interest? Is the crucial division between groups *within* the force, or between the force *as a whole* and the authorities? (ii) whatever the lines of division are, is there a basic conflict of interest between the groups so that sanctions are necessary in negotiation, or is there a fundamental consensus so that presentation of a reasoned case and adequate channels of communication is adequate?

Policemen's views on particular forms of action

The men were asked about their views on four aspects of 'unionateness'. These were whether they thought: (i) the Federation should be more militant in its approach and manner in negotiations; (ii) the police should have the right to work-to-rule; (iii) the police should have the right to strike; (iv) T.U.C. affiliation should be permitted.

In line with the idea of a continuum of 'unionateness' (derived from the work of Blackburn & Prandy 1965, and R. M. Blackburn 1967), I had conceived of these as forming a scale in which successive items represented a desire for a stronger union. In fact it became clear from the interviews that there were two different sets of issues involved. The strategies represented by (i), (ii) and (iii) refer to the approach to negotiations *within* the force, and do in fact form a scale. However, the question of affiliation raised by (iv) raises the problem of how the police should be aligned with political forces in the wider society. It was possible for people to support stronger forms of action within the force while being against aligning the police with the general labour movement. Conversely, it was possible for a person to want affiliation with the labour movement, either as a way of gaining more bargaining strength or because of general political sentiment, while rejecting militant forms of action as inappropriate, either to the police specifically, or to any trade union. This point has since been incorporated into the latest formulation of the concept, which distinguishes between plant or enterprise as opposed to societal unionateness (Blackburn *et al.* 1974).

Support for these various forms of power is shown in Table 5.4.

TABLE 5.4. *Support for types of negotiating method* (in percentages)

(a)   *Should the Federation adopt a more militant approach?*

More	Less	Alright now	Don't know	Total
45	2	49	4	100%

(b)   *Should the police have the right to work-to-rule?*

Yes	No	Don't know	Total
37.5	56.5	6	100%

(c)   *Should the police have the right to strike?*

Yes	No	Don't know	Total
14	82	4	100%

(d)   *Should the Federation be allowed to affiliate with other trade unions?*

Yes	No	Don't know	Total
33	62	5	100%

(Percentages are of total sample of 168.)

The basic conclusion to be drawn from Table 5.4 is that each type of strategy was rejected by a majority of policemen. The right to strike was disapproved of by an overwhelming majority, the rights to work-to-rule and union affiliation were rejected by sizeable majorities, and a slight majority did not even favour a more militant style of approach.

As would be anticipated from the pattern of support for a more union-like body in general, these responses vary a good deal between ranks, as Table 5.5 shows.

Various conclusions can be drawn from Table 5.5. Firstly, on each count constables were considerably more in favour of militant courses of action than other ranks. Sergeants tended to be almost exactly in between constables and inspectors, except on the issue of union-affiliation where they were almost identical with inspectors. Secondly, all ranks rejected the right to strike by considerable majorities, though quite a number of constables, nearly a fifth, favoured it. Thirdly, the supervisory ranks also

TABLE 5.5. *Support for elements of 'unionateness' in different ranks*

(a) *Should the Federation adopt a more militant approach?*

	Constables	Sergeants	Inspectors
	%	%	%
More	55	33	13
Less	2	3	9
Alright now	41	58	74
Don't know	2	6	4
Total	100	100	100
	N = 112	N = 33	N = 23

(b) *Should the police have the right to work to rule?*

	Constables	Sergeants	Inspectors
	%	%	%
Yes	45	27	17
No	49	67	78
Don't know	6	6	4
Total	100	100	100
	N = 112	N = 33	N = 23

(c) *Should the police have the right to strike?*

	Constables	Sergeants	Inspectors
	%	%	%
Yes	18	9	0
No	78	88	96
Don't know	4	3	4
Total	100	100	100
	N = 112	N = 33	N = 23

(d) *Should the Federation affiliate with trade unions?*

	Constables	Sergeants	Inspectors
	%	%	%
Yes	38	24	26
No	56	73	74
Don't know	6	3	0
Total	100	100	100
	N = 112	N = 33	N = 23

rejected the other forms of action by considerable majorities and finally the constables favoured a more militant style of approach by a small majority, were almost evenly divided on the right to work-to-rule, but rejected T.U.C. affiliation.

Desire for these powers varied between different divisions in terms of specialisation. The specialist divisions were less likely to favour granting the police these powers than were the ordinary uniformed men. This is true even when rank was held constant. However, the differences were rather slight, and not usually statistically significant. For instance, 12% of constables in specialist divisions (N=25) favoured the right to strike, compared with 20% of non-specialist constables (N=87). Thirty-two per cent of specialist constables favour the right to work-to-rule, contrasted with 48% of non-specialists.

As argued before, these differences are subdued by the rather motley character of divisions encompassed under the label 'specialist'. It seemed clear that the C.I.D., policewomen and administrative staff were less likely to support these measures, though the separate numbers in these divisions (when rank is held constant) were too small for statistical comparison. There was virtually no desire for any further powers in these divisions. The traffic division seemed closer to the ordinary uniform men. The picture was blurred a little by the fact that the Mounted and Dog section came under Administration in the formal organisation of the force, though its work was clearly rather different. (It was even physically distant from the rest of the police, stationed in its own building on the outskirts of the city.) For various specific reasons, mainly concerning the personality of its commander and some supervisors, and a dispute about recompense for looking after the animals off duty, there was a lot of disgruntlement among constables in the Mounted and Dog section at the time of interviewing. This was reflected in their support for trade union powers. Only four constables were included in the sample from the section but they all favoured all these powers. The sergeants in the section also supported union powers to a greater extent than the average sergeant, though not as much as the constables. The inclusion of this disgruntled section, as well as the traffic division whose responses are fairly close to the uniformed norm, blurs what I think would otherwise be a clear tendency for the other specialist divisions, i.e. C.I.D., policewomen and administration, to reject union powers.

Support for union powers thus seemed to be concentrated among constables in the uniformed divisions, with pockets of support in the Mounted section, as well as to a lesser extent traffic. The other specialist divisions eschewed them almost completely. The same is true of the supervisory ranks, especially inspectors. This pattern of variation between the ranks would seem to confirm the idea that equal representation of ranks on joint Federation bodies functions to reduce overall militancy, and is a control mechanism to mask and dampen any support for unionisation among the constables.

Although the reasoning which underlay support for particular powers was similar to that invoked to justify the general desirability of a union, each one also raised some specific issues which must be examined.

(a) *A more militant style*   Those who advocated this felt that the police would thus get a fairer deal. At present the Federation was too inhibited by concern for decorum and proper procedure. Many of the men arguing this did not actually want to give the Federation more unionate powers.

The Federation have got a gentlemanly, or ladylike, attitude. What they need is a bit of fire in the belly, a bit of iron in the guts, to mix the metaphors a bit. Get in there and fight, say 'No! We don't want to do this.' They're too fond of making gentlemanly discussions and agreements at high level, when they should have a more militant attitude. You don't want some toffee-nosed organisation that thinks itself superior and is not prepared to get in there and fight for what you want for your members. One mustn't necessarily keep thinking of the public good and the high-minded moral aspect. There comes a time when you've got to dig your heels in.   (C.I.D. inspector, long-standing Federation representative)
All we do at the moment is say 'Please, can we have this please?' The words they use, the way they go about it, it's always too slimy, very polite, a bit sort of doff your hat, sir. They should press more, barter harder.   (Uniform constable)

The men who rejected a more militant approach, argued that its detrimental effect on police status would out-weigh any possible gains. Furthermore, militancy was futile unless there were definite powers to back up demands, and these were undesirable. These men believed that 'rational' presentation of a well-argued case was more effective than going through the motions of militancy.

Basically police are easy-going people who'd never support militancy, though they'd moan their heart out. Maybe I live in a Fairyland, but I think the police have got to be seen as being above this sort of thing in order to retain any respect. It brings us into great disrepute. I live in a kind of Fairyland, where I'd like to see the government say to the police: 'We want to keep everyone happy (as I believe this government does) so we'll look after you quietly and you'll get your pay award quietly.'   (Uniform sergeant)

(b) *The right to work-to-rule*   A police work-to-rule could take different forms. 'Go-slows' would reduce work done, within the letter of regulations, e.g. a 'sick-in' or 'blue-flu', whereby a mysterious virus hits the police force causing them to all report sick on the same day (Burpo 1971: chapter 3 gives American examples). Alternatively policemen could rigidly adhere to all the safety and other regulations in detail, thus drastically slowing down the pace of work. The problem with these strategies was that they might constitute violations of the discipline code, as they involved neglect of duty.

The other strategy for a work-to-rule would be to apply the law to the letter, not exercising the normal discretion a policeman utilises as to whether particular cases merit action. It was felt that if the policeman strictly enforced the law this would so overload the system with cases that it would not be able to cope. The results might be even more devastating than a go-slow. The advantage of this method was that doing the job *more* thoroughly could not be seen as a straightforward dereliction of duty. The drawback was that at least in the first instance it hit at the wrong target. Instead of affecting senior officers or the police authorities the initial impact would be on the work load of intermediate supervisors and even more directly the men themselves. Also, the public would be alienated through suffering a larger than usual number of prosecutions for traffic and other offences which they were accustomed to having over-looked.

Many men felt that such actions would be morally reprehensible, and incompatible with their sense of duty and public responsibility. Opinion among uniformed constables was evenly balanced about their desirability. Among the rest of the force they were usually condemned. However, some form of work-to-rule was said to occur sometimes as a means of influencing particular supervisors who have done something which a work group disapproves of. All the various forms of action were seriously canvassed during the period of disgruntlement while the 1970 pay negotiations were proceeding, shortly before my research began. Many men spoke of how near things had come then to some form of work-to-rule, especially in one division, which primarily for that reason was often referred to as the 'bolshie' division.

You could go along the street at the beginning of your tour and get stuck on so much paper work you'd have to come in and write it all out. If everybody did this there'd be no policemen out on the streets. It would be a work-to-rule but they couldn't do anything because you'd be doing the job ultra-efficiency. You'd flood the system, report everyone you saw. Trouble is you'd be getting in the bad books of the public. I don't think it could happen now because we've had some reasonable pay rises and most men are happy. But a bit back in 1970 we talked among ourselves of the ways we could protest legally because of the pay talks. We also thought of everybody going sick on the same day.   (Uniform constable)

The time of interviewing was a low point for support for such action because the police were doing reasonably well in pay terms. But the two forms of work-to-rule were seen as feasible and probably effective means of pressure.

If we worked to rule the British public wouldn't know what had hit them. My idea of a work-to-rule is this. You walk along the street and see people committing any number of offences. Instead of giving them a good telling off and letting them go their way you report them rigorously as per book. You'd have the cells full of the drunks you turn a blind eye to on a Saturday night because all they're going to do is foul the cells up, stink the place out so it has to be disinfected. The courts would be jammed with people down for every motoring offence under the sun. Relations with the public would go [raspberry noise].

(Uniform constable)

The main objection to this strategy was precisely that the system would break down and the public suffer, which was seen as irresponsible and counter-productive. (The casual recognition of the way the system relies on policemen *not* enforcing the law in the technically proper way is remarkable.) Also, the hardest hit, in the first place, would be the working policeman, not the relevant authorities.

It's true that if you did work to rule and went out and made black black and white white, the way traffic wardens do, it would bring the job to a standstill. But God knows what would happen to public relations. And the blokes could never stand the pace, they'd be doing a sight more than now. But you're not getting at the people you want to get at. It isn't our superintendents who are against us, it's the Home Office. And you're not getting at the Home Office by making yourselves work sixteen hours a day! (Traffic inspector)

A work-to-rule by a work-group to defend themselves against particular supervisors for a limited purpose was more feasible, and had actually occurred or been threatened.

There was a group of P.C.s, about half a dozen, at a station I was at. The inspector was on at them. He was one of the old-fashioned ones, who said they didn't do enough work, get your hair cut and all these things. They're known as a belligerent group, a rebel mob. So they said: 'Right, we'll fix him'. They went out and reported everything that moved. Like when you'd normally say to 'em 'get that rear light fixed', they booked them. So they flooded him with cases to process. He could never cope with all the cases. I believe he's retired now, but they're still on the group.   (Traffic constable)

(c) *The police right to strike*   An actual strike was viewed with horror by most policemen, even among the uniform constables who were keenest on the Federation having more powers. The most commonly offered objection was that such action would be disastrous from the point of view of the community. The police were seen as essential to the main-tenance of public order and the containment of crime. They were depicted as sitting on an explosive society which would erupt into violence if not for constant surveillance by the police. Police strikes abroad (especially Montreal 1969) were a potent part of police demonology and narrated with blood-curdling embellishments. The men saw themselves as the only effective restraint on violence and chaos, a view which had clear psycho-logical gratifications as a source of self-esteem, even if it limited their freedom of action. Eschewing the strike weapon was also seen as giving a moral right to preferential treatment in pay negotiations.

> I like to feel that we're responsible people, who're not likely to turn round and jack the job in and leave the country open to anarchy. So that I'm not going to have to sit in the kitchen at night with a shotgun on my knees.
> (Uniform constable)

Some argued against the right to strike on the grounds that it was counter-productive as it would alienate public support.

> While we've got our enemies, we're still reasonably popular. Most people tolerate us as a necessary evil, and quite a few think a good bit of us. We can only do ourselves harm by withdrawing labour. You could strike for half an hour, and in that time X number of people would get killed or assaulted or anything. This can't do us any good.   (C.I.D. constable)

It was felt that not having the right to strike gave superior status:

> If we had the power to strike we could hold the country to ransom. But I would prefer to stay aloof from that sort of thing. I like to think it adds a bit of status to the force, the fact that we can't strike.   (Uniform constable)

A police strike was regarded by many as *intrinsically* wrong, violating the oath taken on joining the force. The right to strike was something they voluntarily relinquished, and they could not renege on their word. A strike was contradictory to the whole nature of the police force. They were responsible for disciplining society and thus had to be a disciplined body themselves. Part of their function was to be a model of orderly conduct and self-discipline. The controllers should not try to shake off their own controls. This would make the very existence of the police force anomalous, a contradiction in terms.

> When we all joined we took an oath of allegiance to her majesty, the King or Queen (depending when we joined). It's a unique service, each officer has his personal responsibility to the Crown, and I feel we shouldn't have the right to strike.   (Administration superintendent)
> We're the last bastion of law and order. Whatever we do implies discipline to the public, we make them comply with the rules of parliament. Therefore our standards must be high, we must be a disciplined body. Because we discipline the public.   (Uniform inspector)

A minority of policemen did wish the right to strike. This was mainly because they saw it as a necessary weapon to defend or further their interests. The possible dangers to the public were either disregarded, or dismissed by the argument that if morale was so low that a strike actually took place, the police force would only be nominally functioning in any case, even if it did not formally withdraw labour. A minority supported it not as a useful defence but as a fundamental right of any worker. They did not envisage it actually being used, and based the case for it on moral rather than instrumental grounds. This view was rare, and mainly found among Federation activists with general sympathies for unionism. They saw a proper police union as essential to mark out the civilian and non-military character of policing. The following argument from the chairman of the Joint Branch Board, a uniform sergeant, illustrates this:

I agree to the right to strike, to withdraw labour. When you join the police force the first thing you learn is the definition of a constable, as a citizen locally appointed but having authority under the Crown. You're a citizen, not a member of the armed forces, nothing special. This point can be driven home in that if you exceed your terms of reference in law, say you're a bit enthusiastic when you arrest someone, you finish up charged with assault yourself, as the individual officer not as a member of the constabulary. A policeman's only authority he got when he was sworn in, and he swears allegiance to the Queen, not the Chief Constable or the Constabulary. The police force is really an abstract thing which organises us into a pattern. So withholding from any man, and when I say this it's a question of principle, the right to withdraw his labour, is unfair penal legislation against him. Of course things would have to be very drastic before we went on strike, like in 1918. But with the best will in the world, had I been a policeman at that time I'd have been one of the ringleaders that walked out and got the sack. Rather then serve in a job where men were so humiliated and subject to such stupidities. By making it illegal they've shown that they don't feel they can give the policeman the credit for knowing the right time to strike. I think more and more of the men support the right. When we're being kicked around a bit they say to me 'we'll go on bloody strike – then they wouldn't do this to us'. But when a person goes on strike it should be, my God, the end of the road, like cutting your throat. No other way out. The only time I would go on strike is if I felt I would otherwise tell the boss to stick my job up his fundamental orifice.

(d) *The right to affiliate with trade unions*   This did not fit into a scale with the other aspects of unionateness so far discussed. Partly it did raise similar issues of the appropriate degree of power that lower ranking policemen should have. But it also raised other problems about where the police should stand in terms of wider political alignments. Some men eschewed industrial action by the police because of the probable harm done to the public, while supporting the right to affiliate with unions in order to strengthen the police in negotiations by gaining support and expertise. Others supported the right of the police to engage in industrial action if necessary, but were opposed to union affiliation because of its political implications. Usually the elements of unionateness went hand in hand, but by no means always.

The main justification given for seeking union affiliation was that it would give the police a lever in negotiations. In addition some felt (especially the Federationists themselves) that they could profit from the unions' skill and experience in methods of negotiation. A few saw it as an aspect of general identification and solidarity with the labour movement.

If we were affiliated with the T.U.C. it would certainly frighten people in the Home Office no end. No doubt about that at all. It would be pretty effective.

(Uniform constable)

There are those diehards in the Police Federation who'd resign on the spot if we had anything to do with trade unions. But I just put this down to the fact that they're short-sighted bigots who joined at the age of nineteen and don't know anything about what goes on outside the police. There could be a lot gained from going to the T.U.C. and being affiliated.   (Uniform sergeant)

On the other hand, a few of the men who supported the idea of T.U.C. affiliation did so not because it would do the police any good, but so that the Federation could teach the unions the art of responsible negotiation without resort to strikes:

We could put our point of view over to the trade unions themselves. I come from a very active family of trade unionists. My father was secretary of the South Wales Miners' Federation. The unionists were bitter against the police force, they always looked on us as tools of the bosses. If we could get through to the unions, become part of them, we could encourage the responsible, middle-of-the-road men.   (C.I.D. sergeant)

Most of the police were against affiliation with the unions. It was felt that the mentality and behaviour associated with trade unionists were antithetical to the efficiency of the police force. It would mean an alignment with the wrong political forces in outside society. Partly this was because the police had to enforce the law on picketing in industrial disputes. Being affiliated to trade unions might expose them to cross-pressures in such a situation, so they couldn't do their job properly:

In a dispute you'd be bound to be biassed, swayed in their favour if you were affiliated with unions. I mean, you can't have brothers throwing brothers about, it's just not done. We ought to be on our own.   (Uniform constable)

Apart from the specific problems that might arise in handling industrial disputes, T.U.C. affiliation was objected to because of what were seen as generally undesirable political tendencies in the union movement. It was regarded as dominated by extreme left-wing elements, including communists, and the intrusion of these into the police force had to be resisted, if the stability of the country was to be preserved. Opposition to left-wing political elements in the unions was itself seen as a non-political stand.

The T.U.C. smells of communism. We would jeopardise ourselves by going in with them. My belief is, well you know for a fact, a lot of unions are affiliated to communism, a lot of the union people are communists. I don't like communist rule. It's all right in theory but not in practice. You've only got to go along M. Rd, there's a Communist Party place there, and they say 'Free political prisoners in Northern Ireland'. Well my answer to that is 'Free political prisoners in Russia'.   (Uniform constable)

I don't get involved in politics. But if we were affiliated to unions we'd be out on strike most of the time. And I don't agree with that, especially where your law and order is concerned.   (Uniform sergeant)

The police should be non-political. But politics come into trade unions. I mean, they're delving into politics all the time. It seems to me there's a load of reds at the top. It's not going to do the country any good if we affiliate with them.

(Policewoman sergeant)

It must be emphasised that the attitudes brought out in the interviews are not fixed, immutable 'facts'. They are informed by a particular historical context and specific situation. Under other circumstances they might well alter, but events would have to be filtered through existing conceptions to produce any changes. The discontent caused by the 1976–7 pay dispute has clearly brought about a marked shift in opinion on these issues.

6

The goals and institutionalisation of representation

The goals of representation

Discussions of trade unions frequently differentiate various aims which the members may wish the union to pursue. A broad distinction between 'economic' and 'cultural' goals has often been suggested, for example in a recent study of the Post Office Workers' Union (Moran 1974). 'A union pursues economic goals when it concerns itself with the provision of remunerative benefits for its members...Cultural goals are pursued if a union commits itself to the support of some social philosophy' (Moran 1974: 6).

'Cultural goals' are manifested by a concern with 'authority relations', at the workplace or in the wider society (Moran 1974: 24). However, a sharp distinction between 'economic' and 'cultural' goals raises several problems.

The first is that, with the concentration of capital and the increasing intervention of the state in economic life, it becomes hard to separate attempts to influence government which are 'ideologically' motivated, and those which are intended to protect or improve members' economic positions.

Secondly, at the level of the work place, it is hard to draw a sharp distinction between issues of pay and work conditions, and the control of work. The relationship between employer and employee involves a bargain in which money is exchanged for effort. There are *two* elements in the exchange, and concern to control the input of effort, and hence the work process, may be an aspect of the wage-bargain, not the intrusion of extraneous 'ideological' concerns. This point is well expressed in Beynon's (1973: chapter 6) account of how Ford workers are engaged in a two-fold conflict, not only over wages directly, but also to prevent speed-ups and other attempts to intensify the work effort. These struggles along the 'frontiers of control' (Goodrich 1920) arise *directly* out of the wage-bargain, rather than any developed ideology of workers' control. Support for the latter may, of course, emerge in response to the day-to-day, piece-meal conflict over details of control. We have already seen in the police context how concern over conditions of work can easily spill over into questioning what management sees as its decision-making prerogative.

The third problem with the distinction between 'economic' and 'cultural' goals is that financial concerns may have moral elements (Beynon 1973: 101). The level of wages represents not merely power to purchase a particular stock of physical goods, but also some measure of the workers' standing and the worth of his effort.

A sharp distinction between 'economic' and 'cultural' goals of trade unionism is untenable. Indeed, the attempt to maintain it can be regarded as a particular ideological position which functions to legitimise the existing prerogatives of management. Under a capitalist system of work relations, the worker offers his labour-power for hire at a certain rate of pay. It is the capitalist, or his managerial proxies, who are seen as having the right to decide what is to be produced and how. The worker may legitimately be concerned to increase his pay and influence some non-monetary aspects of work conditions. But he is not seen as entitled to a say in the methods or purposes of the work itself, even though a manager enlightened in human-relations skills may concede him some limited consultative machinery. However, as argued above, the questions of financial rewards and conditions of work cannot be readily separated in concrete terms from issues of how the work is to be done. These latter may or may not be guided by an explicitly articulated challenge to what management sees as its prerogatives.

Policemen's desire for a say, for example, in how many men are sent to a football ground may derive both from anxiety about the personal interests and the welfare of the men doing the job, as well as the notion that the latter know best what decision ought to be made, and have a right to determine it. Further, what starts off as a demand for money may raise questions about the structure of power, as it becomes realised that this limits the possibility of satisfying the original claim. So ostensibly 'economistic' demands of trade unions have implications for control issues which the men may originally not be aware of. Even if they are unaware at one moment in time, the potential for the raising of clear issues of power is always there. In short, *all* demands made by a union (or the Federation) are politically significant in the broad sense that they raise questions about the structure of power in the organisation. They may not, however, be explicitly politically informed or motivated, and can appear to be exclusively concerned with a delimited issue. The implicit political implications may become clarified as the demand is pursued and obstacles encountered.

Did policemen feel that their representative body should try to modify the authority relations of the force, and gain the lower ranks a say in decision-making? If so, were the existing arrangements in the force adequate for the purpose of allowing the men to influence policy? As argued above, even demands which are not explicitly aimed at the level of policy have relevance for the authority structure of the organisation.

The actual activities and demands of those men favouring a narrowly 'economistic' role do have implications for authority relations. But discussing the goals the men explicitly wanted the Federation to pursue is important in understanding their views of the proper role of representative bodies in the force. It sheds light on their images of the ideal authority structure and the sources of their acceptance of the existing one.

Table 6.1 gives policemen's views on whether the Federation should have a say in running the force.

TABLE 6.1. *Views on desired scope of Federation activities, by rank*

	Total Sample %	Constables %	Sergeants %	Inspectors %
Federation should only deal with pay etc.	32	28	42	35
Present amount of say satisfactory	22	20	24	30
Should have more say	46	52	33	35
Total	100	100	100	100
	N = 168	N = 112	N = 33	N = 23

Table 6.1 suggests that a majority (68%) favoured the Federation having some say, though only 46% felt this should be *more* than existed, and that constables were least satisfied, and a majority of them favoured a larger say.

Participation was rejected *in principle* by a substantial minority, especially of supervisors. While constables wanted more involvement in decision-making, this did not amount to any claim for workers' *control*. Almost all accepted the division between decision-makers and subordinates as legitimate.

Those who argued for more participation by the Federation in decision-making did so predominantly on *pragmatic* grounds. The argument that the lower ranks knew more about the practical needs and problems of police work, by virtue of their immediate involvement in doing the job, was mentioned by 41%. The senior ranks and civilian authorities were seen as out of touch.

P.C.s and sergeants are the police force who keep law and order on the streets. Superintendents and people like that never even go out on the streets, or they might for ten minutes at a time. Take the trouble we've been having with the yobs lately. Friday, Saturday night, when it's at its worst, we know by being on the streets where, and usually when, the trouble's going to be. A senior officer comes along, sees something happen, and says 'I want more P.C.s at that point'. Well we might know by ourselves it's not going to last long there, and we know where the extra policemen would be better put. The same with traffic. It's us that stand out there for one and a half hours every night waving our arms about, and we see all of it, bottlenecks etc. If they took more heed of what we say about points the flow would be a lot easier in the long-run. But if you make the suggestion they say 'Oh, we've being doing it for years and years. We'll keep it as it is.' (Uniform constable)

We should have more say in management. Like we've got instructions at the moment about the use of dogs at football matches which we don't agree with. We're supposed to stay outside with our dogs. We're not allowed to use them other than for barking purposes. They say no dog should go there that's got a tendency to bite. This is a result of an incident which occurred where somebody was bit. Should trouble arise in the ground, we put the dogs back in the van and assist the P.C.s on our own. But we know from past experience that on many occasions there's been only two or three dogs that have stopped a full-scale war. Only a couple of weeks ago some Cardiff supporters went to a match, but were turned away and sent back on the train. They committed so much trouble on the train the driver let them off and refused to go any further. So they thought they'd have a bit of fun down at the Rovers' ground. Two hundred of them come full-scale running in the entrance, bricks, bottles, the lot! Now had that lot got in the ground there would have been all hell let loose. And it was only four dogs that stopped that lot getting in. What we did we shouldn't have because this order's in force. But I mean, we're policemen, we can see what's happening. So we used our common sense. O.K., so people got bit. But they didn't get into the ground! Now they even made us put special reports on what happened up to the Chief! (Dog-handler constable)

A further pragmatic reason for the Federation having more say in policy was that this would give the men a sense of involvement, and increase their responsibility and morale. Eleven per cent gave variants of this Elton Mayoesque argument.

Representation is essential. To improve the efficiency of the force by giving the men rights to get them happy doing the job, as opposed to neglecting their duty by feeling ill-treated, sat upon and suppressed. If you're not truly represented in government, the lower class, the workers, become anti the management.

(Dog-handler constable)

So far we have considered the *pragmatic* arguments for greater participation in decision making. Some supported the Federation having a greater say on the *moral* ground that it was the right of the men. All decisions affected their welfare, so they were entitled to a say. This was suggested by 15%.

Now on this division when the children go back to school we'll have to cover twelve crossings. So that's twelve officers written off for half their tour of duty. Now this leaves the rest of the blokes rushing around like blue-assed flies to get the police work done. We should be able to say 'Well, in this case it's not a busy road, let a teacher do it'. (Uniform constable)

A few also suggested that Federation involvement would act as a check against potential corruption in senior ranks. It would prevent them using their power to further their own, rather than public, ends.

A certain Assistant Chief Constable drives to work and he gets stuck at a road junction. So he thinks 'Good heavens! If there was a policeman doing a traffic point here I could get through in no time at all.' So a policeman will do a traffic point there for the next twenty years.   (Uniform constable)

None of the men suggested any measure of workers' *control*. They all fundamentally accepted a hierarchical authority structure. The most that any wanted was mandatory consultation. Such changes were supported mainly by arguments about force efficiency (even though this may be differently conceived by the various ranks), rather than explicitly 'ideological' arguments about industrial democracy.

The men who do the work obviously know the best how it should be done. The Federation should be able to put suggestions forward more strongly than now. But you can't get workers dictating to bosses and actually running the force. Bosses are bosses because they're bosses.   (Mounted constable)

The demand was for *consultation* not *control*. Most of the men stressed the need for clear lines of authority in the conduct of actual operations. Confusion would be the outcome of any dilution of supervisory responsibility in the field. But there could be greater involvement in policy, without this danger arising. A few did wish greater autonomy in operation (as the dog-handling incident quoted earlier indicates) but by and large a distinction was made between this and policy-making.

The chief arguments *against* the Federation being involved in decision-making were also pragmatic. It was felt, for a variety of reasons, that this would hamper force efficiency. Nineteen per cent argued that senior officers were the best qualified to make decisions, as they had the greatest experience and professional training. They had proved their ability by being promoted up the hierarchy. The average man was too ignorant to play a part in decision-making. Some suggested that Federation officials tended to be even more out-of-touch with practical policing on the streets than were the senior officers. A few also felt that they were too 'militant' to play a role in policy.

If the lower ranks have a say in management you're approaching what I look on as basically a communist principle. There are those who must do the telling and those who must be told. They're either born with it or they're not. It's as simple as that. Some men are happier doing the telling. In any disciplined service you've got to have the tellers and the doers or the structure will collapse. High rank depends on a certain mental ability and ambition. I think it works out reasonably fairly and the *status quo* should be maintained.   (Traffic sergeant)
You'd then have untrained militants interfering with a system that's worked very well for 130 years. The Chief Constable is there to run the show. It's nothing to do with the Federation. Let's be fair, they don't know how to run it. It should be left to the governors who know what they're doing. If they can't do the job properly they should be replaced not undermined.   (C.I.D. sergeant)

A further pragmatic reason for the restriction of participation by the lower ranks is the idea that a clear structure of authority is an exigency of organisation. Democracy is not viable in a work organisation. The police in particular were seen as a body that had to be strictly disciplined because of the requirement for clear, rapid decisions in operational situations. This need for a hierarchical control *structure* was to some degree independent of the question whether or not the incumbents of authority positions had, as individuals, greater ability or expertise in decision-making. This sort of view was argued by 17%.

If you're trying to get everyone running it you might as well have total anarchy. You've got to accept that someone's Chief Constable and his word goes. Someone, somewhere along the line has to carry the can. You can't have a self-governing police force, governed by the ranks. It's like an army in battle. If the general organises an advance you can't have all the soldiers getting together and saying 'No thank you. We'd rather retreat.' We're a disciplined body and somebody's got to make the final decision. (Uniform constable)

The Chief Constable's the man who makes decisions. That's why he's called that! It's a disciplined body of men, and somebody's got to run it. I don't think the Federation should have a vote in what the service does. You can't run the force like the country is run, where the Prime Minister has to put a decision to the Cabinet and the House. You've got to have one person at the top to say yea or nay and not put it to vote. (Uniform constable)

A small number (5%) put forward the argument that hierarchical decision-making was best because only at the top could one have an all-round view of the needs of the force. The Federation had a limited sectional perspective because of its concern with the men's interests. The Chief Constable's role was to balance this against other considerations, such as the needs of senior ranks and the exigencies of operational work.

Some opposed rank-and-file participation in decision-making on moral grounds. Eleven per cent argued that policy-formulation and control were prerogatives of the senior ranks. Federation involvement in this would be an unjustified usurpation of these rights. They had their definite place as representatives of the lower ranks' welfare, and should restrict themselves to this role. Seven per cent put forward the related idea that the division between men in authority and those subject to it was an inevitable feature of the natural order of things and had therefore got to be respected. As one uniformed constable said: 'You've got to have your guvnors!'

I'm not happy with the Federation acting as spokesman on policy issues. If I was Chief Officer I'd be inclined to tell the Federation to mind its own business, not tell me how to run the police force. They can't be the brains behind forward planning, research and development. They're not entitled to be concerned with running the force, or you might just as well do away with ranks. Decisions are part and parcel of senior rank. (C.I.D. inspector)

Three per cent felt that the Federation should not participate in decision-making because it would make no difference anyway. The force was so tightly constrained by financial and other external exigencies that the same decisions would be arrived at with or without involvement of the lower ranks. Furthermore, the ranks had such similar outlooks that participation wouldn't alter anything.

Another 3% objected to Federation involvement in decision-making because it would mean the co-option of the Federation into the management structure. They would no longer be effective spokesmen of the lower ranks, but become a part of the control apparatus. As one uniform constable put it: 'There's enough bosses now, without them creeping in!'

At the moment the P.C.s think the Federation is ours, they're on our side. It's us against them. Whereas if they have influence upstairs it would destroy our confidence in them. Anything the bosses did which we didn't like we'd feel the Federation had a hand in, so we'd turn against them slightly. Now we know they're wholly on our side.   (Traffic constable)

Views on participation were mainly based on calculation of the consequences for force efficiency. Those in favour felt that present decision-makers were out of touch with the practical exigencies of policing, while the federated ranks had more concrete understanding. There was also the argument that it helped develop a feeling of responsibility and involvement in the men. Those against the Federation having a say argued that senior ranks were individually more qualified for decision-making. It was also felt that hierarchical structures were more efficient, especially in a body like the police, which had to be disciplined to cope with operational exigencies.

An intrinsic moral argument in favour of the Federation having a say was that as all decisions affected the men's welfare they had a right to influence them. Some opposed this with the notion that decision-making was the prerogative of senior ranks, or postulated a natural split between workers and bosses as an inescapable fact of social life.

Opinion is fairly evenly split in the force *as a whole* about the Federation having a greater say in decision-making. Uniformed constables are generally keen for this participation. Opposition comes mainly from the supervisory ranks and specialists, particularly the C.I.D. Their objection does not usually extend to the view that there should be no consultation of lower ranks at all. Nearly half of those who feel that the Federation should not have *more* say, think it should have *some*, but believe present arrangements are adequate. Only a relatively small minority favour exclusive concentration on pay and conditions. The demand for the Federation to have a larger say in decision-making does not extend to the assertion of *control* but only more adequate consultation, or some participation.

The institutionalisation of representation

In the last chapter we saw that while feeling that the Federation was relatively powerless, most of the force eschewed the idea of giving it sanctions of a unionate kind. Even among the uniformed constables, only about half favoured any form of more militant approach. However, we have just seen that a majority think it should have some say in policy, and about half feel this should be greater than at present. In what way was this supposed to take place?

The supervisors and about half the constables, seemed to favour a non-militant, institutionalised representative organisation. It would be accepted as an important body, with machinery for regular consultation with the senior ranks and civilian authorities. In turn it would conduct itself as a 'responsible' association. Those constables who desired a union also wanted institutionalised consultative machinery. The establishment of regular meetings between the Chief Constable and the Federation was supported by 92%. These already occurred in the force studied, but not as an obligation on the Chief's part. It was felt that this should be universal practice, and as of right rather than dependent on the individual Chief Constable.

There was also strong support for regular institutionalised meetings with the police authority. Some branches had succeeded in getting representation at Watch Committee meetings, but most only attended as 'observers'. The branch surveyed had not gained access. The secretary told me he had written to the Chairman, 'a bloody-minded autocrat', requesting it. The latter had retorted 'When I want those buggers, I'll send for them.' Regular consultation between the Federation and local authorities still only occurs in twenty-three out of the fifty-three constabulary areas (*Police Review*, 8 April 1977: 443).

A minority felt the Chief Constable ought to be the force's only spokesman. As long as the Federation had adequate channels to meet *him*, he could put their case forward. It was wrong to undermine his authority by a direct approach to the Watch Committee. The Chief Constable had more of the social style necessary to successfully relate to the Watch Committee.

If you make your facts well known to the Chief, and rely on his good will and judgement, he's in a better position to consult with the authority. He can sort of hob-nob with them, you know. (Uniform constable)

The majority, 74%, felt that the Federation *should* have institutionalised access to the Watch Committee. Important decisions about the force were made there, in particular about its finances. It was argued strongly that the members of the Committee were ignorant of police affairs and the requirements of the job. The Chief Constable could put them in the picture to an extent. But it was feared that this would still leave them out of touch with the perspective of the rank-and-file. There was apprehension also that the Chief Constable might be inhibited by requirements of etiquette from putting over the men's views vehemently enough. It was useful and right for the Federation to make direct approaches on behalf of the ordinary working policemen. This would give the Watch Committee a more concrete notion of the details and problems of 'real' police work. The strength of feeling about the shortcomings of the Watch Committee was remarkable.

This is a sore point with me. The Watch Committee are very penny-conscious here. And why a group of plumbers and butchers can dictate to the Chief Constable beats me. It's purely farcical. They don't know sufficient about police forces, but they hold the purse strings.   (Uniform constable)

The police authority, depending which party they are, is either old gentlemen smoking cigars and drinking brandy, or militant trade unionists.

(Uniform constable)

We should be able to go to them. They're the people that foot the bill. Very often a Federation man can stand up and say things the Chief Constable might find hard to say. Like car parking. I'd go to the Watch Committee and play bloody hell with them. I'd say 'We're your employees, you pay our sodding wages. You provide car parks for all other Corporation employees, so why not policemen?' When our Chief goes there he's got to be diplomatic, discreet and courteous. But I'd like to give them a blast. I'd get in there and stuff the discipline code up their left nostril!   (Uniform sergeant)

7
The Federationists and the men

The Federationists

The sample included 7 current and 10 ex-representatives. In addition, I interviewed the chairman and secretary of the Branch Board, and the chairman of the Constables' Board.

Of these twenty with representative experience, six were constables, four sergeants and ten inspectors. This high number of inspectors is not surprising. Representation was not proportional to the numbers in each rank, so it was more likely for an inspector than a constable to be a representative. Furthermore, it was often hard to find an inspector willing to stand, so a reluctant individual was induced to, or there was a rota system, which meant a rapid turnover. Inspectors might also have been representatives in a previous rank.

Among the Federationists there was a hard core of *real* activists. The chairman and secretary of the Joint Branch Board were the key figures. They devoted all their working (and a considerable part of their leisure) time to the Federation. In the eyes of most policemen they *were* the Federation. Other activists were the deputy chairman, the treasurer, and the constables' chairman. This inner circle did not always see eye to eye. There were internal disagreements and hostilities. But they constituted a core who were especially dedicated to the Federation. In the words of the constables' chairman, for example, he was '70% Federation man, 30% policeman', though he added the rider 'but 100% policeman when I'm on duty'. Although only a minority of the Board, they were, by virtue of office and personality, the dominant influence determining the tone and conduct of Federation activities in the city.

The situation was summed up thus by the chairman of the Branch Board:

There are Federation men and Federation men. We've got a Branch Board of twenty-seven and I wouldn't put more than six to eight of them as what I might term ardent Federationists – people who'd come here in spite of any other commitment... Most are men who haven't really got the interest of the Federation at heart. They'd prefer to play sport, and if they're on annual leave they don't come to meetings. The backbone of most Branch Boards is about half a dozen men, and they steamroller it along. These others, passengers you might call them, a lot of them come on the Board because nobody else on the division is prepared to. You've either got it in you or you haven't – it's like an infection.

The activists all attributed their Federation involvement to an inter-action between pro-union sympathy and involvement before joining the police force, and injustices experienced or observed in the job. Their backgrounds had sensitised them to perceive certain situations as griev-ances which should, and could, be remedied by union activity. They all favoured the Federation becoming like an ordinary trade union, with full powers of industrial action. As illustrated already, they justified this on intrinsic moral grounds, as the right of every worker, rather than for instrumental reasons.

I was an ex-trade unionist when I joined at twenty-seven. During my first five years in the job, I gradually became quite disenchanted with the conditions of service, the labyrinth of tradition, the archaic ideas and taboos which have been built up. One feels one's way a bit cautiously at first, but I decided at that stage, which is quite early relatively for most men, to try to do something about it and I went on the branch board with five years service in. I was one of the youngest (in service) members of the Branch Board ever. The official side's mental attitude made me a very hard-core Federationist. By virtue of the Police Act our powers are very restricted – they treat us like children. We haven't got any real weapon apart from public opinion and bringing pressure to bear on local councillors and M.P.s. I would like to see the ordinary Industrial Relations Act apply to the Federation.   (J.B.B. chairman)
I'm trade union minded and had a socialist outlook when I joined. I come from the North, an industrial area, and was a member of N.A.L.G.O. before. This isn't typical of the police, but it led me to be interested in the Federation. I feel we've two sides in the police force too. Superintendents and chief officers are the bosses, and we should become more like a trade union.   (J.B.B. treasurer)

It was not the case, nationally, that most Federationists favoured the Federation becoming like a trade union. Indeed, the activists of the Branch studied were regarded as a particularly 'union-minded' group, though similar views were held by several other large city forces' repre-sentatives. 'We have a notoriously bolshie, militant J.B.B.' (uniform constable).

On the fringes of the activist core was a group that could be labelled 'fellow-travellers'. They were similar in their views on the Federation, but not to the same extent, nor because of a pre-existing involvement in unions. Usually they attributed their interest in the Federation to an incident which had made them aware of the value and importance of the Federation. They had then become progressively more involved with, and influenced by, the activists.

I've been interested in the Federation for many years, since my representative had me cleared of a charge of assault at a disciplinary hearing, arising out of a citizen complaint. This showed me the value of the Federation. Two years ago my colleagues nominated me in place of the rep., who they felt was slipping. I feel we should be like a union. There's no teeth in our negotiations, so the strike weapon is worth having. The official side have a take-it or leave-it attitude. But

we wouldn't actually use it – we're too responsible now. I'm not a communist or revolutionist [sic] – though I've been called that because of my Federation work.
(Constables' representative)

A third category on the Board were the self-conscious 'moderates'. Their main commitment was the job rather than the Federation, but they joined either because of a concern about the supposed domination of the organisation by 'reds', or because they saw taking an interest in the representative machinery as an important part of a professionally dedicated outlook. They were unlikely to support any of the unionate powers desired by the previous groups, and tended to favour the idea of a single professional association. They may well see the Federation as a helpful stage in an upwardly mobile career, as a notch in the belt demonstrating commitment to the job in the eyes of selectors for promotion, as long as 'irresponsible' militancy is shunned.

There are some who are militant and think of authority, in the form of senior officers, as us and them. But you'll find other sobering individuals. There's always somebody else much wiser who balances out the militants.
(Ex-sergeants' representative)

The final type of Federationist was the 'passenger', the 'man who wasn't there when the nominations were made'. Some of these were quite frank about the fact that they had only accepted the position reluctantly and had little interest.

Some of my more enlightened colleagues unbeknown to me submitted my name. I didn't know anything about it at the time. Much to everybody's delight and my horror nobody else stood and I was elected unopposed! Just like that!
(Ex-constables' representative)

The activists were more militant than most members. But there was a small number of (usually young) men who were 'ultra-left'. They wanted a union but felt the Federation too shackled an organisation for involvement in it to be anything but futile.

As it stands at the moment, I wouldn't think about standing for the Federation. I would get terribly frustrated with it, if I wanted to do something as a representative. I haven't been to any meetings in the last two years. In the first year I thought, 'this is my representative body, my unit'. But I came away from the meetings and thought 'well, dear, dear! I shan't go again!' The second meeting was the same as the first. The same bellyaches word for word! Nothing's been done about it. (Uniform constable)

The core activists were not a monolithic group. In terms of general politics some saw themselves as socialists.

I feel it's a weakness that the restrictions on political activity preclude you having an influence where policy is actually made, say the city Labour Party. I'm well known as an individual for strong political views which I've never been afraid to hide, but I'm not aware that as a policeman I've ever been influenced yet in enforcing the law with people where I'm basically in sympathy with their political views. I was always sympathetic to C.N.D. and in my off-duty moments would march for them as an individual with my wife. Yet I've also been a police officer escorting them. I've carted them from Whitehall, the Ministry of Defence, and taken them into custody. O.K., maybe with reluctance, but nevertheless if it is required that I do it as a policeman, it is done, full-stop.

(Uniform inspector)

However, even among the so-called 'reds', who strongly advocated the granting of full trade union powers and status to the Federation, and had generally pro-union identifications, it was more common to find political support for the Tories. As the Branch Board secretary put it:

The Joint Branch Board tends to be even more Conservative than the average policeman (apart from a few left-wing Labour blokes), because they realise it's good for the police. Most policemen tend to be Conservative, at the present time especially. For one very good reason – the Tories have been more favourable to the police with pay and conditions. That's what the average policeman tends to care about, 'what's in it for me?' And you don't have to look far to see why the Tories have been so keen to make sure of a happy, contented police force. The answer's bloody obvious! They're anticipating trouble because of strikes in the next few months, and they want to keep us happy.   (Uniform sergeant)

So the prevailing political sympathy, among the Federation militants as well as the men, seems to have been for the Tories, if only for instrumental reasons. Even some self-styled 'moderates' had a peculiar notion of what this entailed:

I'm a middle-of-the-roader. There's little difference between the parties now discernible, the whole thing's become a farce. A local candidate goes on about how much integrity he has, and then votes the Party whip! You don't vote for a representative but a Prime Minister. And I don't have much time for these last two. Poor old Ted Teeth (as we call him!). A non-entity, no personality. Wilson had a personality. But what kind? The only politician now with any integrity at all is Powell. He's the sort of person the British public wants – they can see he's a man of principle. But perhaps it's a disadvantage to be honest in politics.

(Uniform sergeant)

Thus the Branch Board was divided between some self-styled socialists and a majority of Tories, largely motivated by instrumental considerations as well as ideological conservatism, labelled as 'middle of the road'. At the same time, as we have already seen, the core activists and their fellow-travellers, who constituted the most important third or so of the Board, had strong sympathy and identification with the union movement, and shared the view that the Federation should become a proper union.

Conflicts within the Federation board reflected both structural pressures and individual personality clashes. There were various obvious sources of conflict built in to the structure of the representative system. Three ranks were represented on Joint Branch Board and while on many issues their interests coincided, there were also bones of contention. An obvious one in national negotiations was the question of differentials.

But this was not a matter for local negotiation. There were other issues which did divide the ranks on the local board. Although there were separate boards for each rank, and hence in principle they could each present their own views where there was disagreement, the practice was for separate meetings to be relatively perfunctory and the real business was thrashed out at the joint meeting. Sergeants and inspectors thought that the constables sometimes tended to be over-militant and tub-thumping, and needed to learn the realities of the art of negotiation, while other ranks felt the inspectors were, on occasion, too status conscious and exerted a dampening effect on the board's deliberations. The conduct of negotiations, in the eyes of the experienced activists (who were mixed in rank), required a dilution of the over-enthusiasm of some of the newly elected constables with the sobering effect of the inspectors' immobilism, while the former contributed a forceful edge lacking in the latter. The way in which the lack of moderation of some newly elected men had to be tempered by experience of the realities of negotiation, is illustrated by these comments from the secretary of the Board:

Have you met Constable B.? He was a really fiery Marxist, but he's mellowed a bit since joining the Board. This happens to a lot of people. They become more moderate when they actually become representatives and see the problems in getting anything done.

The deputy chairman noted the same phenomenon:

There's the occasional bolshie chap who's going to put the world to rights, and have a go at all and sundry. My experience of them by and large is that they come and are gone like a meteor. They burn and are brilliant for a brief time, then they burn out and go.

But these men performed a useful function in countering the apathetic acceptance of authority which the activists saw as characteristic of most policemen, and which impeded the effectiveness of the Federation. As the chairman put it:

I've always found it odd that the lads complain the Federation can't do enough for them, but you ask should they have the right to strike, which is the only way you'll get more, and they answer like robots. 'No, of course not... Service to the public etc.' Policemen are an unusual lot. Most are attracted by the thought of the uniform, strutting down the street, a bit of glory. Well, if they like the thought of having authority over the public, they're also likely to be the sort of chaps who'll be paraded and answer 'yes, sir, no, sir'. There's not many ex-tradesmen like us in the job.

The Federation activists, in fact, have to tread a thin line in order to balance the pressures from the relatively few, but vociferous, 'ultra-leftists' who are continually urging it to be more militant, and the majority who are felt not to be sufficiently supportive.

Conflicts are structured into the composition of the Joint Branch Board itself, since it combines equal numbers of constables and supervisors. These remarks by the chairman illustrate the tensions:

> There are occasions where considerations of rank come in and the inspectors would tend to all vote on a class basis. For example, with regard to type of uniform. We discussed this quite recently. The sergeants and constables, they couldn't care less. But the inspectors wanted to retain their own particular style of patch pockets, buttons on the sleeve, and, you know, a bit fiddly. We said we didn't care what the uniform was as long as we all wear it the same. But there was this class division shining through. It's of no significance really. I mean, if they want to dress up as bloody turkeys, I don't care. I wouldn't be one, not a real inspector. . .unless it's a lavatory inspector!

Another example was given by a particularly 'Federation-minded' inspectors' representative:

> We're unusual in having inspectors who are quite democratic. We're apparently the only force in the region who don't have an officers' mess! The other forces all have officers' messes to eat in and ladies' nights and things like that on the style of the armed forces. We're astounded by it. But we do have quite a few arguments on our Board between the ranks. Recently there was one specific occasion when the constables were out-voted, which was to do with an I.R.A. scare. The constables, representing the men who are on the ground, suggested that certain members be armed in preparation for I.R.A. trouble. And this was thrown out by the higher ranks. But the constable is always in the situation where he is out there on the streets and has to act because he has nowhere to go. Whereas a sergeant or inspector can disappear. You know, quite lawfully. We certainly have some who would disappear, though it may be rather hard to prove.

In addition to conflicts based on rank, there were also conflicts between divisional representatives according to the particular interests of different specialist groups. Some specialisms feel largely unrepresented in that they are less likely to have members on the Board. For example, C.I.D. representatives are more often drawn from office personnel than operational detectives, making the latter feel left out of the representative system. Again, sex and age differences are important. Representatives tend to be old in service, and this makes young constables, especially single ones, think of themselves as inadequately represented.

Apart from these structured sources of conflict there were also clashes of individual personality which erupted on occasion. One of these resulted in pressure on the treasurer, an activist, to resign from the Board. This pressure was supported by the other activists. In the words of the chairman:

> There are some men who are empire-builders and after any glory they can get from the post. Some of the big power seekers cannot accept criticism. If a man becomes an officer of the Board and he exercises his powers wrongly, mismanages the job he's given, we see to it that he's removed. And this is what happened in this Board this year. The person concerned was obliged to resign. It was the treasurer. There was a deficit in the petty cash of £14.96 which we

just couldn't find. Not a big sum, but at the same time not a trifling thing. And there have been three or four occasions this year when I've had to speak to this man about the way he was handling the accounts and the manner he was conducting himself. The fact that he had paid out petty cash to himself without authority. And the ironic thing is that when he was elected, the first thing *he* did was nobble the secretary and I and bloody criticise *us* for the fact that *we* made decisions and from now on this had to stop! We work together – *nobody* makes decisions! This money missing came up at the last meeting, and he just sat there and said 'Well gentlemen, there's £14.96 missing and I can't offer any explanation where it's gone. It must have been spent on Federation matters.' The Board done their bloody nut! No word of apology. Anybody else with any common sense would have found the £14.96 himself! He thought he was being so honest and above board about it, bringing it all out in the open. All he did was show everybody that his mismanagement of the books was so gross he was not fit to be trusted with them. In the end somebody put a motion censuring him and asking him to resign. They were saying 'bloody resign!' He was in such a state he called me Mr Treasurer! He said: 'Mr Treasurer, I accept forthwith my resignation!' They'd bent over backwards to try and help him. The average bloke with an ounce of feeling would have gone in the first fifteen minutes.

The contrast between the character imparted to this Branch Board by its activists, with their particularly unionate stance, and that of many other Boards has already been alluded to. The local activists saw themselves as involved in trying to influence the Federation as a national body in the direction of becoming a more union-like organisation. They had some allies in the Branch Boards of several other large provincial city forces who shared similar views, but were pitted against the larger number of county forces where the Federation was a more emasculated body. Another dimension of differentiation was that the largest city force, the Metropolitan, stood on its own on several issues, such as the London Allowance controversy. City forces were seen to have stronger, more militant Federations for various reasons. This was partly attributed to the individual personality characteristics typical of chief officers and men in county as opposed to city forces, deriving from the local cultures. 'There was one county force we recently visited, and we were told there that the Federation was just not the thing. It was still the bloody squire attitude. Do as you're told or get out, which is a bit medieval to my mind' (C.I.D. constable). The perpetuation of such attitudes is encouraged by a structural difference between city and county forces. The different stations and the men on the beat are obviously far more spread out in a county than a city. The greater concentration in urban forces facilitates communication between the men, and the possibility of the Federation gaining support for its initiatives or the men formulating demands to put to it. In the counties, issues which in cities might become matter for negotiation at force level, tend to be thrashed out at divisional level, possibly without formally involving the Federation at all. This inevitably weakens the Federation as an institution in county forces. 'There's strength in numbers, and in cities there's more numbers concentrated in a place' (Traffic inspector).

The Joint Central Committee was seen by the local activists as frequently dragging its feet in negotiations. The Branch Board leaders played the same role (together with some other city forces) in the national body, as did the 'ultra-leftists' *vis-à-vis* those in the local set-up. They were the ginger-group trying to urge stronger and speedier action on the Central Committee, which was forced to balance these demands against the more conservative majority of the membership, as well as the realities and restrictions of negotiation. From the perspective of the Branch activists, the Central Committee often seemed slothful or unimaginative, with the consequence that the men's interests were not adequately fought for, and important positions needlessly lost. In the words of one: 'We think that our Joint Central Committee don't get their finger out and get on with things sometimes. They could be a bit more forceful. They're a bit of a hidden mystery to us.'

The local Branch claimed to lead the way in the practice of holding unofficial regional meetings between representatives of different forces. Some 'old diehard' J.C.C. members were against this, as it was seen as a transfer of power away from them. It was easier for the J.C.C. to speak to large Open Meetings in the provinces if the regional representatives had not co-ordinated their questions or criticism beforehand. The movement towards unofficial regional meetings was resisted by Chief Constables, who envisaged more effective pressure from the various Branch Boards acting in concert. The local officials had been severely reprimanded when news of these meetings was leaked to the Press. (This was aggravated by the fact that the report claimed that militant action was being organised, apparently distorting a conversation with the officials.) The Chief Constable had given the officials 'a rocket, a bloody bollocking. He made us fuck blood.' Even after they claimed the Press had distorted their statement, he remained annoyed about the unofficial meeting, although it had been in the men's own time. He forbade them to use police property for such meetings. 'So if we'd had it in the "Duck and Hounds" we'd have been O.K.'

During the research, the attention of the Branch Board, as well as, to a lesser extent, the men as a whole, became concentrated on the forthcoming amalgamation with two adjoining county forces, under the reorganisation of local government in 1974. Anxiety became sharpened in 1973 when the Chief Constable of one of the county forces was chosen as head of the new amalgamated force in preference to the city man. The latter subsequently rejected the offer of the post of Deputy Chief Constable in the new force. The Federation representatives, as well as many of the men, were distressed, though not altogether surprised, at the authority's choice. They felt sorry for the rejected Chief, with whom they had developed a personal relationship, and who they believed was shattered by his failure to be appointed. 'He's become increasingly Federation-minded now. He told me he wished he was a member, because then it couldn't have happened!' But this element of personal distress was removed when the Chief was offered a job as one of Her Majesty's Inspectors of Constabulary. The Federationists also disapproved of the choice on professional grounds, and because it alarmed them in terms of its implications for the representative body. On the first point, they felt it wrong that the police authority should decide the appointment of the Chief Constable, when more junior promotions were decided by selection boards of 'professional' policemen, not 'laymen' ignorant of police matters. The feeling was that the appointment of the county man was on the basis of presentation of self, rather than virtues and achievements as judged by professional policemen. The county man was considered to work hard at public relations. At Open Meetings, he seemed to spend time with everybody asking for details about their families and so on. The Federationists reckoned he spent a lot of time beforehand learning up people's first names and family situation, to give the appearance of concern for everyone. But it was felt he had rigidly worked out priority ratings of how much time and attention any individual merited. 'Half an hour for a chief superintendent but ten minutes for a P.C.' It was natural that he would impress a committee of laymen. 'He'd go in front of the interview board, salute and stand to attention, very smartly turned out.' 'He was so articulate they had to stop him talking.' Whereas the city man was never the best-dressed of people and would probably just go in and pull up a chair. It was also 'the hardest thing in the world to get him to talk about himself'. These differences of style belied their professional competence, as a fellow policeman would see it. 'If I'd been interviewing, I'd have looked at their achievements as policemen. Why has the county force never been up to strength, while the city isn't seriously under-manned? Because they haven't a reputation which could attract anyone. Why have they an over-average crime rate and an under-average detection rate, in national terms, while we have the opposite? That's what the professional policeman would ask.'

The personality differences between the men were seen as reflected in their different approaches to the Federation, and it was the future of the organisation (as well as their own position and style of negotiation) which especially worried the activists. These fears were confirmed by their early meetings with him on the 'Guardian Board', set up to act as Federation spokesman on behalf of the men during the transitional period. The new Chief Constable objected to the Branch Board circulating its own minutes. He would himself inform the members of all decisions in the regular Force Orders. It was, the activists felt, 'a bloody cheek. We'll have to fucking sort him out!'

The city activists were worried about their prospects of retaining Federation office in the amalgamated force. This was not only personal concern by men who had made the Federation their lives, but also a wish to preserve their negotiating style. 'It's going to be an uphill struggle to gain control of the Board offices, because the county men outnumber us...It's a question of electioneering. We'll have to prove that it doesn't pay to let the Chief play benevolent Great White Father.'

In the event, city activists continued as deputy chairman, secretary and treasurer, but the ex-county chairman became chairman of the new Branch. The erstwhile city secretary lost his position, but not as a result of amalgamation. He suffered an unexpected *contretemps* in the divisional elections and failed to get on to the Board at all. Apparently, his involvement in force-level Federation work had left the division feeling neglected, and a rival had exploited this sentiment. But, altogether, the city Federation men had done well in weathering the reshuffle. A year later the former city chairman was elevated from deputy to chairman, as well as winning a place on the Joint Central Committee, testimony not only to personal political acumen but also the more general 'leftward' swing in the Federation after 1975.

In terms of the general impact on the force, there was the feeling of having been subject to a takeover, and the sense that key supervisory posts tended to be allotted by the ex-county chief to his own men. The result was experienced as an importation of strange county ways into city policing. The tensions arising from the amalgamation surfaced in the local press during the first year. The specific issue over which conflict developed was the application of economy cuts to the police force, and the reversion back to foot patrol, partly motivated by desire to save fuel. Underlying this was tension between the city and county men, reflected in dissension on the Board of the Federation. Thus the county Chief Inspector who had become chairman of the Federation of the amalgamated force approved the Chief Constable's policy in press statements. He praised the partial return to foot patrol as 'a move away from the Fire Brigade type of policing. It would enable the policeman to get back to crime prevention work.' The ex-chairman of the city force issued a contradictory statement to the Press, decrying the way the cuts had been implemented. He attributed the problem to the basic incompatibility between the county outlook and the demands of city policing, and the unhappy consequences of the forced marriage between the two. He argued that morale among the city policemen was low, and there was much unrest, because economies were being implemented in the wrong places. The root cause was the amalgamation, which was 'like trying to cross an elephant with a mouse. We are two different animals'. (Later that year the new Chief Constable did establish a Consultative Committee which has smoothed relationships with the representative organisations.)

To sum up then, the Federationists in the Branch studied could be divided into three main groups. The activists, who set the tone, were all men of general pro-union background and views, who wished to see a more unionate form of representation. Other Federationists, apart from a group of 'fellow-travellers', were either self-styled 'moderates' seeking to counter-balance the activist core, or 'passengers' who were only reluctantly serving as representatives.

The men's attitude to, and relationship with, the Federationists

Did the men identify with the Federationists, as the posters in the office declaring 'This is *your* Federation' imply? What was the pattern of policemen's involvement with, or alienation from, the people claiming to represent them?

The Federationists were generally regarded as a dedicated and socially concerned group of men, who took up office for reasons of public spirit, rather than personal reward. Fifty-two per cent of the men gave what could be broadly classified as 'altruistic' explanations of what motivated Federationists to take up their posts. A further 27% believed it was a mixture of altruism and personal return, while only 8% felt it was entirely based on selfish considerations, (with 13% don't knows). The C.I.D. were more cynical, 25% of them seeing Federation work as a self-seeking 'gimmick'.

The 'selfish' motives attributed to the Federationists were that they got out of 'real' police work with its problems, attended enjoyable Conferences, and were politically 'reds'. It was believed by 10% that activists had better promotion chances. 'Bolshie' representatives might be 'kicked upstairs' to get them off the Federation. (Federationists were believed to be *held back* in promotion by 30%, and many more thought this had happened in the past.)

Look at our rep. He's here two days a week if we're lucky. It's a way of getting off the streets, I suppose. To me the Federation's just a body that exists and you pay a tanner a week for. They're just common or garden agitators. No doubt some have been held back by being a Federationalist [*sic*] but others have been made up because they've become a thorn in the side of the powers that be.
(Uniform constable)
They like the sound of their own voices, and are the type who don't need radios to be heard on the street! Not that they ever go on the streets anyway!
(Uniform constable)

The majority of the men (52%) were less cynical about the Federationists' motives and saw these as mainly altruistic.

Like all policemen, they want to help people, in this case, their colleagues.
(Uniform constable)
They're dedicated to getting the men a decent living wage. They're the doers not the talkers, though some are good arguers.   (Uniform constable)

The good Federationist was 'the rebel, with know-how and courage to fight in front of the governors and be a red, not say "yes, sir; no, sir" to everything'. He must 'prefer to try and better the lot of individual policemen than to seek promotion'. He should 'have enough service in so as not to be browbeaten by the brass, the Big White Chief'. For these reasons most Federationists were 'older men with no prospects of promotion, not "flyovers" who'd be frightened of spoiling their promotion chances if they showed the red flag'.

Identification with the Federation varied between ranks and divisions. There was some feeling among uniformed constables that the Federationists tended to be men 'in posh offices', 'fat-cats', rather than ordinary beat workers. But this was militated against by the fact that many representatives were constables who worked alongside them. The fact that representatives were drawn from the ranks of serving policemen contributes to identification, even though some felt this had its drawbacks in a loss of independence in the face of authority. Supervisory officers had less of a feeling of identification with the Federation, and drew more on the image of representatives as unambitious types, who were more concerned about their rights than the job itself. Alienation was greatest amongst the C.I.D., especially the operational detectives. Usually, though not always, C.I.D. representatives were drawn from one of the inside departments, like scenes-of-crime. The operational men saw the Federationists as not 'real' policemen, but shirkers with little concern for the efficiency of the job, over-concerned with petty trivialities. This is reflected in Table 7.1 showing responses to the question whether or not the Federationist tended to be different from the average policeman in his outlook on the job.

Overall, a majority (56%) felt that Federationists were not different from the ordinary policeman in attitude to the job, and only 38% felt they were. But Table 7.1 shows that supervisors and specialists were much more likely to see them as different than were the uniformed constables. The C.I.D. in particular felt themselves to be alienated from the Federation.

They're professional stirrers, you know what I mean? They do a lot of good work for those who can't look after themselves. I feel I have no need to go to them myself. If you have been treated unjustly you should get round it by yourself. I don't take them seriously myself. It's a terrible thing to say, but the C.I.D. never have. The Federation are anti-authority and anti-establishment even though our governors do what they can do for us. They discuss ridiculous things, like the buttons to have on uniforms, like school-children.   (C.I.D. sergeant)

The alienation of the C.I.D. from the Federation was recognised by the activists. The secretary felt they regarded the Federation as: 'the working-class union, and beneath their dignity. The C.I.D. tend to develop a separate mind from the rest. There's mutual hostility and little interchange.'

The gulf between the C.I.D. and the Federationists rests on structural factors (the nature of the C.I.D. work situation, particularly its individualistic character), and somewhat different conditions in terms of pay, allowances, hours etc. These are interdependent with a difference in ideology between the approach of the 'dedicated professional policeman', as the C.I.D. man sees himself, and the instrumentally oriented 'clock-watcher', as he sees the Federationists. The latter in turn regard the C.I.D. as status-conscious men, who because of the particular advantages of their work situation break ranks with the rest of the membership, and act, in effect, as blacklegs.

TABLE 7.1. *Identification with Federationists*

Are active Federationists different from other policemen?

	Constables %	Sergeants %	Inspectors %
Same	63	45	35
Different	30	48	61
Don't know	7	7	4
Total	100	100	100
	N = 112	N = 33	N = 23

	Non-Specialist %	Specialist %	C.I.D. %
Same	59	48	25
Different	32	50	71
Don't know	9	2	4
Total	100	100	100
	N = 114	N = 54	N = 25

Similar conceptions of the Federation are held by many of the uniform supervisors.

A chap, if he's engaged in an incident, would tend to work on. But a Federation bloke would work out how much overtime or time-off is due him. He'd be thinking about when he's due for a refresher break.   (Uniform sergeant)
Some are keener on the Federation than ordinary police work. They shout and bawl rather than behaving like officers and gentlemen.   (Uniform inspector)
Their concern is with the individual and trivia generally rather than the big issues of the service. They're anarchists who're more left-wing, and stubborn like barrack-room lawyers.   (Traffic inspector)

The majority of the uniform P.C.s see the representatives as basically like ordinary policemen, but gifted with greater organising ability and energy, dedication or knowledge.

> It's good to have acting policemen as reps. We know they're not feathering their own nests. They usually remain one of the men, and don't put on airs.
> (Uniform constable)
> They know our rights better, and tend to be reactionaries [*sic*] who'll react back if we get treated badly.   (Uniform constable)

However, some of the younger uniformed constables feel alienated from the Federation. One young P.C. regarded the Federation as 'the Old Pals' Act...Young, especially single, people are under-represented... The rep's attitude is "you've only just fucking joined the job and you've got fuck-all to say about it".'

This pattern of attitudes is not reflected in actual knowledge of or involvement in the Federation. The men were asked if they knew the names of (a) the secretary and chairman of the Joint Central Committee, and (b) the local Joint Branch Board. The results are shown in Table 7.2.

TABLE 7.2. *Knowledge of Federation officials*

Number known	Constables		Sergeants		Inspectors	
	Local	*National*	*Local*	*National*	*Local*	*National*
	%	%	%	%	%	%
2/2	44	18	70	36	87	70
1/2	38	30	21	36	13	22
0/2	19	52	9	27	—	9
	N = 112		N = 33		N = 23	

The pattern of variation in knowledge is the opposite of that for identification with the Federation (as shown in Table 7.2). The supervisors, especially the inspectors, boast the greatest knowledge of each item. This can be explained firstly by the higher average length of service of the supervisors. They would tend to know more about force affairs in general. The second reason is that, as outlined before, the nature of the representation system means that more inspectors have been involved in Federation posts, however reluctantly. (Specialists tend to have greater knowledge than non-specialists, but not to a statistically significant extent.)

Table 7.2 also shows that the local officials seem better known than the national ones. (The divisional representatives were best known of all; only 7% didn't know the name of their own representative.) The national officials are remote to most of the policemen. Indeed, knowledge of them might have been much lower if not for the fact that the then Chairman of the J.C.C. was involved, during the research period, in two widely publicised *causes célèbres*. The first concerned his son in a drug charge, and the second was his own involvement off-duty in a fight in a pub, which subsequently led to his resignation on medical grounds. The jog to remembering his name was often 'Oh yes, the one who was involved in that case...' This seemed nearly as well known as his activities on behalf of the Federation!

A similar pattern holds for actual involvement in Federation activity. For reasons which have already been given, more inspectors have held Federation posts than among the lower ranks: 43% of inspectors had been a representative at some time in their careers, compared with 12% of sergeants and only 4% of constables. The same pattern applies to attendance at meetings. Forty-one per cent of constables, but only 15% of sergeants and no inspectors said they had never been to a Federation meeting at all. On the other hand, 30% of inspectors, but only 18% of sergeants and 12% of constables claimed to go regularly. Overall, 30% of the force claimed never to have gone to a meeting while 15% said they were regular attenders. (Voting in Federation elections is another index of activity but 74% claimed to vote regularly, and there seemed to be no systematic variation.)

There seems an important division concerning relationships with the Federation between supervisors and constables, as well as between specialist and uniform divisions, with the C.I.D. being particularly distinctive. The uniform constables have the most favourable image of the Federationists, whom they tend to see as similar to ordinary policemen, but with more dedication and skill to represent their rights and interests. The supervisors and specialists, on the other hand, tend to see the Federationists as less professionally concerned with the job, and as instrumentally-oriented, militant men with a grievance, out for their own ends. But partly as a result of the system of equal representation regardless of numbers for each rank in each division, the actual pattern of knowledge of, and involvement in, Federation matters is precisely the reverse. The uniform constables are the least knowledgeable and involved as representatives or in attending meetings, despite their more favourable image of the Federationists.

8
Attitudes to unionism outside the force

Trade unionists have often regarded the police as their enemy, largely because of confrontations about picketing in industrial disputes. An example was the 1970 Pilkington's dispute, during which a member of the Rank and File Strike Committee claimed that: 'The police were definitely Pilkie's private army and you can print that in 10-feet letters' (Lane and Roberts 1971: 196–7).

During the research period, the police handling of labour disputes was a prominent issue in national politics. The interviewing was carried out in the year after the 1972 miners' strike in which the unions involved appeared to reach new levels of success in techniques of organising pickets. In that year there were several confrontations with the police, resulting in union accusations of police bias and brutality against them. On 10 February 1972, the miners succeeded in closing the coke depot at Saltley in Birmingham, which the police had attempted to keep open. Arthur Scargill, the Yorkshire miners' leader, described it as:

a historic day when not just individual unions but British trade unionists decided that they had had enough of police brutality, they had had enough of intimidation by the police in obtaining passage through the picket-lines for scab labour, and they decided to do something about it. (Scargill 1975: 15–19)

The same year witnessed numerous other clashes between the police and trade unionists. Some were over wage claims seeking greater increases than permitted by government Incomes Policy. Others concerned government's efforts to place new legislative controls on union activity by the Industrial Relations Act. This struggle which developed during 1972 between government and unions over control of wages and union organisation, is the background to the following views of policemen about trade unionism. Strikes had acquired a new, explicitly political dimension of confrontation between the unions and the state, not merely specific employers. The police had to cope with the novel tactics developed during this year, including mobile 'flying' squads of picketers and a number of factory occupations.

The police and the courts took various measures to prime themselves for the fight, prompted by the belief that the law was under-enforced. *Police* claimed: 'The police were applying the Nelson touch to obvious breaches of the criminal law' (March 1973: 3). The government thought that no new legislative measures to deal with pickets were necessary, but there should be stricter enforcement of existing law. To this end, anti-picket squads, labelled 'mutual support units', were formed in individual police forces. They consisted mainly of unmarried volunteers under the age of thirty-five, who were given special training for public order situations. These men continued with their ordinary beat duties but were available for use in case of emergency. This reflected the Home Secretary, Robert Carr's, belief that the most effective method of dealing with potentially troublesome situations was a readily available, visible force of police. The new unit in the Metropolitan was used to overwhelm a picket of building workers at St Thomas's Hospital in April 1973. In the 1972 miners' and building workers' strikes, flying picket tactics had been used. Large masses of picketers were rapidly assembled at particular sites, out-numbering the police there. To prevent this happening again, co-operative arrangements were made whereby 'support units' in individual forces could be speedily reinforced by neighbouring ones. The Home Office and Scotland Yard formed a central intelligence unit to deal with industrial unrest. Two Yard officers were to collect and co-ordinate information about the build-up of strike crowds and their movement from area to area, which would be sent out to warn local forces. The new techniques were supplemented by directives to ensure more vigorous implementation. These were intended to allay the fears of Chief Constables who might have been intimidated from a policy of maximum enforcement because of the political dimensions of industrial disputes.

The courts were to deal strictly with offenders, to back up the police. This was made clear in two cases in 1973. In one, a building worker, John Broome, who stood in front of a lorry at a picket outside a site in 1972, was convicted of obstruction under the 1959 Highways Act. The second case was the use of conspiracy charges against some of the 'Shrewsbury 24' building workers, which allowed stiffer sentences than would be possible for charges of intimidation. In 1974 the Court of Appeal decided (in *Kavanagh* v. *Hiscock*) that the police could properly form cordons to prevent pickets from speaking to potential strike-breakers if they 'reasonably' suspected this might lead to a breach of the peace. Together the rulings gave the police powers which could be used at their discretion to prevent picketing which was effective from the union point of view. These cases signalled the government's intention to curb the new effectiveness of picketing tactics. The government was limbering up for the showdown with the union movement which came in the miners' strike of 1974.

In the event it was unsuccessful. A Labour government took office pledged to repeal the Industrial Relations Act and strengthen the legal position of pickets. One response to this, among those who had been disturbed by the 1972–4 successes of the unions, was the proliferation of schemes to organise 'private armies' of volunteers to prepare themselves to aid the police in the event of a serious threat to 'law and order'. These were much discussed in the summer and autumn of 1974, and were condemned by most senior police officers as well as the Police Federation. At the same time, the police lobbied successfully against Labour proposals to give pickets the right to stop persons and vehicles intending to cross picket lines and to try peacefully to persuade them not to do so. It was planned to include this in the Employment Protection Bill which replaced the Industrial Relations Act, but these clauses were eventually dropped. It should be noted, however, that it was already common practice for the police to co-operate with pickets in stopping lorries, for the purpose of peaceful persuasion, where they deemed the situation appropriate. The police objection was to the curtailment of their discretion to judge the particular situation, by granting the right for pickets to stop vehicles in *all* cases.

Clearly, in this historical context the police would be likely to see themselves on the other side of the fence from trade unions. The survey did indeed show that the rank-and-file policeman was inclined to adopt a hostile stance towards trade unionism outside the force, and was prepared enthusiastically to support government attempts to curb union power with their help.

Only a minority of policemen had any experience of union membership, prior to joining the force. Sixty-two per cent had never been a member of any outside trade union (including 21% who had never been employed before). Of the 79% who had been in some outside job before joining the force, 51% had not been union members, while 49% had. This is similar to union membership among workers generally. In 1970, 48.1% of the total labour force were members of trade unions (Bain & Price 1972: 378). Of the 38% of the force who had previously been trade unionists, 48% had been totally inactive, never going to meetings or voting in elections. (Thirty per cent of the ex-members claimed to have both attended union meetings and voted in their elections at least once.) The general conclusion must be that the overwhelming majority of policemen have no significant personal experience of involvement in trade unions.

In terms of inactivity as union members, the police do not differ much from other workers. Low levels of involvement are a norm, from which the policemen who had been union members did not deviate. (The proportions of policemen attending Federation meetings are comparatively high relative to the experience of most trade unions.)

At some time in their careers, 66% had experienced trade unions from the *other* side, as policemen attending at a picket in a labour dispute. The assignment was seen as troublesome by 30% (this was in a city not known for its union militancy). In terms of personal experience, therefore, policemen would be inclined to take a hostile attitude to outside trade unions.

This was confirmed by responses to questions about trade unionism outside the force. Trade unions were said to have too much power by 79%. Of the 18% who saw their degree of power as acceptable, most were from the small minority of ex-union activists. There is an increasing tendency for policemen to join the force as cadets, without trade union or outside job experience, so the trend would seem to be towards a greater preponderance of the view that unions are too powerful.

This proportion of anti-union sentiment is comparable to figures for the general population. The proportion of policemen believing that trade unions are too powerful approximates to that among Conservative-voting, non-union members of the general population quoted in a national study – 77% (Butler & Stokes 1971: 210). The police seem more hostile to trade unions (on the evidence of this question) than the total population, or even all non-union members. However, general public attitudes were becoming more hostile in this period due to government policy and media coverage. The police reflect the critical attitude towards trade union power and picketing which were especially widely disseminated at that time. The police views echo pervasive media themes (Coates & Topham 1974: 159; Hyman 1972: 140–55). The police attitudes were shared by many union members and industrial workers (Nichols & Armstrong 1976: section III). What is significant about them is the *strength* of feeling, which is not brought out in statistical analysis of responses, but is illustrated by the quotes. Due to the nature of their work role, the police are able to give concrete expression to their views in enforcement situations. The police had a deeply felt, often violently expressed, hostility to trade unions. Unions were seen as responsible for the economic troubles of the country, and to engage in irresponsible and damaging strikes. Most supported the principle of unionism *per se*. Originally, or in theory, trade unions were a necessary representative of workers in negotiation with their employers. But the movement had been diverted from its valid purpose of responsible representation. Policemen disapproved of unions having any influence over government and concerning themselves with political goals beyond defending members' working conditions and remuneration (cf. Nichols 1974 for similar attitudes among trade union members.)

When they were instigated they did a fine job, Tolpuddle Martyrs and all that jazz, to secure better conditions for people who had no say. But now the wheel's turned full circle. One of the fundamental causes of the country going to pot is that workers don't work hard enough. All they're interested in is arguing about things which don't concern them, like making policy. As far as I'm concerned you can take all the unionists away, line them up against a wall and shoot the lot.
(Traffic constable)

The perversion of trade unions from their original purpose was attributed to a minority of communist and other militants who abused the apathy of the majority for their own political ends. (This view is reminiscent of Wilson's famous speech during the 1966 seamen's strike, about a 'tightly knit group of politically motivated men'.)

The trouble with trade unions to my mind is they've got so many bloody idiots at the top, who're ignorant, pig-headed and stubborn. They lead the others like sheep. Being a little bit callous, I'm afraid I would sack them on the spot. Whoosh, out! A lot of the trouble with strikes is primarily to do with the leaders, and obviously to my mind backed morally, physically and financially by the communism. When I was in Liverpool we got drafted over to St Helen's, just before the Pilkington's dispute. There was a local coal strike. The gaffer there told them to do a job which was within their realm, and they said 'get lost!' The next minute the shop steward's there. 'Well, we'll get Jack Dash', or some other bloody stupid clown, 'to come down here.' There was a mighty punch up, old 999 and we all pile up there where there's this lot, about 200 of them, having a good old set-to in the yard. The management fired the two trouble-makers, and the whole colliery came to a bloody grinding stop. This is what is ruining the country. Take the dockers. They're bone idle, and riddled with communism without a shadow of a doubt. This containers dispute. They don't want them because they couldn't do any petty pilfering – it's all locked in the containers. I've got a cousin up there, Eddy, on the shop-floor at Fords. He gets £120 gross and does nothing. On nights, most of them play cards, football. He told me they had a coach up there one night, took them down boozing in the clubs till 2 o'clock in the bloody morning. The management play hell about it, but if they say anything they'll all come out on strike.   (Uniform constable)

I wouldn't go back to the situation where it was practically slavery in the early part of the nineteenth century. But nowadays with unions, even the top wallahs are barrack room lawyers. There's a communist outlook on a lot of these unions. The more strikes the better because it will eventually lead to the downfall of the country. But with the ordinary Englishman I don't think they've got a chance. The ordinary English working man does his little job without over-stressing himself, gets his wage packet and goes home at night to put his feet up and watch telly. If he'd get up off his ass he'd sweep the floor of these do-gooders, so the communist system will never work here. You'll never get a banding together of the whole country to fight against the things that are right.

(Uniform constable, ex-trade unionist)

Stricter control of pickets was urged by 51%, though only 15% believed this needed new legislation as opposed to more vigorous enforcement of existing law. Thirty-six per cent thought that senior officers exerted pressure on the men to restrain them from full enforcement, because of fear of aggravating the immediate incident, or apprehension about the political implications of appearing to take sides. The result was non-interference with illegal pickets, and turning a blind eye to offences committed.

People get their knickers in such a twist about where peaceful picketing ends and rioting begins. If I was an officer in charge down there I'd knock the lot off as soon as a person is physically prevented from going about his lawful business.

I don't agree with all this bargaining. You shouldn't bargain with anybody. They either let you through or they don't. And if I saw someone physically restraining a person from going in or putting an iron bar against their lorry, that's it. They'd be straight in, bang! No bother. But the senior officers are frightened of criticism or getting their name in the paper. They're afraid they won't be backed up, it'll jeopardise their chances. There was a case, quite funny actually, about six, seven years ago. I was at this Transport place where a lorry driver was trying to drive in through the pickets who were stopping him. He had his wife and child in the cab. And in the end he just revved up and drove straight at them, and they all jumped out of the way. But one of the blokes, part of the tyre went over his little toes, and he was shouting blue murder that he wanted us to arrest this bloke. So I said to him 'you've got to be joking. You're the engineer of your own downfall. It's your fault not his'. He couldn't see this. Anyway, when the driver came out, the other chap stated that he wasn't going to move out of the road. So he'd stepped outside the law then, and I arrested him. But nothing was ever done about it. The charge was refused.

(Uniform constable)

I don't think picketing is controlled effectively according to the law. In the strikes that have happened recently you'd have had thousands of trade unionists in the dock. But the chief constables and policemen generally don't want to get involved in political matters. They're frightened they're going to commit themselves and look like right-wing Nazis charging in to break up the Peterloo Massacre. They're frightened to get involved and make it look like a political issue. (Uniform constable)

The police don't enforce the law at strikes. We've had incidents where thirty or forty policemen were injured and no-one took action. Someone, somewhere directed the police to play it down, not arrest people for breaking the law. I mean, as a dog-handler, we're not allowed to use our dogs in demonstrations or things like that. Mainly because earlier this year a boy was bitten at a football match. So they're anti-dog now. They could use the horses. They could knock you flying with the horses and push you all over the place. But the dog is far more effective. I mean, a dog will do 200 people in two minutes, whereas a horse sort of takes longer. I believe, see, that the moment they start throwing rocks or something, you should jump on them. (Dog-handler, constable)

Fifteen per cent believed that the police couldn't be more effective without new legislation. The suggested changes ranged from stricter specification of the legitimate numbers and composition of pickets, so that the police could prevent the gathering of large masses and the intervention of outsiders, to the complete outlawing of picketing, as a situation likely to cause breaches of the peace. 'Pickets should be totally abolished. They're like a load of sheep' (uniform constable).

Forty-five per cent felt that the present approach to pickets was adequate. Peaceful picketing was recognised as a right that should be allowed. Enforcement of the law raised delicate considerations, and the police were correct to exercise discretion in overlooking certain violations, in order to prevent incidents escalating into widespread disorder or rioting, and to be sensitive to the political implications of appearing to take sides. A few men were also opposed to stricter enforcement because of the added burden this would place on the police themselves.

As long as they don't interfere with a person's rights, what harm's picketing doing? Because who looks sillier than a man walking up and down waving a banner about? He's a laughing stock to other people. As long as he doesn't go batting anyone over the head with it, let him go up and down in the pouring rain and freezing cold weather. I sit indoors and watch them on telly! I've never had trouble with pickets. This is where the approach comes in. If you go steaming in expecting trouble, you get it. But if you laugh and joke with them, you usually knock some sense into their heads without violence creeping in, I've always found.   (Uniform constable)

The real trouble at pickets was felt to come from a minority of agitators, often not workers themselves, who came from outside to stir up trouble. This is the corollary to the general image of unions being manipulated by small groups of militant members, with the added notion of outside *agents provocateurs*. Students came in for a lot of resentment here.

The trouble we had was not so much the miners. Of fifty arrests only about six were miners. The rest, no disrespect to you, were all students. The workers were well behaved, we had quite a laugh and a crafty fag with them really. We were doing our bit, they were doing theirs. But there's always the rent-a-crowd element that hang on to strikes. You'll see the same rent-a-crowd at them all, a growing number of Communist Party men. I'm not against anyone's politics, they're welcome to it. But they're going more towards a state of anarchy. I like a nice, free country. So at present I'm really anti-Union.   (Uniform constable)
This is a very thorny subject really. Because having seen the miners' and the dockyard pickets, to me they're the hardcore of, dare I say, Communists, Marxists, Leninists, be they what they may, whose sole intention is to go around and disrupt the country, there's no question about it. Some police officers I've spoken to saw the same people picketing at two factories a hundred miles apart on two different weeks. These people are basically rent-a-picket, just industrial agitators.   (Uniform inspector)

There is an association between the men's views on outside trade unionism and their attitude toward the desirability of such an organisation within the police force, shown by Table 8.1.

TABLE 8.1. *Attitude to union power and desire for a union*

		Are trade unions too powerful?		
		Yes	No	Don't know
		%	%	%
Should the Federation become	Yes	34	49	20
more like a trade union?	No	64	44	20
	Don't know	2	4	60
	Total	100	100	100
		N = 118	N = 45	N = 5

These views are also related to previous experience of unions. Only 33% of policemen who had not been union members before joining want the Federation to become more like a union, while 44% of those who had been members wish this change. Clearly neither the view that unions in general are too powerful, nor lack of prior involvement with them, constitute logical or empirical barriers against developing the desire for union power to protect *police* interests. Dissociation between attitudes towards one's own industrial action and that of others is a widespread phenomenon, and permits many trade unionists themselves to subscribe to statements of generalised anti-union sentiment. But the more usual position seems to be congruence between previous experience of unions, attitudes towards them, and views on the desirability of trade union organisation for the police. The norm seems to be both hostility towards outside unions as over-powerful, and, to a lesser extent, rejection of a unionate body in the police force.

PART THREE

The police as an occupation

9

The background and initial orientation of policemen

Who are the police?

Are the police a separate or distinctive group in the community, in terms of social background and career experiences? It has often been alleged that the police stand apart from the rest of society, and that this gulf is encouraged by peculiarities of origin. One recent article argued that 'the police force neither is nor considers itself to be a group of ordinary citizens in uniform' (*Labour Research* February 1975). This goes against much that is claimed by the service itself. For example, the 1929 *Royal Commission on the Police* declared in a famous passage (quoted by the 1962 *Royal Commission*) 'The police of this country have never been recognised, either in law or by tradition, as a force distinct from the general body of the population' (*Royal Commission on the Police* 1962: 10). Some analyses have suggested that a deliberate policy of drawing the police from backgrounds which mirror the general population is a subtle technique of social control. 'Personnel policies may have been instituted and maintained just in order to reduce the risk of total distrust between police and the common people over whom they are watchdogs' (Westergaard & Resler 1975: 187). As the standard historian of the police writes about the nineteenth century: 'It was a deliberate policy to recruit men "who had not the rank, habits or station of gentlemen"' (Critchley 1967: 52).

Policemen today are drawn primarily from working-class origins, most often skilled ones. Their backgrounds, in terms of social class of their fathers, roughly mirror the population as a whole. There seems to be some variation between forces, but there is no national data. Table 9.1 gives the socio-economic background of the present sample (in terms of father's occupation categorised according to the Registrar-General's classification), together with the class composition of the 'chief economic supporter' of all households from the 1971 Census. (Cain's earlier study shows a similar pattern. 1973: 101.)

The majority of the men came from social class III, mainly from the manual rather than non-manual sections of it. By comparison with the general population, the top and bottom of the social scale are somewhat under-represented. The more remarkable thing is the *closeness* of the distribution to the population norm. Certainly there seems to be little in the socio-economic background of policemen, considered in terms of class of father, that would set them apart from the population in general. Like the country as a whole, nearly two-thirds come from manual working-class backgrounds.

TABLE 9.1. *Social class background of police, and composition of population*

Registrar-General's class	Present sample %	1971 Census %
I	2.4	4.9
II	14.9	19.8
III (non-manual)	16.7 ⎫ 53.6	14.2 ⎫ 49
III (manual)	36.9 ⎭	34.8 ⎭
IV	19.1	18.6
V	3.6	7.7
N.A. (military/agricultural background)	6.5	—
Total	100	100

N = 168

There is a relatively high proportion of policemen who themselves come from a police background, in comparison with the population as a whole. Policemen constitute approximately 0.6% of the working population, but in the present sample 14% came from police backgrounds (classified as non-manual social class III by the Registrar-General). Men with police fathers tended to be particularly heavily concentrated in the C.I.D. (46%), and among the more senior officers (22% of inspectors). This peculiarity of background might be a factor in explaining any distinctiveness of outlook in these two groups.

Since the majority of policemen come from manual backgrounds, they have experienced upward social mobility, in that police work is itself classified as a non-manual job. However, it would appear that policemen did not generally use the force as their channel of mobility. Fifty-three per cent of those who had worked outside had been in non-manual jobs immediately before joining the police. This suggests that mobility had taken place *before* entering the force. This is further indicated by the fact that 51% claimed to have earned either more or as much before becoming policemen, and only 48% remembered earning less. Thus financial betterment was not generally a result of recruitment.

This conclusion about the upward social mobility of policemen is further supported by data on their *educational* attainments. These suggest that they do rather better at school than the manual working-class as a whole. Table 9.2 outlines the sample's educational experience, in terms of

TABLE 9.2. *Educational experience of policemen*

School-leaving age	%	Type of School attended	%	School-leaving qualifications obtained	%
14	19.6	Elementary/secondary modern	34.0	None	28.6
15	14.9	Comprehensive	6.5	Less than 'O' level (e.g. C.S.E.)	12.5
16	45.8	Technical	7.7	At least one 'O' level	54.8
17	11.9	Grammar/senior secondary	45.9	Above 'O' levels	4.2
18+	7.7	Private	6.0		
Total	100	Total	100	Total	100

N = 168

the age at which they left school, qualifications obtained, and type of school attended. (The results are similar to the national data presented in the *Man-Management Survey*, Home Office 1970: chapter 2.)

Policemen seem to have done rather better educationally than other children from manual or lower level non-manual backgrounds. Twenty per cent of lower grade non-manual and skilled manual children born in the late 1930s went to grammar or independent schools (Westergaard & Resler 1975: 320). But half of the policemen in the present study had done so. The police are in line with the figures given in *Social Trends* 1975 for the proportion of the economically active population who had 'O' levels in the relevant regions of the country (53%). The police seem to do better than the norm for their class of origin, in terms of proportions attending 'selective' schools, and, to a lesser extent, in obtaining school-leaving qualifications. But they do not perform well relative to the average pupil in these 'selective' schools. Hardly any had qualifications higher than 'O' level. Generally they are not academic 'high-flyers'.

Although police backgrounds mirror the social class composition of the population, their experience of social mobility and educational attainment is different. An orientation towards upward social mobility is reflected in the aspirations they have for their own children. Only 13% would encourage their child to follow their footsteps and join the force as an occupation. Thirty per cent would actively discourage them, mainly in order to urge them to do something which was seen as 'better' in socio-economic terms.

Policemen are often said to be distinctive in their career patterns. It is alleged that they have experienced only a restricted set of work situations, which serves to insulate them from the general population, and to incline them towards a disciplinarian outlook on society. It is argued that they have had only limited experience of outside work, entered the police at an early age, mainly via the cadet scheme, and are particularly likely to have done military service (see *Labour Research* 1975: 31–2).

The present research does not sustain these claims. Seventy-nine per cent of the sample have, in fact, had at least one job outside the force before joining, and 38% had been in more than one. Of those who had worked outside 49% had been at least nominal members of trade unions. It has already been pointed out that this proportion of union membership is similar to that for the labour force as a whole. For the most part union membership was rather reluctant, and not an index of any commitment. But the same would be true of many workers.

It is an exaggeration to claim that policemen have been isolated from the ordinary working world before joining the force. In the sample examined, only 24% had entered as cadets before nineteen, the minimum age of entry. Usually cadet entry *did* signify that the person had been immersed in a completely police environment from leaving school, and this mode of entry *is* becoming more popular. Given the lower wastage rate of cadets, it can be argued that the *trend* is towards a situation where most policemen will lack any prior work experience. As will be seen later, cadets are more likely to become senior officers and thus it can be argued that they have more influence on force policy than their overall numbers suggest.

A trend towards increasing insulation of the force from outside experience is seen in data on the age of entry. Of those who joined before 1956, 42% were between twenty-one and twenty-five years old, 37% were between twenty-six and thirty, and only 20% were nineteen or twenty, i.e. in their first year of eligibility. But for those who have entered the force since 1956, the position is reversed. Forty-nine per cent joined at nineteen or twenty, 29% in their early twenties, and only 22% in their late twenties. This is partly accounted for by the greater likelihood that the earlier recruits delayed entry because of war or national service. But recently about half the recruits have had no extensive experience of other jobs. Among the latest cohort in the sample, those joining between 1968 and 1973, 52% entered at the age of nineteen or twenty. Thus the trend is towards insulation of the police force from prior experience of other sorts of work, though most policemen at present have worked outside.

There is little evidence to support the argument that policemen are particularly likely to have had experience of military service. In the present study, 48% had experience of military life, either in regular or National Service. But this includes men whose service would have been during the war or compulsory National Service. It does not indicate a tendency for policemen to have chosen military service. Among the men who were too young to have been conscripted there was no marked tendency to seek out military experience. Only 8% of the younger men (those in their twenties) had been in any of the armed forces. The proportion is so low in the present crop of recruits, that it cannot be counted as an important factor in explaining the police outlook. This conclusion is further supported by national data in the *Man-Management* survey (Home Office 1970: 19–23). This showed that 46% of constables and sergeants in city forces had never been in the armed forces at all. Only 17% had been in regular, as opposed to war or national, service. Eighty-five per cent of the inspectors and superintendents had been in H.M. forces. But this difference can be accounted for by age, rather than any variations in outlook. Fifty-eight per cent of these supervisory ranks had been in war service, and only 8% in regular. Altogether, these national data confirm the conclusion that, taking account of the age structure and consequent eligibility for war or national service, policemen do not come from military backgrounds to any special extent.

The present study cannot therefore confirm the claim that the police are separated 'from the bulk of the ordinary working-class population' by peculiarities of social background or previous career (Westergaard & Resler 1975: 187). In social class terms their origins roughly mirror the population, with most coming from skilled or other manual workers' homes (though the unskilled are slightly under-represented). Educationally they do seem to over-achieve, and they seem to be characterised by upward social mobility before joining. They have mostly been in outside work, though there is a trend for there to be a greater amount of early and cadet entry. There is no support for the contention that the police are particularly likely to have been in one of the armed forces before joining.

While policemen are not demographically unusual, senior officers, and those in the specialist work of crime investigation, do seem to be. This challenges the frequent assertion that the police force is a career open to the talents. This claim is based upon the fact that there is no direct entry into the senior ranks of any police force (although until recently it was not uncommon for chief constables, especially in county forces, to have had no previous police experience). The myth is illustrated by the career-guidance book *Shall I be a policeman?* A picture of some policemen studying at the Police College is headlined 'The way to the top is open to all'. The text comments: 'There is no back-door, no short cut, to the higher grades in the Police Service' (Wainright 1967: 34–5).

The only *formal* barrier to a recruit reaching the force elite is passing the promotion exams, to sergeant and inspector. These are obtained by many more men than can actually be promoted. Many chief officers have worked their way up the ranks from the bottom, including 'Britain's most powerful policeman' Sir Robert Mark (*Sunday Times*, 3 November 1974). Until recently the key positions within the police service were virtually monopolised by the alumni of the short-lived Hendon Police College, established in 1931 by the then Metropolitan Commissioner, Lord Trenchard, to provide special training and promotion facilities for university and public school entrants. The Trenchard programme was abandoned at the start of the Second World War, largely as a result of Federation opposition. Since the war debate has continued between those who wish to preserve the original Peelian principle of a largely internally selected police leadership, and those who say that modern police supervision requires candidates with better educational attainments and a more 'professional' approach. Bramshill Police College, established in 1948, has, since the introduction of the special and senior command courses, been training men for the elite ranks. Selection for the special course gives forty young constables every year an opportunity for very rapid promotion. Special course completion gives automatic promotion to sergeant, and to inspector after a year's successful service in that rank. The scheme has links with the universities through the Bramshill scholarships, which allow special course alumni to proceed to university. The graduate entry scheme attempts to attract graduates by the carrot of rapid promotion through the special course facilities. It remains true, though, that all policemen *formally* start on the same footing.

The present study suggests that the notion of equal opportunity for the bulk of recruits is false. There are structured differences between the previous experiences of different ranks and specialisms. This should not be taken as proof of nepotism, but is more likely to be due to certain types of background giving the recruit a better chance of performing well according to the criteria promotion boards require for success. A systematic study of the process of selection for promotion in the force would be rewarding. In its absence we can glean some idea of the people more likely to satisfy the operational criteria used by selectors, from the social characteristics of the successful.

In terms of social class of origin there is a slight tendency for supervisory officers and specialists to come from non-manual backgrounds more often than lower ranks do. But the differences are not statistically significant.

However, the difference was marked in the C.I.D., although the numbers are too small for any firm conclusions to be drawn. Fifty per cent of the C.I.D. (N=24) were from non-manual backgrounds. This is mainly because of the previously noted high proportion of men with police backgrounds in the C.I.D. Generally there is little differentiation in terms of social class of origin between ranks and specialisms.

There are greater differences in terms of previous careers and experience. Supervisory officers have been more educationally successful before joining the force. Sixty-five per cent of inspectors and 61% of sergeants went to some form of 'selective' secondary school (grammar or public), but only 46% of constables did so. Specialists are also more likely to have had a 'selective' secondary education. Looking at constables only, 56% of specialists have been to 'selective' schools, whereas only 46% of non-specialists have. But looking at educational attainment within these schools, the differences largely disappear. Twenty-six per cent of inspectors and 29% of constables have got no qualifications at all.

These figures are similar to the national data given in the *Man-Management Survey*. This found that 34% of constables and sergeants in city forces, but 47% of inspectors and superintendents had been to grammar or senior secondary schools. It found virtually no differences between ranks in qualifications obtained, as opposed to type of school attended. The same proportion – about 34% – of city constables and sergeants as of inspectors and superintendents have no qualifications at all.

These statistics on qualifications must be considered in the light of the general rise in educational attainment in the population, and the higher average age of supervisory officers compared to constables. Other things being equal, constables would be expected to have achieved higher educational standards because they are younger. The similar qualifications mask a lower level of educational achievement for constables than supervisors, when the difference in average age is considered. The national study does not give figures for educational attainment of different ranks, holding age constant. But in the present study, while 58% of constables and 48% of sergeants born before 1939 had no qualifications at all, only 27% of inspectors had none. Thus it appears that, when age is taken into account, supervisors are both more likely to have attended 'selective' schools and to have achieved more educational qualifications.

Supervisory officers are also likely to have been more occupationally successful than constables before joining the force. All the inspectors with prior work experience, but only 51% of the constables, had been in non-manual jobs. Specialists are also more likely to have been in non-manual occupations. Looking only at constables with previous work experience, 75% of the specialists, but only 44% of the non-specialists, had non-manual occupations prior to joining the police.

More supervisors have had military experience than constables. Seventy per cent of inspectors, 58% of sergeants, but only 40% of constables, had been in one of the armed forces before joining the police. But this does not signify any tendency for militaristic types to be more readily promoted. It is largely the result of the age differences between the ranks.

A lower proportion of supervisory officers than constables have any experience of outside employment. Eighty-seven per cent of constables had worked in an outside job before joining the police force, but only 66% of sergeants and 65% of inspectors had. There is little difference in this respect according to specialisation. Taking constables only, 89% of non-specialists and 80% of specialists had worked outside. The reverse side of this coin is that supervisors had more often entered the force as cadets. Forty-three per cent of inspectors and 36% of sergeants, but only 17% of constables joined the force after having been police cadets. Specialists also more frequently entered via this route. Looking at constables only, 28% of specialists but only 14% of non-specialists joined as cadets. Bearing in mind the tendency for younger recruits to join as cadets, and the age differences between ranks, these figures minimise the over-representation of ex-cadets among supervisors. The expectation must be that future generations of supervisors will predominantly be men with no experience of outside employment, who joined as cadets. This seems to contradict the claim made in the 1976 *Year Book of the Metropolitan Police Training School at Hendon* that: 'The Cadet Corps. . .is in no sense an officer-producing system, if by this term one means that some special advantage has been conferred on the cadets which will enable them to ascend the promotion ladder more rapidly than their peers.' It is true that they have no *formal* advantages, but they *are* more likely to end up as supervisory officers.

The variations in background between supervisors and constables, and specialists and non-specialists, show that while there are hardly any differences in social class origin, there are patterned contrasts in previous experience. Supervisors and specialists have been educationally more successful. If they have worked outside at all it is more likely to have been a non-manual job. They have more often seen the police as their career of first choice, as indicated by the larger proportion who have never worked outside, and who entered via the cadets. The C.I.D., in particular, are different, both in terms of origin and previous experience. They have a higher proportion of men from police backgrounds (as well as 38% ex-cadets). These contrasts do contradict the myth of equal opportunity for all recruits, despite formal equality. But they cannot be taken as any indication of nepotism or favouritism. Those who have been more successful in career terms prior to entry, and who join with a more dedicated approach (as evidenced by the police being their occupation of first choice), are more likely to do well in the force.

Reasons for joining the police force

Critics of the police frequently claim that the nature of the work, in particular the element of power it confers, attracts men with an authoritarian personality. Lipset, for example, refers to the 'authoritarian traits they bring from their social background' (Bopp 1971: 28). The consensus of research into the personalities of police recruits rejects this conventional wisdom. As summarised by Skolnick:

It is hard to say why men join the police force, but the evidence we have indicates that police recruits are not especially sadistic or even authoritarian, as some have alleged. On the contrary, the best evidence that we have been able to accumulate...suggests that the policeman is usually an able and gregarious young man with social ideals, better than average physical prowess, and a rather conventional outlook on life, including normal aspirations and self-interest. (Skolnick 1969: 252)

This is based on a variety of studies which have demonstrated that police recruits do not seem to differ from the general population in terms of scores on psychological tests for 'authoritarianism'. (For example Niederhoffer 1967: 103–52; McNamara 1967: 163–252; Bayley & Mendelsohn 1968: 14–30.) There is a double-edge to this. While police recruits may not be *more* 'authoritarian' than the population norm, their work makes any elements of such a personality more significant than in most occupations. It does indicate though that the sources of any peculiarities of police occupational culture are not to be located in the individual psychological predispositions of policemen, but in the characteristics of the work.

While the police outlook cannot be explained in psychologically reductionist terms, policemen's initial orientation towards the job is important in explaining how they perceive the situation they encounter. Experience in the job must be filtered through these initial attitudes, and the police culture which emerges is a product of the interaction of objective circumstance and subjective definition. To understand their attachment to the work in general, and the representative body in particular, it is necessary to delineate the goals and perspectives they bring into the situation, as a step towards explaining the meaning it comes to have. (See the account of the 'action frame of reference' in Goldthorpe *et al.* 1968: 284–5.)

There are considerable problems involved in explaining why people choose the occupations they do (Williams 1974). The term 'occupational choice' is itself something of a misnomer. For the working class especially, the range of alternatives is fairly tightly constrained by lack of qualifications in relation to the requirements of different jobs. A complete explanation of occupational entry would require an account of the social processes which underlie the opportunities of different groups of people to acquire qualifications, and the way in which the criteria of suitability for occupations come to be set. Within the socially structured limits of choice, the decision-making process must not be credited with too great a veneer of conscious rationality, a danger implicit in the procedure of asking for *reasons* for choice of occupation. The 'reasons' people articulate for their 'choice' of occupation are not a complete or adequate account of why they actually entered it. Retrospectively recalled reasons, even if offered in all sincerity, are influenced to an unknowable extent by redefinitions developed during the experience of work itself. The relationship between these *post hoc* reasons, and the account which would have been offered at the time, is problematic. Only a longitudinal study could discern the way in which original definitions come to be altered by subsequent experiences. To cover the full range of situations potentially encountered in police careers the time-scale would have to be considerable. This study could only probe the reasons for policemen entering the force as perceived from their present vantage point. In order to overcome this limitation so far as possible, the men were encouraged to describe their circumstances as fully as they could, in response to an open-ended question on why they had joined. This did not impose on them an alien set of categories as a fixed choice might have done. There is, though, the possibility of artificiality of classification at the coding stage. But at least the responses were situated in a more complete picture of their circumstances at the time, and provide a basis for characterising the policeman's initial orientation to work.

Security is the prime attraction of the job, according to most studies of the police, both in Britain and the U.S.A. The editor of the Police Federation journal writes: 'the wish for security is still, after twenty-five years of almost full employment and the welfare state, the most potent recruiting ally of the police' (Judge 1972: 41). This is based on the *Man-*

Management Survey finding that 'security of employment; no strikes or redundancy' was mentioned by 45% of constables and sergeants, and 47% of inspectors and superintendents, as a reason for their joining. In addition, 19% and 21% respectively in these ranks mentioned the pension as an attraction. Thirty-five per cent and 29% respectively gave security as their *main* reason, considerably more than the proportions for any other factor. In the United States too 'At least 2/3 of recruits join law enforcement agencies for materialistic or extrinsic considerations, although a substantial minority do so for idealistic reasons' (Harris 1973: 16).

The present research cannot confirm the results of these earlier studies. Rather it lends support to these prescient remarks: 'Today the security attraction is somewhat of a myth. . .as the economic reasons for joining have increasingly little weight, there is a strong possibility that a more uniform type of personality will be recruited – men attracted solely by the work itself' (Whitaker 1964: 97).

Reasons for joining the police can be classified as *instrumental*, referring to extrinsic advantages of the job such as pay, status or security, or *non-instrumental*, invoking some intrinsic aspect of the work itself, like its interest or social utility. (It is important to emphasise that in a market economy all work is to some extent instrumentally motivated, and the differences are ones of emphasis or degree within this.) Nineteen per cent gave only instrumental reasons, 49% mentioned purely non-instrumental ones, and 33% gave mixed reasons. The police seem to have had a markedly *non-instrumental* initial orientation. That this remains true of their current attachment is suggested by the further finding that only 30% rated pay as the most important aspect of a job. 'Interest and variety' were rated as most important by 53%, and 'a sense of performing a public service' by 13%. (No other factor was mentioned by more than 2% of the men.) This contrasts sharply with the findings of many studies of other workers (e.g. Goldthorpe *et al.* 1968: 37–8; Beynon & Blackburn 1972: 62).

This is probably a confirmation of the change anticipated by Whitaker rather than a contradiction of earlier police studies. Policemen in different generations are likely to be attracted by different factors. This can be seen from the relationship between initial orientation to the job and period of entry, shown in Table 9.3.

Table 9.3 shows that recent recruits gave non-instrumental reasons more often than older generations. This remains true holding rank constant. Among constables joining *before* 1960, 41% gave non-instrumental, 30% instrumental, and 30% mixed reasons. Among those joining *after* 1960, 55% gave non-instrumental reasons, 12% instrumental, and 33% mixed reasons. This does not *prove* that later recruits joined with a less instrumental orientation. It could be that older men redefined their initial attraction as more instrumental than it had been. But the data are compatible with the thesis that recruits were increasingly drawn by intrinsic aspects of policing, as its comparative instrumental advantages decreased due to the relative full-employment and the welfare state. The increasing tendency for the police to be a first-choice occupation supports this.

TABLE 9.3. *Period of entry and initial orientation*

Reasons for entry	Date entered the force		
	Before 1949	1950–59	After 1960
	%	%	%
Instrumental	43	23	11
Non-instrumental	36	40	58
Mixed	21	37	31
Total	100	100	100
	N = 14	N = 65	N = 87

Most policemen, especially in the recent past, were attracted to the job by intrinsic aspects, though many mention instrumental advantages in addition. This does not mean that they see policing as the job they would like in the best of all possible worlds. All were constrained by the realities of the job market. But choice *within* the range of possibilities was governed mainly by non-instrumental considerations. Of those who had previously worked outside, 51% remembered earning as much or more, so that police wages were not an attraction.

The broad distinction between instrumental and non-instrumental motives helps compare the police with other occupations. But it encompasses a variety of more particular considerations. Deeper insight into why people join the force can be provided by examining specific factors within these general headings. (There is no logical or empirical incompatibility between the categories. Some men mentioned several, so that the percentages giving various reasons adds up to more than 100.)

The most frequent reason for joining was *interest and variety*, mentioned by 74%. Police work was seen as not involving a routine. It was not a '9–5 job', and so contrasted favourably with the boredom and repetitiveness of factory or office work, imagined or experienced. Twenty-four per cent talked of its lack of routine, while 17% specifically contrasted it in this respect with other jobs. Twenty-three per cent said they found its outdoor character appealing. Ten per cent singled out the variety of people encountered in the work as specially attractive.

I was attracted to the work. The fact that it was going out meeting all sorts of people, from the basic people up to – one minute you're talking to chaps from

St P. – (a largely immigrant area, with a reputation as a red-light district), the next minute you're talking to mayors. You get such a variety of people to speak to that it certainly broadens your outlook a tremendous amount. I could have earned more if I'd stayed in the hotel trade [he had trained as a chef]. But I was bored inside, you know. (Uniform constable)

This general perception of the job as interesting and varied merges into another set of more specific reasons, which can be labelled the *machismo syndrome*. Thirteen per cent gave an image of police work as 'a man's job', glamorous, tough and exciting with a hint of danger, where you were your own boss. It is not easy to demarcate this category from the attractions of the outdoor life and variety, but these responses seemed to put a greater emphasis on toughness and masculinity.

When I was leaving school I was at the age when it's a bit of an attraction. You know, big white cars and flashing blue lights. (Uniform constable)
It was a bit of an adventure as per the military style. Those adverts, 'Your country needs you!' I like to work with a band of men, more than anything.
(Mounted police constable)

Both the above sets of reasons merge into a third fairly distinct group of points, which can be labelled the *disciplined body syndrome*, mentioned by 28%. This involved an attraction to the idea of a uniformed, disciplined service, with the comradeship and pride involved. Many of these men had been in one of the armed forces before joining the police, and greatly enjoyed the way of life. They had usually left for family reasons, and entered the police as the closest civilian substitute. There is an element of paradox in that part of the attraction of 'the disciplined service' is pre-cisely that it allows more autonomy and independence in the actual work situation, out on the streets, albeit coupled with the element of drill and restriction by a rigid code of rules within the organisation.

I'm a great believer in a disciplined society. I've always been self-disciplined. To have a reasonable society you've got to have some sort of rules. Funnily enough, I'm also a football league referee, which is the same sort of thing. I've got a bent towards it. (C.I.D. sergeant)
It was through having been in the R.A.F. In a uniformed, disciplined body with men. The type of life itself, the discipline mainly. I do enjoy police work. The variety. I think one has a different type of relationship working closely with men than on a factory floor or in an office. A different sort of bond.
(Uniform sergeant)

Twenty-two per cent mentioned a belief in the important social purpose of the police as a factor motivating them. They spoke in terms of the satisfaction of performing a *public or social service*, the importance of enforcing the law. For those who gave this reason there was no clear-cut distinction between social service and law-enforcement, as some studies of the service role of the police imply (e.g. Punch & Naylor 1973). The main way in which they could be of service to the community was through their law enforcement activity as well as any more direct help they might have occasion to provide for people in need.

> Initially I wanted to deal with people. All policemen to come into this job must be basically honest and have the integrity. This is part of the system which you get vetted through. But as individuals you get this honest streak, which is more than the average person. There's something about your individual makeup – right is right and wrong is wrong – and you want to assist people. If I can help anybody I will do, within the rules. But if a man steps out of line and he's well and truly over, I'll rub his nose in it, you know?   (Uniform constable)

In addition to these various sorts of attraction, 29% mentioned some early *personal influence* from another individual, a relative or a friend, who had inclined them towards joining the force.

> My father was a policeman...I was more or less born in the police. I was actually born in that canteen over there. My uncle was in it as well. I was always rather interested in the C.I.D. It's like a paternity, because we lived over there, you see, in those police flats. You're sort of born and bred as policemen and thinking policewise. Seeing all the chaps going out on night-duty, the prisoners come in, and what have you. My brother went into the police too. I liked service life and was quite successful in the army. When you come out in civvy street you miss the service. I like a certain amount of order, I must say that. I'm rather methodical.   (C.I.D. constable)

Nineteen per cent gave only *instrumental* reasons as their motivation. A further 33% gave these in combination with some non-instrumental considerations. Even among those giving instrumental reasons, immediate economic advantage was not the predominant factor. Twenty-five per cent did refer to some immediate financial incentive to join. This does not mean, however, that they were necessarily concerned to maximise their monetary rewards. Most linked this to the stage of the life-cycle they were at when they joined (either newly-wed or beginning to have children). This made financial considerations especially important at that time. The instrumental advantages of police work were more often seen as the long-term prospects of a career, and the security of employment, than the immediate financial gain. Twenty-seven per cent suggested the security of the job as having been one of their attractions. A further 11% mentioned the opportunity for a long-term career with promotion prospects. Seven per cent saw it as a job with some status in the community, apart from any intrinsic or economic attractions. Ten per cent mentioned constraints on their choice due to their lack of qualifications for anything else.

> I'd been with the R.A.F. for six years and I had no settled roots. I felt it was time I had a steady job, where I was assured of at least some evenings at home. It all came to a head when I went on the Berlin airlift, flying packed, loaded aircraft. I don't say one chickens out, but one realises the odds mounting against one. So I wanted something steady. And, of course, I had no trade, you see. My education ended at seventeen, it was fairly grim in those days. I can manage a

machine-gun turret and navigate an aircraft from A to B, but that's no good in civvy street. I'd never been either anti-police or for-police, never interested one way or the other. But I saw it as a steady job, with some security, and after all, getting married I had to think about that. (C.I.D. inspector)

Purely instrumental reasons for joining were rare, especially for the later generations of recruits. It was more usual for them to be mentioned in conjunction with elements of intrinsic attraction to the job.

I was used to a disciplined life from the Guards. It's not my nature on purpose to be in a position to tell people what to do. I'm not particularly vicious as policemen go. As policemen you've got to run virtually the city. But you have to bear in mind the people you deal with are still human beings, and a part of family life. And that's what we want, happy family life. If you sort out a dispute there's nothing more pleasing than to walk out saying you've done a good job. It's just as much pleasure as going into a supermarket and arresting someone for shop-lifting, because that'll cause heartache in the family. When I first came in the job, I went down in salary. But I was attracted because it was a secure job through the years that allows you to accumulate a little bit of something. The bank manager takes more kindly to you, and when you want a mortgage. You become a fixed part of society and the community. You got to live up to the reputation the job has. (Uniform constable)

It was widely acknowledged within the force that people were unlikely to take up police work if they had a markedly instrumental orientation. A third volunteered the comment that no-one would take up police work if they were after money. This fact was often felt to be conducive to proper performance of duty.

Some say it's only a job, but you've got to get involved and contribute to the service, not just sit around waiting for your pension. If a policeman wants to earn more he should leave. Interest is top of the pops as far as I'm concerned. Pay is like a bonus to me. (C.I.D. inspector)
If a job's a job, pack it in. If a job's a pleasure stick with it. You won't find a wealthy policeman unless he's thieving. But it's an enjoyable job that gives a good living wage. (C.I.D. sergeant)
My wife refers to it as my hobby. She says I wouldn't be able to do my hobby if I didn't work. (Uniform constable)
If it was only a living you wouldn't tolerate being kicked and having your parentage doubted. (Policewoman inspector)

While it may be the case that the police do not primarily see themselves as attracted to the job by instrumental concerns, this does not mean that they are indifferent to pecuniary considerations. While only 19% saw their reasons for joining as being instrumental, we have already seen that 30% rated pay as the most important aspect of a job. This seems to suggest that more policemen come to see their job instrumentally than start off that way. Sixteen per cent specifically volunteered an account of how they had lost their original interest and/or idealism in response to various frustrations, usually failure in promotion or perceived victimisation. They had come to adopt a basically calculative approach to the job. In effect they had become 'uniform-carriers' or 'clock-watchers'.

Whether you do anything or not you get your wages at the end of the month, whether you go looking for stuff or just hang around on corners. Hence you get uniform carriers who just do their corner. The 50% who are sat on their asses inside are lazy swines, but the other 50% have been eaten out by the system. They came in with flags flying, all ready for it, and halfway through their career they realise because their face didn't fit, they weren't masons or whatever, their flags come down to half mast, and suddenly they look around, see the other uniform-carriers and say 'right they are, aren't they?' (Uniform constable)

I'm here mainly for the bread. They think we come here to do the police service a favour. Well we do to begin with. But mainly we're grown men, even if we're not treated like that, and I'm here for a standard of living. Not like Oliver, 'please sir, may I have some more?' (Mounted police constable)

The general picture is of 'satisficers', people who are not 'maximisers' of economic rewards but neither are they indifferent to them (Simon 1966: 9–11).

The general trend seems to be for more recent generations of recruits to be drawn by intrinsic interest, as the relative instrumental advantages of police-work, particularly its security, became less outstanding with the maintenance of comparative full employment in the post-war period. The rise in unemployment in the last few years has contributed to a slight easing of the problem of attracting and holding recruits, which had been endemic in the fifties and sixties. There has been concern about the implications this has for the quality of the new recruits, in terms of genuine commitment to a police career. In a debate on 'present trends in recruitment' in the House of Commons on 15 January 1976, Mr Jenkins (then Home Secretary) referred to 'a substantial increase in recruitment in 1975' both in London, and England and Wales as a whole. Mr Jessel, Conservative M.P. for Richmond upon Thames, asked him: 'Can he estimate how far the improvement is due to a positive wish to join the police and how far to a fall in other job opportunities due to economic conditions outside the force? Is the government doing anything tangible to ensure that the new recruits stay in, if and when the economy picks up again?' (*The Times*, 16 January 1976). As Mr Jenkins replied, there are no firm data available on the motivation of current recruits, and only speculation is possible. The data given above on the changing pattern of motivation in the post-war period do suggest, though, that there is some substance to the notion that in times of unemployment more recruits are attracted by the security advantages of the police as a career. This does not mean necessarily that they are any less committed or capable men. Indeed, general economic hardship may well mean that the police are presented with a better qualified selection of recruits to choose from. It is possible that, whatever their merits as policemen, people who join with different orientations will develop contrasting attitudes to the representation they have.

There is some tendency for supervisory ranks to define their initial attraction, and current attachment, to police work in *intrinsic* rather than instrumental terms more often than constables (holding constant the period of entry). However, neither relationship is strong enough to be statistically significant at the .05 level. Among constables joining before 1960, 41% give non-instrumental reasons, 30% instrumental, and 30% give mixed reasons. Of inspectors who joined in this period, 57% give non-instrumental reasons, 24% instrumental, and 19% mixed. Sergeants in this generation give predominantly mixed reasons (57%), with 22% respectively stating solely instrumental or only non-instrumental reasons. Only two inspectors and ten sergeants in the sample joined after 1960. Both these inspectors and seven of the sergeants gave purely non-instrumental reasons. Supervisors are also slightly more likely to rate non-instrumental aspects of work more highly. Pay is rated the most important aspect of a job by 31% of constables, but only 22% of inspectors. But 'interest and variety' is rated most highly by 61% of inspectors, as opposed to 52% of constables. 'A sense of performing a public service' is felt to be most important by 17% of inspectors, but only 11% of constables. (On all these points sergeants are almost identical with constables.) These differences, while not statistically significant, are nonetheless suggestive of a less instrumental orientation among inspectors than constables (or sergeants). This could be due either to a process by which people joining for non-instrumental reasons are more likely to be promoted, or a tendency for those who fail in promotion terms to redefine their attachment as more instrumental. Whether either (or both) these processes operate could only be properly tested by a longitudinal study.

Specialist and non-specialist divisions also differ in reasons given for joining, and evaluation of the most important aspect of a job. Specialist divisions were less likely to see their attachment in instrumental terms. These variations were not statistically significant either. In specialist divisions, 50% gave non-instrumental reasons for joining, compared to 42% of non-specialists, while 10% and 17% respectively gave instrumental reasons. (40% in both gave mixed reasons.) Pay was ranked the most important aspect of a job by 26% of specialists, but 32% of non-specialists. Interest was ranked more highly by specialists, 65% of whom put it first compared to 48% of non-specialists. The reverse was true of desire to perform a public service. This was ranked first by only 7% of specialists, but 16% of non-specialists. Thus there is a slight tendency for specialists to see their attachment in less instrumental terms, but the difference is small.

The conclusion is that most policemen view their choice of job as governed more by *intrinsic* than instrumental considerations. The latter play only a secondary part for most policemen. The intrinsic attraction is the job interest and the nature of the work situation, rather than commitment to the goals of the work or the public contribution it makes, though this was of importance to a minority. Within this broad characterisation there are certain variations. Supervisors (especially inspectors), and to some degree specialists, are less inclined to see their choice as having been taken on instrumental grounds. Recruits in the immediate post-war period were more influenced by security considerations than the later generation, who grew up in a full-employment world. This may well reverse itself if present economic trends continue. For most of the men, the police represented an opportunity to do work which was seen as intrinsically more attractive than available alternatives, as well as providing a reasonable and secure, though not particularly high, economic return.

It is plausible to argue that the initial orientation men had towards the job will be related to their attitudes to police unionism. People joining primarily for extrinsic considerations could be expected to be more concerned about having a strong representative body, capable of defending or advancing their material interests. Table 9.4 supports this hypothesis.

TABLE 9.4. *Initial orientation and desire for a police union*

		Reasons for joining		
		Instrumental	Non-Instrumental	Mixed
		%	%	%
Should the Federation be	Yes	52	34	35
more like an ordinary	No	39	63	58
trade union?	Don't know	9	3	1
	Total	100	100	100
		N = 31	N = 82	N = 55

It seems clear from Table 9.4 that those who join for purely instrumental reasons are more likely to want the Federation to be like an ordinary trade union than are those who give either purely non-instrumental or mixed reasons. This relationship continues to operate when rank is held constant. Among constables, 55% of those joining for instrumental reasons want a union, but only 35% of those joining for non-instrumental reasons.

The relationship between an instrumental orientation and desire for a union could partly be explained by both being connected to common background experiences, such as previous trade union membership. More importantly, it is likely that the orientation towards the job on joining

influences both progress within it in objective terms, e.g. success in promotion, and also sensitises a man towards perceiving and interpreting
certain situations as unsatisfactory and requiring union protection. It will
be seen subsequently that dissatisfaction with the job, in particular its
more instrumental aspects, is related to the desire for a union.

It can be suggested that one of the sources of the overall tendency of
policemen not to support police unionism was the generally non-instrumental nature of their attraction and attachment to the job. This makes
it less likely that they will experience grievances of a kind for which union
organisation might seem the appropriate answer. Within the force, part of
the explanation of variations in support for a police union is the difference
in initial orientations. The recent development of demands for union
status may be partly attributable to an influx in the last few years of more
instrumentally oriented recruits, attracted by the security of police work
at a time of high unemployment.

10

Orientation to work

The concept of 'orientation to work' as a crucial element in understanding the attitudes and behaviour of workers was introduced to industrial sociology by Goldthorpe *et al.* (1968). It was part of the 'action frame of reference', derived from the tradition within sociology which stressed the interpretation of subjective meanings, most familiarly associated with the influence of Weber (1964: 88). This was viewed as a corrective to previous perspectives in the study of workers' behaviour. The 'technological implications' approach was held to explain workers' behaviour and feelings in an over-deterministic way by the objective character of the work organisation and their place within it. (For examples see Blauner 1964; Woodward 1958.) It was argued that workers' attitudes and actions were not *determined* objective factors of their situation, but interpreted in terms of an 'orientation' to work, which allowed for the possibility of different responses to what was the same situation as defined by the observer. Contrary to the 'human relations' approach, however, Goldthorpe *et al.* did not regard these subjective meanings as stemming from fixed needs and psychological processes within the individual, but rather as socially generated and sustained (or modified). This directs attention not only to interaction in the place of work, but also to the sources of orientations in the experience of workers in the wider social structure.

There is a certain ambiguity in the notion of an 'orientation to work', as used by Goldthorpe *et al.* The concept seems to be used in two rather different ways. One is to regard the 'orientation to work' as providing an *explanation* of various elements of consciousness and behaviour which, while different from the factors stressed by previous theoretical perspectives, remains nonetheless a mono-causal account. In this sense, the 'orientation' to work is treated as 'the wants and expectations which men bring to their employment, and the interpretation which they thus give to their work', which 'shapes the attitudinal and behavioural patterns of their working lives as a whole' (Goldthorpe *et al.* 1968: 184). This will explain 'not only their relationship with their mates, supervisors and managers in the immediate work situation but also, for example, their stance towards their firm as an employer, their "image" of the industrial enterprise, their style of trade unionism and the manner in which they envisage, and plan for, the lives ahead of them'. These 'values and motivations that lead workers to the view of work they have adopted must be traced back...to typical life situations and experiences'. In this usage the 'orientation' is narrowed down into being synonymous with the reason for attachment to the firm, deriving from out-of-plant experience. It is used then to explain the general characteristics of attitudes and behaviour at work.

However, at other points Goldthorpe *et al.* imply a rather different usage of the notion of an 'orientation to work'. Instead of seeing it as a factor in a causal explanation, they treat it as the *principle* or *rationale* which runs through and informs all of a worker's disparate feelings and responses. For example, at one point they set up a typology of three ideal-typical orientations, each constituted by four dimensions: the meaning of work; the quality of the worker's involvement in the organisation; the degree of psychological self-realisation in work; and the extent to which there is a sharp dichotomy between it and non-work life. The three orientations, 'instrumental', 'bureaucratic', and 'solidaristic', are principles of organisation, which form the particular attitudes held on each of these four separate dimensions into a coherent whole, with an internal rationality of its own. No *one* aspect of work, say reasons for joining or staying in a particular job, necessarily has causal primacy over the others. The orientation is 'the way in which workers order their wants and expectations relative to their employment'. It informs all aspects of the work experience, including the relationship to non-work life, and the future life-plan of the worker (38–40).

This latter sense has been particularly stressed and utilised by Beynon and Blackburn. They emphasise how the concept of orientation to work 'offers the possibility of treating the worker as a whole person...The way in which work is experienced depends neither on work factors nor orientation alone, but on the interaction of the two. Furthermore, an orientation to work should not be thought of as arising outside and brought into the work situation, but as something which derives from the individual's total experience...The rejection of the adequacy of explanations based on technological determinacy and system needs should not lead us to adopt one which replaces an analysis of the work situation with one based on prior orientations...Orientations to work are related to structural features of the workers' biographies...The way in which work is experienced is a complex evaluation of the various objective features of the particular work situation, which is based on these orientations.' (1972: 3–4.)

In the following account of policemen's 'orientation to work', I define this concept in the way Beynon and Blackburn do. It refers 'in a general way to a central organising principle which underlies people's attempts to make sense of their lives'. There are certain dangers implicit in developing a model of such an orientation, and these must be further considered before proceeding. This more general usage of 'orientation', as the underlying rationale of the worker's experience, does not have the same empirical status as the narrower one, which treats it as the reasons for original or current attachment to the job. The latter, more limited, usage is, in principle, directly ascertainable by questioning the worker about why he entered, or stays in, his job. There are, of course, technical problems in conducting such an enquiry so as to avoid distortion or retrospective redefinitions. But the researcher is trying to ascertain a process of reasoning which operates, more or less, at a conscious level. The postulation of an orientation in the sense of 'a central organizing principle' is an 'ideal-typical' construct. As Weber stressed, such types 'are pure mental constructs, the relationship of which to the empirical reality of the immediately given is problematical in every individual case' (1949: 103). The purpose of developing these models is that the ideal-type is formulated so that it gives us an interpretation and understanding of subjective meanings in a clear way. It provides a conceptual tool of understanding which allows some degree of purchase on reality, but not a straightforward description of what is observable. As Weber puts it, the types 'in each case involve the highest possible degree of logical integration by virtue of their complete adequacy on the level of meaning. But precisely because this is true, it is probably seldom if ever that a real phenomenon can be found which corresponds exactly to one of these ideally-constructed pure types' (1964: 110). For example, the ideal-type of an 'instrumental orientation to work' is unlikely to be found with all its ramifications in every, or possibly even any, worker whose behaviour is made sense of by that notion. The argument is that we can gain a subjective insight into their action by regarding it as informed by an instrumental orientation, compared to others. The usefulness of the notion is not absolute, but depends on the scope of the questions asked. Thus, for instance, it may be that when 'affluent workers' as a whole are contrasted with 'traditional workers', it makes sense of their behaviour to attribute an instrumental orientation to them. If, however, the purpose is to illuminate differences *within* the group of 'affluent workers', the behaviour of some categories may be better understood in terms of their relative non-instrumentality. The constructed orientation is a hypothesis of the observer, not the direct outcome of an attitude survey. Its use is that, because it is developed as a subjectively meaningful structure of which we have a clear understanding, it provides an insight into the consciousness of the workers. But its status as an observer's construct, rather than the direct result of observation, must always be remembered. Otherwise the danger is that it will be reified, and an artificial degree of logical integration and articulation will be attributed to the people studied. The attitudes expressed by actual men may be internally contradictory even though they approximate sufficiently closely to a type for us to gain understanding of their consciousness through its use. Nor are 'orientations' fixed. The way in which we can comprehend how people make sense of their lives may have to change as they encounter new situations which alter their ideas. But these new experiences are defined in terms of previous orientations, so these remain useful.

The particular aspects of policemen's attitudes to the job which are discussed in this chapter are the extent and sources of satisfaction and dissatisfaction; conceptions of the force as a social organisation, revolving around a set of disciplined relationships between different ranks; career aspirations and assessments of the promotion system; notions of professionalism and the impingement of police work on private life. It emerges that, overall, policemen seem fairly close to the 'bureaucratic' orientation to work which Goldthorpe *et al.* attribute to salaried employees in general (39–40). There are, however, certain distinctive features of the police view, which can only be discerned after we consider their images of their role in the social structure, as well as internal variations around the central theme of a 'bureaucratic' orientation.

Satisfaction with police work

Assessment of the extent of satisfaction people have with their work is notoriously fraught with difficulties (Blauner 1960: 486–7). The close connection between self-esteeem and work is probably the main reason why studies of job-satisfaction, based on direct questions, reveal an overwhelming preponderance of satisfaction, even in situations which outside observers have seen as involving great deprivation (Blauner 1960: 474). Apart from the possibility that men, deliberately or unconsciously, exaggerate the extent of their satisfaction to protect their ego, the notion of job satisfaction is rather nebulous. Does it mean satisfaction relative to a realistic range of alternatives, or in some absolute sense? How does a person balance out several aspects of work, which may be evaluated in different directions, in order to arrive at some overall response? Is it meaningful to speak of *job* satisfaction in abstraction from other areas of a person's life? How far do feelings of satisfaction fluctuate from time to time according to immediate events and circumstances? Finally, how far should the person's own assessment of his satisfaction be accepted, in the face of what appear to be 'objective' sources of deprivation? Perhaps satisfaction with what seem to be meaningless or oppressive work situations should be interpreted, with Marx, as an alienated adaptation to an animal rather than human level of life? It is clear that there are considerable, and perhaps insuperable, problems in assessing even the subjective extent of satisfaction with work.

This does not mean that no aspects of satisfaction with work can be studied. Growing awareness of the problems involved in measuring satisfaction has led to three responses. Firstly, while it is generally conceded that the assessment of an *absolute* level of satisfaction may be a chimerical pursuit, it is widely argued that it is nonetheless meaningful and possible to *compare* different workers or occupations in this respect (Blauner 1960: 487). Secondly, job satisfaction is often assessed by more indirect questions relating to behaviour, rather than bluntly asking how satisfied the respondent it. For example, Blauner refers to surveys which attempt to get at job satisfaction by such questions as whether or not the worker would rejoin the same job in the hypothetical situation that he had his life over again, or won £1m. However, while these questions may be of some use and interest in *comparing* workers, they cannot be taken as an absolute index of satisfaction with work. The third development has been to analyse what aspects of a job workers consider important, and how they evaluate their own work in these terms. This gives some idea of what they look for in work, and the way they see their job as satisfying these desires. Again this can help compare workers in terms of their satisfaction with work, and delineating the sources of this in particular jobs. The arguments above suggest that an absolute notion of job satisfaction is not meaningful. We can have some comparative account of how different groups of workers assess their jobs in response to different questions, and the aspects they find gratifying, but this is a far cry from the attempt to measure some unitary dimension of 'satisfaction with work'.

In the present study, various questions were asked which attempted to provide a basis for comparing the police with other workers in terms of satisfaction, and also to pinpoint the sources of this. In order to have as direct a basis as possible for comparison with the other occupations studied by Blauner, I asked whether or not the men would rejoin if they had their lives over. The problem with this question is its extremely hypothetical nature. The men may suppose that if they started over they would change other aspects of their life too, so that they would have a broader range of choice. Thus it may not be a valid indicator of how they feel about their actual work. The pattern of response to this question was what could be expected on the basis of previous studies of satisfaction with work. The response overall was that 51% felt they would become policemen again if they had their lives over, 38% said they would not, and 11% didn't know. The hypothetical character of the reply, and the fact that it is not an adequate characterisation of their present feelings, was brought out by the reasons given by those who would *not* rejoin. The usual statement accompanying this reply was that the respondent would try to do better at school, now that he realises the value of this, in order to get a more prestigious job with higher pay. The point is that the range of comparison evoked by this question is perhaps unrealistically wide. Nonetheless, just over half the men on this basis give the 'satisfied' response. The proportions in other occupations discussed by Blauner are presented for comparison in Table 10.1.

Policemen seem to be similar in degree of 'satisfaction', as tapped by this question, to skilled craftsmen. They score lower than what Blauner calls 'professional' occupations, but higher than most manual ones, even skilled. Blauner argues that 'occupational prestige' is 'the one best explanatory factor' in accounting for variations in satisfaction, largely because this 'subsumes within itself a number of factors which contribute heavily to differences in satisfaction', such as 'the level of skill the job entails, the degree of education or training necessary, the amount of control and responsibility involved in the performance of the work, the income which is typically received' (Blauner 1960: 477). This makes sense both of the comparison of the police with other occupations, and the internal variations within the force. In the Hall–Jones study of the prestige ranking of different occupations, policemen were graded just above skilled manual workers like fitters or carpenters, at the same level as a routine clerk, and below most non-manual or professional workers (Hall & Caradog-Jones 1950).

TABLE 10.1. *Proportion in various occupations who would choose same kind of work if beginning career again*

Professional occupations %		Working-class occupations %		Present research %	
Mathematicians	91	Skilled printers	52	All policemen	51
Physicists	89	Paper workers	52	Constables	47
Biologists	89	Skilled automobile workers	41	Sergeants	55
Chemists	86	Skilled steelworkers	41	Inspectors	61
Lawyers	83	Textile workers	31		
Journalists	82	Unskilled steelworkers	21		
		Unskilled automobile workers	16		

Source: Blauner 1960: 477; and present study

Satisfaction as tapped by this question relates to rank, as Table 10.1 showed. However, the differences were not statistically significant. The relationship may be weakened by differing *aspirations* between ranks. Specialists did not seem more satisfied than non-specialists. Among specialist constables 48% would rejoin, but so would 47% of non-specialists.

Asked whether they would encourage their children to join the police, only 13% said they would; 29% would discourage them. But 32% felt they would leave it to the child. Girls, but not boys, would be discouraged by 9%. While more seem inclined to discourage than encourage, this does not necessarily reflect job dissatisfaction. Usually the reason was a desire for children to do 'something better' in socio-economic terms. (There was no variation in this between ranks.)

At some time, 59% had thought of resigning, 27% seriously. This was not related to rank. More constables (40%) than inspectors (30%) had *never* thought of resigning, but this was because inspectors had been in service longer. The proportion of constables and inspectors with similar lengths of service who had never thought of resigning was the same. The majority of policemen, regardless of rank, have thought of leaving at some point in their careers, though only for a minority was this a serious consideration.

The reasons for considering leaving, and for deciding to stay on, give an insight into the *sources* of dissatisfaction with the job, and the nature of its hold. Resignation was considered more often because of dissatisfaction with *intrinsic* aspects of the job itself, or internal discipline, than *extrinsic* grievances like pay. (As some men gave more than one reason, percentages total more than 100.)

Resentment of the discipline system, or actions of individual supervisors, were mentioned most often (30%). On the whole, the degree of discipline was not felt to be irksome. Discipline was seen as having lessened over the last decade or so. Many grievances were generated by the *older* style, or were idiosyncratic, involving either exceptionally strict individual officers, or personal victimisation.

After three and a half years I was still at the same station. I don't know if that's what I was worth [laughter] or they'd forgotten about me. When you talk to policemen from other divisions you feel 'Cor, the things I've got to put up with'. Police in different areas got totally different jobs although they've got the same uniform on. I had two attempted murders under my belt in my probation period, which is really good, and a rape case not long after. You meet many people who after eighteen months say 'Oh, I had my first prisoner, drunk and incapable'. I was proud I had those cases under my belt. Then I had another job done through observation off-duty, and didn't get anything for it. I saw three yobboes running out of a shop, hotly pursued by a shopkeeper... There's me with the wife, and I saw it, and thought 'Well here we go'. Accepting it, like. Swing me old car round, just out of instinct more than anything. Chase after them. Jump out of the car as it was still going along. My missus grabbed hold the hand brake, and it pulled up demolishing a dustbin. So I run after the yobboes and catch one. We're down squabbling and fighting! I'm not that big, you know! And then somebody's obviously rung 999 and the police from that division arrive. I tell them I'm an off-duty policeman, and they let me have the prisoner. It's usual practice, if you're off-duty and from your own observation get a prisoner, you get a commendation. Well, I didn't hear a word! – So I think, I won't ever do that again. Obviously, if an old lady was getting beat up I'd step in, but anything else, I've no time for it. My ambition when I came in was, well it still is, to know the job inside out, go as high up the ladder as I can. So then I was offered a job as a rep., selling insurance. I play golf with the manager and he approached me. I thought very seriously about it. He said 'you've got the gift of the gab, you can do it. Make £50 a week on commission.' But I thought, 'I've got a comparatively nice wage coming in every month, a police house, a six-month-old baby son. I'm not going to take the big step of moving to another job at this stage.' I decided to stay, and lo and behold a vacancy occurred and I got the job of area P.C. I was getting in a rut, no job satisfaction. But now I feel at least someone upstairs in the brass knows I can work by myself.

(Uniform constable)

Various problems with the work itself were mentioned as prompting thoughts of resignation: hostility of the public towards the police (18%); the frequency of jobs which were seen as impossible or extraneous to the policeman's notion of 'real' police work (18%); dirty, uncomfortable and physically unpleasant jobs (11%); excessive paperwork (9%); and lack of a visible, discernible end-product (6%).

Public hostility often led to a desire to leave.

I've thought of leaving many times. I got to the point where I was scanning the papers every night. This was about twelve months before Unit Beat came into operation. I had a particularly rotten beat, a rough area of town, full of dogs, yobs and kids. And they're all on to you. It's bred into them from the time they're so high. Not all of them obviously. But 90% of them. Well over 90%, I should say. It's soul-destroying, it really is. And I thought, 'Well, I'm not having this'. Wages were a bit lower at the time, so I thought 'I can find a better job than this'. I was losing interest weekly, scanning the papers. Wrote away for jobs. Then the panda came looming on the horizon, and I thought if I've got to do this, at least I can do it in comfort. So I hung on. Then I progressed on to motorcycles. Give me motorcycles every time. You've got to be motorcycle minded, but it's for me.   (Traffic constable)

A few of the men saw this hostile attitude of the public as stemming from the intrinsically antagonistic and adversarial character of much police contact with people, which they found difficult and unpleasant. They would prefer a job which allowed them primarily to have co-operative rather than conflictual relationships.

I don't think it suits me. A lot of the contacts we have with the public are difficult ones. It's the very nature of the job really, where you've got to be aggressive with people. Well, you haven't *got* to be, but there's some aggression in it by nature isn't there? It doesn't have to come over necessarily but you have to be firm with people and this sort of thing, and I'm not basically like that really. It's taken me seven years to find out. Like, I've got a real fad about litter. I just find it so disgusting that anyone could consider putting a piece of paper or a matchstick on the floor. And yet I find it incredibly difficult to stop any ordinary housewife or chap going about his day's work and say: 'Right! You pick that up or I'll report you!' Which I ought to do. But I find it hard because he's probably not aware he's being anti-social. He's probably a decent enough chap. Yet you can't let them off every time or they'll just do it over and over. I find it very difficult, unless I get in a bad mood and then it's easy! I thought of doing some sort of social work, but I haven't the qualifications. Same for teaching. But I think I really fancy some sort of clerical job, where I could be performing more of a useful and friendly service. Somebody would come in and ask me things, and I would help them.   (Uniform constable)

I found the attitude of mind hard in the early years. I think I was too friendly with people. I probably still am. I didn't develop the police attitude towards people. I was possibly too easy-going, and at first I never liked to report anyone. I never used to put in enough reports. I was always being badgered that I hadn't arrested enough people. I was always too keen to give them a second chance. The depressions it's given me over the years! I don't think I've changed a great deal, but the service has changed beyond all recognition from when I joined. In 1955 you did as you were told, but nowadays we're all on the same level and you speak to the inspector just as you would anybody. And my job's different. I'm an area constable now. I'm not resident on the area, but I'm there everyday. It's more or less like a public relations officer really. We still do the job of reporting people, but mainly it's getting to know the people on the patch, the community. I have a very good relationship, I think. I have a friendly approach which I use often in these circumstances.   (Uniform constable)

Eighteen per cent gave as part of their reason for wanting to leave the high proportion of jobs that they regarded as not appropriate for the police to do. The general view seemed to be that crime prevention and detection were the most important, key elements of their task, but there was little resentment at the bulk of duties which involved various sorts of help being provided to members of the public. Certain assignments were, however, especially resented, usually because they were seen as useless, or work which should be handled by other agencies. In some cases the frustration which such work produced was so great as to be a factor in prompting thoughts of resignation. The particular tasks mentioned as generating this discontent varied somewhat from division to division, according to its specific policing problems. On the central division there was a large business area where the panda system was not in operation. The work involved ordinary foot patrol, which at night, when the area was deserted, consisted largely of checking premises. This produced a sense of purposelessness in many men there. Some of the older ones in other divisions also cited the apparent meaninglessness of this style of patrol as having made them want to leave in their early days on the beat.

Among the C.I.D. a major grievance was the amount of time spent on preparing cases in a form suitable for court appearances and to fit the requirements of criminal statistics compilation.

We all get bogged down with statistics in the police service, and you know as well as I do what statistics are like. Everybody gets a little frustrated from time to time when some junior clerk in the Home Office demands the statistical figures on how many left-legged Irishmen stole what have you. And this tends to breed discontent.   (C.I.D. inspector)

Some men in the Mounted and Dog section felt frustrated by the emphasis in the force on using animals largely for ceremonial rather than strictly police purposes. (This view was not universal, and others were proud of the section's record of trophies and other distinctions.)

It's questionable whether the mounted branch do all that much good in the city. It's not the fault of the men, but the whole organisation of the thing is wrong to me personally. It's got the most fantastic record for these horse shows and things around the country. It's now become an absolute phobia. The Watch Committee love it, 'our great police horses'. It's a load of rubbish. They shouldn't be going around in shows, but getting down and doing the job. When I was in the Met. it was different. The old chief super. used to say 'Don't look at yourself as a mounted policeman, look at yourself as a police officer on horseback.' This is of primary importance. You're in a specialist section, but you're a police officer every bit, through and through. They should be out on patrol doing the normal job of a police officer, instead of chasing round the countryside.

(Uniform constable, ex-Mounted)

Thus to some extent the particular tasks which were seen as frustrating, because of their apparent uselessness or extraneous character from the standpoint of a specific notion of 'real' police work, varied according to the circumstances of each division. But there were certain duties which seemed to crop up fairly regularly in the routine work of the ordinary territorial divisions which produced this feeling. The ones most often referred to were domestic disputes and traffic control, especially school-crossings.

Domestic disputes have been mentioned by several previous studies of police work as a much disliked task (e.g. Wilson 1968: 24). Such disputes present the policeman with a frustrating situation, which at best offers no rewards, and at worst can produce accusations of failure to do one's duty and/or having exceeded it. The frequency of such events in routine patrol work was pointed to by 14% as a reason for wanting to leave.

Things like domestic disputes, I don't see that's our job at all. They're messy, unpleasant things and we never do any good. We can't solve – I mean, if you've got a man and a woman arguing, if it's going to become a breach of the peace, they're keeping the neighbours awake, O.K. But quite often you get a phone-call, or your radio comes through, and you go to an address. A woman outside the door: 'My husband won't let me in.' So he lets her in. When you hear her story, he's a pig. And his story about her, she's an alcy. What can you do? All you can do in the end, you say, 'well, you must go down and see the magistrate's clerk'. And you come back from it and make a report. There's been no offence committed. It's not our job, we shouldn't have to go, but we always do.

(Uniform constable)

A related source of dissatisfaction, mentioned by 15% who had thought of leaving, was the degree of boredom and lack of scope for initiative in much police work. This was especially remembered as having been true before the panda system was introduced, when most work involved walking the beat. It was still true, in the eyes of those who remained on foot patrol in the centre of the city. The panda drivers felt that some shifts or areas presented monotonous, routine work.

If I could have foreseen what the job would end up like when I saw the recruiting literature, I wouldn't have bothered. I'd have fought shy of it. It's monotonous all the way through. I go home physically tired, but I feel I haven't used my brain at all. I become a cabbage when I'm at work. These ads. are all wrong. Dull it *is*. (Uniform constable)

If you were in a quiet part of the city, the beat was soul-destroying. Shaking bloody door-knockers. To think of twenty-five years doing that! When I started you just walked around. Frightening yourself to death seeing yourself at 3 o'clock in the morning in a shop-window and thinking it was a fellow walking towards you. You just couldn't put up with it if you had any inspiration.

(C.I.D. sergeant)

Many referred to the physical unpleasantness of some of the jobs, especially the handling of dead bodies. 'We're the nation's scavengers, the clearer uppers of mess basically. Though there are rewarding sides, like getting prisoners, wrong-doers' (traffic sergeant).

Excessive amounts of paperwork were also complained about. 'There's an awful lot of time-wasting jobs. Interminable form filling! Police stations, eventually they'll sink under the weight of paper, I'm sure of it!' (uniform constable).

The sense of frustration was summed up with the phrase 'there's no end-product to police work'. So much effort was expended with apparently no demonstrable result.

So far we have considered those aspects of the job itself which prompted the desire to leave. A set of more *extrinsic* considerations were also involved. Inadequate pay was cited by 27% as a reason for having thought about resigning. This does not necessarily represent a purely calculative, maximising approach to financial rewards. The pay was not so much seen as inadequate in relation to its purchasing power over material objects, but as a morally insufficient recompense or recognition for the job done and the effort put into it. Conditions of work were mentioned by a large proportion of the men as problematic in some way. Twenty-one per cent referred to the inconvenience, physical and mental strain, and disruption of home and social life induced by the shift system, and the sometimes unpredictable hours. Seventeen per cent spoke of the lack of proper equipment and decent physical facilities at work. Another 17% mentioned various ways in which police work directly interfered with their private life, apart from the consequences of the shift system. They talked of ostracism by the public in out-of-work life, the difficulty of relaxing or switching off, the occurrence of jobs while off-duty which forced them to intervene. Nineteen per cent mentioned frustration with the promotion system.

Inadequate pay was, we have seen, cited by 27%. But, as argued above, this did not necessarily indicate a materialistic outlook. Rather the sense of grievance felt about levels of pay was usually in terms of its inadequacy as a measure of the importance or difficulty of the work done, especially in relation to other groups who were perceived as less deserving, but earned more.

There's a bloke across the road from me. He's a labourer at the yeast factory.

Well, he takes home round about seventy a week. A labourer mind! And he's thick, you know! (Uniform constable)

People say you should go where your bread and butter is. There's far easier and better ways of making money than the police force. You can't make money in the police. You're working for a fixed salary. If I'd known what I know now when I joined, I'd have gone into business. Because we're just hitting our heads against a brick wall. Particularly in the C.I.D. a lot of your service is involved with business firms, business people, and you see how easily they make money. I could name half a dozen people in this city who've had no education whatsoever, one that cannot even read or write, yet he's a millionaire. I remember saying to him 'Reg, if only I'd had an education'. And his answer straight away was 'That's where you're wrong. If I'd had an education I'd be a clerk on the Council!' And he's probably right. Knowing what I know now, I wouldn't join the police, it's stupidity. Take these licensees, I mean. They're doing more than our Chief Constable! (C.I.D. inspector)

Conditions of service were also frequently invoked as the reason for contemplating resignation. Twenty-one per cent singled out the burden of shift-work, and unpredictable hours caused by jobs coming up suddenly which required staying on, or unexpected court duties. Single men felt this a considerable inconvenience in social life or courting, married men saw it as putting great strain on domestic relations.

I thought of leaving, especially earlier in my service. I thought, 'Well, do I like shift work? No, I don't!' It causes upsets in the family. Everybody gets this problem. In fact, I don't mind saying, policemen are very high on the list for matrimonial problems, very high indeed. (C.I.D. sergeant)

Until such time as they can devise a system whereby crime stops at midnight on Friday, you'll never have satisfactory conditions. (Uniform constable)

The other frequently mentioned complaint about conditions was the lack of equipment and poor physical facilities at work. Seventeen per cent gave this as a reason for thinking about leaving. To many others, though, there was a certain pride to be taken in the ability to put up with rough physical circumstances and overcome them. It was part of the outdoor, 'man's life' which had initially attracted them. Nonetheless, for some it was a source of discontent, especially when it was seen as avoidable, rather than bound up with the job.

If you go out to T. Road, there's a toilet which was built in 1893. Putting it crudely, it must be the coldest crapper in the world, in the winter. If you got on to the public health people, they'd be there like a shot, and say 'These men cannot sit here!' (Uniform constable)

Police work was also seen as interfering with private life in a more direct way than the inconvenience caused by the hours and shift-system discussed above. Seventeen per cent mentioned this as a factor in thinking of leaving. Particularly resented was the way in which members of the public were seen as treating policemen badly in social relationships, as not accepting them readily as companions.

It's not the money that makes me want to leave. I don't know how the old blokes find it, but I didn't realise so many people dislike the police. It's an in-built complex they have. To give you an example, I spoke to a woman the other day when I was at a dance-hall. She saw my helmet on the back of my car. She said: 'Are you a copper?' So I said 'No, it's my dad's', because I could tell by her tone what she thought. And the bloke I was with – you see, it was two blokes and two girls, said 'Yes, he is a policeman'. She said: 'Stop the car', which I did and she got out. I thought Christ, you know. She must have had some grudge or other – maybe her last boy-friend was one. But it's a lot of people like that, so we tend to mix more with people at work. If I thought all the public didn't want us I'd leave the job straight away.   (Uniform constable)

Promotion frustrations were frequently mentioned (19%) as reasons for having considered leaving. The offer of another job acted as the trigger for their thinking of leaving to 11%.

The most frequently mentioned alternative job was sales representative (18%). Its appeal was that it could be more lucrative, and did not require paper qualifications, but an ability rapidly to assess social situations and handle them by verbal dexterity, which experience on the beat imparted. Setting up in business was considered by quite a few (12%). The attractions were the financial prospects, together with 'being one's own boss'. Becoming a licensee, which had the same attractions, was mentioned by 4%. Other jobs in which police related skills could be used were: private security work (4%); a police force abroad (4%); ambulance-man (2%); one of the armed forces (11%); probation work (4%); social work (3%); driving instructor (3%). Teaching was attractive to 12%, as a job with reasonable status and pay, and a clear social function. Other forms of white-collar work had been considered by 11%. Some who had a manual skill prior to entry thought of returning to it (9%). A miscellaneous variety of alternatives was mentioned by 7%, ranging from working on an oil-rig, to a 'good worthwhile job' of unspecified character.

Some men stayed on because they felt bound to the job despite dissatisfaction with it. The longer the service a policeman has already put in, the greater the odds against him leaving, in that he has a shorter time to go before he can claim his pension. Also the prospects of retraining for another career become more daunting. So the man is trapped by the combination of lack of outside alternatives with equal security, and the lure of retiring with a pension. At the same time, if he remains in the job which causes him dissatisfaction, and fails to be either transferred or promoted, his sense of grievance accumulates. This generates a pool of extreme malcontents only bound to the job by the 'cash nexus', and with multiplying resentments. During the 1960s and 1970s, premature wastage of policemen resigning before reaching their pensions was often pointed to as a, if not the, major manpower problem of the service. While more than half of those who left were still in their first two probationary years of service, it was recognised that 'the gravest problem was the resignation of policemen in mid-career' (Martin & Wilson 1969: 87). The present analysis of reasons for considering resignation among officers still serving is only an indirect guide to the motives of those who actually do leave. The factors causing discontent among those who contemplate leaving, but (so far) have not actually exercised that option, may well differ from those prompting resignation itself. But the above reasoning suggests that concentration on the manifest problem of actual wastage, important as this is, may deflect attention from the perhaps equally serious issue of the creation of a pool of highly discontented and unmotivated men, held to the job only by its security and the coldness of the outside world. Growing unemployment in the labour market can only exacerbate this situation.

Of those who had considered leaving 88% gave reasons for staying which reflected attachment by these sorts of extrinsic factors. Forty-six per cent spoke of the security of the force, and the prospect of the pension. Forty-two per cent mentioned the difficulties of finding a job outside without academic or other paper qualifications. This had deterred them from even applying for other jobs, or was blamed for their rejection for posts. Some had considered applying for various training courses, but had been deterred by the costs of this, both direct and the opportunity cost of forgone earnings (18% mentioned this). However, not all were held to the job by these instrumental considerations alone.

The other set of reasons for staying on, after having considered leaving, was the disappearance of the problem(s) causing dissatisfaction. This could be because of a personal resolution of the difficulty, through promotion or transfer to another division. Alternatively, or in addition, it could be because of a general change in the circumstances of the whole force. Most often cited here were a pay rise; the trend towards a relaxation of standards of discipline and the introduction of 'man-management' styles of supervision; and the switch to the Unit Beat system of policing, which gave the men a greater variety of work as well as the chance to work in cars, instead of on foot at the mercy of the elements. Some 41% gave their reason for staying as their own promotion or transfer. Another 18% mentioned one or more of the more general changes. Thus approximately half those who had considered leaving, stayed because of an improvement in the situation which was producing their grievance. But the others stayed solely because of the hold of the extrinsic factors of security and lack of alternatives. In other words, about a third had considered leaving, and had decided to stay, not because of the resolution of their grievances, but because of the instrumental disincentives to resignation.

No one type of factor seems outstandingly important in prompting thoughts of leaving. Pay and conditions of service, relationships with the authority structure (including promotion chances), and the intrinsic nature of the work itself were all mentioned with a considerable degree of frequency as factors leading to the idea of leaving. This contrasts with research on the sources of *actual* wastage. The Home Office survey on this discovered that pay was the major reason given by 40% of men who had resigned (Judge 1972: 40). As argued above, the attitudes of the men who actually do *resign* are unlikely to mirror those who only *consider* it, but remain in the force.

From a policy point of view the implication of the above analysis is the importance of ensuring that interest in the job is kept alive by the prospect of promotion or transfer. This also prevents the continuation of service for long periods under a supervisory officer who may be disliked. As has been shown, in many cases discontent which could have resulted in premature wastage was headed off by a timely transfer or promotion.

All the different attempts to examine job satisfaction which have been made in this section, seem to pinpoint a section of acutely dissatisfied men which is about a third of the force. This is the proportion suggested by the fact that 32% have seriously thought of leaving and are held only by the cash nexus, 38% would not join the police again if starting their careers now, and 29% would actively discourage their children from joining.

Some further insight into the sources of satisfaction may be gained by examining the way the sample as a whole (as opposed to just those who had thought of leaving) evaluated certain aspects of the work. This is shown in Table 10.2, together with the proportions rating each as the most important aspect of a job.

Police work is rated as more interesting and varied than most occupations by an overwhelming majority, and over half also rate this the most important aspect of a job. A further third rate it the second most important aspect. This would account for the general satisfaction that was revealed in the previous part of this section. There also seems to be considerable feeling that one's workmates were more congenial than would be the case in outside work, though this is not seen as such an important aspect of a job. Pay is ranked as most important by 30% (and second by another third). The prevailing view (of nearly three-quarters) is that pay is only quite good by outside standards, and only a small minority are either very satisfied or dissatisfied with it. The conclusion must be that while most men feel they would like, and indeed deserve, more pay, this was not (at the time of interviewing) an acute source of discontent for most. A minority did view pay as most important and also very or quite unsatisfactory. As has been seen, this figured in considerations of leaving, and most importantly in actual resignations. No other aspect of work was rated as of equal importance to pay and interest by anything but a small minority. More than half felt that police work gave more of a sense of performing a public service than most jobs, but there was some degree of cynicism about this among the rest. Only a small number saw working conditions as pleasant in the police, and nearly a third viewed them as actively unpleasant by general standards. This does not seem to have been of much salience, and it has already been suggested that it might have been a source of pride to many. There seems to be a split concerning the degree of autonomy from close supervision. Forty-four per cent see the police as very good in this respect compared to most jobs, but 48% see it as less so, 7% seeing it as bad. The question of supervision will be more fully explored in the next section when it will be argued that there is variation over time in general standards, as well as within the force at any one moment. There is also a contrast between the degree of supervision inside the station and in the outside work situation. Altogether, the table would seem to confirm that the sources of what discontent exists are pay, conditions of service, problems with supervisors and doubts about the meaning or purpose of some of the work. Overall though, there was a fair degree of satisfaction with the work, based on the interest, variety and sense of social belonging it provided.

TABLE 10.2. *Rating of various aspects of police work*

	Comparison with other jobs				
	Very good %	Quite good %	Not good at all %	Total %	Proportion rating this as most important aspect of a job %
Interest and variety	86	10	3	100	53
Pay	14	73	11	100	30
Good workmates	74	23	1	100	1
Sense of performing public service	58	27	13	100	13
Pleasant work conditions	12	55	32	100	2
A supervisor who doesn't breathe down your neck	44	48	7	100	1
			N = 168	Total = 100	

This sense of satisfaction helps to account for the general rejection of the idea of union representation which was earlier identified, as well as what support there was for it. Most men seemed relatively satisfied with the job, and hence did not feel a need for stronger representation. Among those who were less satisfied, there was more support for having a stronger representative body, as Table 10.3 shows.

This relationship between job dissatisfaction and desire for a union remains as strong when rank is held constant.

It holds for other items of 'unionateness' too. For example, 52% of constables who would *not* rejoin support the right to work to rule, while only 36% of those who *would* rejoin do so. It also holds for other indices of dissatisfaction with the job. For example, of those who have never thought of leaving, only 27% want the Federation to be more like a union. But of those who have thought of it, though not seriously, 40% do. Of those who have seriously considered resigning at some point, 48% support the idea of a union.

TABLE 10.3. *Job dissatisfaction and support for trade unionism*

		Would you join again if you had your life over?		
		Yes	No	Don't know
		%	%	%
Would you want the	Yes	29	50	32
Federation to be more like	No	64	45	68
a trade union?	Don't know	7	5	—
	Total	100	100	100
		N = 85	N = 64	N = 19

Job dissatisfaction thus clearly seems related to the desire for a union. However, it is evidently neither a necessary nor a sufficient condition of it. Some who are dissatisfied do not wish to have a union. This is because they see unionism as either a morally illegitimate and/or a practically inappropriate way of coping with their dissatisfaction. On the other hand, some who are satisfied with their job *do* want a union. As shown in the chapter on the Federation activists, in some cases a commitment to unionism as a general principle exists prior to experience of the job itself. To others, unionism may seem a way of improving certain aspects of the job, e.g. pay, even though the situation as a whole is favourably evaluated. But in general there was a relationship between job dissatisfaction and desire for a union.

Relationships between the ranks

The image policemen have of the social organisation in which they are employed is an important element of their orientation to work, and helps in understanding the character of their unionism. The present section explores this image, and how it varied within the service and over time. Capturing such imagery is extremely difficult. Some previous studies of workers have asked questions intended to tap it directly, such as the frequently used 'football team' analogy (e.g. Goldthorpe *et al.* 1968: 73–5. For a general critique of the 'teamwork' question, see Ramsay 1975: 396–9).

Attempting to tap so subtle and elusive a notion directly, presupposes what is problematic, namely whether the workers had a clear view of this image at all. An 'image' of the organisation is a construct imposed on a variety of situations and relationships, which may be experienced differently. It is a synthesising notion, asking what is the overall view, given that different ranks and other positions within the organisation share interests in some respects, and are in conflict over other issues. It is not a simple addition of points of shared or conflicting interests, as some areas may be perceived as more important than others, and people may differ on the degree of importance of various issues. Groups are subject to complex processes of 'fission' and 'fusion' in terms of where shared interests lie, according to the particular context of discussion. A direct question may penetrate this web of overlapping interests at various points, and the meaning of any response is not clear.

It was, therefore, my intention to consider only the more limited question of how the men viewed the supervision they received and the discipline to which they were subjected. However, as already discussed in chapter 5, it turned out that the responses to the question whether the police should be represented by a single association, reflected assessments of the nature of interest groupings in the force. Using the responses to this question as a means of estimating perceptions of the relationship between the ranks avoids some of the strictures levelled at more direct questions like the football team one. It was not *presupposed* that the men had a clearcut image of the social organisation of the force. This only emerged from the reasoning used in relation to the question of representation.

The direct question leaves ambiguous the level of analysis the person is using. Is he talking about economic interdependence, or the degree of co-operation in the work process, or the extent of harmony in face-to-face supervisory contacts? The single association question does not involve this ambiguity. It indicates whether the men feel that the degree of similarity, as opposed to conflict, of interest between ranks allows or precludes joint representation, when balanced out according to the individual's priorities. As was shown earlier, opinion roughly divided on this. Forty-four per cent suggest that the degree of consensus made it desirable to have a single representative body, 43% felt the elements of conflict were too great, while 13% didn't know. The ranks varied on this, with 38% of constables, 45% of sergeants but 70% of inspectors putting the 'consensus' view.

These generalised images of the police force as a work organisation are extrapolated by the men from their experience of interaction with other

ranks. In order to understand them, it is necessary to consider how policemen regarded the supervision and discipline they received. The quasi-
military character of the police force, with its elements of drill, uniform
and a strict hierarchy of ranks might be expected to generate some feelings
of resentment at the degree of discipline. In fact, although views varied,
there was no general feeling that the discipline was irksome. This is
conducive to a consensual image of the police force.

The men were asked to evaluate the present state of supervision.
Thirty-five per cent felt present standards were satisfactory. Thirty-one
per cent felt there was too little discipline. Only 11% thought there was
too much. Twenty-four per cent felt variation between individual supervisors and different situations was too great for any overall assessment to
have much meaning. It certainly seems that only a small minority felt
there was too strict supervision or discipline. Most viewed it as acceptable,
or if not, their criticism was of excessive laxity.

The ranks varied in their assessment of supervision and discipline. The
proportions viewing it as satisfactory were much the same in each rank.
But more constables than supervisors felt that there was too much discipline. Supervisors, especially sergeants, were more likely to criticise it as
inadequate, as Table 10.4 shows.

TABLE 10.4. *Rank and evaluation of the system of supervision*

	Constables %	Sergeants %	Inspectors %
Discipline too little	23	52	35
Discipline too much	16	3	4
Discipline satisfactory now	34	36	39
Discipline varies	27	9	22
Total	100	100	100
	N = 112	N = 33	N = 23

Which division men were in affected their views, although there was no
difference between specialist and non-specialist ones as a whole. The
C.I.D. were the most likely to see standards of discipline as deficient.
Fifty-eight per cent thought there was *too little* discipline, and only 21%
thought the present level was satisfactory. (This was true even among
C.I.D. constables. Forty-five per cent felt there was too little discipline.)
The other division to stand out was the city centre one, which had the
highest proportion seeing discipline as *excessive*. Twenty-four per cent of
them felt this, as compared with only 11% of all uniformed constables.

(This was mainly because this area was still policed on the old foot patrol system.) There was much talk about younger recruits being more recalcitrant to discipline than older generations. There was no evidence to support this. Seventeen per cent of constables in their twenties felt there was too much discipline, but so did 13% of older ones. (It might, of course, be the case that the discipline present recruits experience is less strict than for previous cohorts, and that the younger men would resent past standards.)

The belief that standards of discipline had become less strict, especially in the last decade, was supported by 88%. (Nobody disagreed; the rest were young in service and felt they had not been in long enough to perceive a change.) Sixty-three per cent approved of the relaxation of discipline, but 37% defined it as a deterioration of standards. Sergeants were the most likely to feel the change had been for the worse (59%), constables least likely to (29%), with inspectors in between (38%).

The change in supervision and discipline was experienced and explained in several ways. The police are subject to a Discipline Code of formidable length and complexity, and are often referred to as a 'disciplined service'. (See *A Handbook of Police Discipline*, Police Federation 1965.) There has been little change in the content of this code in recent years. The changes in complaints procedure introduced by the Police Act 1964 increased the chances of a policeman having to face disciplinary proceedings. In what way, then, has discipline declined?

A distinction must be made between supervision and discipline in the course of police work outside the station, relationships between ranks inside the station, and controls over out-of-work life. In each of these areas it was felt that supervision and discipline had relaxed. The change was attributed to various intertwined factors, the relative importance of which was hard to evaluate. After 1968 most city forces had begun to introduce the Unit Beat system of policing instead of the older Fixed Points system. This involved a changed relationship between ranks. Since the mid-60s the Home Office had encouraged new styles of 'man-management' in police forces, and supervisors were increasingly trained in 'human relations' skills. It was felt that general attitudes to discipline were changing. Younger supervisors and recruits reflected these new values and imported them into the force. These changes influenced not only the extent of control over work, but also the formal and informal social organisation within which it was carried out, modifying somewhat its quasi-militaristic character.

A parodoxical contrast has always existed between the relative autonomy of the policeman in the work situation, and the quasi-militaristic character of formal police organisation, with its uniform, retention of military titles, drill, parading and strict sartorial standards. This has been accompanied by continuous debate about the appropriateness of the military analogy, with the Federation in particular rejecting its validity. But some elements have remained, backed up by various arguments. Precisely because of the low visibility of the policeman outside on the job, coupled with the power and responsibility he held, it was believed necessary to inculcate in him 'self-discipline' through the trappings of militaristic organisation. Some types of police work, notably crowd-control, involve large numbers of men in situations requiring disciplined co-ordination. It is often argued the police perform their function of maintaining order in society partly by example. The appearance of an orderly, disciplined body is held to be crucial to their role as exemplars. Whatever the validity of these arguments, they are certainly widely accepted by the men, especially the older ones. It may be that many policemen feel an intrinsic attraction to militaristic organisation, an idea supported by the numbers who cite a liking for a uniformed, disciplined service as a reason for joining. Certainly many paid testimony to their belief in the value of discipline, both outside and inside the force.

Anything that's disciplined is far more efficient. If you don't have discipline everything begins to get a bit ragged and lax. I'm all for the parade, yeah, left, right, left, right, quick march and all the rest of it. It gives you that confidence to deal with things, you got a purpose in life. Nothing's allowed to get shoddy or ragged. Take a person who's got dirty shoes, hasn't shaved, clothes never seen an iron or a press – that's the sort of job you'll get from him! A person with a smart appearance smacks of efficiency from the start.   (Uniform constable)

The men have to be made to appreciate that everything revolves around them, around law and order. If they're not prepared to discipline themselves, how can they discipline people outside. After all, life is really a set of rules, and rules are discipline. If we don't comply with the normal set of rules of life, we've got anarchy, people going hither and thither shouting 'We've got this right and that right!' We've got to work together as a group under one head. If we all go different ways how can we be governed, how can there be any order, how can anyone walk abroad? The policeman is the person who has to encourage people to comply with a normal set of rules by his example.   (Uniform inspector)

Many previous studies have argued that the nature of police work limits the ability of supervisors to control the actions and decisions of subordinates. 'The police department has the special property. . .that within it discretion increases as one moves *down* the hierarchy' (Wilson 1968: 7). Working out on the streets, the constable usually has considerable discretion about how to act, and his decisions are only subject to review after the event if the consequences become problematic, for instance through a citizen complaint. Throughout the development of police forces, administrators have devised a variety of systems of organisation to maintain some degree of control. But the formal rules of supervision are filtered through the patrolman's culture, and the actual operative procedures are the result of this set of informal understandings, which the wise supervisor shares (Rubinstein 1973).

Since 1968 most British city forces have moved over to the Unit Beat system of policing. Under the earlier Fixed Point system, the constable had been allocated a certain area to cover by foot patrol. He walked around this beat in a given direction, checking properties, dealing with incidents that might crop up, and, hopefully, deterring the would-be wrong-doer by his presence. In addition, emergencies and 999s were dealt with by mobile units from the traffic division, under the direction of the Information Room. A sergeant tried to maintain some element of control over the three or four men in his section by designating certain fixed points on each constable's beat, at which he would meet him at a particular time. Briefings took place at a formal parade and inspection was held a quarter of an hour before the start of the tour. A rather rigid (although it worked out more flexibly in practice) and para-militaristic set of rules was thus superimposed on the autonomy the constable had in the work situation itself. As Cain (1973) has shown, there were patterned evasions of these rules, which she called 'easing behaviour'. Nonetheless there was a rather tight system of constraints on the subordinate, within which he had to operate.

The Unit Beat system involved both a set of technological developments and a social reorganisation of the work. Among other benefits it was supposed to bring, such as a speedier response to calls, it was also seen as giving policemen a greater degree of responsibility and autonomy, and hence, it was hoped, it would raise morale. Divisions were sub-divided into Unit Beats, which were covered by a team who would co-operate in the exercise of their duties. Patrol was by the now familiar panda driver who, in addition to driving around seeking incidents, was in contact with the station via his personal radio, so that he could speedily be dispatched to calls on his beat. To maintain personal contact with the public, an Area Constable was also allocated to the beat, who if he did not live on it, was at least expected to do his daily shift of work there, getting to know the people and picking up relevant knowledge about the area. He was allowed a considerable degree of flexibility in determining exactly where and when he would work his eight hours. Despite the role of the area man, the complaint has frequently been heard that the Unit Beat system has resulted in a loss of contact with the public. When the fuel crisis resulted in many forces abandoning, or at any rate considerably modifying, the Unit Beat system, 'restoring contact with the public' provided a rationale that sounded less calculative. The third member of the Unit Beat team was the collator, a constable whose job it was to assemble all information about the area into a systematic body of knowledge for future policing. Each sub-division was also covered by a sergeant, who would drive round ready to help out or take the lead where needed.

The change re-arranged the formal roles of different ranks, and hence the limits within which actual behaviour developed. The sergeant in effect became one of the team of active policemen, and would often attend incidents himself, instead of having a primary role of control and supervision. The tour of duty of the patrol constable became less structured, due to the abandonment of fixed points. But he was under continuous supervision by the radio-controller, a fellow constable, who could send him to calls at any time, check up where he was or ask for information. In theory, this put the constable in a more tightly constrained situation. In practice, various strategies could be adopted by the constable to avoid calls on the radio if he wished. In most areas there were certain 'blind-spots', where it was known reception was impaired, so the driver could claim he had been there when called. Or he could claim he had left his car to deal with something, or that his set was damaged. Nonetheless, there are clearly limits to the extent such devices could be used, and as Cain and others have shown, constables (apart from the minority of disgruntled 'uniform-carriers') do not adopt easing behaviours at the expense of what they regard as 'real' police work. The Unit Beat system has placed a greater work-load on the motorised constable, in that he is inevitably dispatched to many more incidents than would come his way on foot. As many pointed out, he is now more likely to arrive in the *middle* of an incident. When sent on foot or push-bike, he would often have arrived after things had quietened down. Control by the highly structured system of fixed points has been replaced by the more continuously present radio contact. The new system, together with changes in values (and the generally lower age of supervisors), has modified the nature of relationships with sergeants. The latter have become less controllers than part of a team. Most supervisors tolerated certain forms of easing behaviour, such as unofficial tea-breaks at the station, as long as these remained within limits defined by the shared values of the group. The supervisor who did not respect these conventions was usually brought into line by some means. As one constable said: 'We're the inspectors' graveyard. You have some inspectors, the blokes talk about him – "cor, swine!" They send him over here. Give 'em six months, he's completely changed. Because people take no notice of him. When they come down to it, they're nothing, you know.'

The others in the system were also subject to less structured control. The area man in particular had considerable autonomy, even over his time of work. He was meant to be evaluated largely by the quality of information with which he provided the collator. Some area men complained that, in practice, the proper role of maintaining close relations with the public on their patch was hindered by their being given tasks which were not really part of their duties (such as delivering summonses), but which fell on them because of manpower shortages. A frequent complaint was that the Unit Beat system had never been put into practice properly because of manpower problems.

At the same time as the introduction of Unit Beat policing, there was increasing emphasis on training supervisors in 'man-management' skills, discouraging the previous degree of drill and discipline. There is some cynicism about the change actually brought about in hard-line old-timers by a lecture or two extolling the virtues of democratic leadership. A cartoon in the Federation magazine some years ago depicted the saga of a grumpy old sergeant, pictured as walking roughshod over his constables with a grim look on his face. The crusty tyrant was then sent on a 'man-management' course and returned to continue trampling all over his men, but with a benign countenance! Any changes are not attributed to overnight conversions on the part of existing supervisors. Rather they are explained by the increasing number of young supervisors as promotion patterns have changed. These have from the start been trained in the new skills, and they reflect the less disciplined outlook of the younger generation. Recent generations of recruits are said to be more recalcitrant to the old rules and changes have had to take place, especially because of manpower shortages. Various aspects of the old militaristic style have been modified. Parading has been abandoned, or become more informal. (It is anyway less important as a source of information dissemination, given the personal radios.) Restrictions on appearance, such as rules about hair-length and facial hair, have been relaxed to some extent (probably not enough in the eyes of the younger men who wish not to be excluded from civilian peer-groups, but to the great dismay of many of their older colleagues).

The typical view is that the changes have brought about a welcome toning down of discipline to a more acceptable level.

It's changed a lot. When I joined we were treated almost like idiots, as if we had no sense, but now we're treated more like men. As an individual, I've not really been controlled by a sergeant at all in the last four to five years. I have a section sergeant, he exists, he's there, but I've been left to get on with it as an individual, doing the panda driver's job. This doesn't always apply to other shifts or divisions. One sergeant's very unpopular with his shift because he won't let them have the tea-break, strictly unofficial, the others tolerate. But it's a poor policeman that can't get a cup of tea on the streets! The supervisor's always available if necessary, and for the most part they attend emergency calls. With the exception of one sergeant who doesn't usually bother! But the sergeant knows if he exercises too much control, he visits his men too often, they begin to think 'Doesn't he trust me? Doesn't he think I can do the job? Does he think he needs to hold my hand?' He probably has to for probationers, because now we're 90% mobile, how the hell does the probationer learn the job? But he's not really in a position to exercise any control over the P.C. when he's sent out on patrol. No-one is these days. This personal radio system is a lovely advantage. If we want help we can get it immediately. And the public benefits because they have a response to their 999 calls within two or three minutes, subject to the work load. But it's not perfect by any stretch of the imagination. There are vast numbers of black spots where you can't get a message in or out. If you have a piece of apparatus that's not 100% effective, there's always the man who'll take advantage, fail to receive a message – in other words, he ignores it. Because he knows nobody can prove he got the message, unless there's somebody stood on his shoulder. So to that extent supervision has fallen down. Most of the time we play fair, we answer. Not for any high-minded reasons, but we just do. But obviously there are blokes who don't come to work to do any, but just for the ride. This applies in any industry. Some of them shove off a bit quick, without a radio, because there's not enough to go round. I'm not saying they're committing crime or going into people's houses, shagging the missus, or any of this nonsense. Just they may be disinterested or lazy, can't be bothered. If a nasty job comes up, a sudden death, and it's a bit pooey, he says 'Oh, I don't fancy that, I shan't hear it'. He points his car in the appropriate direction, and goes deaf! If the sergeant happens to see him three minutes later, he can pull the batteries out of the bloomin' thing and say he was just checking it. I know it's done, and to this extent supervision's impossible.

(Uniform constable)

These changes were deplored by a minority, largely older constables, sergeants, and in particular, detectives. The C.I.D. constable has always had a considerable degree of autonomy in working on his case-load. Relationships with supervisors in the C.I.D. have always been less formal, with less control over appearance. The C.I.D. men do not gain by the more relaxed supervisory styles of the uniform branch, and tend to look askance at a generation of men who do not have to experience the same rigours as they did. Possibly, also, they are drawn from a self-selected group of men with disciplinarian attitudes. One third of the total (and a majority of the C.I.D.) condemned the relaxation of discipline.

In a body like the police you must have discipline. One should show other people through example. Take the subject of hair. Now mine is long compared with when I joined, when we used to call it the 'crop-cut'. It's alright for you, because you don't have to wear a hat. Provided it's neat and tidy, that's all right. But I've seen policemen who look ridiculous. I saw one, who shall be nameless, the other day...I thought it was Coco the Clown! Little bonnet perched on top of his head, and his hair was sticking out like this...I was with my mother-in-law, and she almost collapsed on the floor laughing – my father-in-law had been a policeman for thirty-one years. The C.I.D. have their hair longer, but that makes no difference, because the only time people know *they're* policemen is when they're nicked, and then that's it. There used to be some respect. You'd call a sergeant 'sergeant' even if you thought he was a B.F. But now you hear the young blokes in the games room, and it's all first names. A bloke might be given a job to do and he says 'Balls! Get stuffed!' Well, that's a bit naughty. In the old days they'd have made his life a misery!   (Uniform constable)

A few of the younger men felt that whatever changes there might have been, discipline remained too tight, allowing them little initiative and demeaning their self-respect. This attitude was especially found in the central city area where the Unit Beat system had not been introduced. There were still interferences with a policeman's private life which rankled with the younger men. Partly these were indirect consequences of the work, such as restrictions on sartorial styles, partly the direct effect of the

Discipline Code, with its expectations of policemen adhering to a strict moral code.

The discipline could do with relaxing a bit. Things like hair-cuts! I wouldn't like shoulder-length hair, but I'd like it longer than mine. The older blokes say 'Ah! If you were here back in 1920!' Things may have relaxed since then, but for 1973, I don't think it's terribly good. A couple of blokes here have their hair too long, so they're sort of kept off the streets. They've just sacked a probationer too. As a probationer, you can't afford to upset anyone till your two years are in. I'd like longer hair. When you go out you find people always know you're in the army or the police. Obviously it'll change in time, but time's no good when you're young, is it? When I'm forty I won't bloody want it any longer. For instance, if you have an affair, which a lot of people do nowadays, I mean it's not bad, is it? In this job you can't have any public aspersions cast on you whatsoever. If it became public that you were having it off with somebody else's wife or something, you'd rise no farther. I don't see why they make a big fuss personally. I don't suppose they will in years to come. Perhaps the women might still feel it a bit.   (Uniform constable)

The fact that *most* of the men accept the legitimacy of the authority structure, and that criticism is more likely to be on the grounds of the inadequacy of the present standard of discipline rather than its excessiveness, helps us understand the general rejection of the idea that policemen should be represented by a more unionate body. The men do not, on the whole, see their supervisors as another side against whom they need stronger weapons. The movement away from an older, more harsh and rigid standard towards a more acceptable one, bolsters the view that the present supervision system is legitimate, and that modification can occur without stronger representative powers. The link between acceptance of the discipline system and rejection of unionism, is supported by Table 10.5.

TABLE 10.5. *Evaluation of the discipline system and support for unionism*

		Evaluation of discipline			
		Too much %	Too little %	All right %	Varies %
The Federation should	Yes	56	37	28	43
be more like a union	No	44	60	64	50
	Total	100	100	100	100
		N = 18	N = 52	N = 58	N = 40

Table 10.5 shows that over half of those who felt the discipline is too much supported the Federation being more like an ordinary trade union. On the other hand, nearly two-thirds of those who felt the level of discipline was either satisfactory, or too low, rejected unionism. (Those who

saw discipline as varying between individuals and situations were almost evenly split.) This suggests that those who see discipline as oppressive are likely to see unionism as a desirable defence. Among those who see discipline as variable, more visualise the need for unionism in some situations than among those who see the existing structure as satisfactory, or would like it to be even tighter. The generally accepted legitimacy of the system of discipline and supervision partly explains the tendency to reject unionism.

Personal aspirations and the promotion system

Every young policeman carries a chief constable's baton in his truncheon pocket. Indeed, the phrase is much more accurate than the old canard about field marshals, for the service has nothing to compare with the military in the way of direct entry to officer rank. Every recruit, at least in theory and regulation, starts off on the same footing.   (Judge 1972: 164)

Realistic chances of promotion are less than this statement, and a lot of recruitment advertising, imply. In the force studied there were nearly five times as many constables as sergeants, and over eleven times as many constables as inspectors. We have already seen that certain background characteristics indicate a better chance of success in the promotion stakes.

The system of promotion involves essentially two components. First, a necessary but not sufficient condition of promotion from constable to sergeant, and from sergeant to inspector, is passing a written examination. Second, a number of those who have passed the qualifying examination will be selected by paper-sift to be interviewed by a promotion board, where the final choice is made. During the 1960s certain changes were introduced in promotion procedure, with the net effect of increasing the pool of contenders and accelerating the pace of mobility. Since 1967 the written examination has only been in police subjects, whereas before that it included a general educational component. This has increased the number of successful candidates. The regulations have been changed to allow exams to be taken earlier, and hence increase the speed with which promotion can occur. The old regulations did not allow a constable to sit the exam for promotion to sergeant until after four years' service. It is now possible to take the exam after two years' service, and be eligible for promotion to sergeant after three. It is just possible to be promoted to inspector after only four years' service, though only an infinitesimal proportion are such 'high-flyers'. Nonetheless there is an increasing number of very young inspectors, in their twenties or early thirties, mainly the products of the special course at Bramshill. The pace of promotion has dramatically altered since a decade ago, when experience and seniority seemed necessary conditions, and a man would be doing well to reach sergeant rank inside ten years.

A 'middle generation', who were qualified and awaiting promotion under the old system, have lost out. They are now undercut by an increasing number of other qualified competitors, and a shift away from the tried and experienced man, towards those showing 'leadership potential' through academic ability. Because the criteria for promotion are not straightforwardly standardised, there is ample scope for the disappointed to see the system as unjust.

There was considerable interest in promotion, but a more realistic perception of the actual prospects. Well over half in each rank were interested in being promoted, although only just under a third actually expected to be. Table 10.6 shows the proportions of constables and sergeants qualified for promotion.

Fifty-two per cent of constables and 58% of sergeants are still potential competitors for promotion, in that they have already passed the exam, or at least have future plans to take it again or for the first time. Forty-six per cent and 41% of constables and sergeants respectively have withdrawn from the competition, either because they have failed the exam and are not planning to resit, or because they have never taken it and do not plan to. Declared interest in promotion is shown in Table 10.7.

TABLE 10.6. *Rank and promotion examination performance*

		Constables %	Sergeants %
(a)	Passed relevant exam	19	33
(b)	Failed, will resit	16	6
(c)	Failed, won't resit	31	19
(d)	Never taken, no plans to	16	22
(e)	About to take for first time	17	19
	Total	100	100
		N = 112	N = 33

TABLE 10.7. *Rank and promotion aspirations*

		Constables %	Sergeants %	Inspectors %
Are you interested in	Yes	55	61	91
(further) promotion?	No	43	39	9
	Total	100	100	100
		N = 112	N = 33	N = 23

Almost all inspectors, and over half the constables and sergeants declared an interest in further promotion. The smaller proportion of constables and sergeants stating an ambition for promotion is partly explicable by the fact that nearly half of these ranks are neither qualified nor preparing to become so. All inspectors are potentially eligible for promotion without further examination. It may also be that experience of promotion to inspector raised expectations of further success, and that men who are promoted that far were more ambitious to begin with.

Expectations are more realistic than these aspirations. Table 10.8 shows the proportions in each rank who said they actually expected to be promoted, together with the approximate proportion that were likely to be, given the rank structure.

TABLE 10.8. *Promotion expectations and chances, by rank*

		Constables %	Sergeants %	Inspectors %
Expecting promotion		27	33	30
Not expecting promotion		60	24	26
Don't know		13	43	44
	Total	100	100	100
Approximate chance of promotion		20	44	25
		N = 112	N = 33	N = 23

Expectations did not seem wildly unrealistic. Not many more constables and inspectors anticipated they would be promoted than the proportion who were likely to be (calculated roughly by the ratio of all officers in higher ranks to the number in that rank). A smaller proportion of sergeants expect promotion than actually had a chance. In each rank, a fair proportion say they do not know what their personal chances are. This seems reasonable in the absence of concrete knowledge of what governs the selection procedure in practice.

It is inherently difficult to ascertain the extent to which a man's acceptance of his rank is 'genuine', and how far it involves a scaling down of ambition to protect his ego from a sense of failure. A longitudinal study of whether or not aspirations were altered in the face of lack of achievement would help illuminate this. As it stands, there is the possibility that a declaration of lack of interest in promotion may mask various levels of deception, either of the researcher or of oneself. While promotion brings more money, formal status and power, there may be genuine reasons for not pursuing it. Some may prefer 'real' police work at constable level to the more supervisory or administrative responsibilities of higher ranks. There may be a wish to retain the *camaraderie* of being one of the lads. Some men may attach more value to family life than the grind of studying for exams. Whatever the degree of rationalisation on the part of those who declare themselves uninterested in further promotion, the disparity between aspirations and expectations reveals a significant extent of explicitly perceived frustration with lack of opportunity. This is further supported by assessments of the legitimacy of the promotion system.

The men were asked to give their opinions as to what governed promotion, apart from the exam. Clearly, their views were not necessarily a valid account of what *does* account for promotion. But they give a useful insight into whether the men perceived the system as legitimate, and how they explained success or failure. These accounts could be classified into those defining the system as 'just', based on assessments of ability and merit, and those which saw it as 'unjust', influenced by social status, connections, outside groups (the Freemasons were often mentioned here), luck or victimisation. (Promotion could also be attributed to a 'mixture' of just and unjust criteria.) Assessment of the system's justice was related to aspirations and expectations, as Table 10.9 shows.

TABLE 10.9. *Promotion aspiartions, expectations and evaluation of the system*

Are you interested in promotion?		No		Yes	
Do you expect to be promoted?		No	Yes	No	Yes
		%	%	%	%
	Just	9	—	7	55
Factors governing promotion	Unjust	60	(2)	64	—
(*as seen by the men*)	Mixed	20	—	23	30
	Don't know	11	—	7	15
	Total	100	—	100	100
		N = 35	N = 2	N = 44	N = 47

Of those who did not expect to be promoted, nearly two-thirds saw the system as entirely unjust, a further one-fifth saw it as partially so, and less than a tenth saw it as wholly just. There was a slight tendency for more men to see the system as unjust if they were interested in promotion but felt they would not succeed, than if they did not have such aspirations. But this difference was not significant. Of those who both wanted and expected to be promoted, more than half saw the process as totally just, and none saw it as completely unjust. The mechanism underlying this relationship is not clear. It could be that those who come to feel they have no chance of promotion are induced to see the procedure as illegitimate, or that an initial perception of the system as unjust causes opting out, or other factors underlying both failure and definition of the promotion system, or a mixture of these processes. Only a longitudinal study could sort out the relationships more fully. Some support for the interpretation that it is failure which generates a more cynical view of the opportunity structure is given by Table 10.10, which shows the relationship between length of service and assessment of the fairness of the promotion system. While the longer serving men tend to be more cynical in their views, we cannot firmly conclude anything about the causal process involved from such a cross-sectional comparison.

TABLE 10.10. *Length of service and assessment of the promotion system*

		Less than 10 years service %	10–20 years %	More than 20 years service %
Factors governing	Just	50	31	30
promotion (as seen by	Unjust	23	33	37
the men)	Mixed	13	28	26
	Don't know	12	8	7
	Total	100	100	100
		N = 40	N = 72	N = 56

Table 10.10 is compatible with the view that failure to be promoted in line with one's ambitions is a source of cynicism about the justice of the system. This is also supported by the fact that the higher ranks were less likely to be cynical about the system than constables. Forty per cent of constables, but only 15% and 17% of sergeants and inspectors respectively saw the system as totally unjust. The older constables are the most likely to see the promotion process as unjust. Only 25% of constables but 52% and 57% of sergeants and inspectors respectively regarded it as completely fair. The reasons offered to support the judgement of the 35% who regarded the system as completely 'just' were rather stereotyped accounts. The fact that all started off formally equal was often referred to.

The police is different from other jobs in the respect that everybody starts off as a constable. It's not a case that if someone talks with the right accent he's in, it doesn't work here. Background is of secondary importance. What gets a bloke planted in this job, as long as he's not obviously externally sort of dumbish, is how well he does the job. I don't mean just bringing in prisoners, but the whole job. (Uniform constable)

Those who mentioned 'unjust' reasons, either totally (32%) or in part (24%) gave less stereotyped responses. The main factors that were mentioned were: background, social graces, nepotism, the influence of the 'Freemasons' or 'lodges', victimisation of 'bolshie' Federationists, promotion of 'yes-men', overemphasis on academic qualifications as contrasted with ability as a 'practical' policeman, and pure luck, 'being at the right place at the right time'.

The most common of these 'unjust' factors was the charge that social connections counted for more than ability (specifically mentioned by 40%). There were various permutations of the idea that what was important was 'not what you know, but who you know'.

It's knowing someone in the job. You find that if say the chief superintendent's son joins, they push him into different jobs so he gets experience. One P.C., whose father was a chief superintendent seemed to get commendations right, left and centre for things nobody else would get commended for. If you've got somebody in the hierarchy they can help a lot to push you through. You can usually see those that are destined. One chap had been to Clifton College and was a doctor of music. The inspector would say how wonderful it was to have a chap like him, with his background. So when there were reports he'd write them out for him to copy and they looked perfect. But you find a chap say from the country, he may be a better policeman but he's just left to soldier on on his own. This chap who'd been to college was helped in every direction. He left eventually – it was women trouble with him. He tried a bit of this wife-swapping, and he was discreetly pushed out, advised to leave. (Traffic constable)

A specific example of the importance of connections was the alleged influence of the Freemasons on promotions. It was clear from many conversations that the idea that Freemasons or similar 'secret societies' dominated the force was a common part of police folk-lore. Twenty-eight per cent singled this out as a determinant of promotion.

When they advertise for policemen, they say 'Opportunity for promotion, or to specialise'. They should put three paragraphs underneath it, as follows, (a) Your face fits in all ways. In other words you never say 'no' or disagree with anything. (b) The right background. (c) The fact that you have to be a mason. People say it doesn't go on. But my father-in-law's a mason, and the chappie who lives next door is a mason. They keep on at me: 'Come on join... You'll be all right.' There was this chap who was leaving, because he was fed up. He said it was rotten from top to bottom from the point of view of masons. So he decided to leave, and he went to be interviewed by the editor of the *Evening Post*. He told them all the truth, that he felt the police force was run from the place at the bottom of P. Street, and he said 'I don't mean the Council House!' You know what he meant...The biggest Lodge in town is there! We all knew he said this, but it wasn't printed. You see, the editor is himself one of the top boys of them! I've been in the Royal Hotel sometimes when they have these do's. You can see them come out – lines upon lines of C.I.D. and uniform officers. I've been up for promotion or selection for C.I.D. My name never even appeared on the interview list. I was narked about this, as I'd been working so hard. And when I saw that three masons were in the first five, I was just sick. So I resigned myself – I would just be a uniform carrier.   (Uniform constable)

Nineteen per cent claimed that men who were recalcitrant to authority, like militant Federationists, were held back in promotion. One had to be a 'yes-man' to get on. We noted earlier that 30% of the force believed being a Federationist was a barrier in a career, and many more felt that this had been a problem in the past (as noted there, a cynical 10% thought that 'bolshie' Federationists were promoted out of the way. They were also aided by the general principle that it was good to have your name known, even if, as one man put it, it's for 'being in the fertiliser!').

They may butter somebody up by promoting him to sergeant, thinking it's going to sweeten him. But if he carries on the same way, there's no doubt about it, he'll not get any further. It's bound to affect your promotion chances. What goes down on your little file down town nobody ever sees. They may say 'Good old Harry, old so-and-so's on the Federation, good bloke.' But that's as far as it goes. There's one chap who's in this force who's an inspector, extremely capable. If he hadn't been on the Federation he'd be a superintendent by now, as regards capability. But he defends most of the cases when policemen are upon the sheet. So this ruins his chances completely. I've no doubt about it, because he's very, very capable on the streets *and* on paper, which doesn't often work out.
(Uniform constable)

Twenty-eight per cent complained that promotion was now governed too much by academic qualifications. It favoured people who were good at paperwork, rather than the best 'practical' policemen. Some of those in the generation who suffered from the switch to younger promotion railed bitterly at the policy of promoting 'whizz-kids' with too little experience of the exigencies of operational policing.

Years ago when a supervisor came up to you, whether sergeant or inspector, he could tell you how to do the job. But now you've got these sergeants promoted that are paper tigers. They've got their ability on paper work, but you put them down where you've got crowds or an ugly situation, and these boy sergeants they ask you, 'Christ, what do we do here?' These whizz kids have to ask the bloke with fifteen to twenty years' experience what to do.   (Uniform constable)
They promote you on exams, but they're all irrelevant questions about hijacks etc. We're on the bloody ground, not in the bloody sky! There's too many office wallahs!   (Uniform constable)

Eight per cent saw promotions as dependent entirely on luck, to the exclusion of merit.

I was in a particular station – I was a panda driver at the time, and the telephone rang, and I answered it. I just happened to be there, in the office. I picked up the phone, and it was a superintendent's clerk. He obviously thought he was talking to the station officer. He said there was a vacancy on the motor-cycle training course, and could I suggest someone. I said: 'Oh, yes'. And so I told him my name, and he said 'Righto', and put me down. Rotten devil!
(Traffic constable)

Some who criticised the system claimed they were not themselves interested in promotion. Many detectives felt that a condition of being promoted was to move back into uniform, and they preferred to stay in the C.I.D. with their present rank. There was also the view that to get ahead required sacrificing family life, because of the hours spent in study. It was often felt to be at the expense of comradeship, and ambitious men were depicted as pushing, ruthless types. The extent to which these points were rationalisations for lack of success cannot be ascertained, but as we have seen approximately 40% of constables and sergeants denied any interest in promotion.

With the present overemphasis on bookwork, hardworkers, especially if they've got a family, are just too knackered to study. Anyway, I wouldn't want to go back into uniform.   (C.I.D. constable)
I don't want to be promoted, because the lads see the inspectors as tin-gods. I don't want to mix with the snots. It's best to be a working P.C.

(Uniform constable)

Nonetheless, for those who were concerned about promotion, frustration with failure was a major source of dissatisfaction with the job, and of desire for a trade union as a means of protection. Table 10.11 shows how perception of the promotion system as legitimate or not was related to job satisfaction (as assessed by the question whether or not one would rejoin the force).

TABLE 10.11. *Assessment of the promotion system and job satisfaction*

		Assessment of promotion system			
		Just	Unjust	Mixed	Don't know
		%	%	%	%
Would you rejoin force?	Yes	57	39	55	56
	No	32	51	35	25
	Don't know	11	10	10	19
	Total	100	100	100	100
		N = 58	N = 54	N = 40	N = 16

Table 10.11 shows that those regarding the promotion system as based on completely unjust considerations were more likely to say they would not rejoin the force, than those seeing promotion as either completely or partially just (or who don't know). Views on the promotion system are an important source of support for the idea of police unionism, as Table 10.12 suggests.

Table 10.12 shows that desire for a union was higher among those who regarded the promotion system as either partly or completely unjust, than among those who saw it as just (or don't know). Perception of the promotion system as unfair was thus an important source of support for unionism in the police force.

TABLE 10.12. *Assessment of the promotion system and desire for a union*

		Just %	Unjust %	Mixed %	Don't know %
		Assessment of the promotion system			
Would you like the	Yes	19	54	50	19
Federation to be	No	74	43	45	75
more like a union?	Don't know	7	4	5	6
	Total	100	100	100	100
		N = 58	N = 54	N = 40	N = 16

Police professionalisation

An important element in considering policemen's orientation to work is whether they see themselves as 'professional'. Police administrators and spokesmen have often seen 'professionalism' as virtually a panacea for police ills. This is especially so in the U.S.A. where, since the 'progressive era' in the first two decades of this century, the ideology and practice of 'professionalism' has been developed by a series of liberal police thinkers (Carte & Carte 1975). This largely involved attempts to extricate the police from control by local political machines, and gain some degree of independence for the chiefs of police. This was linked with an ideology of police work as a neutral, technical function providing services for the whole community, and being 'above politics'. The administration of this service should be in the hands of the 'professional experts'. The skills and techniques necessary for this required an 'up-grading' of personnel, in terms of entrance and training standards. In Britain, where chief constables have always enjoyed a greater measure of independence, discussion of 'professionalism' has revolved more around the question of standards of recruitment and training. It can be seen as a bid for higher status, appropriate pay and conditions to go with this, and a consolidation of independence from civilian control.

Many police spokesmen talk in terms reminiscent of Balzac's view of the policeman as the noblest professional, combining the roles of soldier, priest and artist (Chapman 1970: 99–102). The 'F.B.I. Pledge for Law Enforcement Officers', in which new agent vows to 'always consider the high calling of law enforcement to be an honourable profession', paints a portrait of the police officer as a latter-day saint and saviour of mankind (Niederhoffer 1967: 24–5). The question of whether the police are a profession is barren if approached in an essentialist spirit, to ascertain whether the police fit the criteria of professionalism established by 'experts'. But it is clearly an issue discussed by the police, and one that needs to be explored as a part of the policeman's orientation to his work. This must be from a phenomenological point of view, elucidating the *policeman's* perspectives, rather than comparing it to the definitions of the sociologist.

'Trait' and 'functionalist' theories of professions both adopt a *consensus* approach (Johnson 1972). The *trait* model seeks to describe the core characteristics of 'true' professions. The *functionalist* approach attempts to explain these traits (e.g. service orientation, codes of ethics, specialised knowledge, lengthy training) by their necessity in occupations vital to the 'central values' of society. Such theories beg the question of what is a profession, and accept practitioners' self-definitions of the nature of their occupation (Johnson 1972: 26).

Others see professionals as distinctive not in any special qualities of skill, dedication etc., but in *control* of the market. A 'profession' operates its own licensing system, recognised by state and public, defining competent practice, entry to the work, and discipline of members. The group claims access to esoteric knowledge which laymen cannot judge for themselves, as well as dedication to public service rather than personal returns (Hughes 1963: 65). This is essentially a strategy to control the work and market-situation with similar purposes to trade unionism, but different power resources.

The control approach avoids the egregious value assumptions of the consensus models. Nonetheless, it presupposes that the analyst knows what a profession is, although it makes problematic the process of 'professionalisation', the power-struggle by which a group succeeds in establishing this mode of control. But many occupations which lack such control still describe themselves as professionals.

This suggests the utility of an altogether different approach to the study of professions. A *phenomenological* approach can be adopted, examining how the members of an occupation themselves define it. The truth value of these definitions is bracketed, while they are looked at to illuminate the subjective viewpoint of practitioners (Hughes 1958: 44–5). The question of the extent to which an occupation does control its situation, and the process by which this is achieved are clearly crucial ones, but so is the exploration of the way practitioners themselves define the nature of their work, regardless of whether their usage of terms like 'professional' fits the sociologists'.

It must be emphasised that the police are not now, and unlikely ever to be, a profession in either the consensus or control model sense. It is not the sociologist's task to comment on whether the value or complexity of the skills utilised by policemen is comparable to that of the 'classical' professions. But in terms of the degree of education required for entry, and subsequent formal training, the police are markedly lower in attainment. There is an ideal of service, and an oath to abide by it. The enforcement of this, though, is not by peers but by superiors in a bureaucratically structured hierarchy of authority. It could be argued that this is the whole purpose and point of the efforts of certain police administrators to achieve a raising of standards towards the ideal of 'professionalism'. But a sceptical note must be expressed about the degree of progress to date towards the formulation of an explicit, specific body of professional knowledge, necessary and sufficient for practice, which can be taught through formal training procedures.

Nor does police organisation fit the model of 'professional' control. It might be argued that policemen are analogous to 'professionals' in that (at least until recently) discipline was handled internally without an independent element. But this was not a system of collegial control by peers. Rather it was bureaucratic control by a hierarchy of authority levels, modified by the discretion allowed the constable. Although the issue of independent elements in the discipline process is often couched in terms of 'lay' versus 'professional' control, the latter does not fit the model of the 'classic' professions.

Seventy-four per cent of policemen felt the police should be seen as a profession. What did this mean to them? The essential reasoning was that police work should be considered as different from, and worthy of higher status than, 'just any job', i.e. manual or routine non-manual work. The claim to professionalism was not so much a bid for control, as a claim for status. However the influence of a folk version of the trait model was evident. The claim to special status had to be justified in terms of some elements of this model. It was backed up by arguments seeking to establish that the police had special skills or abilities, and/or that their job involved crucial responsibilities and powers, and/or that it was characterised by an ethic of service.

The assertion of specialist police expertise had to cope with the problem that police work does not in fact have particularly stringent academic entry requirements or extended periods of training. Nor is it immediately obvious that there is a specific skill policemen uniquely have. This was handled in one or both of two ways. The first was to try and assimilate the police to what was regarded as an established profession. Usually this was the legal profession, and the policeman's knowledge of law was favourably compared to it. Others were the army, seen as 'The Professionals' in line with the famous recruiting campaign, social work or medicine – the police were 'doctors for the community's sickness'. The other strategy was paradoxically that the police could be seen as specialist non-specialists, expert jacks-of-all-trades. Their speciality was adaptability, the ability to cope with any and every eventuality. This was associated with two ways of regarding police training. Either the formal training, especially its legal element, was stressed, or the argument was invoked that experience on the streets gives the policeman a distinctive skill, the ability to handle all kinds of people and situations more readily and confidently than most 'laymen' could. The element of dedication, the character selection before entry, and the degree of restrictions on out-of-work life, were also referred to as demonstrating the ethic of service, and a vocational rather than instrumental orientation.

Seventy-one per cent of those who felt it ought to be seen as a profession argued that the policeman possessed an expertise and skills unique to him. He had a special flexibility, an ability to cope in a smooth, unruffled and competent manner with all the unpredictable contingencies of his work.

It's a profession in the strict sense of the word. You're a professional, you know what to do, when perhaps the ordinary man in the street wouldn't know. You're not a professional in the sense that you're a specialist in any one field. You could describe it that you're a professional jack-of-all trades. When it comes to illness or an accident, a doctor would know more than I would, you know more sociology, and a fireman would know more about a fire. But I'd know more than all of them about a little bit of each. We're the professional jack of all trades, you start the ball rolling and wait for the specialists to take over... It's a job with a bit of this and a bit of that, but a lot of crime! (Uniform constable)

The training was specified by 21% as a source of this expertise. Apart from formal training, the 'academy of the streets' was regarded as imparting unique and special skills.

Some attempted to assimilate police work to another occupation regarded unequivocally as a 'profession'. Law was referred to as analogous to police work by 15%.

Your knowledge of the law needs to be as good as what a solicitor's is or anyone in the legal profession. In fact, you go to court and cross brains with the big guns, the barristers and judges and people that are paid many thousands of pounds a year. High court judges are in the £10 000 plus bracket, barristers £30 000 plus, aren't they? Your policeman comes lower down the scale, most of them well below £2000. But his knowledge of the law needs to be as high and efficient. (Constable, dog-handler)

Five per cent compared police work to social work, also seen as a profession:

I do think it's a profession. It's a social service type job, you train for social service like welfare workers and probation officers. The policeman is really just that. You're expected to stick your neck out: someone's in the river, you jump in. You go looking for missing persons and even the biggest rogue under the sun comes to you and says 'my son's missing, would you go and have a look?' If you could, you'd turn around and say 'stuff you mate! You didn't help us when we asked you a question about that robbery, why should we help you?' Things like that make it a bit of a different job.   (Uniform constable)

Nine per cent saw parallels between being a policeman and a doctor:

It's a profession really. You're dealing with the human brain, like doctors are. We're a body of men that give their life wholly and solely to the work we're doing. I don't think any doctor would ever deny a call of mercy from anybody, and I don't think a policeman would either.   (Uniform constable)

The dedication and integrity required, a vocational rather than instrumental approach, and the discipline code restrictions on private life, were seen by 26% as making the police a profession.

Even the village chappie is a professional because there's restrictions on his private life.   (C.I.D. constable)

The career structure was mentioned by 21%.

It's a profession because a person joins with a set number of years ahead of him. He thinks to himself 'This is my profession for thirty years of my life.' Not many who join anticipate leaving before then. That's why I'd say it was a profession, or a way of life even.   (Uniform constable)

The public status of the police was seen by 23% as a sign of its professionalism.

It's got more status than the ordinary job. The P.C. Plod image is going. Policemen are no longer thick as two planks, all brawn and no brain.
(Uniform constable)

Finally, 18% justified regarding the police as a profession by referring to the responsibility the job carried, and the considerable powers vested in the constable. An aspect of the 'professional' occupation was its concern with life-and-death matters.

Yes, it's a profession. As you appreciate, we've a lot of unique powers. All the strong powers. The powers under circumstances to detain a person, take his liberty away. You can't say a man is unprofessional who's able to do this. And if things go wrong, the ball is thrown right back at him and he's in for a hard time.   (Traffic sergeant)

The 21% who felt the police should *not* be considered a profession, mainly argued that the standard of training required for performing the work precluded this. Recruits had too low educational and social status. The police had no special skills apart from 'common sense'. For these reasons, they could not regard themselves, or hope to be regarded by others, as professionals.

You don't have to have the qualifications of a professional in the police. Most policemen I've met, it might be your opinion too, are a bit on the thick side. Some are as thick as a builder's plank. How they got in, I don't know. Anyway just passing exams in arithmetic, spelling and law doesn't mean you're a good policeman. It's what we call 'the Ways and Means Act'. There's no such act, but it's common sense, which is what you need out on the streets. You can get the policeman who's got all the law up there, he's practically a lawyer, yet he's hopeless dealing with a yob. The law's no use when you're dealing with a yob, or knocking on someone's door to say 'I'm very sorry, but your son's been killed in a road accident.' The law doesn't come into it, it's common sense, being a bit wise to the ways of the world. No, it's not a profession, the coppering lark.

(Traffic constable)

A few of the men, primarily among the leading Federation activists, rejected the notion of police professionalism on the grounds that it was a ploy to reduce pay demands by a conferral of meaningless status, and appealing to a sense of responsibility. The chairman of the Branch Board said:

We're not professionals. Being from working-class stock I associate professional men with someone whose got a degree or academic qualification, like a doctor or solicitor. He charges a fee, rather than being an employed man working for a salary. It only applies to a small proportion of the population who've devoted themselves to something, a real vocation. I'm a worker, of the working-class, paid wages, and that's it. I come to work, get paid a regular salary – wages and salary mean the same thing, money, don't they? The word salary has a bit of snob-appeal, but it doesn't make your money any more does it? No, I don't think we'd do ourselves a lot of good by calling it a profession. I think it's just snob value.

Table 10.13 shows that seeing the police as a profession is related to rejecting the idea of a union. This supports the Federation activists' view that 'professionalism' may be a badge of status that reduces the demand for more power to gain material rewards.

TABLE 10.13. *Conception of police as a profession and desire for a union*

		Are the police a profession?		
		Yes	No	Don't know
		%	%	%
Should the Federation be	Yes	33	52	44
more like an ordinary	No	61	43	56
trade union?	Don't know	6	5	—
	Total	100	100	100
		N = 124	N = 35	N = 9

The same pattern holds for other elements of unionism. For example, whereas only 31% of those who see the police as a profession want to have the right to work-to-rule, 57% of those who reject the conception of the policeman as professional want this right. It seems plausible to argue that the widespread view of the police as a professional body partly accounts for the general rejection of the appropriateness of union organisation. The latter is seen as interfering with the status which is aspired to. Furthermore, the pride taken in 'professional' status is a source of satisfaction with the job which moderates the perceived need for strong representation. In addition, the notions of integrity linked with the idea of a 'profession' precludes the adoption of the 'irresponsible' tactics associated with the image of trade unionism. So the notion of the police as 'profession' is an important element of their orientation to work. It is to the policeman an aspect of status, enabling him to feel better than 'the ordinary worker'. It is justified by the characteristics of police work as he sees it. 'Professional' status means that union powers are to be shunned as demeaning, even if they could give the policeman more leverage in negotiations.

Police work and private life

An occupational community is, in very general terms, one in which the worlds of work and non-work are closely interdependent, each world permeating and affecting the other. From the available evidence the police display this sort of work/non-work convergence in an extreme form.   (Salaman 1974: 45)

Salaman has developed a theory about the determinants of the existence and character of an 'occupational community' on the basis of evidence from a number of studies. Members of occupations tend to form themselves into communities if they are 'socially marginal', i.e. regard themselves as being higher on the social status hierarchy than they are seen to be by others, or their work is 'inclusive' in the sense that it affects non-work life. Inclusiveness can result from pervasiveness, that is, the number of activities for which the culture of work sets norms; organisational embrace, that is, the extent to which the organisation's hierarchy deliberately and explicitly sets out to control the life of members; and restrictiveness, that is, the way in which some types of occupation limit men's non-work life, as a result of the intrinsic exigencies of the work rather than deliberate policy. Work involvement of a positive moral or emotional kind is a *necessary* condition of occupational community, for otherwise the other factors which inhibit the formation of relationships with outsiders might result in social isolation. Occupational communities tend to develop when positive expressive rather than instrumental involvement with work is augmented by barriers to interaction with others.

The police are characterised by all these factors, and this makes it understandable that they should exhibit a marked convergence between work and non-work life. We have already documented their expressive rather than instrumental orientation to the job, and the relative degree of satisfaction with it, so they satisfy the necessary condition of positive intrinsic involvement.

The police are also characterised by social marginality. They seek a higher social status, that of 'professional', than that accorded them by others. This inclines them to turn inwards for validating interaction. Even more important is the fact that policemen experience themselves as rejected as social companions by outsiders, because of fear engendered by their authority role.

The police are also subject to all the factors which make for occupational inclusiveness. They are members of a well-developed and demarcated occupational culture, with its own particular argot and conceptions of itself, of the social world, and of the relationship between the two. The organisation explicitly lays down a code of rules regulating conduct, which is sufficiently extensive and general to control most aspects of a man's life. The shift-work and frequent unpredictability of hours limits the practical possibilities of interaction with others outside the job. So does the tendency to house policemen together in what sometimes amount to 'police colonies'. Finally, the policeman is expected to carry out any necessary activity in connection with incidents which might arise even when he is off-duty.

It is hardly surprising that all the policemen felt that their work affected their private lives. There was less agreement about the legitimacy of this intrusion and the extent to which it should be resisted as far as possible.

Thirty-two per cent felt that the policeman should *not* allow his work to interfere with his private life. Another 34% agreed, with the qualification that it was impossible not to let it sometimes. Twenty-seven per cent felt it inevitably did interfere, so there was no point in evaluating whether it should. Only 7% found the extent of interference with private life acceptable.

Fifty-five per cent of the men rejected the view that a policeman should never stop being a policeman. This is at odds with the often repeated notion that the policeman has a 24-hour responsibility. While most policemen conceded this, and felt they would involve themselves in what they saw as important tasks if they cropped up off-duty, this was not regarded as the same as activity on-duty. The threshold of perceived importance for off-duty intervention would be higher. Several men stressed that they saw any involvement in incidents off-duty as derived from their role as private citizens with appropriate know-how, rather than as employees of the police authority. They would try to minimise such interventions, and to find time and space to stop 'being a policeman' because, as one detective put it, 'if you were a policeman 24 hours a day you'd have a lot of nervous breakdowns!' On the other hand, 23% of the men agreed with the view that the policeman should never stop being a policeman. A further 21% argued that the policeman simply cannot stop being one, so there was no use speculating whether he ought to.

These attitudes are related to rank and specialism. On the whole, supervisors and specialists, particularly the C.I.D., are more likely to perceive both the inevitability and the legitimacy of work interfering with private life. While 45% of uniform constables felt that the policeman should not let his work interfere with his private life, only one uniform inspector agreed. Only 24% of the specialist constables agreed with this, and of these only one was a detective. Fifty-seven per cent of all inspectors and 54% of all detectives felt that work simply must interfere with private life, compared with only 25% of uniform constables. While the factual spillover of work into non-work life was recognised by all ranks and specialisms, the extent and accepted legitimacy of it was greater for supervisory officers and detectives than for uniformed constables.

How had the men experienced work intruding into 'private' life? Social marginality was often referred to. Fifty-two per cent mentioned examples of suspiciousness, hostility or ostracism by members of the public. This encouraged policemen to seek social companions from among their fellow officers.

The fact that you're a policeman influences not only your life, but your wife's and children's. My boys come into contact at school with people who are a bit anti-police at times. My eldest has told people that the fact that his father's a policeman is none of their bloody business, and if they can't talk about anything else they should seek other company, as bluntly as that. I don't think he's actually showed them a knuckle sandwich or anything, but they do get a certain amount of hardship at school. On one occasion a teacher rang me to complain about my son's language at school. She made the fatal mistake of saying 'and him a policeman's son too'. I said 'if my son used bad language that's one thing, but the fact that I'm a policeman is no bloody business of yours or your bloody teachers!' She's showing an infantile bloody mentality to bring that into it. 'My son is subjected to far more discipline and self-control than 90% of your pupils. If he did swear you've got my permission to thrash him if necessary. But I will not have my child held up as an example to others because his father's a policeman!' (Uniform sergeant)

The inclusiveness of the occupation was mentioned in various ways. Forty per cent spoke of the psychological intrusion into off-duty life, due to the 'police mind' into which they had been socialised. Primarily this was manifested by a continuous habit of observation and suspiciousness which it was impossible to break off in non-work life.

You drive along and you see things, or read circumstances differently to your wife or friends. And invariably matchboxes and cheques are covered with car-numbers and this sort of thing. You go to the football, and you tend to be more aware, to keep your eye on the yobs. Or you notice odd things, like an old chap standing by a school. (C.I.D. constable)

The perceived reserve of the public is thus reciprocated by an ingrained habit of suspiciousness on the part of the policeman. The emotional effects of the work also spill over into 'private' life. The men try to fight this, but often find it impossible. 'You often take your moods home with you, come home moody and quarrel with the wife. You can't just switch off' (uniform sergeant).

Some are more successful in combating the emotional consequences of the work. But the resulting attitude of cynicism or lack of emotion may well take a more indirect toll of the quality of personal relationships.

Before I joined the force I didn't like the sight of death much. It doesn't worry me now. If there's a serious road accident I just thank Christ it's not me and carry on with the job. That's the only compassion and sympathy I feel. It makes you hard to some extent. Some things that upset my wife won't even touch me at all. She thinks I'm a bit bitter and hard sometimes. If I go to a serious stabbing, I'll look at the bloke, take all the details and get him to hospital. Then I'll just go and eat my tea again like normal.   (Uniform constable)

The inability to cast off the police perspective when off-duty some-times results in action. Thirty-nine per cent volunteered accounts of at least one occasion in which they had actually become involved in an incident while off-duty. But it was stressed that they would not deal with what were perceived as unimportant jobs. Different terms of discretion govern action on and off-duty.

I live in a police house, five of us in a row. One night we heard a car screaming around. I got out of bed, and so did my mate next door. A woman down the road said she'd nearly been knocked down by this car. So we got in my friend's car, and found this car abandoned outside a house. We knocked on the door. Of course, we were both in pyjamas! We said we're police officers, but the chap said 'you're not coming in'. So we showed him our warrant cards. Then a back window broke, and a man ran from the back of the house. We tried to chase him but lost him. He was caught next day. My wife moaned, 'why did you have to get out of bed?' But if that woman had been injured or he'd injured somebody else, you wouldn't be able to ease your conscience. It's my job to do something about it. But you have to strike a happy medium. If I saw two kids riding on a bike I'd say 'Well, there's an offence, but I'm off duty.'   (Uniform constable)

Off-duty activities were governed by the personal morality of the police-man rather than organisational constraints. Nonetheless these were also operative. Given the notion of the policeman's 24-hour responsibility, if failure to deal with an important incident subsequently came to light, the officer would be liable to a discipline charge for neglect of duty. There was also the carrot of commendation for a good piece of work. But many of the men stressed that their intervention in occurrences while not 'at work' was as a citizen rather than specifically a policeman.

If you're going out for the night with a girl-friend or the wife and somebody holds up an old lady and hits her over the head, obviously you don't say 'I'm off-duty now'. But you've got to know where to stop. I mean I could lay on the beach with jock-strap, boots and helmet, I'm a policeman, P.C. Fuzz. I don't go around with my warrant card in my hand. But you've got civil obligations. Like if a lady's being battered, a man's got to do what a man's got to do. Whether you're a policeman or not. But if you see a bloke riding without lights and you're off-duty, you leave him alone.   (Mounted constable)

While primarily governed by the informal value system and thus an example of what Salaman calls 'organisational pervasiveness', the obligation to do certain tasks even off-duty is also influenced by formal, explicit controls and hence shades into 'organisational embrace'. A more obvious example of the latter are the rules deliberately laid down to control a policeman's out-of-work life.

It was widely felt that the enforcement of these had relaxed recently, though not sufficiently to satisfy some of the younger men.

Life is getting less moralistic and there are many things you could get away with outside without being frowned upon. But the moral standard here is stricter, but less so now than it was a few years ago. Like having a bit on the side. A policeman could do it, though they might clamp down.

(Uniform constable)

The policeman is also subject to what Salaman calls 'organisational restrictiveness', i.e. the way that the organisation of work by its nature inhibits social interaction with outsiders, regardless of any design to achieve this. In particular, the shift-work and relative unpredictability of hours (due to unforeseen events cropping up which keep a man overtime) serve to restrict the circle of associates for the policeman. Forty-five per cent referred to this sort of interference. It was especially prevalent in C.I.D. work, which more often involved unanticipated events that necessitated staying on beyond normal hours.

In the C.I.D. overtime is really just part of the job. You don't watch the clock, like in uniform. If something important comes up, you can't say 'bugger that! I'm going home'. (C.I.D. constable)
The C.I.D. man gives his wife a framed photo, because that's all she'll see of him! (Uniform sergeant)

For all these reasons police work involves a strain on the family life of the men. Twenty-seven per cent mentioned that policemen were more likely to have domestic problems than the average worker. This was especially so in the C.I.D. As one detective sergeant put it: 'Every 'tec has been nearer the divorce court than most other people. You never see the kids, meals are always being spoilt, you're always being driven.' Apart from the above sources of domestic problems, it was often argued the aura of masculinity and glamour surrounding the job made policemen more likely to get involved in liaisons which threatened their marriages. 'Policemen have one of the highest divorce rates in the country. There's always a bit of spare round the corner, because of the glamour of the job' (uniform constable).

A priori the strong occupational community of policemen might be expected to provide a basis for the development of unionism, as it involves a collective sentiment of solidarity with colleagues. As Salaman has noted, some sociologists have seen occupational community as linked to class-consciousness in that 'it was significantly related to the development, or maintenance, of a "them–us" view of the world, with its associated radical implications' (1975: 219). This was largely due to the association of the notion of 'occupational community' with certain traditional working-class occupations (such as miners, dockers and ship-builders) with noted histories of militancy. The model of the traditional worker implied by these communities was contrasted with a model of the privatised worker in non-traditional industries, whose class-consciousness had mellowed. However, as Salaman argues, a strong sense of occupational community 'is an entirely different thing from a class-conscious view of the world. Indeed the them/us view could, hypothetically, lead to a strongly re-actionary political line' (Salaman 1974: 129).

The case of the police bears out this argument. They are characterised by an extreme degree of occupational community but a rejection of trade-union organisation (though trade unionism cannot be taken as in itself an index of *class* consciousness). The crucial issue seems to be the source of 'occupational community'. In the police it largely results from positive involvement and satisfaction with work, plus the perceived hostility of outsiders. Both factors generate a consensual view of the force itself, precluding the formation of strong organisation against superiors in the hierarchy. This is supported by the fact that desire for a union is linked with the assertion of the need for a more privatised existence. Thirty-seven per cent of those who feel that the policeman should *not* let his work interfere with his private life, want the Federation to be more like a union, compared to 27% of those who feel he should. Of those who say the policemen *should* try to stop being a policeman off-duty, 42% want a union, compared to 26% of those who say he should *not*. The connection between desire for privatisation and for a union is not necessarily a causal one. It would be more plausible to interpret both as a reflection of the degree to which work is regarded from an instrumental point of view.

The nature of the police role

There has been much debate in recent years about whether the police should perform a wider, social service role. The traditional conception of the police function stresses law-enforcement and order-maintenance. Rowan and Mayne (the first commissioners of the Metropolitan Police after its foundation in 1829) emphasised *crime prevention* in their force instructions. 'The primary object to be attained is the prevention of crime. To this great end every effort of the police is to be directed.'

The Royal Commission on the Police Report (1962) specified eight police functions. The first five were different aspects of order-maintenance and criminal law-enforcement. The sixth was the control of traffic, and the seventh miscellaneous government duties like checking applications for British nationality. Only the eighth hinted at a social service role: 'They have by long tradition a duty to befriend anyone who needs their help, and they may at any time be called upon to cope with minor or major emergencies.'

Contrary to the impression given by these official statements, the bulk of police work (measured in terms of time, or number of incidents dealt with) consists of service calls for help (Banton 1964: 49; Cumming *et al.* 1964; Punch & Naylor 1973).

There seems to be an emerging consensus amongst some senior officers and academic commentators that the large proportion of social service tasks in the actual activity of the police ought to be more explicitly recognised and encouraged in training and force organisation ('Police Insist on Social Work Link', *Guardian* 30.9.74). A body of evidence suggests, however, that such concerns are seen by most policemen as at best extraneous, and at worst counter-productive, from the point of view of their 'real' work as controllers of crime. Disagreement with the tendency to encourage a social service conception has surfaced in press discussions with policemen, as in the controversial interviews published in *The Times* in 1971, where two anonymous senior detectives spoke of the need for 'hard-line' policies to control crime. (These reflected the internal controversy at Scotland Yard which preceded Robert Mark's appointment as Commissioner. Evans 1974: 111.) More recently, the Federation 'law and order' campaign has put forward similar views.

The *Man-Management Survey* showed that a representative sample of policemen felt that their prime role was crime prevention and detection. Asked to list various aspects of police work in order of importance, the sergeants and constables in city forces placed 'prevention of crime' at the top of the list, 'protection of property' second and 'detection of crime' third. Only then did they mention 'assisting members of the public'. 'Social and welfare work' came seventh on the list. (The results for county and borough forces, and inspectors and superintendents, were almost identical. Home Office 1970: 163–4.)

This research confirms the view that the bulk of serving policemen, especially constables, espouse a 'narrow' conception of the police role. Fifty-five per cent thought that they had to do jobs which they should not do. Amongst constables 58% thought this, as did 55% of sergeants, but only 39% of inspectors. These tasks were invariably the types of activity defined by Punch and Naylor as 'service calls', e.g. domestic disputes, school crossings, coping with the mentally ill, rescuing animals or handling dead bodies. Even those who accepted the propriety of these calls on police resources often regarded them as legitimate only because they indirectly served the primary police purpose, through improving relationships with the public and hence enlisting their co-operation in the 'fight against crime'. We have seen that some of the men did join the police for public service motives. However, the way most of these men interpreted the notion of being of service to the public was by performing the specific police function of combating crime.

The men recognised that they were called on to perform a variety of tasks which could not be encapsulated under the narrow heading of crime prevention or detection. When asked whether police work was like any other job, 81% said it was not. The chief reason was the variety and unpredictability of police work. This made it necessary for the policeman to be adept at rapid assessment of people and equipped with the social skills for handling them.

It's no good going to S.B. [affluent suburb] and talking like a navvy from S. [adjacent council estate], or going to S. and talking like one of the city gents from S.B. You have to be adaptable. My wife often accuses me of being Jekyll and Hyde. It's difficult, but you are enforcing, however mildly, people to do things which are against their will and foreign to their nature.   (Uniform constable)

Excitement and pride were derived from the variety of challenges encountered in police work. But many of these tasks were not their proper role. Especially frustrating were the frequent calls to domestic disputes:

We're a psychiatrist, solicitor, sociologist, doctor, first-aider and midwife all rolled into one when they put the uniform on. It's impossible. You haven't the expertise, and some problems are insoluble by their nature. If a husband and wife don't get on and we're called to a domestic dispute, there's no easy magic wand we can wave over it. My grandfather used to say: 'When there's no solution to a problem, it becomes a fact.' But people won't accept facts.
(Uniform constable)
With domestic disputes, the husband and wife going hammer and tongs, you've got to separate them, calm them down, before you go. And you're not doing a policeman's job, you're doing a socialist's [sic].   (Uniform constable)

With domestic disputes the reason for resentment on the part of the policemen was not the perceived lack of importance of the task. Rather it was the apparent impossibility of coping adequately, at any rate with the limited expertise imparted by police training. Another set of jobs cited as ones the police should not be asked to do were those which were seen as unimportant, and hence a diversion of police time from central tasks. Examples here were school crossings, fetching cats out of trees, or letting people into houses when they had locked themselves out.

The majority felt that crime control, narrowly conceived, was the proper role of the police. 'This idea of performing a public service is a load of codswobble as far as I'm concerned' (uniform constable).

It was made clear by many of the men that their interest in dealing with crime stemmed more from the fascination of the chase, than the idea of performing a necessary social function.

I don't go round with a sense of righteousness, that I'm protecting the public and all that. In my job we're catching thieves and bringing them to justice. I don't think about it as a public service, I just feel 'that's one thief less'.

(C.I.D. constable)

All police work's like a game. You get the people who do wrong and the people that try and catch them. Sometimes the wrong doers get caught, sometimes they don't. If they get caught and copped, if they get nicked and weighed-off, fair enough. If they don't, there's no point getting emotionally involved and saying 'I'll get you next time'. There may never be a next time, or he may get you. I've seen policemen get bitter over these blokes who get away with something, if they didn't really screw him down. It upsets them three or four days afterwards. But if I feel I've done my best to clobber him I say 'good luck to him!' The worst thing that can ever happen to you in this job is to get emotionally involved in anything. Oh, God, Tut, tut! Terrible!   (Uniform constable)

A minority of constables and sergeants, and most of the inspectors, accepted the propriety of the police being called upon to do a wider variety of jobs than crime control.

It's not like any other job. There's a terrific amount of job satisfaction, and it all or largely stems from that portion of the job where you're virtually a sort of social worker, the 90% of the time you spend doing all sorts of social jobs. Policemen are students of the world, and in most cases they're in a position to give advice, probably more so sometimes than the social worker whose job it is to patch things up.   (Uniform inspector)

There was unpleasantness and frustration which arose from having to perform difficult tasks, but this just had to be tolerated. One device for coping was the development of a sick form of gallows humour as a tension-release mechanism. A common police phrase was 'if you can't take a joke you shouldn't have joined this job'. (One man's motto was 'The difficult takes some time. The impossible, just a little longer.')

There are a lot of things we do which are unpleasant. It's your job because past people in the police force have done it, so there you are. You don't take great delight in it. One of the most harrowing jobs I had was to go and tell a young woman of about thirty that her husband and three sons had been killed in a road accident. I was just unfortunate enough to be in the station when the call came through. People commit suicide, and they find some diabolical ways of doing it. You've got to cut the body down with its rope round it, or drag it out of a pool of blood. It's got to be done. You try not to take much notice, and to joke about it. If you don't joke about it, it plays on your mind. So you make light of it: 'Poor chap, he'll have a headache in the morning!' Something like that.

(Traffic constable)

Another example of the role of humour as tension release is given in the following incident:

We got a body out of the river down at S.M. It's a beauty spot just over the hill there. It had been there six weeks – an old man missing from the local mental hospital. It took four of us to get it out, and as we brought him up the gas escaped from him and it stank, see? Well by this time the path was filled with people. And we walked away, and what happened was, we had a laugh. You've got to do that or just give in. I'm certain the people thought 'Look at them policemen laughing and smoking, and they've just got that poor old man out of the river!' (Uniform constable)

The conception the men had of the nature and purpose of the job was related to their attitude to unionism. Those with a narrower conception of the police role, who felt that they did many jobs which were not 'real' police work, were likely to favour the Federation being more like a trade union. Forty-two per cent of them wanted this, compared with 33% of those with the broader conception. They wanted a stronger representative body that could protect them from having to perform duties seen as 'extraneous'. The relationship was not very close though, because there was a contradictory process in operation as well. Those with the narrower conception were more likely to feel a sense of alienation from the public. As one detective constable remarked: 'You've got to upset people to be a policeman, or you're not doing the job properly.' This attitude produced a degree of identification with policemen in more senior ranks, as opposed to the public, which mitigated against a conflict view of the force itself and support for unionism.

Overall orientation to police work

The orientation to work typical of policemen approximates to a 'bureaucratic' one (Goldthorpe *et al.* 1968: 239–40). This is characterised by the following features: (i) 'The primary meaning of work is as service to an organisation in return for steadily increasing income and social status and for long-term security – that is, in return for a career. Economic rewards are regarded not as payment for particular amounts of work done or of labour expended, but rather as the emoluments appropriate to a particular grade and function or to a certain length of service.' We have seen that the majority of policemen were initially attracted, and are retained, by intrinsic aspects of the work rather than income maximisation. In so far as instrumental considerations play a part, this is largely the attraction of a long-term career. Pay was not seen as direct payment for work done. As one constable put it: 'We're not paid for what we do, but what we might be called upon to do.'

(ii) 'Arising from this, the involvement of workers with their organisation contains definite moral elements rather than deriving from a purely market relationship...It is unlikely, thus, that in this case involvement can be neutral: it will tend normally to be positive, where moral expectations are being faithfully met, or perhaps strongly negative if it is felt that commitments of a moral kind are not being honoured.' We have seen that most policemen were strongly committed to their work and relatively satisfied with it. In so far as they were unsatisfied with certain material aspects, this was underpinned by a moral rather than purely materialistic argument, concerning inadequate recognition of the importance of, or effort put into, the work. A minority of men, particularly among long-serving uniform constables, were disgruntled about failure of career aspirations to be met, and were quite alienated from the job.

(iii) 'Work represents a central life-interest, in so far as the individual's career is crucial to his "life-fate"...Ego-involvement in work is strong.' The policeman felt his work to be unique. He was part of an occupational culture regarding itself as distinctive, and cut-off from social interaction with other people.

(iv) 'Consequently, workers' lives cannot be sharply dichotomised into work and non-work. Their organisation and their colleagues may, or may not, continue to form the basis of social life outside work; but self concepts and social aspirations formed through work necessarily carry over into non-work activities and relationships.' The extent to which the police constituted an occupational community, with marked convergence between work and non-work life, has been documented.

This orientation to work is not conducive to support for unionism. It is related to a consensus rather than conflict image of the organisation. The worker is imbued with a sense of dutiful service in return for fair treatment. Aspirations are of an individual kind, aiming at promotion through one's own effort. However, if the work situation changes in the direction of acquiring a more anonymous, impersonal character and promotion channels come to be blocked, support for unionism may develop (Lockwood 1958: chapter v). We have seen that support for unionism in the police is related to the development of dissatisfaction with work, largely linked to frustration with lack of promotion opportunities, and hence cynicism about the fairness of the system. While the modal orientation of policemen approximates to the 'bureaucratic' model, the content of their work gives them some distinctive characteristics. The adversarial nature of much police activity, stemming from their primary crime fighting role, underlies the development of a culture which sees itself as separated sharply from other social groups. This sense of alienation from the rest of society adds to the barriers against police unionism.

11

Police and outside society

I had intended to question policemen about their political views, conceptions of the stratification system and their place within it. This would have permitted the exploration of links between attitudes to unionism, political ideas, and images of the class structure. Unfortunately the Chief Constable and the Home Office did not give permission for these questions to be raised, on the ground that they threatened the notion of the police force's political impartiality.

It was my impression that most policemen subscribed to a version of what has been called the 'myth of classlessness' (Westergaard 1972). They felt that social divisions were being eroded and people mixing more freely with each other. In the discussion of attitudes towards outside trade unions, mention of class was (like Sherlock Holmes's dog barking in the night) conspicuous by its absence. Very few men saw trade unions as an organisation representing the working class, though many did regard this as their historic role, invoking the image of a past society polarised between two sharply differentiated classes. By contrast with this conception of the past, trade unions were now seen as too powerful, rather than as representing the less privileged or influential groups in society.

Many policemen did subscribe to an *ideal* of egalitarianism. This was brought out by the fairly frequent comments about how they tried to enforce the law impartially regardless of social status, and indeed would relish the chance to take action against a member of the 'elite' if the chance arose. 'Nothing would give me greater pleasure than being able to arrest the Lord Mayor' said one constable. This is not to deny the evidence of other research about the differential treatment of people belonging to different social strata. (For some British data, see Shaw & Williamson 1972; Box & Russell 1975. American evidence is summarised in Box 1971: chapter 6.) Stereotypes of criminality are related to class and race, as are the opportunities for privacy, and it is this which underlies the social structuring of police action, although individual policemen may nonetheless subscribe in principle to egalitarian values (Stinchcombe 1963; Piliavin & Briar 1964; Chapman 1968; Young 1971).

While policemen may no longer think it valid to see society as polarised in *class* terms, they are aware of status distinctions. This is evident in frequent comments about the need for skill and flexibility in dealing with people from all parts of the social spectrum. 'You deal with everybody here. From the basic form of human life in the jungle conditions of the bad areas, to the elite of the town. The posh dinner parties that go on. You have to handle them all' (uniform constable).

Policemen do see people in different occupations as enjoying and meriting varying degrees of social respect. They see themselves as deserving to be on a par with more skilled non-manual workers or 'professionals', even though they are not secure about their acceptance as peers by those strata. Their conception of a status system differs from the notion of a class structure in that it is based on merit and social contribution rather than power and ascription, and does not involve polarisation but a finely differentiated scale.

This is not to say that society was seen as completely fair and equal in the chances it bestowed. It was recognised that certain sections suffered chronic multiple problems and contributed seriously to crime figures. Their offspring did not enjoy the same opportunities as others. As one constable put it 'it's hard for a kid if his mother's tomming it, and his dad's always in the boozer'. At the other extreme, some were obviously born with silver spoons in their mouths. But these were limited enclaves of problem families, and a small social elite. For the most part, society was differentiated by gradations of status in which the individual could rise by dint of effort, as indeed many policemen had done.

Policemen did have a characteristic social philosophy, although the salient issues in it were not those of class and inequality. They analysed society in terms more directly relevant to their experience of it as policemen. This social perspective emerged clearly in response to an openended question about whether the problems facing the police were getting better or worse.

The first noteworthy point was the almost unmitigated pessimism characteristic of the men's replies. Eighty-one per cent felt that things were getting worse, and this was often expressed in most emphatic, even apocalyptic, terms. Virtually none of the rest saw things as getting better. They were either young men who felt their experience was too short for them to discern trends, or a few who saw police problems as always having been bad and likely to remain so. The healthy society was depicted as one based on a considerable measure of discipline and acceptance of authority. Various tendencies were undermining these preconditions of the good society. We were heading towards disorder, which not only made the police task vastly more difficult, but also threatened to undermine 'civilisation' itself. The only solution to this was a reassertion of control by authorities in society, which would involve giving the police more powers and backing them up by severer sanctions against offenders. This was made problematic by the degree to which authorities were under the sway of ideologies which aggravated the situation. Politicians were seen as, at worst, influenced by radical beliefs which made them anti-police, or at best as effete and naive, albeit well-intentioned, men who were out of touch with the true condition of society. The courts failed to deal with offenders effectively because of the influence of 'do-gooders' with theories about the sources of crime which were over-indulgent to criminals. The shackles of 'due-process' of law frustrated the honest efforts of the police. The policeman had to contend not only with his obvious enemy, the offender, but also with the other members of the system of authority, whose ignorance of the real life of society outside the charmed circles they inhabited led them to emasculate police action.

These views have been translated into political activity, as described in chapter 2. At the end of November 1975, the Federation initiated a campaign to gain public support for pressure on parliament and the courts to review penal policies and end 'the drifting into a lawless society ...we have gone too far with the liberal, lenient approach'. Local Branch Boards became active in this effort. The secretary of the board in the force studied urged the public, via the local newspaper, to 'write to your M.P. or councillor if you think the courts are too soft'.

The background to this public activity by the Federation can be made clear by an analysis of the views of rank-and-file members. The campaign is the result of long-standing grievances about social changes.

The reasons given for the pessimistic view of police problems lay the blame on trends in society which were undermining authority and restricting the ability of the police to cope with the situation.

Fifty-three per cent offered variants of the view that authority in society generally was coming under attack. They spoke of trends towards permissiveness, the erosion of discipline, and declining standards of conduct. Twenty-four per cent blamed the courts, who were too lenient in their treatment of offenders, while a further 11% attacked the 'do-gooders' who pleaded for understanding the criminal, and were seen as sympathetic with the offender at the expense of the victim.

There's too much emphasis on the psychological side of it in the courts. You know, people steal because they're bloody greedy or too lazy to work. But there's too many influences saying the only reason he stole was some psychological reason. Nowadays, if a kid steals a packet of cigarettes, psychiatrists say it was because his mother was hit by an empty cigarette carton when she was carrying him! A kid steals a packet of cigarettes because he wants to smoke! We've got the stage of everyone trying to do good and sort them out. They've introduced all sorts of legislation to try and keep the prisons empty, suspended sentences etc. And it's all snowballed on, they're more crowded than ever. Eventually you've got to come down with the heavy hand again. (C.I.D. constable)

We're living in a sick society at the moment. We're going through a spate of do-gooders who do no good! When you've got them you've got bloody problems. They shout and shout to create problems, or they'd be out of a job! They create this myth for themselves, juvenile bureaux, the probation service. I don't think half of it is justified. They're getting rid of the deterrent all the time. They'd rather waffle round rather than give a short, swift dose of corrective punishment. Bang! It's done!   (Uniform constable)

Everything used to be orderly. At 10 o'clock when they came out of the pubs, they went on their way home. They were taught to be well-behaved and respect things. Today, people question too much. It's going so far that in the end you'll have anarchy. If people go on demanding their so-called rights and live their lives irrespective of anyone else, there must be a day of reckoning, akin to the Roman Empire. Live now, pay later. A lot of things boils down to morals, not that one wants to be narrow-minded. In the past, discipline was strong at schools, and also because of poverty. A man was feared of his job. We've lost in many things.   (Uniform inspector)

Forty-three per cent felt that there was an erosion of the power of the police specifically. This was partly the fault of the 'do-gooders', such as the National Council for Civil Liberties (sometimes nick-named the 'Council for the Prevention of Policemen Doing Their Duty!'). The other explanation given was the higher standard of education nowadays, which made people more sophisticated and knowledgeable about their rights. An educated society was harder to police.

The problems have got worse only because the do-gooders clap on to it, the Freedom of Civil Liberty people. Whereas before hand you could deal with the job and say what you liked. I don't mean go round thumping people and things like that. I don't agree with that. I don't agree with this so-called hitting a man when he's in a cell and all that sort of thing. That's definitely out. But pushing him around a bit... If he's in a football match, well, he's just got to accept it. But the thing is now if you do that, for example you're in a football crowd and someone throws a penny at you and hits you in the back of the head, or thumps you in the ribs or kidneys. You immediately turn round and grab him, and as you do someone just sees you grab him, they don't see what happened before hand. The next thing is that person is making a complaint against the police!   (Uniform sergeant)

Related to the increasing control over the police due to greater awareness by people of their rights, and the vigilance of organisations concerned with civil liberties, was a perceived decline in respect. This was also a consequence of the changing attitudes to discipline and authority. It was felt that nowadays people were far less inclined to listen to what policemen said, and more likely to protest or answer back rudely. Policemen were very anxious about what they perceived as a general reduction in the respect accorded them by the public. Twenty-eight per cent singled this out as a factor making problems worse.

I don't think the public today backs up the police force sufficiently. The permissiveness of society has gone so far now that as time goes on the police job won't be workable. People want the police force purely for their own ends, not because it's representative of law and order for society. They look on it as an unnecessary evil. Except when they need us, and then they want everything, when they're in trouble. We're the whipping-boys of society. We can do no right. And this is becoming more so. There is, of course, a hard-core of people who think we're wonderful, mainly the old people who grew up with different standards of conduct, discipline like. But generally the way we're going the job will be impossible to do within a short space of time. The public neither wants nor deserves a police force, in my opinion.   (C.I.D. sergeant)

Problems have got much worse by virtue of the attitude of the public towards the police force, and the general lawlessness throughout the country. It's more difficult to interview prisoners and persons in general. We've got this animosity, an increasing animosity, which has come about in the last ten years. A division (which includes a largely immigrant area) is so bad now we call it the jungle. There's not enough deterrent for the hardened criminal. I'm all in favour of going back to the Middle Ages, when they cut off a finger if you stole an apple. Well, perhaps that's going too far. But stiffer penalties than are now current. [At this point two other detectives entered. 'Don't be surprised if you hear some scrapes and bangs in here in the next few minutes, it just means we're having a fight', D/C B. told them. One replied as they were leaving: 'Why? Is he one of those Civil Liberties blokes then? We'll come and help you out if he is!' (laughter)].   (C.I.D. constable)

Up to the end of the war a policeman was able to exercise his authority and influence far easier and he was taken more notice of, more respected than he is now. You've only to look at the number of assaults on police by these young hooligans. Years ago I could go up to twenty yobs and say 'Right! On your way.' And they'd all mumble and grumble but they'd go. Now I go up to them I think 'Am I going to get a bloody good hiding here or not?' The chances are that if I jumped in with both feet and got stroppy, before I could look round one of them behind me would have given me such a thump round the neck I wouldn't know what was happening for the next three hours. Disrespect of rule of law is so apparent. A few years ago the Federation issued a document called 'The Thin Blue Line'. Well, that's what we are. If revolution ever did become seeded in this country the police force would be in such a tenuous position that overnight we could become completely disregarded. We're 90 000 men. If you had a bloody good organisation and wanted to disrupt the country, you could take over every police station in the country within twenty-four hours. We're such a small body of men compared with the population. We depend on their respect, and that's going.   (Uniform sergeant)

Certain particular problems were felt to have become aggravated recently. Foremost among these was increasing violence. There was a larger number of violent crimes, and the policeman was more likely to be met with violence in handling cases. This made them feel apprehensive about their work. Thirty per cent singled this out as a problem which had grown worse.

Our biggest problem is the increase in violence. You've only to be in the Operations Room for five minutes to realise. There's violence going on all over the city. It's not just London like you read in the papers. It's going on here. Go out on any tour of duty, just go in the Operations Room, you'll see it. Take this latest incident last Saturday night, when two policemen got injured. There was this fracas in M. [an immigrant area] 2.30 a.m. Sunday morning. The police got there right in the middle of it, and it was terrible. I was there – a good inspector should be out there when there's rough stuff, as much as any of the men. One of the two men injured – and this the papers didn't tell you – he was a dog-handler! Now I ask you, if a man with a dog isn't safe, what's an ordinary bloke, no dog to protect him or anything, going to be like?   (Traffic inspector)

Problems of crowd control on occasions like pickets, political demonstrations, and football matches, were felt to be increasingly prevalent. The following account of the famous Grosvenor Square demonstration in 1968 by a policeman who had been involved in trying to handle it encapsulates these problems. Twenty-one per cent referred to crowd control issues as a source of greater difficulty.

All I could see was the proverbial 'thin blue line'. And my God, it was thin! And the sheer volume of *them*! You could see them coming about three-quarters of a mile off. Nothing but a seething mass of people coming down from Oxford Street. And just this little, thin blue line and twelve horses behind them. It was a frightening sight when they came down because we'd heard they'd been having trouble all the way. It looked quite honestly that we were going to be swept away before the tide, and it's lucky we weren't... I saw crowd hysteria as it really is, some people had really been stirred up! Probably about 5–10% of the crowd were hostile and they worked the atmosphere up. The hate wasn't being thrown at the Americans – it was at us! We were the enemy, there on the receiving end. Before we started moving anyone backwards, we were hard at it for about an hour and a half. On TV it looked like a brief punch-up! And then afterwards, I must confess things ran a bit amok, because we'd taken a right hammering that day. When it was getting dark, we split up into groups, and were chasing all the hangers-about away. I think the press coverage was very fair. I saw things on our side that were very much kept out of the press. There were God knows how many complaints by the Civil Liberties people. I went up on twelve different complaints! I handled one bloke a bit roughly, and that was the subject of one complaint. The rest of it was a load of rubbish. But there was the casual boot that went in and this sort of thing from the P.C.s. Let's face it, when things get hot... But things happened that shouldn't. One bloke went absolutely berserk. He set about a girl on the ground with his truncheon, he'd done all kinds of diabolical things with it. To give you an idea, there were sixteen statements against him by other police officers, and he was dismissed. Only too right – we don't want blokes like that. But in the crowd, when it all builds up, you can't say how people are going to react.   (Uniform constable)

Apart from politically motivated crowd situations, many policemen were alarmed by the development of violence at football matches and other places of entertainment where there were large gatherings of young people.

Years ago at a football match, it only wanted one policeman in the middle of a crowd of kids arguing and shouting, and he would calm them down. Nowadays you can get ten policemen there, and they get their heads kicked in! They seem to have little or no respect for you. Only last week, I was on night duty. We had a motorcoach pull up outside the station about half past one in the morning. The driver had a group of youths aboard and had just come from the Mecca dance hall. One of them had smashed the back window. The driver wanted the police to come and quieten them down. It was impossible. The abuse was more when we got off the coach than before. There's no respect at all, whereas years ago the policeman commanded a bit of respect. I used to be frightened of the police force when I was a kid. I used to be scared of the copper who lived up the road, he was a terrifying sort of figure. But that's all gone now.

(Uniform constable)

Trouble was especially likely to come, it was felt, from certain sections of the population, particularly the young and blacks. Thirty-three per cent referred to changes in the behaviour and attitude of youth towards authority as a source of their worsening plight. There were new patterns of deviance, among sections of the young, especially students, who had not previously been problematic to the police.

There's no deterrent or respect in society. If you catch a criminal, the magistrate listens to the probation officer. 'Well, don't do it again! Suspended sentence.' I'd prefer to bring back hanging and the birch...and National Service. Do them good, these yobboes, going round a bit with the old sergeant-major. The younger type couldn't care less if you tell them anything. No respect, you see it as you go round. Years ago you'd get a clip across the ear from the old-time bobby. Not that I believe in going round thumping people. But football and things like that, you ought to hear them! Everything boils down to discipline. Their parents give no discipline nowadays. Everybody's out to work or bingo, the kids got to fend for themselves. A lot of the kids get fantastic money now.   (Uniform constable)

Race was mentioned by 23% as a worsening problem (35% in the division which contained the city's largest black community). It was felt that immigrants subscribed to different moral codes and hence were more likely to break the law. They were perceived as hostile to the police and likely to offer violent resistance. (A Birmingham study demonstrated that the association between race and crime resulted from the 'ecological fallacy'. The concentration of black immigrants in zones of transition suggests an *apparent* association of race and the high criminality of such twilight areas. But immigrants were not in fact responsible for the high crime rates. This may well be true of the area referred to by policemen in this study as the 'ghetto' or the 'jungle'. Lambert 1970: 283–4.)

On our area we have colour problems. I get people coming into the office, we had a delegation the other week. Complaining about noisy parties. On our patch if they put on a party it'll last for three days! And not just a couple of people. You got hundreds there, milling round. People ring up 'Can you do something?' Well, you can't expect one policeman to walk into the middle of a hundred coloured people who are anti-police and turn the radio off. You'd have a dead policeman next thing you know. So I tell people 'He's only a man in uniform, he's not Superman. Take the uniform off and I'm the same as you. I've got my fears.' They expect you to have BATMAN written across your chest or something! I don't like being punched, but if there's fights you've got to break it up. I've always told young policemen, 'If you're sent to a fight, take your time. When you get there he's exhausted, and you're still fresh.' The public expect too much. If anything goes wrong it's the bloody policeman's fault. We're the kicking-boy and the hero.   (Uniform constable)

S.P. (the immigrant area) is a terrible place, shocking. Whatever job you go to, you know you're going to have trouble. You always look out for a knife or a fist or something. It's a drunken Irish labourer or someone. They've got all sorts over there. West Indians, Indians. They're always fighting, at one another's necks. You've got Hungarians, Poles. And your local layabouts that mix in with them. Prostitutes. It's a right den of iniquity. Even the T Rd. Station is diabolical.

Every time I go there I suffer from what I call T Tummy! You'd get depressed if you didn't have a sense of humour. We're here to be run around by the public today, rather than a police *force* that could just command people.

(Uniform constable)

You get ghettos of people of a particular race or colour who are completely anti-police. Here on this division we have the S.P. area, which is a ghetto of multi-nations and multi-colours, and a concentration of a lot of common lodging houses. Families on the very lowest income and employment bracket. They are a cause of a lot of the crime and vice in the city. The race aspect is so bad. You get so many coloured prisoners. I very rarely see a coloured man who is pro-police... So I don't exercise a colour bar, but I must admit that if my daughter wanted to marry a coloured man, I would most certainly object.

(Uniform sergeant)

Fifteen per cent claimed their problems had become worse because of a general increase in workload. This was partly the result of recruitment and wastage problems, partly because with panda cars the constable attended more incidents and arrived more speedily, before trouble had cleared itself up. 'With Unit Beat policing you get the problem of more 999 calls. We more or less said to people "Well folks, we have cars. You can have instant policemen now, please dial 999"...The problem of success' (uniform inspector).

Most policemen had a pessimistic image of society as becoming far more problematic for them. Their conception of the good society revolved around a notion of order, respect for authority and discipline. These values were all perceived as being under threat. Society was divided not so much into a system of classes as into groups presenting different problems for the police. There were the hard-core 'villains', the young and the blacks who represented an ever more recalcitrant turbulence over which the policeman is expected to maintain control. This task was made more difficult by betrayal from within the camp of the 'respectable' members of society, who ought to be on his side. Politicians, judges and lawyers all failed to back him up, and, instead of giving help, were more inclined to impose legal restraints on his means of action. At worst this was because they were themselves hostile to the existing system of society, as the police-man viewed it. At best they were well-intentioned, but misguided, 'do-gooders who do no good'. Older people retained some vestiges of respect, but often made unrealistic demands. The policeman was not seen as a human-being, but an automaton in uniform.

I continually find that the majority of people outside feel a little bit astonished to find out that we're human. This comes home to you occasionally. One after-noon I wanted to go to the toilet. I walked into the one by the traffic lights. And three or four blokes were all staring at me. All I could think was − ! They seemed to be saying 'Fancy! A policeman! He's got one the same as everybody else!' This puts it in a nutshell.   (Uniform constable)

Previous studies have also described an 'occupational culture' in which the police see themselves in conflict with all other segments of society, whether 'deviant' or 'respectable'. There are dangers involved in speaking of *a* police 'occupational culture', and distilling its characteristics from studies done at different times and places. The nature of police work and the people doing it are historically and socially variable. Nonetheless, there are certain broad parallels between the police outlook described in several studies, though there can be no *presumption* of similarity. An early American study, completed in 1951, explored how the 'theme of an enemy public that threatens and criticises binds the policeman's group to isolation and secrecy' (Westley 1970: 49). In the mid-1960s Skolnick argued that 'elements in the police milieu – danger, authority and efficiency...combine to generate distinctive cognitive and behavioural responses in police: a "working personality" '. The crucial characteristics of this were: endemic suspiciousness, concern with potential violence and danger, social isolation coupled with internal solidarity, and a conservative emotional and political perspective (1966: chapter 3). The first sociological study of the British police contrasted the situation here with that in the U.S.A. Contrary to assumption, it concluded that American police seemed *less* socially isolated (Banton 1964: 215). The British police are more subject to rules controlling work and non-work life, because their role has more of an exemplary character. The result is greater social isolation. A later study depicted a British city force as 'a tight, integrated whole facing a community, which is seen as segmented and in part undesirable' (Cain 1973: 232). Strong norms of solidarity developed due to the need for support in the work situation, and to hide from senior officers both illegal acts, and illicit 'easing behaviours' making work-life more tolerable.

The present study has tried to show that there is *conflict* as well as consensus in the police force. But despite internal conflicts a closing of ranks tends to occur *vis à vis* 'outsiders'. This militates against unionism. Conflicts within the force will usually be limited by an overriding solidarity against mutual enemies. The policeman's analysis of his problems, and the remedies for them, is likely to pit him against the labour movement in the political sphere. But while the 'police culture' is inimical to unionism, the force is far from monolithic. Around the central tendencies of the 'policeman's working personality' there develop various permutations, both of an individual kind, and also structured by the division of labour. These variations will be the subject of the next chapter, which develops a typology of police perspectives. But these variants must be seen in the context of a basic value-system stressing internal solidarity, conflict with outsiders, and a philosophy of order, conservatism and stability.

12

Understanding police unionism: a typology

There are variations within the force in the distinctive police outlook. Various *typical* patterns can be distinguished: the 'bobby', the 'uniform-carrier', the 'new centurion', the 'social worker', the 'professional', and the 'Federation activist'.

The *'bobby'* is the 'ordinary' policeman, at best exuding the cosy avuncularity of George Dixon rather than Z Cars, at worst, the image of Mr Plod. He views the police as a way of earning a living which, at the same time, has certain intrinsic attractions over other possible employment. There is no particular social purpose he wants to achieve, but he is not alienated from his work. Intrinsic interest is the most important thing in a job, and police work provides this. He stresses the importance of discipline, both in the force and society, and bemoans the decline in standards which he sees. But this concern does not amount to a crusade, and is not depicted in any grand metaphysical terms. He will apply the law with the discretionary commonsense supposed to characterise the good copper. He will welcome the fact that he can help people in various ways rather than feeling this a distraction from 'real' police-work, though he may well be frustrated by the apparent insolubility of some of the social problems and situations encountered. He is contented with uni-formed patrol work, which he sees as the core part of policing. He may have promotion ambitions, but is not altogether frustrated by failure to achieve them. He has the compensation of not disrupting his family life and *camaraderie* with his colleagues the way that the more single-minded pursuit of 'success' by the 'high-flyers' and 'whizz-kids' does. The system of promotion is not seen as completely just, but criticism will be in terms of over-emphasis on 'irrelevancies' like paper qualifications rather than actual corruption. The basic legitimacy of the present hierarchical struc-ture of authority is accepted. At the same time, decision-making could be improved by paying more attention to the views of the 'practical man on the street', for senior officers may become 'out of touch'. But ultimately decisions must be made by them, and a clear-cut line of authority and responsibility works better than 'rule by committees'. The Federation has a role to play in facilitating the communication of rank and file views, and in advancing their interests. It would be nice if it had more 'teeth', but there is no way this can be achieved without threatening the responsibility of the police to the public. He assumes the good sense of the authorities in recognising the importance of the police, and thus giving them a fair deal. The 'bobby' recognises problems in mixing with the public, but regrets these. He strives to maintain relationships with outside friends, and succeeds to some extent despite obstacles. 'Some of his best friends are civilians.' He tries to limit the disruption of home life by the job. He has a basic sympathy for the role of trade unions as a protection against exploitation, which existed in the 'bad old days', but sees 'the wheel as having turned full circle'. The present power and behaviour of trade unionists is unacceptable. Altogether, there is a fit between his expectations and actual situation as a uniformed constable.

The '*uniform-carrier*' is the man with a basically instrumental and calculative approach to work. He is the type who believes that 'a policeman will never answer the phone if he can help it – it might be a job at the other end!' Or 'Why should I read *Police* in my own time when I can read it in the firm's time?' He may well not have joined with this initial orientation. Men who had been attracted by the extrinsic advantages of the job often became more intrinsically committed. It was widely argued that without this moral commitment the work would be impossible, that no-one would do some of the 'dirty' jobs involved in policing just for the money. Typically, he had once had other goals in mind, perhaps promotion or a particular specialism. Failure to achieve these had produced an outlook that made him get by with as little work as possible. He was tied to the job by the 'cash nexus' rather than any moral commitment. By the time he had faced up to the frustration of early aspirations he was trapped by the lack of equally lucrative alternatives at his stage in life. He is disillusioned about the job and its purposes. This functions to neutralise any potential guilt about not carrying out work tasks. He is embittered about policing and sees it as performing no useful service anyway. His life is sharply dichotomised between work and non-work, and he will actively involve himself in outside pursuits which constitute his central life-interest. He seeks out civilian company as far as possible. He is cynical about the authority structure of the force. He doubts the capabilities of senior officers, and suspects corrupt processes underlying their promotion. The supervisors are viewed as placing work demands upon the men which must be resisted by a variety of strategies. But he is also alienated from his colleagues, and his resistance is individualistic not collective. He would ideally like a more powerful Federation or union to advance his pay and conditions. At the same time, he is quite uninvolved in the Federation as it stands. Indeed, it is regarded with suspicion, as an alternative career path holding out 'cushy numbers'. It is not so much the representative of the men's interests as a part of the management structure, functioning to control them. He is not morally committed to trade unionism, but he also does not condemn their activities. They are pursuing, as best they can from their own point of view, the strategy of 'looking out for number one' which, in a world without ideals, is the only sensible course of action. In short, the 'uniform-carrier' is alienated from all aspects of the work organisation, including the representative system.

The *'new centurion'* is the man with a mission (Wambaugh 1972: 88). He is dedicated to a crusade against crime and disorder. Usually he will end up in the C.I.D., and most detectives approximate to this type. If he is in uniform he will probably have ambitions to be a detective. He is relatively unconcerned about pay, except as a sign of appreciation. He will be prepared to work long hours despite the ensuing disruption of family life. Indeed he has hardly any private life outside the force. He has a social perspective which is police-centred. The police force, or rather the active sections of it, are the repository of all truth, wisdom and virtue. They alone understand and respect the requirements of a 'civilised' social order. The public are either villains who actively threaten society, or inept wishful-thinkers placing unreasonable demands on the 'centurions' who are trying to protect them, hampering their efforts by mollycoddling the 'enemy'. The hierarchy of the police force are oversensitive to the views of 'do-gooders'. They are more concerned with public relations than 'real' police-work. They have been promoted not so much for their qualities as operational policemen as for irrelevant paper qualifications, or social skills which impress interview boards. The law is an ass. It allows criminals to escape their just deserts through exploitation of loopholes. If the 'new centurion' has found his niche in the C.I.D., or still hopes to, he is likely to be relatively content and committed to the job, despite his cynicism about society and the police force in general. If he has not found the appropriate position for his outlook, he may become increasingly embittered. In either case the 'centurion' has no respect for the Federation, which he will see as another lot of office-bound shirkers. But he is in favour of the real, active policeman having more power to determine policy, relative to the 'do-gooding' fraternity. He would even favour some sort of union to represent their views more forcefully. However, he is hostile and unsympathetic to trade unionists in general, who are seen as yet another disruptive element. His unionism would be more concerned to influence policy in a hard-line, reactionary direction, than with bread-and-butter issues, as the example of much American police militancy in the 1960s showed.

The *'social worker'* is also relatively unconcerned with the financial aspects of the job. He joined because he saw the police as a way of helping people, not in the indirect sense of thief-catching, but the specific service aspects of the job. Despite the high content of service calls, he finds little outlet for his aspirations in police work. This is because of the conflict-ridden nature of most tasks. He might be fortunate enough to find one of the few niches in the force which do allow a particular emphasis on the service aspects of policing, e.g. community relations, juvenile liaison or area P.C. Otherwise he is likely to leave, if frustration becomes acute early in his career, or become a disillusioned 'uniform-carrier', tied only by the security and financial return. He would have preferred another job like social work or teaching had he been adequately qualified. Police work was chosen as a substitute which was less demanding of educational qualifications. He may have toyed with the idea of leaving to take further educational courses, but was deterred because of the financial difficulties involved. He is not keen on the Federation, and takes little interest in it, because of his relative lack of concern about the job's instrumental aspects. He sees it as adequate, and does not approve of any move in a unionate direction, as this would clash with his ethic of public service. He is likely to have little knowledge of outside unions, and accepts the normative view that they are too powerful. While seeing society as moving in the wrong direction, towards a deterioration of moral standards and discipline, he does not use the apocalyptic terms typical of the 'new centurion', nor will he support hard-line recipes of stricter punishment. The 'social worker' will be keen to maintain outside social connections, and probably be involved in voluntary youth or church work. He will lament the suspiciousness and hostility felt to characterise the attitude of outsiders. This will be puzzling to him, given his conception of the police force as a public service.

The '*professional*' policeman is mainly to be found among the more senior officers or the career-conscious constables. I had originally thought of calling this category the 'senior officers', but felt this would be misleading as, on the one hand, it can be found among ambitious constables, while on the other not all senior officers share this perspective. Some senior officers have the views attributed to the 'social worker' or 'new centurion' types. Conversely, some young probationary constables talk as if they were Sir Robert Mark. The keynote of this category is *judiciousness*. The 'professional' gives all the 'right', sensible, balanced responses. For example, while the overwhelming majority of policemen have no hesitation in saying that the problems facing the job have got worse, the 'professional' takes a qualified, more long-term perspective. 'It all depends what you mean by worse.' In some respects, things have got worse, in others they have improved. The 'professional' always seems to be in front of a promotion board. His image of the ideal force is a bureaucratic, hierarchical organisation in which each man performs a specialised function for which he is most suited. He sees the point of all existing arrangements. If you made him lavatory cleaner, he would say, to quote one, 'I see the function in it.' It would be one of the tasks a man ought to acquaint himself with in order to get the broad, all round view of police work necessary to equip one for leadership. Police work is about social service *and* crime-busting *and* peace-keeping *and* traffic control etc. It is a multi-functional organisation, and there can be no narrow definition of 'real' police work. Incidentally, it also provides some men with employment and a livelihood. Within this ordered schema the Federation has its place, as a means of communication to ensure both the morale of the troops and wise command policies. But it must know its place, as it does. The 'professional' will view the Federation with a benevolent eye, and may well see a stint as representative as useful experience for a potential commander. Unionism is inappropriate; the Federation should become more of a 'professional association', as part of what is seen as the panacea for police ills, an 'upgrading' of the occupation. This means a raising of educational standards, an intensification of in-service training and even the encouragement of police research. If the 'new centurion's' view of how to get a better policeman is, to put it crudely, to give him more weapons, the 'professional's' is to send him on a sociology course. 'Upgrading' the police would go hand in hand with improvements in salaries, and is a more potent way of achieving this than irresponsible militancy. The 'professional' is basically sympathetic to trade unions, which also have their function, although he is likely to feel that 'they've got out of hand a bit, don't you think?' He does not deliberately maintain barriers against civilians socially, but feels that the hours and shifts of police work inevitably constrain private life. His dedication to his career may well put strains on his family life, and his identification is primarily with the job.

The *'Federation activist'* is a rarity, and we have already discussed these men in an earlier chapter. Not all representatives are activists – many reluctantly fill the post because no-one else will. The activist usually had a commitment to the labour movement before entering the force, and this sensitised him to the need for the Federation. Usually they joined with a 'trade' behind them, attracted by the security of police work. They stress the right of every worker to a trade union, and they would like to see one in the force. But theirs is a far cry from a generally radical perspective. Some activists do have liberal views on politics. But most combine dedication to unionism, in and out of the force, with what can only be labelled as reactionary views on other political and social issues, such as crime and punishment, race and international relations, the expression of political dissent, and the control of morality by the state. Nor would it be right to view them, *pace* the views of some older senior officers, as in any way subversive of the force hierarchy. They accept the discipline and authority structure, and only seek more adequate representation of the men's interests within this. They are no more likely to condone 'uniform-carrying' or rule-bending than most supervisors are, because these individual ways of expressing discontent weaken the claims put forward in collective bargaining for better pay and conditions. The Federation activist must be clearly distinguished from the 'uniform-carrier'. His support for union powers is based on general principle rather than dis-satisfaction with the job, and he is highly committed to the police in a positive and moral, not calculative, way.

These categories are all 'ideal-types' (Weber 1949: 84). They are constructed so as to highlight certain tendencies amongst policemen, and no concrete case can necessarily be found to fit any one type in all details. Most individuals hold views which are contradictory with each other. Some do approximate to a type, and a case-study will be given to illus-trate each. The decision to fit a case into a specific type is a subjective one. Classification is based on the *overall* impression given, rather than an arbitrary cut-off point for the number of characteristics of the pure type which the concrete case must satisfy. That is to say, when cases are labelled as, for example, 'new centurions', this is the result of the overall tendency and character of the man's responses, rather than an operational decision that he must have say eight or nine out of ten defining characteristics. The types *can* be summarised by their attitudes to ten aspects of the job. These underlay the allocation of cases to the types: (1) initial attraction; (2) current attachment: what is seen as the most important aspect of a job; (3) job-satisfaction; (4) degree of privatisation; is the 24-hour respon-sibility of policemen, and the interference with private life, resented?; (5) attitude to police unionism; (6) attitude to Federation officials; are they seen as different from the typical policeman, and as selfishly or altruistically motivated?; (7) views of the promotion system; (8) consensus or conflict images of relationships between ranks; (9) conception of the proper police role as 'wide' or 'narrow'; (10) views on outside trade unions. The responses characteristic of each type are summarised in Figure 12.1.

Most policemen could be said to approximate to one type or another, in the sense that they fit most of its characteristics. Ultimately the decision whether they fit one or another category is subjective, because in so far as they deviate from a type it may be in any one or more than one dimen-sion, even though the overall impression might be clear. The questionnaire items cannot in themselves be taken as indices of the types. This is because the meaning attached to a specific response depends on the overall orientation of the person. Both 'uniform-carriers' and 'new centurions', for example, share a 'conflict' view of relationships between ranks. The meaning of this in each type is, however, quite different. To the 'uniform-carrier' the supervisors are the 'bosses' seeking to extract a maximum of effort. The 'new centurion' sees the conflict not in such instrumental terms, but as a difference in policy and ideology between the 'practical' and 'desk' policeman. To him, horizontal lines of conflict between specialisms may be more salient than the vertical gulf between supervisors and men. Twenty per cent seemed to approximate to the 'bobby' category. Almost all of these were uniformed constables. Some were uniformed

Fig. 12.1. *A Typology of police orientations*

	Bobby	Uniform-carrier	New centurion	Social worker	Professional	Federationist
Initial attraction	Mixed or instrumental	Could be either	Non-instrumental	Non-instrumental	Non-instrumental	Instrumental
Current attachment	Interest and security	Pay	Interest	Public service	Public service or interest	Interest
Job satisfaction	Moderate to satisfied	Completely unsatisfied	Satisfied	Satisfied to moderate	Satisfied	Satisfied
Privatisation	Moderate privatisation	Privatised	Work pervades non-work	Moderate privatisation	Work pervades non-work	Moderate privatisation
Unionateness	Wants a little more power, but not real militancy	Wants union for instrumental reasons	Wants more say but not a union	Rejects, because responsibility	Rejects, because unprofessional	Wants as a basic right
Support for Federationists	Sees them as altruistic	Sees them as self-seeking	Sees them as shirkers	Sees them as altruistic	Sees them as useful for communications	Sees them as necessary

FIG. 12.1. (continued)

	Bobby	Uniform-carrier	New centurion	Social worker	Professional	Federationist
Promotion system	Mixed reasons	Completely unjust	Unjust: based on irrelevant criteria	Just	Just	Just or mixed
Relations between the ranks	Mainly consensus	Conflict	Conflict	Mainly consensus	Consensus	Contained, limited conflict
Role of police	Includes some social aspects, but mainly crime prevention	No valid function at all	Narrow, should concentrate on crime	Wide, largely a social service	Includes many functions	Includes many functions but must limit
Outside trade unions	Basic sympathy but too much power now	Identifies with them as selfishly concerned	Against as disruptive of order	Too much power now	All right if they are responsible	Moral identification with unions

sergeants, and there were a few in the traffic division. Fifteen per cent were closest to the 'uniform-carrier' type. Again, virtually all were uniformed constables, with a few uniformed sergeants and traffic constables. Twenty-four per cent were 'new centurion' types (50% of the C.I.D. approximated to this type). It seemed to stretch higher up the rank structure than the first two categories, and some uniformed inspectors seemed to fit it. The 'social worker' type was rather rare. Only 6% seemed to come close to it, and these were mainly young constables. Twenty-one per cent fitted the 'professional' type. These were primarily, but not exclusively, specialists or inspectors. The 'Federation activist' is statistically an unimportant category. The inner caucus of the Federation is only six or seven men. It was impossible to fit 11% into any of the categories, because they seemed to straddle two or more.

Since data was collected only at one point in time the process by which people develop into these types could not be traced. It is suggested that they result from the interaction of initial orientation to the job and experience within it. This distinction is itself largely a tenuous one, as events are perceived through the perspective the man brings into the job, and his reaction to occurrences depends on his interpretation of them. But the man's career development is not a simple unfolding of his initial orientation. He encounters a situation which, whatever the variations in the subjective meaning and definition of it, nonetheless imposes objective constraints. The 'action' perspective validly emphasises that a worker's response to his situation cannot be regarded as a simple, determinate reaction to it. He brings into work a subjective interpretative scheme and set of values which filter his response, but a 'definition of a situation is, after all, a definition of a *situation*' (Beynon & Nichols 1971: 11). There are limits to the validity of W. I. Thomas's famous dictum that 'if men define a situation as real, it is real in its consequences'. Men's definitions have important consequences, but so do the real social situations they encounter, in which other men with conflicting definitions and resources have varying amounts of power to act in ways which satisfy or frustrate their expectations.

The suggestion made here is that varying kinds of initial orientation may interact with subsequent experience so as to produce a relatively stable and satisfactory 'fit' between expectations and situation, resulting in a 'bobby', 'new centurion', 'professional' or 'social worker'. Alternatively the situations which are encountered may frustrate expectations, and result in either resignation from the force or 'uniform-carrying'. For a very few, the availability of definitions stemming from a strong union background suggest an interpretation of problems as soluble through representative organisation, and these men become the dedicated Federationists. Some suggestions about relationships between initial orientation and subsequent career patterns can be made.

It has been noted that (a) C.I.D. men come more often than others from police backgrounds; (b) they, and uniform inspectors, are more likely to have entered as cadets, or at least made the police their career of first choice; and (c) inspectors tend to have better educational qualifications prior to entry, and if they have worked outside at all, to have been in higher status jobs. The suggestion is that men with police or cadet backgrounds are more likely to have elements of the 'police mind', such as a trained suspiciousness and a sense of discretion congruent with that of the supervisors, than are other recruits. They are more likely from the start of their careers to work in ways that mark them out as suitable detectives. Those with better educational and/or occupational attainment before entry are more likely to impress as having 'leadership' potential, as are those whose dedication to the police as a 'professional' career is indicated by early or cadet entry. On the other hand, those who initially see police work as attractive because of its extrinsic advantages such as security, are unlikely at the start to have the appropriate values and know-how for success. However, their progress in career terms is certainly not ruled out.

The way in which these career paths work out in practice can be seen in case-studies of men who illustrate each type. These are not representative, in that they fit one or another type more closely than most do. But they usefully highlight the processes at work.

Case 1: The 'bobby'

Constable T. is a 49-year-old uniformed man, whose present job is as a collator. This involves co-ordinating the information about an area which is provided by the Unit Beat men. He has been doing this for three years, and had spent the other twenty years of his service as a patrol constable. Being station-bound suits him in view of his age, but he had really preferred outside patrol. 'The best part of the job really is being in contact with the public.'

He joined in 1950 at the age of twenty-six. He had been in the army during the war, and before that had worked for some years as a clerk in an aircraft factory. His main attraction to the police force was instrumental. For clerks 'the money wasn't rising, the prospects weren't too good. . .and they were crying out for policemen in 1950'. He earned a pound more in the force, and 'that £1 meant a lot'. But there were also intrinsic attractions: 'Having been in the army and out in the open-air, the clerical work didn't exactly suit me.' He was not really 'police-minded'. 'There's been no member of the family in the police force at all. . .I'd never thought about it before.' He is fairly satisfied with police pay. 'We can't grumble today, compared with lots. I don't live a very high life, but I live within my means, as we all should do. But I suppose we can all do with a bit more.' The most important rewards in a job were social. Pleasant work-mates were the most important thing to look for in a job. 'They're essential, let's face it.'

He was 'not a particularly ambitious man. I never flogged it.' He had sat and failed the promotion exam early on in his career, and 'then I didn't bother again'. Promotion is seen as just. It depends on 'personality' and 'dedication', plus a certain element of driving ambition. 'You've got to do a bit of pushing, mind.'

Ordinary beat work is regarded as the essence of the job, and what he'd liked best because of the social contact. The collator's job is a 'bit remote', though still useful, and best suited for someone like himself who 'can't get about like I used to'.

He views the public in friendly terms. 'When I go home, I relax as much as I can and forget about it. If an incident occurs whereby help is required, well then, it's the same as any citizen.' He sees himself essentially as a civilian doing a job, and maintains a 'private' life.

He is quite sympathetic to trade unions, and does not feel they have too much power, though they sometimes 'abuse' it. 'The ordinary man's got to have a watchdog.' The police, however, are a special case, and the Federation is adequate for them. 'We stand for the government...The British public looks upon the police force as something which sort of stands for the government, and therefore it has respect for it and expects it to toe the line, not take industrial action.' Anyway, it doesn't need to take militant action like industry 'because if the Government is doing its job by the police force and the public, then the police force is looked after'. Affiliation with unions might be a good thing as it would 'pool experience, and improve police–public relations'. But striking or working-to-rule are rejected because of the unique nature of a job 'where there's injury and death about'.

He is morally committed to the purposes of the job, which he sees as wider than crime-control, though this is a crucial aspect. The policeman must be expected to do all jobs which come his way. The problems facing them have got worse, but in quantitative terms of workload rather than any qualitative change. The policeman ought to have more say in communicating the grass roots view of problems, but this must be limited to 'talking and discussing things'. The basic legitimacy of the command structure must be respected.

His overall satisfaction is perhaps best reflected in the fact that his son has followed him into the force. He does have some vague feeling of regret at his not having been 'very academic' at school, which would have allowed him more scope in job choice. He doesn't think he would rejoin if he could relive his life, 'though I've got nothing against the police force, no complaints about my job'.

Constable T. typifies the 'bobby'. He was drawn into the job by a mix of instrumental and intrinsic attractions, though primarily the former. He has been quite satisfied with the job, and content to remain a uniformed patrolman, which he sees as the core of the service. He was never especially ambitious, and tries to maintain a private life outside the force. He sees the Federation as a useful 'watchdog', as are outside trade unions for industrial workers. The police cannot have a stronger body, because of their special responsibilities.

Case 2: The 'uniform-carrier'

Constable R. is a 54-year-old uniform P.C. He joined in 1947 at the age of twenty-eight, having been in the army during the war, and then holding a clerical job with B.O.A.C. for a couple of years. He had also been in the regular army prior to war service. He recalls his motivation to join the police force as primarily financial. 'I looked round for another job, but this was the best paid job going at the time.' But police work also had certain intrinsic appeal. 'I'd been used to wearing a uniform. There was a certain regimentation about it to which I had become used, giving and taking orders. We went on the square and we paraded and marched about. This was a thing I could do well...I enjoyed it to begin with.' A further intrinsic attraction was the respect he had been brought up to have for the police. 'Like most members of the public, from a distance I had admired policemen. My recollection was of stalwart looking individuals who came round and put things right, and all this business... Some are brought up to hate policemen, but I wasn't. I always admired them, and thought, well, that's all right, be a policeman.'

No trace of this initial respect remains. He has become very embittered both by failure to be promoted, and by his transfer out of the C.I.D. after several years. He regards this as 'what the trade unions call victimisation', and sees it as a punishment for his having been too 'outspoken'. He sees the force hierarchy as riddled with nepotism and corruption, and dominated by Masons. 'I know there's an old boy network in most establishments, but the extent to which it's perpetrated in this job makes the mind boggle.' The fact that 'the last thing they look for in promoting people is efficiency', makes no difference to the job. Supervisory incompetence is of no consequence because the police force has no real function to perform anyway.

We're not required to be efficient, we're non-productive, it doesn't matter if a man can do his job or not. It would be different outside in business. If you suddenly appointed someone as head of department who was a clown, who couldn't do it, straight away the department goes to pieces. In an enterprise like this, it's of no consequence who you sit at the top of the Christmas tree. It's the rank and file that do the work. Anyone can sit up there.

Masonic influence is seen as extending beyond internal promotion, to the determination of force policy.

The public at large accept the fact that the law is administered by a body of men who are presumed to be completely unbiassed in every respect, politically and what have you. But how can you be when some of us are subject to outside influences? If we join a secret society and we have some blood brothers or some Klu Klux Klown [*sic*] and one of them suddenly commits some breach of the law, and I'm sworn as his blood brother, how can I be unbiassed? If only the public at large were aware of the fact! We're precluded from belonging to a political party, not that I'd want to, but I do object to the fact that some people belong to all kinds of funny little organisations which hide themselves behind doors and go through all kinds of strange rites. It's an offence! There's an act which says the practice of witchcraft is illegal! Yet these silly sods, they dress up in all sorts of peculiar garb, and the whole thing is a mutual aid society. Let's have a police mutual aid society, let's all help each other. But when you bring in outside interests it gets a bit dicey, I think.

The policeman needs an organisation to protect him. The Federation is useless in this respect. It was established as a control device to prevent policemen having an effective representative body, and it continues to function this way. 'It was a sop, that's all when it was first created. That was in 1919 and nothing's happened to it since.' The Federation, like the force itself, is run by a corrupt group of men.

It's another gimmick, a way of exploiting the job. Getting something out of it you wouldn't otherwise get. I don't think they're dedicated people, hoping to achieve anything for us, quite honestly. Someone's got to be elected, and they offer themselves. But cast us all away on a desert island, and a leader would emerge, but I'm sure it wouldn't be one of the Federationists! . . . Why do they take up office? It's a gimmick, like knowing the boss's daughter, or playing golf with him. Some chaps get disgruntled because they don't get promotion, so they think if they make themselves a big enough nuisance, they'll promote them to get rid of them.

It would be hard to give the police force more power in negotiations. This is not because of the responsibility they have to the public, or other such moral arguments. It is simply that the force has no importance at all.

It would make us look rather foolish if we worked to rule and found out that people accepted it, and said 'Carry on this way, it's a lot better than it was before!' I don't think strike action is the answer as far as the police force is concerned. It doesn't hurt anybody. People go on strike in industry, it hurts somebody in the pocket, and this is what tells. Here we're not productive, we don't produce anything, people don't care if we're here or not.

Affiliation with trade unions is ruled out, because there is already too much outside influence in the force.

At the moment, there are very few, if any, communists in the police force. Well, there are many in trade unions, that's obvious. I don't want to see this country turn communist. Mark you, there are other, more insidious bands of people, who perform miracles in their own quiet ways behind closed doors, which are peculiar to the police force. I can join a secret society like that, and in collusion with other people who have an interest, thereby deploy individuals in a way that would be beneficial to us both. Are you with me?

Although he condemns many activities of outside trade unions, and admits to ignorance about them, he shares a certain sympathy for their situation and realises that from *their* point of view their actions may be justified.

I think picketing should be abolished altogether. I can't quite see the necessity for it, to be quite honest, between you and me... It depends from which point of view you look at it, you see. As a member of the public inconvenienced by strikes you feel 'Oh! the ... unions!' But I dare say if I was in a similar position I might be inclined to do the same thing.

Constable R. tries to minimise the extent to which work interferes with his private life, but recognises certain difficulties in mixing with civilians because of their suspiciousness.

As soon as the job starts to affect your private life it's time to pack it in. It's rubbish, nonsense to say the policeman should never stop being a policeman. You shouldn't be one when you're off duty. If they're going to have that, make us all members of M.I.5 and give us spy cards! But when you join the job you do virtually ostracise yourself from being an ordinary member of the community, because of the way people react to you when they know you're one.

These views are all informed by a generally instrumental and cynical approach to life. 'Words like dedication are old hat, they've gone out of the window. It's the survival of the fittest again. You've got to look after number one today.' The only reason he stays is for the pay, and to collect his pension at the end. In return he tries to get by with as little as possible. The policeman 'should exploit his job to the full advantage'. Police pay was totally inadequate by outside standards. He had often felt, when as a detective he had occasion to learn how much money some people had, 'why the hell am I doing this, when I could be sitting there getting that man's money?'

Constable R. is completely alienated from the police force. He sees it as unfair, useless and frustrating. He is only tied to it by the cash nexus. His original respect for the job has been transformed into hostility through the experience of what he sees as victimisation and unjustified failure. There is no practical way of changing this, though he would welcome any powers that did. The situation of the police force is a reflection of a generally sick and corrupt society, based on ruthless self-seeking.

Case 3: The 'new centurion'

Constable E. was a 31-year-old panda driver. When I met him he was in a uniform division, though he was transferred very shortly afterwards to the C.I.D. He had originally joined another force at the age of nineteen, and transferred to his present force after five years, for entirely personal reasons. He had had nothing but odd jobs previously, and had done two years at a further education college making up for failing 'O' levels at school. He had considered the R.A.F. as an alternative career, but his father, who had spent his life in it, dissuaded him.

His early experiences growing up in R.A.F. bases on the continent had inclined him towards a uniformed service career, preferably the police force. 'I've always given it serious thought, since I was twelve or thirteen. As a young boy you're persuaded by adults around you. I was in Germany, and other parts of Europe, for three years, and I saw different police forces there. You get influenced a good deal by the glamour, especially on the Continent.' He was impressed with European police forces, whom he viewed as less shackled by legal restraints on their action. 'The police on the Continent are...um...unreserved. In this country, we are reserved as policemen really. On the Continent, act first, ask the questions afterwards, regardless of circumstances. In this country, the other way round, we have to think.' He sees policemen as having 'an honest streak, more than the average person', which draws them to wish to help people by enforcing the law. He joined at the earliest possible opportunity, and 'the pay never worried me at that time'.

His frustrations with the job are not related to failure to have financial demands met. They result from pressure from senior officers, and the courts and legislature, not to do the job the way he, as the man actually on the scene, knows best. On the one hand, there are cases where, he feels, there are too many pressures limiting his discretion *not* to enforce the law in all its rigour. For example, he describes a case where three lads, about ten or eleven years old, had knocked bricks off a car-park wall.

Now at this stage I had three courses of action. I could have gone in with both feet and arrested the boys... Or I could have gone round to those kids' homes, seen the fathers, got all the rubbish you need for statements. Or, as I did do, said 'Over to you, Mr Complainant' and let him decide. He said he was not bothered, he was quite happy to let them off. So I said 'Well, fair enough'. As an individual policeman, in my own mind, I did it the right way. But you get these circumstances whereby you have a sergeant or inspector or even a higher rank, dictating to you. 'You will arrest that man.' Now, he's a third person, he's not in the job from the start, he doesn't know the family. And he comes along and sticks his big head in, and says 'knock 'em off!' I feel like saying 'bugger off!' But he's the gaffer, he's in charge, and that's the trouble.

On the other hand, for reasons best known to themselves, the courts mysteriously under-enforce the law in serious cases.

You come to the courts, where you get a bloke indecently exposing himself, or indecent assault, rape, something like this. And they get a psychiatrist's report and put him on probation! Whatever you say, this man is of sound mind. A little bit kinky, but a sound mind. He should do time, not two years' probation... There's no comparison on the offences. Like capital punishment, which undoubtedly was a deterrent. The vast majority of people who knew they were convicted were a bit strung up. Tried to get on the bandwagon, insanity and so forth. Now if you get the bloke who's genuinely round the bend, then I say let's help him the best we can. But these people who rob banks and go armed. You don't need all this psychological rubbish. This is murder, Capital Murder, and that bloke should be strung up!'

The source of much of the trouble is the promotion system and its injustices. This is not because of personal corruption, but the use of the wrong criteria. Too much attention is paid to the academic qualifications of candidates, and too little to the more relevent question of experience and success in real police work. The practical policeman has no time for the studies necessary for promotion.

If you're working shifts, pounding the beat and getting soaking wet through all night, do you want to go home to bed, or to start reading law books? But if you're into a little nine-to-five job in an office somewhere, see the difference... Due respect to them and the system, they're bloody idiots! They haven't got the experience. The members of the public, they go past the constable or sergeant and straight to the inspector. It's natural. But what have they got? A glorified boy-scout, still wet behind the bloody ears. And a sergeant with twenty years experience alongside him! No wonder they lose the respect of their supporters. All right, they might know it up here, I mean, not being disrespectful to you, they've been to university perhaps, got B.A.s. It's all very well, make them chief superintendent tomorrow, but for Christ's sake, don't put them out on the street!

The practical, experienced policeman should have greater discretion to apply the law as he sees fit in view of immediate circumstances rather than preconceived, theoretical notions.

I'm not saying I'm God Almighty by any means, that I should be allowed to do exactly as I please. But I am saying that if I go to an incident or a scene of something or other, I draw my conclusions as to what's going on and what should be done. And then you get these young inspectors, with four bloody years' service in, coming round and telling me 'Oh yes, as per paragraph sub-section this, that and the other, you haven't done it right!' This is what gets my goat. I feel like turning round, and telling him to bugger off! In fact, I have done on occasions.

Given the way the system works, the 'new centurion' would rather continue without promotion than go through the necessary motions and stop being what he sees as a proper policeman. 'I know you might say I'm a bit jealous because I haven't got a nine-to-five job. I could get one if I wanted, but I'd cease to be a policeman, because you're away from the public. Sure, sat on your backside, pen-pushing, doing statistics. Anyone can do that! But you're not being a policeman!'

The Federation ought to have more power to put over the case of the rank and file policeman. He is against trade unionism in general, but believes the Federation must have some 'leverage', a 'spur' to goad the authorities with. 'I've got no time for these trade unions, but you must have some leverage, whereby if circumstances govern it we can withdraw our labour.' Not, like the unions, for 'some stupid tiddly reason that could be negotiated or thrashed out quite easily'. The power is necessary not for 'bread and butter' matters, but to protect policemen doing their job.

If, for argument's sake, a policeman is in trouble whereby he assaults somebody, the attitude is that a policeman should never assault anybody. Full-stop! If he's in a position whereby he's outnumbered five to one, and he gets in first, him or me, that's wrong. He should have ten pints of shit knocked out of him and then stand up and say 'I arrest you'. If he doesn't the policeman is convicted of criminal assault and kicked out of the job.

The 'new centurion's' perspective is centred on the colleague group of rank-and-file policemen. The senior ranks are out of touch at best, and corrupt at worst, unlike the integrity of the 'centurion'.

The biggest row I ever had was with an ex-chief superintendent. I seriously considered punching him one straight between the eyes...I'd nearly got knocked down on the main road 3 a.m. one morning by a white MGB. He was going like a maniac, overtaking everything in sight, forcing everyone off the road. I got in the middle of the road to stop him, and he nearly knocked me down! I got his number, traced his name and address to S.B. [affluent suburb]. I rang up and the man said he was the owner. I asked 'who was driving it this morning.' 'Oh, that'll be my son, I expect'. I asked him to send his son to the station. In he walks. 'I didn't see you' he says, and all that rubbish. I said I'd report him for driving in a dangerous manner and failing to stop on the indication of a uni-formed police officer. Give him his due, he seemed genuinely sorry. Anyway, I put it all on paper, and then this thing came back. 'Caution!' So I marched into the office and said to the super 'I understand you've given Mr so-and-so a caution?' 'Yes'. 'May I ask why? On what grounds?' The first thing he said was 'Well, after all's said and done, he is an apprentice chartered accountant. And his father is the commandant of the Special Constabulary'... This is done by senior officers, especially when they're old in the tooth. They're safeguarding their retirement. And we get penalised in the end.

The public outside the force are also regarded with varying degrees of suspicion and hostility. The basic division perceived by the 'centurion' is between the villains, or potential villains, on the one hand, and the respectable public on the other. For the villains, there is little sympathy.

My patch...is a bit naughty, Nice new houses, but the bloody animals that live in them! There are some people who are decent, conduct themselves reasonably, but they're a minority. Last night, 9 p.m., I got called to a house over there. Domestic dispute. Supposed to be a fight going on, husband and wife having a set-to. So I goes in there. Deadly quiet. And what it was, this tart, that's all I can say she was, a tart, had been thown out of her house, 'cos she's been having it off with some other bloke. She had two kids by this bloke, but her husband accepted them into his house. Along with the five they had, that was seven kids. And the husband got to the stage where he said 'Out!' Off she went, seven kids and all, down to her sister's. The husband gets papers served on him for a separation, and comes round to the sister's house, playing merry bloody hell about it. Which is where I came in. By the time I get there, he's gone. And there's these two bloody women, sluts, down and out bloody sluts. She's got seven kids, five by her husband and two by the other. The sister's been divorced twice, got nine kids. So she said: 'What am I going to do? There's us two, and sixteen kids!' I said 'Putting it bluntly, my dear, I should have it cut out!' They're so bloody ignorant! They start swearing, and what have you. They get it back! If anyone starts f-ing and blinding at me, he gets it back, because I'm a big believer, you meet force with bloody force! It's not just here, it's all over the country. Millions of them in homes like that. They're animals, thick. They were born in shit, and they'll die in shit! If you give 'em money they spend it on booze or bloody bingo! How do you legislate for morons like that?

The line between villains and potential villains is increasingly blurred, as groups like students or trade unionists become involved in law-breaking.

You see, it's even you students. I know there are a minority who go to university genuinely to study, and you get no trouble with them. They don't go smashing up the universities, having bloody great riots, getting on the band-wagon. But like at L.S.E., where they have these sympathy do's with trade unionists. How they can sympathise with a group of workers when they've never done any work themselves beats me! I mean, I've got sympathy for deep-sea fishermen. It's bloody rough out there in the winter. If they came out on strike, I should suffer, because I like my fish. But I'd never start bloody canvassing and lobbying on their behalf.

The respectable public are themselves viewed with hostility and suspicion. They are in turn divisible into two groups. The ordinary public, who are the potential victims of the villains, and those involved in the criminal justice system, e.g. judges, M.P.s. The latter are seen as at best naive and out of touch with the real world, at worst for mysterious reasons sympathetic to villains who they see as potential subjects for 'do-gooding'. The courts are not apprised of the tricks the villains get up to, and easily fooled by appearances into giving woefully inadequate sentences.

You get a bloke in court, he says 'Plead guilty, your Worship'. 'Yes, my man. You broke into so-and-so's shop. What have you got to say for yourself, my good chap?' 'I'm very sorry, sir! Won't do it again, sir!' And he stands there, with his bloody Brylcreem, and posh suit. The judge thinks 'How could a man like this do it? Must be something at home upset him...Probation!' But you know by yourself that all the bloody stuff he's got on is nicked anyway, there's not a bloody carpet on the floor that's his own. Excreta and what have you all over the bloody walls. Bread and jam and crumbs all over the bloody place... But the courts don't see this.

Legislators are equally out of touch. 'M.P.s turn round and ask "Are people losing faith in the Houses of Parliament?" They are, because they're idiots. They're not idiots as individuals, but collectively they're ignorant. They're making decisions about something they just don't know nothing about.'

The rest of the respectable public are naive, and even though they are well-meaning, the policeman must be wary of them. Their naivety is illustrated by an occasion when a mate of Constable E.'s had to show a B.B.C. team round his patch.

They had a team from Woman's Hour came to this station, two or three years ago. A couple of headshrinkers and so forth. They went out with W.... And he had a tanking! [Laughter]. The jobs that came up! As if it were planned! [Laughter]. He was rocking for a bloody month afterwards! The jobs he got involved in! And they had tape-recorders and bloody all, the B.B.C. They were amazed. The standard of what kind of people the police are dealing with. You heard it all over the tape. Terrible, these women shouting obscenities. They said: 'I never thought I'd hear a woman say that!' They were amazed and taken aback. 'This isn't England...I mean, I've been to Roedean!' and all this. It's a completely different life altogether to them, they couldn't understand it.

But while the naive simplicity of the 'law-abiding' public may be a source of amusement, the policeman must always be careful that it doesn't land him in trouble.

They drop you right in it. It's happened many a time. I was out on the pandas when they first started. And there was this bloke doing sixty-five miles an hour on the B. Road. Sixty-five miles an hour! This was about 8 p.m. I eventually nailed him on the city boundary. I told him: 'What in ... do you think you're doing? I don't mind forty, but sixty odd is a 100% more than you should be doing. Now why?' He said, 'My wife's in labour. I've had a phone call from the hospital.' He's full of it. So I say, 'On your way, but watch it!' So he went off, beating the wind. Roars off! A fortnight bloody later he writes to the Chief Constable. He explains all the circumstances, and wants to thank me. I got dragged in there and given the thickest bollocking ever for condoning him going at sixty-five miles an hour. He dropped me right in it. They think they're doing you a good turn, but they don't.

The policeman must therefore be continuously watchful in interaction with the public, even the well-meaning, respectable sections. The practical policemen are essentially on their own, can only rely on each other. They are surrounded by potential danger and threats from all other groups. 'We're a tight-knit community. We've got to stand by each other because we're getting it from all angles. We get it from the outside, the general public, we get it from solicitors, from Q.C.s, we get it from our own bosses.' This gives the operational policeman a perspective and understanding unique to him, which no other group, with their more limited position in society can share. The police, in effect, are the touchstone of truth, able to transcend the limitations of all other groups whose vision is blinkered by the confines of a specific social status. 'As police officers we see life as nobody else sees it. At the top and at the bottom. You only see it at the top. A dustman only sees it at the bottom. As policemen, we're going up and down the ladder, all the time.'

The inducement to do a job with such responsibility and lack of appreciation can only be dedication, not financial reward. 'The only incentive is the desire to do the job. I have the desire to do the job, as an individual thing. It's the way I feel.' But pay is important as a mark of relative standing and public esteem. 'Years ago, before I joined, a policeman's pay was well above average. They were scrambling to get in, and they only took the cream, you had the better class coming in. Now they're not getting the men in, so they'll take anybody.' Nonetheless, while pay is important as a mark of status and determinant of the quality of recruits, police work is not to be regarded primarily as a job. It is a vocation, and the basis of a community unlike any other. 'It's a sect – it's like a religion, the police force.'

The outlook of the 'new centurion' is one that sees the 'real' policemen as the basis of social order and morality. They are opposed and hindered in their effectiveness not only by the 'villains', but also respectable but ignorant ordinary members of the public, and even their own superiors, who owe their positions to academic and social skills and graces, rather than police ability. The 'new centurion' feels that the only way of coping with crime and villainy is the tough approach. But this is not to be equated with rigorous enforcement of the law as written. On occasion the policeman uses his discretion not to enforce the law as it stands, when this would run counter to his commonsense morality, or in his 'expert' judgement of the concrete situation, be counter-productive. Despite his general opposition to trade unions, the 'centurion' feels that the Federation, or any other police representative body, must have much more power to put over the rank-and-file perspective, and alleviate their treatment as a pariah group.

Case 4: The 'social worker'

G. was a 27-year-old area constable. This role is the most likely one in the Unit Beat system to provide an outlet for the social work orientation, since it involves responsibility for a specific area and encourages a more continuous, wider relationship with the public than driving a panda car and responding to calls signifying trouble.

Constable G. joined in 1965 at the age of nineteen, having already done two years as a cadet. His attraction was clearly social. It was 'the fact that we are able to help people. I see my job as a social job. It's needed to keep the peace, to protect people's lives and property. Some of the people I come into contact with are inevitably the criminal kind. Not necessarily hardened criminals. I try to help them if I can, especially younger ones who've got into a state. This is the part of the work I like doing in the police force, this is why I'm an area constable now.' He was not attracted by financial considerations, and claimed to have earned twice as much in a temporary job he had before joining. But the security was a welcome factor. The real attraction was intrinsic: 'My brother was in the police force, and he told me the job was very interesting. It varies not only from day to day, but hour to hour.' He would really have preferred a more directly 'social' job, had he possessed the necessary qualifications. He had at one stage applied to a teachers' training college, and been accepted for the course. But by then he had domestic responsibilities, and felt he could not take the drop in income. 'If I ever leave, I'd like teaching, something to do with children anyway. But there was domestic reasons made me reject the offer [at teachers' training college]. I couldn't really afford to drop so much. The grant was only a third of what I was earning, and I had a mortgage commitment.'

Despite having seriously thought of leaving, and only being held at that stage by financial considerations, he was now satisfied with his job, and would join the police again if he had to start over.

We've probably got more schools on my ground than any other area in the city. . . A lot of juveniles, who are going through a stage of not having any clubs or anything to do while they're off from school. They've been given this extra year at school, and they just don't know what to do with themselves. The only thing I feel we can do for them is rent a playground, but a lot of residents are against that. The kids are always in trouble. I can't blame them to a certain extent. There's no facilities whatsoever for them. No youth leaders. So a lot of the kids have broken into houses, pinched mopeds, bicycles, this sort of thing. There are a lot of old people up here too, and they're always complaining. Old people can't stand a lot of noise. I give them as much attention as I can.

The 'social worker', unlike the 'new centurion', is sympathetic to, and concerned to help, all sections of the public, including the 'villains'.

I feel as though I've had a lot of success. I've got myself reasonably friendly with quite renowned criminals, well to the police force anyway. Some armed criminals who are very anti-police. I sometimes get invited to their house for a cup of tea and things. Sit down and chat. I feel that's an achievement in itself, and it really helps in some cases. One or two of the houses on this estate have improved their standard quite a bit. You go and tell them a bit about yourself and the things you do, what you think they should do. Not all of them, but one or two of them, have come along and improved their standard of life a bit.

Although he recognises that police work inevitably affects his private life, he tries to minimise this and to maintain outside friendships.

I try to keep my private life separate if I can. I try to keep the majority of my social friends outside the force, as much as I can. It's inevitable, of course, that you can't the whole time. . .I have very close contact with the schools on my ground. I'm on Christian name terms with many of the teachers, which is a good thing. I know my local magistrates well, and my local Councillors. They can be brought a bit closer to the police force by the area constable's work.

The lack of interference with private life was perhaps helped by the fact that his present wife was a policewoman, with similar ideas. (His previous wife had been a teacher.)

She does this school liaison scheme. She feels it's a tremendous job, a group of policemen going into schools to talk to kids about police work. They love it... The kids today are far less scared of policemen than they used to be. Whether that's good, I'm not 100% sure. I'm able to find out a lot more from the kids, but I know that while they'll talk to me, they'll still carry on housebreaking when I'm not there.

It should be noted that his conception of the 'social work' role of the police is integrally related to crime prevention. Constable G. does not see himself as a general public servant. He resents having to perform duties such as school traffic crossings, which he feels ought to be done by teachers or parents, and delivering summonses, which is seen as extraneous to the area man's real job, and possibly even counter-productive.

While attached to the work for primarily non-instrumental reasons, he is ambitious for promotion, and passed his exams early in service. He is quite frustrated with his failure to date. He attributes this partly to the influence of the Masons. 'The only ones getting promoted were the ones in the know: Lodges, clubs, Freemasons is the prime one. I wasn't prepared to join myself. If I can't get promoted because of my ability, I'd rather stay as I am.' He has, in fact, reconciled himself to the situation now, and is content to derive the satisfaction he does from the work itself and home life. 'I don't eat, drink and sleep promotion as do some policemen...I'm not ultra ambitious. I'm not prepared to go through all sorts of courses which will disrupt my home life, in the name of trying to get promotion.'

Despite these doubts about the justice of the promotion system, he accepts the legitimacy of the rank structure, and sees relationships as primarily consensual. They ought all to be represented by one association. 'It would be better if we were united rather than separated.' There is no real conflict between ranks. 'We're left to our own resources on the whole. The supervisors don't breathe down your neck.'

The police, like public services generally, are not given sufficient priority in government expenditure. 'The public ought to pay more for social service work, teaching, things like that which are important to the community. They're lacking in numbers, purely because the job's not well paid. Our pay isn't bad, but we could do with better pay. But so could other jobs like nursing, teachers, social workers.'

The answer to this is not trade union power, which is incompatible with the social responsibility of the job. The Federation ought to receive more sympathetic attention from government precisely because it renounces militancy. 'We don't hold our employers over a barrel to get what we want. We do ours by negotiation over a table. The government and the Police Council ought to realise we don't want to strike or work-to-rule. And because of this, we ought to be listened to more sympathetically.' The Federation does its best, and certainly the representatives are well-intentioned, dedicated men, 'blokes who are keen on helping the other'. But the government is not responsive enough to police needs. Other unions, with their disruptive tactics, achieve more, but they ought 'to adopt our line, the Federation line', so that 'there would be far less strikes in this country'.

Despite Constable Gs.'s inclination towards social work, and understanding view of 'villains' in general, he shares the opinion of many policemen that crimes of violence have been encouraged by the leniency of the 'do-gooders' who have 'reduced the harshness of sentences'. Precisely because of his generally humanitarian concern he sees 'crimes of violence' as in a category apart, and requiring tougher sanctions.

Crimes of violence towards other men are inhuman, and should be dealt with severely. I'm not saying death sentences, I'm against the death penalty. But more severe sentences so that people realise violent crime will not be tolerated. I cannot stand seeing people hurt other people physically, and I would never give them the kid-glove treatment. But I would be considerate to an ordinary housebreaker, even a hardened thief, if he doesn't resort to violent tactics.

The 'social worker' differs from the 'centurions' primarily in not perceiving the same gulf between police and public. He differs from the 'bobby', and *a fortiori*, the 'uniform-carrier' in his considered commitment to the job's social purpose. But unless he finds a suitable specialised niche, or succeeds in defining crime prevention as a social service, this type of policeman is likely to become rapidly frustrated, and either seek another career outside, or become ambitious for promotion and gravitate towards an increasingly 'professional' outlook. If all fails, the outcome is likely to be 'uniform-carrying'.

Case 5: The 'professional'

Chief Inspector P. is a 35-year-old officer in charge of a sub-division. He is what many policemen dub a 'whizz-kid'. He joined the force in 1958 at the age of twenty, having spent two years in the police cadets after leaving school, and then two years in the R.A.F. His father had been a butler, and then a chef. Chief Inspector P. had been to a grammar-school and left at sixteen after obtaining some 'O' levels. Since being in the force he had been continuously on the move from one division to another, done various specialist jobs, and several training courses, all the while moving up the rank structure quite rapidly. This wide experience typifies the 'high-flyer'.

His original attraction to the job had been primarily social.

It goes back to an appreciation at an early age that one wanted to do something more than just go out and earn a living... And to me the police service was the obvious embodiment of a social service, which was doing something concrete, specific and obviously beneficial to the community. And this is what I wanted to do. My closest pal and I at school made this decision at roughly the same time. We joined the cadets together, but after National Service he joined what can only be described as a pop group. He's since joined the force, and is now detective-sergeant in the Vice squad.

His attitude to life remains non-instrumental.

I sometimes think there must be easier ways to earn a living. But you come back to the question, what is it you want in life? Is it just to earn a living? Quite frankly, for me it isn't. The constrictions on using your mental faculties that you find in industry I'd find claustrophobic. I'd find minimal job satisfaction. You've got to be fairly blinkered to say you are achieving something if after thirty or forty years of working life you've just supplied people with material objects which become obsolescent and discarded. But there's always a need for what we provide.

His conception of the force structure is the converse of the 'bobby's' or the 'centurion's'. To him, the senior officers best embody and represent the proper view of policing.

The views of the service are reflected more by the comments of divisional officers than the Federation... Particular individuals like Sir Robert Mark, now Commissioner of the Metropolitan Police, who since his days as Chief Constable of Leicester has been particularly outspoken on a number of subjects associated with the police. More regard is paid to the things he will say than to Reg Gale, who is chairman of the Federation... The Association of Chief Police Officers is the one authoritative body the government will go to to seek views... The management structure is made up of people all of whom have been through the ranks, so they are aware of the difficulties and problems...sometimes there are overriding pressures in other directions which require a job to be done a certain way, perhaps to the disadvantage of the men who actually have to do it.

The enlightened superior will, however, afford *some* scope for consultation of the men's views. 'More notice is now taken of the Federation. I think there is room for more involvement in discussion. They reflect the views of the men who actually implement new policies, more than the Chief Officer who's geared more to the administrative side.' But as argued above, it cannot have the main say, which must be left to the senior officers with their all-round view. The supervisor should, however, adopt a non-authoritarian, man-management style of leadership.

The very nature of police work is that you entrust the individual to do his own job in what he sees at the time, in the prevailing situation, to be right. It's not so much control from above to me as self-control, self-discipline... Until the late fifties it was much more the formula of the armed forces for discipline. But that's been breaking down, and it's more open now.

The granting of trade union powers to the police would be a retrograde step, contrary to professionalisation. It is argued for by backward-looking people, who fail to see its irrelevance. The Federation is adequate as it stands. The only desirable changes would be in the direction of a professional association for the force.

We are limited in what powers the Federation ought to have. Within those limits it's quite adequate... The more traditionalist in outlook in the police service feel we should have the right to withdraw labour. But I accept that the police are in the same sort of situation as the medical profession and others who consciously waive such rights... It's opposed to my concept of what we're here for.

The way forward for the police force is increasingly to satisfy the traits associated with professionalism, so that it can become accepted as such by others. 'We see it as a profession. For many of us it's also a vocation. But I don't think it's seen as such by other professional bodies. I regret this. I think the Police College ought to be developed into a police university which, on completion of a period of study, awards a recognized academic qualification, recognised both internally and externally.' This would aid the selection process for promotion. It is already correctly based 'on your ability to do the job at the next rank...not particularly what you've already achieved.'

The improvement of professional training would facilitate the measurement of this. He is still personally keen on promotion, and confident of success. 'I feel I'm competent to do chief superintendent rank, and arguably beyond that...One's attitude to this changes as you progress. When one first joins, you join to do the job as constable, and thoughts of promotion are remote. It's only subsequently when opportunities come up that your attitude changes.'

As a profession, the police must accept restrictions on, and interference with, private life. 'The job doesn't end when you go home after eight hours' duty. There's an innate consciousness that you live on the job virtually. The nature of the job is such that you can't stop.' For example, the policeman must accept the restriction on outside employment. 'He ought not be subject to some other person. The police service is his primary responsibility.'

In terms of his opinions on matters of social and force policy, Chief Inspector P. consistently takes the balanced view, seeing both sides of the case. Problems facing the police? 'In some areas they've got better. We've become our own P.R. men, and have gone out of our way to explain to the public what we're trying to achieve. Certain areas of difficulty have got worse, for example the immigrant problem.' Civilianisation of police jobs? 'There are arguments both ways...I would encourage it in some areas, discourage it in others.' Trade unions? 'There's a lot of advantages in their having the powers they have, but some abuse it...But one must remember there are also hundreds of other unions that are not involved in disputes or attempting to overthrow the government.' Discipline in the police force? 'One can always think of instances where too much or too little control is exercised.' Like Buridan's ass, the judicious officer always sees the virtues of both sides of every situation. There are no panaceas to any problem, apart from 'professionalism', that is the ability to shun the simple view.

The work of the police force is and must be varied. It cannot be said to be solely crime-fighting or any such narrow conception. 'The job is not just law enforcement. It's a response to a social need which takes many, many forms. There are jobs which one is required to do which go beyond the limits of what some see as strictly police work. Some define these limits more closely, others have a more extended vision of what the police job is.'

Those who see the police role as maintaining the social order are mistaken. The police are vital in preserving a free, democratic way of life. Within this, their prime function is the provision of services to people in need.

I like to think one can contribute something to prevent us going the way we see evidence of police forces going in some other countries. In other words, that we remain the buffer between the establishment and the ordinary member of the public, rather than the instrument of the establishment. I know most people don't see us in that light. I see it this way, but there are times when one must take a stance which appears to support the *status quo*, to keep the establishment going or to back it up. But more often than not you're providing a fire brigade response to assist the average member of the public who is inadequate to deal with the unexpected. The one agency to whom he invariably turns is the police and the range of activity is enormous. You fill the role in the first instance of perhaps a hundred different specialists. This is its great attraction, of course.

The 'professional' thus has an image of the force as a multi-functional, bureaucratic hierarchy of dedicated, trained men. Authority must be concentrated at the top. The senior officers have a broader perspective, based on their wider experience, and greater ability as measured by professional qualifications. But there must be consultation, and a man-management rather than authoritarian leadership style. The men must be represented by a body that communicates their views, but they do not need any sanctions in a smoothly running, consensual organisation. The police perform a wide social role in a democratic society, and are incorrectly analysed as a tool of the *status quo*.

PART FOUR

Conclusions

13
Conclusions and implications of the study

Different theoretical perspectives on the police imply contrasting models of the appropriate form of work organisation. These were described in the first chapter. The *conservative* image of the policeman as the protector of a differentiated but consensually validated social order implies quasi-militaristic internal police organisation. The police are to be a strictly disciplined, hierarchically structured organisation. The duty of the lower ranks is to obey the decisions and orders of their superiors. This is appropriate because the patrolman operates away from the immediate observation of his commanders, and drill, and the self-discipline it engenders, are needed to ensure he acts in the expected way. Discipline is especially necessary on those occasions when the police act as a co-ordinated body of men in the control of crowds. Finally, strict discipline and obedience enables the police force to act as a model of the ideal organisation of society, to symbolise legal order. In this view, while the wise commander will be concerned about his men's morale and welfare, this ought not to be forced upon him by representative organisation. Concessions in this direction may be necessitated by the men's demands and actions, but they must be curbed as much as possible.

In the *liberal* view, police efficiency in the enforcement of law must be tempered by consideration for the rights of citizens to privacy, and of the accused to fair treatment. The ideal is a democratic police service, exercising authority by consent rather than force. Proper representation of the subordinate ranks is not only their right, but also conducive to the inculcation of police commitment to democratic values. There is ambivalence about the extent of union power they ought to have. Some see full unionisation as a vehicle of democratisation, at any rate in the long-run. Others, more impressed by the evidence that lower-rank personnel are readily politicised in support of reactionary positions, argue that policemen must accept limitations on the normal rights of workers. They look to the control of police forces by more liberally minded senior officers as the guarantee of conformity to democratic values.

To *radicals* the police force acts to buttress a repressive social order, even if it conforms to norms of legality and due process, as defined by a parliamentary democracy within a capitalist society. In so far as they have gone beyond regarding the police merely as authoritarian opponents of social change, the radical image of policemen has been of falsely-conscious dupes of the ruling class. Objectively, it has been argued, policemen are propertyless workers, who potentially could be organised into unions as parts of the labour movement. As with liberals, however, there has been ambivalence about police unionisation, in view of the frequently right-wing character of police politics. The purpose of this study has been to explore the views of policemen themselves towards their work organisation and representation. These have to be understood in relation to their work and social situation, rather than seen as 'false' by the standards of an *a priori* ideal.

The historical development of police unionism in Britain was described in chapter 2. Towards the end of the First World War, the clandestine Police and Prison Officers' Union gained rapidly in strength, fuelled by the erosion of the real value of pay through rapid inflation, together with resentment engendered by harsh and sometimes unjust discipline. Two strikes were called in 1918–19, in the course of a struggle for recognition, improved pay and better conditions. The government, especially alarmed by the growing links with the trade union movement in a context of general labour militancy (and with the example of the October 1917 Russian Revolution before it), succeeded in outlawing the union and substituting a tame official substitute, the Police Federation. The limitations of its constitution, together with the buoyant recruitment situation during the inter-war Depression years, made the Federation a fairly ineffectual body. The problematic manpower situation, brought about by post-war full-employment and inflation, stimulated the emergence of the Federation in the 1950s as a more independent organisation, and the establishment of collective bargaining machinery. The Federation has utilised its new status and resources (as well as the continuing manpower shortage) not only to press for improvements in pay and conditions, but to claim a voice in the determination of policy. Since the mid-6os it has come to be consulted frequently on legislation, and is increasingly prominent as the public spokesman of the police rank-and-file. The 'law and order' campaign marks the culmination of this trend. The growing social and political unrest of the late 1960s, and especially the struggles between the Conservative government and the trade union movement in the early 1970s, considerably strengthened the police hand in negotiations. Recently, the rapid rise in unemployment has, for the first time since the war, eased the recruitment situation, and undermined the police bargaining position. But in the period of the fieldwork, the police were in an especially favoured position with regard to pay negotiations.

This was reflected in the overall assessment of the adequacy of the Federation. Fifty-two per cent felt the Federation was an adequate representative body. This was partly because the moral responsibility of policemen precluded the full powers of a trade union. But rejection of unionism was buttressed by the belief that it was not necessary, in view of the strong bargaining position enjoyed by the police due to their vital role in maintaining order, especially at a time of crisis. This demonstrates a major reason for the tendency of policemen to reject identification with the union movement. Some writers have suggested that, because of their common position as propertyless wage-earners, the police share similar objective economic interests to the working-class. This may be true under some circumstances, as the 1918 developments indicate. But the experience of the early 1970s suggests that the police may often be diametrically opposed to the labour movement in terms of economic interest. Due to the need to ensure police morale in times of social crisis, when they are called upon to control union picketing and political demonstrations, their bargaining strength may be greater precisely at those times when that of other workers is under attack. In so far as this is true, their failure to identify with the labour movement is not 'false consciousness', but based on rational economic considerations. Although a majority of policemen felt the Federation was, on the whole, adequate to represent them, a considerable minority, 45%, disagreed. This response was related to rank. The inspectors were overwhelmingly satisfied with the Federation, but more constables were dissatisfied.

The assessment of the Federation varies in terms of its specific performance on particular activities. The one area of Federation work which was seen as outstandingly successful was the help given to men on discipline charges. This is paradoxical in view of the explicit exclusion of this activity from the Federation's statutory terms of reference. Nonetheless, although its involvement in this area is unofficial, it underlies much of the support the Federation enjoys. Since it is in the first instance a local activity, this partly explains why the branch level of the Federation is regarded as more successful than the national. In the field of collective bargaining over pay and conditions, the Federation is seen as only moderately successful. The determinants of pay and conditions are largely beyond the Federation's reach. Pay is determined by demand and supply factors which, in the absence of powers of industrial action, the Federation cannot influence, but only utilise to support its claims. Other aspects of pay, such as overtime or allowances, are the arena of a continuous struggle at local level to ensure that the men actually receive their due when general rates are applied to individual cases. The Federation was credited with success over some 'conditions of service', for example, mitigation of harsh discipline and improved hours. It was felt it could do more on others, for example, ensuring the 'tools' for the job, but some were beyond its grasp in principle, for example, the clemency of the weather. 'Welfare' was regarded as a successful area of Federation activity. The Federation was seen as quite unsuccessful in relation to 'professional' issues concerning how the work should be done. Its public relations efforts were not widely appreciated, it was not the principal channel for communication of information, it was seen as contributing little to force efficiency and as having virtually no say in legislation. It may be, however, that the recent 'law and order' campaign will alter this assessment.

Overall, there was a general satisfaction with the structure and powers of police representation. A majority rejected the idea of a police trade union, although opinion was again related to rank, and among constables there was a considerable body, though not a majority, in favour of a more powerful and militant representative body. Affiliation with trade unions, and the right to strike, were generally ruled out. The reasons for opposing these were that they are seen as irresponsible and undermining force discipline, as well as exposing it to undesirable political influences. These outweighed any potential advantage to policemen. (It must be remembered, however, that the police were anyway in a strong bargaining position at this time.) Among the inspectors, there was majority support for a single professional association to replace the Federation, reflecting a consensus image of the relationship between ranks. Sergeants were evenly divided on this, but constables tended to be against it. The general conclusion would seem to be that the Federation commands more support overall than either a trade union or a single professional association would. However, there is considerable dissatisfaction among constables with its adequacy as a bargaining body, and among those dissatisfied with it a majority would like a union (although not necessarily one that was affiliated with the T.U.C., and without the right to strike, though with the right to resort to more limited industrial action). The situation was one in which there were considerable contradictions and tensions, both between different individuals and ranks, and ambivalences within the consciousness of individuals. There was a dynamic instability, and while the situation at the time of interviewing seemed to result in a favourable evaluation of Federation adequacy, other historical contexts would be likely to produce a very different picture. The inclusion of inspectors (with their more consensual image of the force) in the Federation in the same numbers as constables functioned, as intended, to lower support for trade unionism.

A majority of constables, but not of supervisors, wanted the Federation to have more say in decision-making. A majority in all ranks agreed it should have *some* say in policy, but supervisors were more inclined to feel that consultation was already sufficient. There was virtually unanimous support for the Federation to have a right of regular access to the Chief Constable, rather than being dependent on the individual's whims. A substantial majority felt there should also be proper access to the police authority, which was seen as ignorant of police matters and exerting a pernicious influence.

Most of the force identified with the Federationists, saying that their attitudes to the job were no different from the ordinary policeman; this was more true of constables than supervisors. The C.I.D. seemed peculiarly alienated from the Federationists, whom they saw as 'clock-watchers', not dedicated policemen.

Various types of representative could be distinguished. A hard-core of dedicated activists filled the executive positions, like chairman and secretary. They tended to have a long-standing commitment to trade unionism, and had worked in outside 'trades' before. Their union sympathies and experience inclined them to Federation work. They all believed the police ought to have a proper union as a matter of right, and pressed for this at national Conferences. These activists had the reputation of being 'bolshie reds'. This was in police terms, however, and their general political and social philosophy was by no means necessarily radical, apart from their trade union commitment, though a few were avowed socialists. Another group of representatives were essentially 'passengers'. Usually inspectors, these men had stood only because it was their 'turn' and no-one else would. The other distinct group were the ardent 'moderates', who wanted to be a counter-weight to the 'bolshie' elements. Some saw a term of 'responsible' Federation work as an asset in the climb to the top.

There was general agreement that outside trade unions were now too powerful, although they were originally justified as protection for the down-trodden working-man (seen as a relic of the past). Union activities, like picketing, ought to be more strictly controlled. While the generality and vehemence with which these views are held by policemen must be noted, they are, of course, widely felt sentiments, shared by many trade unionists themselves. Where the police differ is their role in relation to unions, which sometimes permits them opportunity to give their feelings practical expression. Policemen have *not* generally been shielded from membership in outside unions. Support for outside unionism is neither a necessary nor a sufficient condition for wanting a *police* union.

Police attitudes to trade unionism can be illuminated by the characteristics of their orientation to work. Policemen came mainly from skilled manual working-class backgrounds. Of those who come from non-manual origins, many had police fathers. Policemen were educationally successful, compared to their social origins, in terms of type of school attended, but did not perform especially well academically. Those who had worked before joining the force, had usually been upwardly socially mobile *prior* to entry. Supervisors and specialists were slightly more often from non-manual backgrounds, and more educationally successful. The C.I.D. disproportionately had police backgrounds. Supervisors and specialists were less likely to have worked outside, and had made the police their career of first choice, often entering as cadets. These differences cannot be taken as evidence of nepotism. They probably indicate a relationship between prior experience, initial orientation to the job, and subsequent career success. There was no tendency for policemen to have military experience more often than the population in general, when age was taken into account. Nor was military experience related to subsequent success. So policemen were mainly from skilled manual working-class homes, and, especially in the case of supervisors, oriented towards upward social mobility, as their educational and previous occupational experience suggested. This would tend to weaken their interest in *collective* strategies of a union kind, as opposed to individual career advance. It would, however, incline them to support upgrading the status of the police as a 'profession', as a means of collective social mobility.

The reasons given for joining the force contradicted the conclusions of previous studies, which indicated that policemen were attracted by instrumental concerns of pay and security. Most mentioned intrinsic attractions such as interesting, varied, exciting work and the attractions of a uniformed, disciplined body. Only 19% gave purely instrumental reasons. This cannot be taken as a universal constant. The motivation people have for joining is related to the economic circumstances of the labour market at the time they joined. Older men, recruited in a period when memories of the pre-war depression lingered, were more often drawn by the instrumental advantages of a secure livelihood. Younger men, accustomed to a full-employment economy, more often considered intrinsic attractions of the job itself. Non-instrumental factors only influence choice within a structurally determined range of alternatives. Even for those who saw it as intrinsically attractive, police work may not have been their career of first choice in the best of all possible worlds. But there was a tendency for those joining in the late 1950s and 1960s to do so for non-instrumental reasons, and as a career of first choice. (It is likely that the recent development of mass unemployment, and the growing instrumental attractions of the police as a secure occupation, result in a different initial orientation among current recruits.) Men drawn by an intrinsic attraction were more likely both to be occupationally mobile in the force and to reject unionism.

Policemen's *current* orientation to their work shows them to be more satisfied than most manual and lower-grade non-manual workers, but less so than 'professionals'. Satisfaction with work was related to opposition to unionism. On any measure of satisfaction, there seemed to be a hard-core of dissatisfied men, constituting about a third of the force. The main sources of dissatisfaction were problems with supervisors (especially in the past when discipline was harsher), difficulties with the work itself, e.g. public hostility, 'dirty' or useless jobs, excessive paperwork, and discontent with pay and conditions, such as shift-work. It was generally agreed that discipline had become more relaxed. Partly facilitated by the change to Unit Beat policing, there was more team-work and a 'man-management' style of supervision. The majority approved of this trend.

But a substantial minority, mainly older supervisors and the C.I.D., deplored it. About half the men thought of the force in consensus rather than conflict terms, but this was more common among supervisors. Those regarding supervision as too strict were more likely to support unionism. A most potent source of discontent and desire for a union was frustration about promotion. Most of the men wanted promotion, but few expected it. This produced a jaundiced view of the promotion system as unjust.

The police *were* seen as a profession by 74%. This was an assertion of superior status, a claim to be more than just an ordinary worker. Desire for a union was more common among those not seeing the police as a profession. The extent to which police work pervaded non-work life was generally recognised, but not always seen as desirable. Those wanting a greater degree of privatisation were more likely to support unionism. 'Occupational community' has often been regarded as a factor facilitating unionisation and militancy. The example of the police shows that it is certainly not a sufficient condition of commitment to unionism.

Many commentators have suggested that because a large part of police work consists of providing various kinds of assistance to the public, other than law-enforcement, the police ought to be seen as performing a broad, social service role. However, most policemen, especially constables, rejected the wider conception. They either saw their service to the public in terms of law-enforcement, or were not concerned about public service at all. The social aspects were objected to as extraneous to proper police work, or at best seen as indirectly related to it by fostering good public relations. Those who felt they had to perform tasks which were not rightly their duty were slightly more likely to favour a union. But this relationship was not close, because there was also a pressure acting in the opposite direction. Those favouring the narrow, crime-fighting conception of the police role were more likely to play down internal differences and to close ranks.

Altogether, it was suggested, the policeman's orientation to work approximated to that which Goldthorpe *et al.* describe as 'bureaucratic'. Work was seen as service to an organisation in return for a long-term career, characterised by moral involvement rather than an instrumental cash nexus. It was a central life-interest and source of identity, so that life cannot be sharply dichotomised into work and non-work. Aspirations were of an individualistic kind, in terms of mobility up a promotion ladder. There was a collective bid for status as 'professionals'. Consensual images of the organisation predominated over perception of conflict within it. All these points militated against commitment to unionism. This was strengthened further by the typical police conception of their role in society and social philosophy. The policeman's perception of being surrounded by hostile or non-comprehending outsiders fostered a feeling of internal solidarity, overriding conflicts within the organisation. The police analysis of the problems they face, and the solutions for them, is a conservative one, in terms of declining standards of discipline and the need for a re-assertion of authority. This further cuts them off from the labour movement, which tends to attract those favouring a more liberal approach to social and penal policy. The typical police social philosophy encourages an internal solidarity and suspicion of outsiders which separates them from the labour movement and aligns them with more conservative forces.

Within the central tendencies of the police outlook there are systematic differences in the force. Six types of policemen were distinguished. It was argued that they could be understood in terms of an interaction between varying sorts of initial orientation to the job and subsequent experience within it. The 'bobby' was the man for whom uniformed patrol work proved a satisfactory task. He had joined for security, but to some extent had an intrinsic attraction to a varied, outdoor life. He sees his job as primarily peace-keeping, which might involve both law-enforcement and service aspects. He regrets the extent to which the job interferes with private life, and seeks to maintain outside contacts in so far as possible. He has a basic sympathy for outside unions, but feels they have overstepped the mark. He views the police force as a primarily consensual organisation, and rejects unionism though he would like some more power. The Federationists are seen as altruistic men doing their best for the others.

The 'new centurion' is either a detective or has aspirations to be. Crime-fighting is the main police task, and what he joined for. His initial orientation and current attachment are non-instrumental. He views all people apart from operational policemen with suspicion, as villains, or naive do-gooders. The police are a misunderstood pariah group. They need stronger powers, even a union, but not one linked with outside bodies. The Federationists are office-bound shirkers, as are the senior officers. If doing the work he wants to, the 'new centurion' is satisfied; otherwise his cynical outlook stretches to include the police force too, and he becomes a 'uniform-carrier'.

The 'uniform-carrier' is attached to the police force solely by the cash nexus. A few started that way but most have become so through frustration of early idealism or ambition. The Federationists and the senior officers are viewed as corrupt self-seekers. Unions do much wrong, but this is a natural reaction to a Hobbesian world. The 'uniform-carrier' is completely alienated from all aspects of the police force apart from the pay. He seeks to have nothing to do with it outside work-hours, and as little as he can get away with during work.

The 'social worker' is the person who joined to perform a public service. Typically he would have preferred an alternative occupation like social work or teaching, but did not make the grade educationally. He either finds a niche that allows him work that is not primarily involved in adversary contacts with the public (e.g. community relations, schools liaison, area constable), or leaves if he discovers the work doesn't suit him early on, or becomes a 'uniform-carrier' if resignation is no longer viable. He rejects unionisation because of a notion of public responsibility. He supports the Federationists as altruistic 'social workers' for the policeman. He maintains plentiful outside social contacts. His image of the police force, and its relationship with the public, is consensual.

The 'professional' joined with ambitions to reach the top, and set out to gain the necessary qualifications and experience. His life is geared round this goal, and his private existence subordinated to it. The police force is viewed as a multi-functional hierarchy, based on consensus. Consensus is maintained by always pursuing the middle, judicious position on any issue. The Federation is useful as a channel of communication for the good 'man-manager'. But it must not get out of its place. A police union must be rejected as 'unprofessional', though moderate unionism is appropriate for manual workers. If he achieves his ambitions, the professional will be satisfied. If not, he may gravitate towards 'uniform-carrying'.

The 'Federation activists' typically had a sympathy for unionism before joining, and identify with the labour movement. They usually joined for security in times when their 'trade' was bad. They see unionism as a basic right of policemen, and necessary to check potential official abuses. But they are satisfied with their work, and see the conflict in the police force as contained and manageable by negotiation. The activist will maintain some contacts with outsiders, within the limits of the time left over by Federation work. The true Federation activist is a rarity in the police force.

What are the implications for the future development of the Federation? Is a police union likely to emerge?

Until recently certain trends were making the 'bobby' more of a rarity. On the one hand, the relative decline during the post-war period in the instrumental advantages of police work, due to the maintenance of comparative full employment and rising wages in industry, meant that recruits were increasingly drawn by intrinsic attractions of the job. These were primarily the excitement and variety offered by the work. Some regarded the force as a species of social work for the unqualified, and others as a route to a high status job through promotion. The tendency was for there to be increasing numbers of recruits who were predisposed to a 'new centurion' outlook, with a greater number of potential 'social workers' and 'professionals' too. Changes in the content and structure of the work were congruent with this. The advent of the Unit Beat system as the main type of patrol offered more scope for dealing with incidents, but also reduced the extent of ordinary interaction with the public which was not of a conflictual kind. The increase of specialisation and more rapid promotion opportunities offered more scope for those with 'social work' or 'professional' inclinations. But both changes in the character of recruitment, and the work itself, have tended to discourage either the 'bobbies' or the 'Federation activists'. The traditional peace-keeping style of the bobby was being eclipsed by what has been called 'fire-brigade' policing (i.e. merely providing a service in response to emergency calls) complemented by various specialisms, such as detection, community relations, and juvenile bureaux. The decrease in the recruitment of ex-'tradesmen' with union experience and sympathies, who had been attracted by security rather than glamour or ambition, also meant that the pool of Federation 'activists' was drying up. The likely impact of all these changes would have been a further decline in support for police unionism, and the evolution of the Federation towards a more decorous 'professional association' type of body, possibly even amalgamating with the superintendents. The trend towards assertion of a voice on 'professional' matters of legislation and social policy, reflected in the 'law and order' campaign, fits these predictions.

However, the recent worsening of the economic situation has partly counter-balanced these trends. Firstly, rising unemployment has made the police once more an attractive occupation for instrumental reasons, so that recruits who may not be 'police-minded' and who may have had experience of outside 'trades' are entering. Secondly, financial stringency together with a re-evaluation of the Unit Beat system, has resulted in some forces partially returning to old-style foot-patrols. These two factors may guarantee the perpetuation of the 'bobby' and the old-style 'activist', and hence some degree of potential support for police unionism.

The bargaining position of the police has not continued to be as favourable as in the early 1970s. The rise in unemployment has increased the supply of recruits. The 'demand' for policemen is somewhat lessened with the decline in union and political militancy, following the end of the 'confrontation' policies of the Heath government, together with the 'discipline' imposed by unemployment. Public expenditure cuts have induced some forces not to try and recruit up to official establishments, and in particular to cut back on cadet programmes. Rapid inflation means continuous decline in the real value of police pay which would necessitate frequent readjustment to keep up with outside increases.

These factors were all reflected in the 1975, and even more clearly the 1976–7 pay negotiations. The development of rank-and-file demands for the right to strike, the withdrawal of the Federation from the Police Council and its request for a review of the representative machinery have been described in chapter 1.

The growth of support for the right to strike and a 'free association' is remarkable in view of the considerable opposition to them found in the survey. To some extent it may be attributable to a difference in the general orientations of many policemen. Among the newer recruits more are likely to have been attracted by instrumental considerations than was true for the sample, reflecting the change in economic conditions. Such men are more likely to be sensitised towards reacting with considerable hostility to frustration of economic expectations. The increase in recruitment after 1974 means that the force consists of a higher proportion of young policemen, who may reflect a more recalcitrant mood towards discipline (a favourite explanation among policemen themselves), and have not yet been fully socialised into the 'responsible' stance of older generations.

However, it is not necessary to place too much explanatory weight on possible changes in the individual orientations of policemen. The growth of a more militant mood is quite comprehensible as a response to changing economic and social circumstances, given the police outlook found in this study. While in 1973 policemen generally rejected the right to strike, and to a large extent were opposed also to weaker union powers, the analysis of their reasons for this suggests that this was conditional on expectations being met. Although opposition to unionism was justified by the responsibility of policemen to the public, this attitude was buttressed by the belief that the importance of the police force would continue to result in 'special case' treatment. The failure of this expectation has added frustration with financial rewards to the long-standing grievances with social policy, which were already stimulating the Federation to adopt a more outspoken style. In previous decades such dissatisfaction would undoubtedly have induced many policemen to resign. This option is now cut off because of high unemployment. If policemen are to seek redress for their grievances they must do so in the job. In pursuing their demands they can no longer point to difficulties in attracting recruits. Rather they have to defend against cutbacks in expenditure. Nor can they rely on the need to 'keep the police sweet' to which many of them attributed the favourable rises of the early 1970s. The years from 1974 onwards have witnessed a dramatic decline in the intensity of industrial conflict, due to T.U.C. acquiescence in the 'social contract' and the 'discipline' of unemployment. In view of these changing circumstances the demand for the right to strike is hardly surprising. Even in the better bargaining situation of 1973 a considerable proportion of constables wanted stronger powers of representation. Whether the accumulation of grievances will be sufficient to erode policemen's interpretation of their 'responsibilities' to the extent of actually supporting strike *action*, as opposed to referenda requesting the Federation to seek this right, has yet to be seen. The outcome of the 1976–7 unrest is uncertain, and depends largely on general political and economic developments. It is probable that the return of a Conservative government would reduce the pressure for police unionisation. The Conservatives have declared their willingness to treat the police as an exceptional case in pay policy, and condemned Labour for stimulating police militancy by not doing so. In the event of a Conservative government failing to achieve a pay policy that has union consent, and facing industrial unrest, the bargaining position of the police would no doubt improve as in the early 1970s.

Whatever the outcome, the experience of militancy in 1976–7 and the contemplation of unionism and the right to strike, undoubtedly constitute a marked shift in police consciousness. Even if the pressure diminishes, the issue of unionisation has come on to the agenda, and will no doubt be revived in any future period of frustration.

This indicates one element in the contradictory class position of the police. Their situation as salaried employees always has the potential of generating pressure for unionisation. However, when industrial confrontation makes them especially important, their economic interests are opposed to those of other workers. More generally, the way policemen define the source and solution for their *non-economic* grievances drives them into positions of a conservative kind, and cuts them off from the labour movement. These aspects of policemen's problems are a more perennial concern than the economic frustrations that might lead to police unionism. Therefore despite the surfacing of demands for unionism in periods when the policeman's problems as a salaried worker are highlighted, the more salient content of the policeman's work separates him from the union movement. The assertion of a police voice on social policy, usually in support of right-wing strategies, is a more stable direction of police association activity, and ultimately a greater cause for concern than economically motivated unionism.

The continued assertion of a voice in social and penal policy can be predicted. The Federation is likely to continue to become more institutionalised in the decision-making machinery of the police force, at national and local level, as well as to be an articulate public spokesman for the police viewpoint. At the moment the views it promulgates on social and penal policy appear to be illiberal and to support more punitive measures. It might be, however, that if rank-and-file policemen were given a greater say as of right in police decision-making, through the Federation, they would necessarily have to consider a more rounded view. A case can be made for bringing a wider range of viewpoints into play in the process of determining police policy and the priorities in allocation of resources. Banton has argued that the role and constitution of police authorities should be expanded, so as to allow a greater variety of interests and perspectives to be represented. He has suggested they should include representatives of different interest-groups in the community who have a claim to be concerned in the process of peace-keeping. As well as increasing the representation of interests from the 'community', 'means will have to be found for associating the rank-and-file more effectively with policy formation. Representation on committees of the peace is one way of doing this' (Banton 1974). Such representation would meet the demands for regularised access as of right to the police authority, and lessen the sense of exclusion from decision-making. The initial contributions of rank-and-file representatives may involve the advocacy of repressive or punitive social and penal policies. But the long-run consequences may be a greater depth of understanding of the viewpoint of sections of the 'public' who are policed. The historical improvement of police conditions was associated with a greater degree of fairness and impartiality in the administration of the law by policemen. 'The movement which has brought greater justice for policemen has also brought greater justice by policemen' (Banton 1970: 2). In the future too, incorporation of policemen into the decision-making bodies which affect their working lives may encourage an ultimately more liberal and generous view of the interests of different sections of society.

It must not, however, be expected that any major changes in police outlook or behaviour can be achieved merely by alterations in internal organisation. It has been seen that policemen, especially detectives, tend to develop a hard-boiled, cynical, even bitter perspective on life. This is not surprising as long as their role is one of handling some of society's dirtiest work. There are limits to the extent to which this could be changed in the absence of wider reforms which are beyond the control of policemen themselves. To a large extent, a society gets the policemen it deserves.

Postscript and appendixes

Postscript: The Scarborough 'Events' 24–6 May 1977

The 1977 Annual Conference of the Police Federation might seem to mark a radical shift in police consciousness and espousal of trade unionism. The increasing bitterness and militancy which built up during the tortuous and protracted pay negotiations of 1976–7, culminating in the laying-down of several Conference motions concerning unionisation and the right to strike, have been described in chapter 2. This postscript is intended to summarise and evaluate the dramatic happenings at the May Conference, which were much publicised by the media.

On Tuesday 24 May, in a heated, emotionally charged debate, the delegates voted overwhelmingly to seek the right to strike. (As seen in chapter 2, referenda in many local police forces during the early months of 1977 had shown considerable rank-and-file support for this.) On Wednesday 25 May Merlyn Rees faced a predictably hostile reception to his speech as Home Secretary. (The previous week's *Police Review* cartoon had depicted him anxiously selecting a suit of armour!) Rees was mobbed by coachloads of jeering police who had turned up in such large numbers that they could not get into the capacity-filled hall. They hurled verbal abuse ('Out, you bum!'), and one officer was rebuked by a superintendent for pummelling the top of the official car with his fists. A policewoman sported a tee-shirt with the slogan 'Stuff Merlyn Rees'. The delegates inside the Conference Hall adopted precisely opposite tactics. An emergency closed session immediately before Rees's arrival decided to maintain complete silence while the Home Secretary spoke. They did not stand as he entered, nor clap after his speech. The rows of delegates pretended to read their newspapers or doze off as he delivered his text. Mr Rees's unpopularity, due to the months of unsuccessful pay negotiations, had been capped by his unilateral decision the week before to enforce a pay increase amounting to the Official Side's initial offer, which the Federation had already rejected before walking out of the Police Council the previous July.

On the face of it, the sudden shift in police attitudes seems to be an example of the 'explosion of consciousness' thesis, much discussed in the late 1960s (Mann 1973: chapter 6). It is reminiscent of the 1966 Vauxhall strike, where the workers who shortly before had appeared to exhibit a harmonistic image of the firm when interviewed for the 'Affluent Worker' project, sang the 'Red Flag' and demanded that the directors be 'strung up' (Blackburn 1967; reply by Goldthorpe *et al.* 1968: 195). Such an analysis rests on a contrast between 'possible' and 'actual' consciousness, which as Mann has argued, is often, but not necessarily, presented in an excessively idealist fashion (Mann 1973: 45). 'Possible' consciousness becomes manifest as an explosion into action in specific conflicts, bursting out of the bounds of normal 'actual' consciousness, which is all that empirical sociology can tap. This account underestimates both the contradictions and tensions in consciousness which research *can* convey, and the fragility, narrowness and superficiality of many of the slogans emerging in 'explosions' (Mann 1973). It is also important to distinguish between *industrial* militancy and *class consciousness* in a wider sense. Despite the apparent radicalism of the slogans that may accompany militancy over essentially narrow, economistic demands, it is quite possible for workers to combine militant trade unionism or industrial action with wider social and political attitudes and practices of a conservative or even reactionary character (*vide* the recent Ulster Protestant workers' strikes).

These general reservations about the 'explosion of consciousness' thesis apply *a fortiori* to the police case. The police occupy a *contradictory* place in the class structure (Wright 1976: 40–1). It would be incorrect to argue that they are 'truly' workers, whose normal conservative and anti-union views are shown to be 'false' consciousness in crises. 'While every worker is a wage-earner, not every wage-earner is a worker' (Poulantzas, 1973: 30).

The police *are* wage-earners, and they are controlled by a hierarchical authority structure. These elements of their work situation stimulate grievances and demands for representation, as has been apparent at many points in the book. But their social role is to preserve an existing economic and political order. This usually generates consciousness of a conservative character. In particular, their role in labour disputes augments their media-derived images of trade unions and results in a hostile attitude towards unionism. This even modifies the effects of their economic position as wage-earners. While at an abstract level the police are similar to all workers with only their 'labour power' to sell, the determinants of the price of this are often diametrically opposed to others. In situations where governments attempt to hold down wages through non-voluntary means, police bargaining power is strengthened. Thus often the economic, political and ideological dimensions of the policeman's class position divide him from workers. The recent years of voluntary incomes policy have placed him economically in a similar situation to all employees. The Labour government was concerned to prevent a special case which would undermine T.U.C. assent to the 'social contract'. This has driven the police into expressions of a more unionate kind. But these co-exist with other facets of a profoundly conservative nature, as manifested, for example, in the 'law and order' campaign. The permanence of the unionate demands is questionable. A change in the political scene, such as the election of a Conservative government, might well result in a return to the situation of the early 1970s, when the economic demands of the police were given special case treatment. All this is not to argue that the position and consciousness of policemen is immutable, but solid changes would require wider social transformation.

The recent events, notably the demand for the right to strike, *are* significant. There is discernible a growing tradition of union consciousness through the pay disputes of 1970–75–76/7. Future crises will occur with a rhetoric of militancy more readily available. But so far there has not been an espousal of unionism, as a more detailed account of the Scarborough Conference makes clear. The delegates were united in seeking a review of negotiating machinery and condemning the government, and to a slightly lesser extent, supporting the right to strike. But within this solidarity some cracks are visible, and there was rejection of affiliation with the T.U.C., as well as evidence of continued hostility to the labour movement.

The inspectors are far less committed to the assertion of militancy than the constables, with sergeants still in between. In some forces where referenda were analysed by rank this was very clear, although the preponderance of constables meant a clear victory overall for the right to strike. The Constables' Conference expressed some concern about a possible inspectors' split from the Federation, should any strike move become serious. Among all ranks there remains profound anxiety about strike action. The more militant seemed ready to strike, and the possibility of wildcat action by a minority cannot be ruled out. The majority would still be most reluctant to take action.

Most significantly, T.U.C. affiliation was rejected by Conference (as well as those referenda which raised the issue), despite support from the J.C.C. Red-baiting rhetoric pervaded these debates. The image of the union movement was of a left-dominated body. Many delegates expressed fears that their discontent had been deliberately engineered by the left-wing of the Labour government to drive them into the T.U.C. 'If Michael Foot supports what we're doing, there must be something wrong with it', said one. A young Metropolitan constable who introduced explicitly Marxist terminology into his speeches (itself a sign of the change) was roundly heckled and jeered. He argued: 'We're no different from other workers. We may wear funny clothes and do society's dirty work for them. But we come from the same stock as other workers. [Boos] We have only our labour power to sell, no capital.' This was punctuated by catcalls of 'commie' and 'where's your party card?' Much resentment of the Labour government was expressed, not only for their rejection of police pay demands. They were generally castigated for their liberalism, for being more interested in 'releasing from prison pimps, perverts and bombers' than the police. Over-sensitivity to the demands of radicals, a 'vociferous minority', was felt to underlie the new Complaints Board established under the Police Act and due to commence work the week after Conference. (The Federation advised non-co-operation by members.) The government was too influenced by groups like Radical Alternatives to Prison – 'there's one alternative to prison – going straight'. The fit between policemen's working role and a general conservative ideology remains apparent, despite the surface shifts.

Many delegates expressed scepticism about the Conservatives too, but there was general hope that they would be more favourably inclined to support the police in the manner to which they wished to be accustomed – a hope bolstered by Mrs Thatcher's speech to the Conservative Women's Conference reported during that week, pledging more spending on the police.

Altogether it seemed that while there was a much more militant mood than at past conferences, and the 'activists' were no longer voices crying in the wilderness, there was no hard support for unionism. Tensions and contradictions *were* more apparent, but it is likely that a favourable pay deal would undercut much of the militancy. The most general support was not for unionism, but for a pay review body which would regularly provide increases based on research on general earnings movements and take the police, 'like the Queen and the National Debt', out of the ordinary procedures of collective bargaining. The view that favourable treatment could not be guaranteed without sanctions did not seem to have taken firm hold. Pay grievances were attributed mainly to particular failings of the Labour government. In this context support for the right to strike appears more of a gesture, an expression of frustration and discontent, than a permanent shift to the left. The police still seem to prefer being a special case, with appropriate treatment, to any identification with the working class.

Appendix 1

The introductory letter sent to the sample

I am working on a study of the Police Federation, which will form the basis of a Ph.D. thesis. I am interested in finding out what the Federation means to policemen, their attitudes towards it, and the way that this is influenced by their experiences at work. I am interested in the views of all policemen on this subject, so please do not feel that if you are not especially involved with the Federation you cannot be of help to me.

All the results of the survey will be collected and analysed completely anonymously, as I am not concerned with the views of individuals as such. The data will in fact be grouped for the purpose of presentation, and no views will be traceable to individuals.

I have the permission of the Home Office, the Federation, and the Chief Constable to conduct this survey. However I am not connected in any way with the police force, but teach in a university.

You were selected by a random method for inclusion in the survey, and therefore your co-operation is very important in order to ensure the representativeness of the results. I hope I can count on your consent to participate in this study, and that you may find the interview of interest to you.

I believe that the information yielded by this survey will be of interest to all members of the force, as hitherto there has been no comprehensive knowledge of how members of the Federation regard their organisation. It may also prove of practical value to the police service and to Federationists, and produce improvements in the facilities and services provided.

Thanking You,

Robert Reiner (B.A.(Cantab), M.Sc.(London))

11th October 1972.

Appendix 2

The interview schedule: questionnaire on police attitudes

Introduction [points in introductory letter repeated]

(Section A) Work history

To start with, I wonder whether you would mind telling me some things about your career so far?
1. Firstly, in what year did you first come to work in the ... Constabulary?
2. Had you ever worked in a police force elsewhere?
   (*If yes, ask 3; if no, go on to 4*)
3. In which police force had you previously worked, and between what years?
   (*Go on to 4*)
4. Did you first enter the police force as a cadet?
5. Have you ever worked anywhere except in the police force? I would like you to include in your answer any military service you may have done.
   (*If no, move on to 7; if yes, ask 6*)
6. (a) What was the last employment you had before you took up your present work as a policeman?
   (*Try and get (i) job title (ii) kind of work, i.e. skill and responsibility level*)
   (b) When did you have that job?
   (c) For how long did you have it?
   (d) Did you have any jobs before that?
   If yes: What were these?
   (e) When, and for how long, did you have each of these jobs?
7. Have you ever thought seriously of leaving the police?
   If yes: (a) Why?
   (b) Have you done anything about it?
   If yes: What was that?
8. Have you been on any training courses since you joined the police?
   If yes: What were these?
9. What is your present rank?
   If sergeant: In what year were you promoted to sergeant?
   If inspector: In what years did you receive your promotion (i) to inspector, (ii) to sergeant?
   If chief inspector: In what years were you promoted (i) to chief inspector, (ii) to inspector, (iii) to sergeant?
10. What is the type of work you do in the police force?
    Could you briefly describe what this involves?

(Section B) Attitudes to the Federation
Now I wonder if we could move on to discussing some of your attitudes to and relations with the Federation?

11. First of all, just speaking overall, do you feel that the Federation is in general an adequate representative organisation? Why do you say this?
12. How would you feel about making it more like a trade union?
13. What would you feel about setting up a single professional association as the representative body for all policemen, regardless of rank?
14. The Federation could be said to perform various services for policemen. How influential do you feel it is in the following areas? (*Show card A*)
15. Do you feel that the Federation should be given the following rights:
    (i)   right of affiliation to the T.U.C.
    (ii) right to strike
    (iii) right to work to rule
    Could we now discuss the way in which officers of the Federation work.
16. Firstly, why do you think people take up office in the Federation?
17. In your opinion, are active Federationists different from other policemen in their outlook in any way?
    If yes: In what ways?
18. (a) Do you think that Federation service helps, harms or has no effect upon the promotion prospects of policemen?
    (b) What are your reasons for thinking this?
19. Do you feel that the Federation should be more or less militant than at present in its approach to negotiations, or is the present approach satisfactory?
    If more or less: Why?
20. (a) In your view would it be desirable or undesirable for the Federation to have an official right to consultation on a regular basis with the Chief Constable?
    (b) Do you think the same should apply to the police authority?
21. Some people say representative organisations should be strictly concerned with getting higher pay and better conditions for their members. Others think they should also try and get workers a say in management. Which of these two views do you favour?
    Why?

(Section C): Involvement in Federation

22. Have you ever held any of these offices in the Federation? (*Show card B*)
    For each one held: For about how long did you hold this post?
    If none held: Have you ever stood for such a post?
    If yes: What happened?
23. When did you last attend a Federation open meeting? And before that? And before that one?
24. Did you vote in the last election for Federation posts?
    Did you vote in the one before?
25. Have you ever made any suggestions to the Federation about any actions they should take?
    If yes: By what means?
    What happened to these suggestions?
26. Have you ever made any suggestions about police organisation or conditions by any channels other than through the Federation?
    What means did you use?
27. Have you ever talked about work and conditions to your divisional representative or any other Federation official?
    Can you remember what happened?
28. Could you possibly tell me the names of (i) the present J.C.C. secretary and

chairman, (ii) your J.B.B. secretary and chairman, (iii) your divisional representative?

(Section D): Other union experience

Now I wonder if you could possibly tell me something about your experience of unions outside the police?

(*N.B. 29–31: only to be asked of people who had previously been employed outside the police.*)

29. Had you ever been a member of a trade union in your previous employment?
    If yes: Which was this?
30. (a) Did you ever attend (i) shop meetings (ii) branch meetings
    (b) *If yes:* Would you say you attended regularly?
31. (a) Did you ever vote in elections for (i) shop stewards (ii) union branch elections?
    (b) *If yes:* Would you say you voted regularly?
    If no to 30 or 31: Why did you not vote or attend meetings?

ask all:

32. Do you feel that trade unions in general have too much power in this country? Why?
33. In what ways, if any, do you think picketing should be controlled?
34. Have you ever been involved in handling pickets?
35. Did this particular assignment cause you any special problems?
    If yes: What were these?

(Section E): Work attitudes

Could you tell me a little now about your attitudes to police work in general?

36. Do you feel that supervisory officers in the police exercise too much or too little control over the men or is the present situation satisfactory. Why?
    Has this changed in your experience? *If Yes:* In what way?
37. Do you agree or disagree with the following views? (*Show card C*)
    For each item: Why do you say this?
38. Would you say that sometimes the police get called on to do types of jobs which are impossible or unnecessarily difficult or unpleasant?
    If yes: Could you give some examples?
    Should these be regarded as police duty?
39. (a) In your view should civilianisation be encouraged or discouraged in general?
    What, if any, limits should be placed on civilianisation?
    (b) In general, do you think the police should be allowed to do outside jobs?
    If yes: What, if any, limits should be placed on the type of jobs allowed?
40. Do you think the police are a profession?
41. Have the problems facing the police worsened, improved or remained much the same, in recent years?
    To what sort of problems are you referring?
    Why has the change taken place?

(Section F): Personal orientation and aspirations

Now could you tell me some things about your attitude to your job?

42. Here are some of the things often thought important about a job (*Show card D*). Could you rank them in order of importance?

Are there any other things that you would consider to be important in a job?

43. As far as each of these things is concerned, would you say police work is first rate, pretty good, average, not too good, or very bad? (*Show Card D again and note answer for each*).
   For each: Why do you say this?
   Are there any other things you particularly like or dislike about police work?

44. Are you interested in being promoted?
   (i) *If yes:* How far would you hope to reach?
   (ii) Have you taken any promotion exams? Do you intend to?

45. How far do you expect to reach?

46. In general, what factors do you think influence promotion chances?

(Section G): Demographic data

Finally, I'd like to learn a little about the kinds of background and home life policemen have.

47. In what year were you born?

48. Are you married?

49. Have you any children?
   If yes: How many?
   How old is each?

50. What was the highest educational level you reached?

51. What type of school did you attend?

52. What sort of work did your father or guardian do when you were eighteen? (*Or what was his last job if he was no longer alive or had retired?*)

53. Had he been in that kind of work for most of his life?
   If no: What were the main jobs he had before that?
   (*For all job descriptions try and ascertain same points as in 6a*)
   Are there any comments you would like to make about the interview?
   Finally, may I thank you for your co-operation.

Card A.

1. In securing higher pay
2. In securing satisfactory conditions of work
3. In communicating a good public image of the police
4. In the communication of information and views within the service
5. In influencing legislation in the interests of policemen
6. In the provision of welfare benefits
7. In fostering the efficiency of the police force
8. In providing help in questions of discipline charges

Card B

(i)   Divisional representative
(ii) Branch board member
(iii) Secretary of (a) constables' Branch Board
                  (b) sergeants'   "   "
                  (c) inspectors'   "   "
                  (d) joint   "   "
(iv) Chairman of (a) constables' Branch Board
                  (b) sergeants'   "   "

      (c) inspectors'   "   "
      (d) joint   "   "

(v) Treasurer of (a) constables' Branch Board
                  (b) sergeants'   "   "
                  (c) inspectors'   "   "
                  (d) joint   "   "

(vi) Member of a central committee
(vii) Officer of a central committee

Card C

1. When it really comes down to it, police work is just like any other job.
2. The police should only be concerned to do what he must to earn a living.
3. The policeman shouldn't let his work interfere with his private life.
4. The policeman is obliged to perform police duty even if it involves overtime or other interference with his private life.
5. The policeman should never stop being a policeman.

Card D

Interest and variety
Good pay
Good workmates
A supervisor who doesn't breathe down your neck
Pleasant working conditions
A sense of performing a public service

[These items were presented to the men on individual cards. They were shuffled before each interview, and spread out when question 42 was asked. This was done to avoid the order of presentation influencing the result systematically.]

Appendix 3

The Prohibited questions

The following are the questions I was *not* permitted to raise. They are taken, with some modification, from 'The Affluent Worker' study.

Questions on class perceptions

1. People often talk about there being different social classes – what do you think? What underlies this distinction between classes?
2. Do you think that divisions between social classes in this country are becoming greater, less great or remain as before?
3. Into which social class would you see yourself as belonging?
4. Some people say there's one law for the rich and another law for the poor. Would you agree or disagree, on the whole?
5. Do all people in this country have a fair chance in life, regardless of their background?
   Why do you think this?

Questions on politics

1. Do you feel it makes a great deal of difference whether the Conservatives or Labour win an election, or doesn't it make much difference?
   If difference: In what ways would it make a difference?
   If no difference: Why do you feel that it won't make much difference?
2. How do you feel you will vote in the next General Election?
3. Could you tell me how you've voted in the last few elections (i) 1970; (ii) 1966; (iii) 1964; (iv) 1959?
4. *If the same vote in each:* Now you seem pretty attached to the Conservative/ Labour Party – can you tell me why?
   For each change: Why didn't you vote as you had in the previous election?

Bibliography

Alex, N. 1969. *Black in Blue.* New York: Appleton, Century, Crofts

Alex, N. 1976. *New York Cops Talk Back.* New York: Wiley

Allen, V. L. 1958. 'The National Union of Police and Prison Officers', *Economic History Review*, vol. XI, no. 1, pp. 133–43

Bain, G. S., Coates, D. & Ellis, V. 1973. *Social Stratification and Trade Unionism.* London: Heinemann

Bain, G. S. & Price, R. J. 1972. 'Union growth and employment trends in the United Kingdom, 1964–70', *British Journal of Industrial Relations*, vol. X, no. 3, pp. 366–81

Banks, J. A. 1969. Review of 'The Affluent Worker', *British Journal of Sociology*, vol. 20, no. 1

Banton, M. 1964. *The Policeman in the Community.* London: Tavistock

Banton, M. 1970. 'Social order and the police', *The Advancement of Science*, vol. 27, no. 131, pp. 48–56.

Banton, M. 1972. 'Labour–management relations in an American police department', *The Police Journal*, vol. XLV, no. 4, pp. 302–11

Banton, M. 1964. 'The keepers of the peace', *New Society*, 5 December 1974, vol. 30, no. 635, pp. 604–6

Bayley, D. H. & Mendelsohn, H. A. 1968. *Minorities and the Police.* New York: Free Press

Becker, H. S. 1963. *Outsiders.* New York: Free Press

Belson, W. A. 1975. *The Public and the Police.* London: Harper & Row

Bent, A. E. 1974. *The Politics of Law Enforcement.* Lexington, Mass.: D. C. Heath.

Berkley, G. E. 1969. *The Democratic Policeman.* Boston: Beacon Press

Beynon, H. & Nichols, T. 1971. 'Modern British sociology and the affluent worker'. Unpublished paper, Bristol 1971

Beynon, H. & Blackburn, R. M. 1972. *Perceptions of Work.* Cambridge: Cambridge University Press

Beynon, H. 1973. *Working for Ford.* London: Penguin

Blackburn, R. 1967. 'The unequal society' in A. Blackburn & A. Cockburn (eds.), *The Incompatibles.* London: Penguin

Blackburn, R. M. 1967. *Union Character and Social Class.* London: Batsford

Blackburn, R. M., Prandy, K., Stewart, A. 1974. 'Concepts and measures: the example of unionateness', *Sociology*, vol. 8, no. 3, pp. 426–46

Blauner, R. 1960. 'Work satisfaction and industrial trends in modern society', reprinted in R. Bendix & S. M. Lipset (eds.), *Class, Status and Power* (2nd ed. 1967). London: Routledge & Kegan Paul. Page references are to this edition

Blauner, R. 1964. *Alienation and Freedom.* Chicago: University of Chicago Press

Bopp, W. J. (ed.) 1971. *The Police Rebellion.* Springfield, Illinois: C. C. Thomas

Bowes, S. 1966. *The Police and Civil Liberties.* London: Lawrence & Wishart

Box, S. 1971. *Deviance, Reality and Society.* New York: Holt, Rinehart & Winston

Box, S. & Russell, K. 1975. 'The Politics of Discreditability', *Sociological Review*, vol. 23, no. 2, pp. 315–46

Bulmer, M. (ed.) 1975. *Working-class Images of Society*. London: Routledge & Kegan Paul

Bunyan, T. 1976. *The Political Police in Britain*. London: Julian Friedmann

Burpo, J. H. 1971. *The Police Labour Movement*. Springfield, Illinois: C. C. Thomas

Butler, D. & Stokes, D. 1971. *Political Change in Britain*. London: Penguin

Cain, M. E. 1973. *Society and the Policeman's Role*. London: Routledge & Kegan Paul

Capune, W. G. 1971. 'U.S. police associations', *The Criminologist*, vol. 6, no. 20, pp. 13–22

Carte, G. E. & Carte, E. H. 1975. *Police Reform in the United States*. Berkeley: University of California Press

Centre for Research on Criminal Justice 1975. *The Iron Fist and the Velvet Glove – An Analysis of the U.S. Police*. California: Centre for Research on Criminal Justice

Chapman, B. 1970. *Police State*. London: Pall Mall

Chapman, D. 1968. *Sociology and the Stereotype of the Criminal*. London: Tavistock

Chapman, S. G. 1962. *The Police Heritage in England and America*. East Lansing, Michigan: Michigan State University Press

Cliff, T. 1975. *The Crisis*. London: Pluto Press

Coates, K. & Topham, T. 1974. *The New Unionism*. London: Penguin

Cook, W. 1967. 'Policemen in society: which side are they on?, *Berkeley Journal of Sociology*, vol. 10 (Summer), pp. 117–29

Critchley, T. A. 1967. *A History of Police in England and Wales, 1900–1966*. London: Constable

Cumming, E., Cumming, I., Edell, L. 1965. 'Policeman as philosopher, guide and friend', *Social Problems*, vol. 12, no. 3, pp. 276–86

Daniel, W. W. 1969. 'Industrial behaviour and orientation to work: a critique', *Journal of Management Studies*, vol. VI, no. 4, pp. 366–75

Evans, P. 1974. *The Police Revolution*. London: George Allen and Unwin

Gammage, A. Z. & Sachs, S. L. 1972. *Police Unions*. Springfield, Illinois: C. C. Thomas

Goldthorpe, J. H., Lockwood, D. Bechhofer, F. & Platt, J. 1968. *The Affluent Worker: Industrial Attitudes and Behaviour*. Cambridge: Cambridge University Press

Goodrich, C. L. 1975. *The Frontier of Control*. London: Pluto Press (first published 1920)

Hall, J. & Caradog-Jones, D. 1950. 'Social grading of occupations', *British Journal of Sociology*, vol. 1, no. 2, pp. 31–55

Halpern, S. 1974. *Police Association and Department Leaders*. Lexington, Mass.: D. C. Heath

Harris, Richard 1970. *Justice: The Crisis of Law, Order and Freedom in America*. London: Bodley Head

Harris, Richard N. 1973. *The Police Academy: An Inside View*. New York: Wiley

Hinz, L. 1975. 'Police unions and associations in the German Federal Republic'. Unpublished paper delivered at the Third Bristol Conference on the Sociology of the Police, 15–18 April 1975

Home Office 1919. *Committee on the Police Service of England, Wales and Scotland, Report* (Chairman: Lord Desborough). London: H.M.S.O.

Home Office 1949. *Committee on Police Conditions of Service: Report: Parts I and II*, Cmnd. 7674 and Cmnd. 7831 (Chairman: Lord Oaksey). London: H.M.S.O.

Home Office 1970. *Man-Management Survey*, Report No. 5/70 of the Home Office Police Research and Development Branch. London, January 1970

Hughes, E. C. 1958. *Men and their Work*, Glencoe: Free Press

Hughes, E. C. 1963. 'Professions', *Daedalus*, vol. xcii, No. 4, pp. 655–68

Hyman, R. 1971. *Marxism and the Sociology of Trade Unionism*. London: Pluto Press

Hyman, R. 1972. *Strikes*. London: Fontana

International Association of Chiefs of Police 1958. *Police Unions*. Washington D.C.: I.A.C.P.

Johnson, T. J. 1972. *Professions and Power*. London: Macmillan

Judge, A. 1968. *The First Fifty Years*. London: Police Federation

Judge, A. 1972. *A Man Apart: The British Policeman and his Job*. London: Arthur Barker

Juris, H. A. & Feuille, P. 1973. *Police Unionism*. Lexington, Mass: D. C. Heath

Labour Research 1975. 'The police and the state', *Labour Research*, February 30–3

Lambert, J. 1969. 'The police can choose', *New Society*, vol. 14, no. 364 pp. 430–2

Lambert, J. 1970. *Crime, Police and Race Relations*. London: Oxford University Press

Lane, T. & Roberts, K. 1971. *Strike At Pilkingtons*. London: Fontana

Laurie, P. 1972. *Scotland Yard*. London: Penguin

Lemert, E. 1967. *Human Deviance, Social Problems and Social Control*. Englewood-Cliffs, New Jersey: Prentice-Hall

Lipset, S. M. 1969. 'Why cops hate liberals – and vice versa', *Atlantic Monthly*, 1969. Reprinted in Bopp (1971) pp. 23–39

Levi, M. 1977. *Bureaucratic insurgency: The case of police unions*. Lexington, Mass.: D. C. Heath

Lockwood, D. 1958. *The Black-Coated Worker*. London: Allen and Unwin

Lockwood, D. 1966. 'Sources of variation in working-class images of society', *Sociological Review*, vol. xiv, no. 4, pp. 249–67

McNamara, J. H. 1967. 'Uncertainties in police work: The relevance of police recruits' background and training' in D. Bordua (ed.) *The Police: Six Sociological Essays*, pp. 163–252. New York: Wiley

Maddox, C. W. 1975. *Collective Bargaining in Law Enforcement*. Springfield, Illinois: C. C. Thomas

Mann, M. 1973. *Consciousness and Action Among the Western Working Class*. London: Macmillan

Marshall, G. 1965. *Police and Government*. London: Methuen

Marshall, G. 1971. 'The Government of the Police since 1964'. Unpublished paper delivered at the First Bristol Conference on the Sociology of the Police, 25–28 February

Martin, J. P. & Wilson G. 1969. *The Police: A Study in Manpower*. London: Heinemann

Millerson, G. 1964. *The Qualifying Associations*. London: Routledge & Kegan Paul

Moran, M. 1974. *The Union of Post Office Workers: A Study in Political Sociology*. London: Macmillan

Nichols, T. 1974. 'Labourism and class consciousness: the "class ideology" of some northern foremen', *Sociological Review*, vol. 22, no. 4, pp. 483–502

Nichols, T. & Armstrong, P. 1976. *Workers Divided*. London: Fontana

Niederhoffer, A. 1967. *Behind the Shield.* New York: Doubleday

Nott-Bower, W. 1926. *Fifty-Two Years a Policeman.* London: Arnold

Picton-Davies, G. 1973. 'The police service of England and Wales between 1918 and 1964, with particular reference to problems of personnel, recruitment and command'. Unpublished Ph.D. dissertation, London School of Economics

Piliavin, I. & Briar, S. 1964. 'Police encounters with juveniles', *American Journal of Sociology,* vol. 70, no. 2, pp. 206–14

Police Federation 1965. *A Handbook of Police Discipline.* London: Police Federation

Poulantzas, N. 1973. 'On social classes', *New Left Review,* no. 78 (March-April), pp. 27–55

Prandy, K. 1965. *Professional Employees.* London: Faber

Punch, M. & Naylor, T. 1973. 'The police – a social service', *New Society,* vol. 24, no. 554, pp. 358–61

Ramsay, H. 1975. 'Firms and football teams', *British Journal of Industrial Relations,* vol. XIII, no. 3, pp. 396–9

Reiner, R. 1976. 'Reds in blue?', *New Society,* vol. 38, no. 731, pp. 14–16

Reiner, R. 1976. 'The blue-coated worker: a sociological study of police unionism', Ph.D. thesis, Bristol University

Reynolds, G. W. & Judge, A. 1968. *The Night the Police Went On Strike.* London: Weidenfeld and Nicolson

Royal Commission on the Police 1960. *Interim Report* Cmnd. 1222. London: H.M.S.O.

Royal Commission on the Police 1962. *Final Report* Cmnd. 1728. London: H.M.S.O.

Rubinstein, J. 1973. *City Police.* New York: Farrar, Strauss & Giroux

Ruchelman, L. 1974. *Police Politics: A Comparative Study of Three Cities.* Cambridge, Mass.: Ballinger

Salaman, G. 1974. *Community and Occupation.* Cambridge: Cambridge University Press

Salaman, G. 1975. 'Occupations, community and consciousness' in M. Bulmer (ed.) *Working-Class Images of Society,* pp. 219–36. London: Routledge & Kegan Paul

Scargill, A. 1975. 'The new unionism', *New Left Review,* no. 92 (July–August) pp. 3–33

Shaw, M. & Williamson, W. 1972. 'Public attitudes to the police', *The Criminologist,* vol. 7, no. 26, pp. 18–33

Silver, A. 1967. 'The demand for order in civil society' in D. Bordua (ed.) *The Police: Six Sociological Essays,* pp. 1–24. New York: Wiley

Simon, H. A. 1966. 'Theories of decision-making in economics and behavioural science', in American Economic Association/Royal Economic Society *Surveys of Economic Theory,* vol. III pp. 1–28. London: Macmillan

Skolnick, J. 1966. *Justice Without Trial.* New York: Wiley

Skolnick, J. 1969. *The Politics of Protest.* New York: Ballantine

Stinchcombe, A. 1963. 'Institutions of privacy in the determination of police administrative practice', *American Journal of Sociology,* vol. 69, no. 2, pp. 150–60

Taylor, I., Young, J. & Walton, P. 1973. *The New Criminology.* London: Routledge & Kegan Paul

Taylor, I., Young, J. & Walton, P. (eds.) 1975. *Critical Criminology.* London: Routledge & Kegan Paul

Wainwright, J. 1967. *Shall I be a Policeman?* Exeter: Wheaton

Wambaugh, J. 1972. *The New Centurions*. London: Sphere
Weber, M. 1964. *The Theory of Economic and Social Organisation*. Glencoe: Free Press
Weber, M. 1949. *The Methodology of the Social Sciences*. Glencoe: Free Press
Westergaard, J. 1972. 'Sociology: the myth of classlessness' in R. Blackburn (ed.) *Ideology in Social Science*, pp. 119–63. London: Fontana
Westergaard, J. & Resler, H. 1975. *Class in a Capitalist Society*. London: Heinemann
Westley, W. 1970. *Violence and the Police*. Cambridge, Mass.: M.I.T. Press
Whitaker, B. 1964. *The Police*. London: Penguin
Williams, W. M. (ed.) 1974. *Occupational Choice*. London: Allen & Unwin
Wilson, J. Q. 1968. *Varieties of Police Behaviour*. Cambridge, Mass.: Harvard University Press
Woodward, J. 1958. *Management and Technology*. London: H.M.S.O.
Wright, E. O. 1976. 'Contradictory class locations', *New Left Review*, no. 98 (July–August), pp. 3–41
Young, J. 1971. 'The role of the police as amplifiers of deviancy' in S. Cohen (ed.) *Images of Deviance*, pp. 27–61. London: Penguin

Index

action frame of reference, 158, 168–71, 236
Aitken, Jonathan, M.P., 38
Allen, V. L., 23
amalgamation of police forces, 49, 53, 130–2
  policemen's attitudes to, 75, 130–2
Angry Brigade, 60–1
Area constable, 74, 247, 265
Armstrong, P., 141
Association of Chief Police Officers, 30, 44, 51–2, 251
Association of Scientific, Technical and Managerial Staff, 42

Bain, G. S., 4, 140
Banton, M., 4, 53, 214, 227, 268–9
Bayley, D. H., 157
Bechhofer, F., 158–9, 168–9, 171, 185, 217–18, 263, 274
Becker, H. S., 3
Belson, W. A., 73
Berkley, G. E., 7
Beynon, H., 85, 114–15, 159, 169, 236
Blackburn, R., 274
Blackburn, R. M., 4, 9, 94, 103–4, 159, 169
Blauner, R., 168, 171–3
'blue-flu,' 34, 36, 107
Bopp, W. J., 34, 157
Bowes, S., 8
Box, S., 219
Briar, S., 219
Bulmer, M., 94
Bunyan, T., 8
bureaucratic orientation to work, 4, 169, 171, 217–18, 263–4
Burpo, J. H., 5, 34, 107
Butler, D., 141

Cain, M. E., 3, 4, 10, 149, 189–90, 227
Callaghan, James, 31–2, 34, 36, 43–4
Campaign for Nuclear Disarmament, 126
capital punishment, 7, 46, 77–80, 92, 242–3

Capune, W. G., 34
Caradog-Jones, D., 173
Carr, Robert, 61, 80, 139
Carte, E. H., 202
Carte, G. E., 202
Centre for Research on Criminal Justice, 8–9
Chapman, B., 202
Chapman, D., 219
Chapman, S. G., 7
Chief Constable (of local force)
  and discipline, 90–1, 95, 246
  and local Federation, 72–3, 85–7, 121–2, 130–2, 260
  and policing, 71
  as decision-making authority, 85–7, 118–19, 251, 260
  in relation to other ranks, 87, 99, 102
  involvement in the research, 10–12, 219
  selection of, 130–2
Chief Constables
  and discipline, 72
  and Police Council, 52–3
  and Police Federation, 27, 44, 46, 50, 54, 27–8, 85
  and police unionism, 21
  and policing, 37, 46, 139
  and political control of police, 53, 202
  in relation to other ranks, 111, 194
C.I.D. (Criminal Investigation Department)
  alienation from Police Federation, 68, 70, 93, 134–5
  and Federation representative structure, 49–50, 134
  and Freemasons, 199
  and promotion, 201
  as part of sample, 12–13
  attitude to work, 230, 236–7
  autonomy of, 192
  disciplinarian attitude, 70, 162, 186, 192
  effect of work on private life, 210, 212
  grievances of, 176, 179

C.I.D. (Criminal Investigation Department)—*contd.*
image of police force as a work organisation, 96–7
opposition to police unionisation, 106
social origins of, 150, 155, 162, 237
civil liberties, 3, 77–81, 222–4, 257
class consciousness, 9, 11, 94–5, 213, 219–20, 273–4
class images of society, 94–5, 219–20
class structure, ix, 8–9, 11, 45, 149–50, 152–4, 158, 173, 219–20
Cliff, T., 8
Coates, K., 141
Collator, 189, 237–8
Commissioner of the Metropolitan Police, 21–3, 51–2, 154, 214, 251
Commissioner of the City of London Police, 21–2
communists, *see* radicals
complaints against the police, 46, 77, 79, 88–90, 124, 187–8, 219, 222, 224, 276
Conservative Party
and police pay, 36, 42–3, 45, 60–1, 126, 267–8, 275–6
and police unionism, 38–9, 45, 267–8
and trade unions, 126, 138–9, 241, 258
on law and order, 42, 61, 80
conservative view of the police, *see under* social theories of the police
conspiracy charges, 139
courts, police view of, 46–7, 221–2, 242, 245
crime
and police pay, 32, 37, 60
and police role, 1, 109–10, 176, 213–16, 218, 228–53 *passim*
police view of, 34, 45–9, 79–80, 215–16, 219–26, 242–3, 248
punishments for, 45–6, 77, 220–3, 225, 242–3, 245, 250, 276
criminology, 3
Critchley, T. A., 53, 149
crowd control, 3, 6, 34, 36–7, 71, 116–17, 188, 224, 257
Cumming, E., 214
Cumming, I., 214

democratisation of police, 7–8, 21–2, 257
Desborough Committee, 24–7, 30
discipline, *see under* police
discretion, *see under* police
Dixon, P.C. George, 229
Dog section, 49, 106, 117–18, 143, 223
domestic disputes, 177, 214–15, 244–5

easing behaviour, 189–92, 227
Edell, L., 214
Ellis, V., 4
Evans, P., 214

false consciousness, 9, 258–9, 274
F.B.I. (Federal Bureau of Investigation), 5, 202
Feuille, P., 7, 34
Fixed Points system, 187, 189
Foot, Michael, 275
football matches, problems of policing, 71, 86, 117, 224
Freemasons, 197, 199, 239–41, 249
Frost, David, 74

Gale, Reg., 73–4, 251
Gammage, A. Z., 34
Goldthorpe, J. H., 158–9, 168–9, 171, 185, 217–18, 263, 274
Goodrich, C. L., 114

Hall, J., 173
Halpern, S., 34
Harris, R. N., 159
Hayes, Jack, 21–2
Heath, Edward, 35–7, 126, 266
Holmes, Sherlock, 219
Home Office
and control of police forces, 37, 53, 99, 109, 139, 176, 187
and police pay, 60
and police unionisation, 11, 21, 111
and the Police Federation, 27, 33, 35, 54
and the research, 10–11, 15–16, 57, 219
on the Police Council, 30, 51

ideal-types, 169–70, 233–6
Industrial Relations Act 1971, 35, 37, 124, 138–40
instrumental orientation to work, 5, 159–60, 162–7, 169–70, 208, 213, 229–30, 237–8, 241, 267
International Association of Chiefs of Police, 7
I.R.A. (Irish Republican Army), 38, 60, 128

Jardine, James, 44
Jenkins, Clive, 42, 63
Jenkins, Roy, 33, 39, 45, 61, 164
job satisfaction
measurement of, 171–84, 228–53 *passim*, 262–3
sources of, 174–84, 201, 215–18, 262–5

Johnson, T. J., 203
Joint Branch Board
  and 'law and order' campaign, 46,
    221
  and the members, 136
  and the research, 10–11
  constitution of, 26, 50
  divisions in, 123–33
  work of, 69, 85–6, 121, 123–33
Joint Central Committee
  and police unionisation, 35, 275
  and the local branches, 130, 132
  and the members, 136–7
  and the research, 10–11
  constitution of, 51
  in early years of Federation, 26–9
Joseph, Sir Keith, 38
Judge, Anthony, 20, 22–3, 25, 27–9, 51,
    158, 182, 194
Juris, H. A., 7, 34

Kavanagh v. *Hiscock*, 139
Kempster, John, 20–1

labelling theory, 3
Labour Party
  and law and order, 46, 275–6
  and local politics, 125
  and picketing, 139–40
  and police pay, 33–4, 42–3, 61, 126,
    267–8, 274–6
  and police unionisation, 8, 22, 25,
    38–9, 42–3, 275
  and the Police Federation, 36
Labour Research, 8, 149, 152
Lambert, J., 3, 225
Lane, T., 138
Laurie, P., 82
law, police view of, 34–5, 45–9, 76–81,
    204–5, 207, 221–3, 226, 245
'law and order' campaign, 7, 35, 46–9,
    77, 214, 221, 258, 260, 266, 275
legislation, *see under* Police Federation
Lemert, E., 3
Levi, M., 34
Lewis, Arthur, M.P., 43
liberal view of police, *see under* social
    theories of the police
Lipset, S. M., 157
Litterick, Tom, M.P., 38–9
Lloyd-George, David, 22–5, 29
Lockwood, D., 4, 9, 94, 158–9, 168–9,
    171, 185, 217–18, 263, 274

McNamara, J. H., 157
Macready, General Sir Nevil, 23–6
Male, Les, 40, 46, 48
man-management, *see under* police:
    discipline and supervision

Man-Management Survey, 10, 57, 152–
    3, 155, 158–9, 214
Mann, M., 9, 273–4
Mark, Sir Robert, 74, 154, 214, 231,
    251
Marshall, G., 53
Martin, J. P., 21, 29–30, 32, 181
Martucci, Joe, 41
Marx, K., 171
Marxist theories of the police, 275; *see
    also under* social theories of the
    police: radical
Mates, Michael, M.P., 39
Maude, Angus, M.P., 42
Maudling, Reginald, M.P., 77, 80
Mayne, Richard, 213
media, police treatment by, 13, 73–4,
    92
Mendelsohn, H. A., 157
methodology, 9–17, 219
Metropolitan Police, 10, 19–25, 28, 31,
    37, 42, 51–2, 129, 139, 154, 156,
    177, 275
military model of policing, 5–7, 21, 111,
    161, 186–8, 191, 251, 257
Millerson, G., 94
Moran, M., 114
Morrison, Herbert, 29
Mounted police, 49, 106, 143, 176–7

National Council for Civil Liberties,
    222–4
National Union of Police and Prison
    Officers, 19–26, 34, 258
Naylor, T., 161, 214
Nichols, T., 141, 236
Niederhoffer, A., 157, 203
Nott-Bower, Sir William, 21

Oaksey Committee, 30–1, 51
occupational choice, 158; *see also*
    policemen: reasons for joining
occupational community, 208–13, 218,
    263
occupational culture, 226–7
orientation to work, 5, 157–218, 236,
    261–4; *see also* bureaucratic orien-
    tation *and* instrumental orientation

Pamplin, Dick, 74
panda driver, 189–90, 241
pay, *see under* police
'permissive society', 46–8, 77, 79–80,
    221–3, 275–6
picketing
  police control of, 4, 36–7, 112, 138–
    40, 259
  policemen's attitudes to, 142–4, 224,
    241, 261

Picton-Davies, G., 22–3, **28**
Piliavin, I., 219
Platt, J., 158–9, 168–9, 171, 185, 217–18, 263, 274
Police (Monthly journal of the Police Federation), 35–8, 40–1, 45–8, 51, 75, 138, 229
police
    authorities: and control of police force, 53, 99, 121–2, 130–1, 260; and Police Federation, 27–9, 57, 67, 121–2; attitude to police unionisation, 21–3; on Police Council, 26, 28, 30, 40–1, 51–2; police attitude to, 121–2, 260; reform of, 53, 268–9; types of, 52–3
    cadets, 141, 152–4, 156–7, 262, 266
    conditions of service: and job satisfaction, 175, 178–9, 181–3, 262–3; before 1918 strike, 21; effects of Federation on, 68–93; in 1970s, 39
    discipline: and Police Federation, 26, 28, 63, 69–71, 85, 88–92, 124; and police role, ix, 6–7, 39, 63, 110, 119, 161, 187–93, 257; and police unionisation, 20–1, 39, 193–4; changes in, 69–71, 174, 181, 187–93, 262–3; code, 71–2, 88, 187, 211–12; policemen's views on 69–71, 89–92, 174, 181, 185–94, 262–3; responsibility for, 53, 72, 88, 92, 187, 189–90, 204; system of, 20–1, 88–92, 187–91
    discretion, 3, 108–9, 140, 188, 204, 209, 211–12, 242
    efficiency, 82–7, 116–19
    manpower, 27, 34, 37–9, 60, 164, 190, 258, 265–7
    masculinity, 68, 161, 179, 211–12
    militancy: examples of, 5, 21–5, 34–6, 70, 87, 107–9; policemen's attitude to, 103–7, 125, 260; recent growth of, 4, 39–45, 266–8, 273–6
    oath of office, 62–3, 110–11
    overtime, 39, 66–7
    pay: determinants of, 27, 32, 35–9, 42, 45, 60–1, 65–7, 258, 266–8, 274–6; disputes over, 21, 29–45, 113, 258, 266–8, 273–6; level of, 21, 27, 29–34, 36–45, 65, 237, 258, 266–8; policemen's attitudes to, 60–1, 65–7, 159–60, 162–3, 165, 174, 178–9, 181–3, 207, 217, 237–8
    political control of, 8, 32, 52–3, 202
    powers, 77–81, 139, 206, 220, 222–3
    professionalisation, 154, 202–8, 231–2, 250–3, 262–3, 265–6
    promotion system: policemen's attitude to, 178, 180–1, 195–202, 218, 228–53 *passim*, 263; working of, 28, 53, 154–7, 191, 194–5
    public image of, 73–4, 222–3, 226
    public relations: adversarial nature of, 175–6, 218, 227; and police industrial action, 108–9; anxiety about, 31–2; Federation role in, 46–8; in non-work life, 178–80, 209–13, 218; in work, 215, 238
    right to strike, 5, 6, 20–1, 27, 35, 39–45, 54, 62–4, 100, 103–7, 109–11, 127, 238, 260, 266–8, 273, 276
    right to work to rule, 87, 103–9, 184, 207, 238, 260
    role of: and police bargaining power, 60–2; and police unionisation, 4–9, 109–10, 257–8, 274–6; conservative character of, ix, 4, 45, 269, 274–6; debates about, 4, 6–9, 213–14, 219–20, 226–7, 257–8, 263; policemen's conception of, 109–10, 175–8, 213–18, 227–53 *passim*, 263–5, 269
    shift system, 67, 71, 178–9, 209, 212, 262
    solidarity, 209–10, 217–18, 227–53 *passim*
    strikes: Birmingham 1919, 25; Boston 1919, 5, 34; Detroit 1967, 5; Liverpool 1919, 5, 34; London 1872 and 1890, 19–20; London 1918–19, 5, 22–5, 28, 35, 38, 111, 258; Montreal 1969, 5, 109; Vallejo, California, 5
    supervision, 69–71, 85, 116–19, 142–3, 181, 183, 185–94, 262–3
    unionisation: correlates of rank-and-file support for, 97, 104–7, 124, 144–5, 166–7, 183–4, 193–4, 201–202, 207–8, 213, 217, 258–65, 275; debates about, 4–9, 38–9, 42, 257–8; growth of rank-and-file support for, 4, 19–25, 41–5, 258, 265–8, 273–6; reasons for rank-and-file attitudes to, 4, 42, 44–5, 60–4, 97–9, 103–13, 217–18, 228–37 *passim*, 258–60, 263–8, 274–6
    unions, ix, 4–9, 19–25, 34, 258
    wastage, 39, 174–82
Police Act 1919, 26–7, 43
Police Act 1964, 43, 49, 51–3, 82, 88, 124, 187
Police Act 1976, 276
Police Advisory Boards, 30, 52
Police College, Bramshill, 154, 194, 252
Police College, Hendon, 28
Police Council, 26, 28, 32

Police Council for Great Britain, 30–3, 36, 40–4, 51–2, 65, 266, 273

Police Federation
and communications within the police force, 74–6, 92, 260
and conditions of service, 68–73, 92, 259
and discipline, 26, 69–71, 85, 88–93, 259
and efficiency, 26, 33, 82–7, 92–3, 116–19, 260
and legislation, 45–9, 76–81, 92, 258, 260
and pay, 57, 65–7, 92, 258–9
and public image of police, 73–4, 92, 260
and welfare, 26, 33, 81–4, 86, 92–3, 115, 120, 259
as control device, 25–7, 50, 106–7, 240, 258, 260
as pressure group, 7, 45–9, 76–7, 92
conflict between areas, 31, 37, 41, 57, 124, 129–30, 132, 136
conflict between ranks, 58–9, 95, 97, 103–7, 120, 126–8, 134–7, 259–61, 275
conflict between specialisms, 58–9, 75, 96, 106, 128, 134–7, 261
conflict within branch board, 126–33
history of, 19–49, 258
involvement in decision-making, 27, 32–3, 54, 71, 83, 85–7, 93, 115–22, 251, 258, 260, 266, 268–9
officials: relations with members, 7, 74–6, 123–37, 228–53 *passim*; types of, 7, 10–11, 26–8, 123–37, 199–200, 207, 232–3, 261
policemen's evaluation of, 57–93, 99–103, 258–60
policemen's involvement in, 49, 75–6, 123–6, 136–7, 261, 265
policemen's knowledge of, 74–6, 136–7
powers of: members' views on, 54, 57–93, 97–8, 103–13, 258–60, 266–268, 275–6; politicians' views on, 26–32, 38–45, 267–8
structure of, 26–32, 49–54, 75–6, 95–103, 260
unrepresentativeness of structure, 24, 26–7, 50, 75, 106–7, 123, 260
see also Joint Branch Board *and* Joint Central Committee

policemen
aspirations of, 152, 172–4, 180, 194–202, 217–18, 238, 261–3
class consciousness of, 8–9, 11, 213, 219–20, 258–9, 274–6
class position of, ix, 5, 8–9, 38, 45, 149–50, 152–5, 173, 207, 219–20, 274
conception of role, 175–6, 213–17, 258–9, 261–5, 268
differences between generations: in age of entry, 152–6; in assessing justice of promotion system, 198; in attitude to discipline, 187, 191–3, 267; in attitude to Federation, 125, 128, 136; in attitude to police unionisation, 266–7; in educational attainment, 155–6; in involvement in Federation, 128, 134; in orientation to work, 265–6; in previous experience, 152–6; in promotion chances, 194–5; in reasons for joining, 159–60, 164–6, 262
differences between ranks: in attitudes to promotion system, 195–6, 198–9; in defining efficiency, 85, 93; in evaluation of discipline, 92, 186–7, 263; in evaluation of Federation, 58–9, 259–60; in identification with Federation officials, 134–6, 261; in image of relations between ranks, 185; in involvement in Federation, 123, 136–7; in job satisfaction, 173–4; in knowledge of Federation, 136–7; in orientation to work, 233, 236; in reasons for joining, 165–6; in social background, 153–7, 237; in support for police unionisation, 97, 104–7, 259–60, 275; in support for professional association, 95–6; in view of police role, 214; on branch board, 26–7, 50–1, 127–8; on Federation involvement in decision-making, 116, 260; on Joint Central Committee, 26–7, 50–1; on Metropolitan Representative Boards, 24, 26; on relation between work and non-work life, 210; roles in Unit Beat policing, 189–92; statistical significance of, 14
differences between specialisms: in evaluation of conditions, 68, 70; in evaluation of discipline, 186–7, 263; in evaluation of Federation, 58–9; in identification with Federation officials, 134–6, 261; in job satisfaction, 173–4, 176–7; in orientation to work, 233, 236; in reasons for joining, 165–6; in social background, 154–7, 237, 261; in support for police unionisation, 96–7, 106–7; on branch board,

differences between specialisms—*contd.*
128; on relation between work and
non-work life, 210, 212; roles in
Unit Beat policing, 189–92
educational background of, 150–2,
154–7, 162–3, 181, 199–200, 204,
206–7, 237, 250, 261–2
image of relationship between ranks
of, 95–103, 116–20, 184–6, 213,
228–53 *passim*, 263
isolation of, 4–5, 8, 38, 72, 125, 127,
149–50, 152–4, 179–80, 189, 209–
13, 217–18, 226–7, 241, 246–7,
263–4, 268–9
job security of, 27, 84, 158–60, 162–
4, 180–1, 262
military experience of, 152–4, 156,
161
moral responsibility of, 5–6, 62–4,
100–1, 110, 204–6, 249, 258, 267
political views of, ix, 7–9, 11, 34, 45–
9, 60–2, 111–12, 124–6, 141–4,
219–20, 226–7, 230, 232, 238, 253,
257–8, 261, 263–4, 268–9, 274–6
reasons for joining, 157–67, 228–53
passim, 261
social mobility of, 150–2, 154, 261–2
social origins of, 5, 149–57, 162, 199,
207, 237, 261–2
status of, 4, 21, 30, 32–3, 73–4, 110,
162–3, 173, 204, 206–9, 246, 262–3
suspiciousness of, 210–11, 227
types of: the 'bobby', 228–9, 237–9,
264–6; the 'Federation activist',
232–3, 265–6; the 'new centurion',
230, 241–7, 264–5; the 'professional', 231–2, 250–3, 265–6; the
'social worker', 230–1, 247–50,
264–5; the 'uniform carrier', 229–
30, 239–41, 264
work and private life of, 71–3, 174,
178–9, 187, 193, 201, 206, 209–13,
218, 227–53 *passim*, 263
Police Review, 20, 121, 273
policewomen, 13, 49, 96, 106
politicians, police view of, 36, 39, 42,
46–8, 60–3, 73, 77–80, 121–2,
125–6, 220–1, 245, 273, 275–6
Poulantzas, N., 274
Powell, Enoch, 48, 126
Prandy, K., 4, 94, 103–4
Price, R. J., 140
promotion system, *see under* police
professional associations, 92, 94–103,
125, 232, 260, 266
professionalisation of police, *see under*
police
professions, 203–8

punishment, *see under* crime

race, police views on, 48, 219, 225–6
radicals
among the police, 22–3, 39, 125–7,
135, 240, 275
police view of, 34–5, 45–8, 77, 98,
112, 141–4, 240, 275–6
radical view of police, *see under* social
theories of the police
Ramsay, H., 185
ranks, *see* policemen: differences between ranks
Rees, Merlyn, 42–3, 273
Resler, H., 149, 152, 154
Reynolds, G. W., 20, 22–3, 25, 29
role of police *see* police *and* policemen
Rowan, Sir Charles, 213
Royal Commission on the Police 1960,
31–2, 73, 149, 213–14
Rubinstein, J., 188
Ruchelman, L., 34
Russell, K., 219
Russian Revolution 1917, 22, 38, 258

Sachs, S. L., 34
Salaman, G., 208, 212–13
sampling, 11–14
Scargill, Arthur, 138
Shaw, M., 219
'Shrewsbury 24', 139
Silver, A., 5
Skolnick, J., 3, 8, 34, 82, 157, 227
Smuts, General, 22–3
social change, police view of, 34–5, 45–
9, 77–80, 187, 191–3, 212, 220–6,
275–6
social mobility, *see under* policemen
social origins, *see under* policemen
social theories of the police
conservative, 6–7, 257
liberal, 7–9, 257
radical, 8–9, 257–8
social work/service role of the police,
161–2, 165, 182–3, 204–5, 213–17,
230–1, 247–50, 263–5
sociology
of occupations, 3–4, 203–4
of the police, 3–4, 203–4
Spackman, P.C. W., 24
Special Constabulary, 38, 244
status system, 94, 173, 219–20
Stevenson, Judge Melford, 48
Stewart, A., 104
Stinchcombe, A., 219
Stokes, D., 141
students, police view of, 15, 35, 72, 144,
245

Superintendents' Association, 30, 44, 46, 52, 101
supervision, *see under* police
Syme, John, 20–1

Taylor, I., 3, 6
Thiel, P.C. Tommy, 22–3
Topham, T., 141
T.U.C. (Trades Union Congress), police affiliation with
  police attitudes to, 21–2, 41–4, 103–6, 111–12, 238, 260–1, 275
  politicians' attitudes to, 8, 21–3, 27, 30–1, 38–9, 42–4, 54
Trade Union and Industrial Relations Act 1974, 44
trade-union consciousness, ix, 9, 44–5, 274–5
trade unions
  policemen's attitude to, 4, 8–9, 21–2, 97–8, 100–3, 111–12, 124, 138–45, 219, 228–53 *passim*, 261, 274–5
  policemen's experience of: as members, 112, 140–1, 152, 261; controlling disputes, 4, 36–7, 60, 138–45; organisational links with, 21–3, 25, 42, 46–7
traffic
  department, 49, 86, 96, 106
  police control of, 73–4, 78–9, 90–1, 117, 214
Thatcher, Margaret, 276
Thomas, W. I., 236
Trenchard, Lord, 28, 154

'uniform carriers', 84, 164, 180–1, 190, 200, 229–30, 236, 239–41, 264–5
unionateness, 9, 103–4, 111, 184, 193
union character, 94–5, 184, 234–5
Unit Beat policing, 33, 61, 181, 187, 189–92, 226, 262, 265–6

violence, police views on, 34, 45–8, 60, 109, 223–5, 227, 250

Wainwright, J., 154
Walton, P., 3, 6
Wambaugh, J., 230
wastage, *see under* police
Watch Committee, 52–3, 99, 121–2, 177; *see also* police authorities
Weber, M., 9, 168, 170, 233
Westergaard, J., 149, 152, 154, 219
Westley, W., 3, 227
Whitaker, B., 159
Williams, W. M., 158
Williamson, W., 219
Willink, Sir Henry, 32
Wilson, G., 21, 29–30, 32, 181
Wilson, Harold, 126
Wilson, J. Q., 177, 188
Woodward, J., 168
workers' control, 114–16, 118
Wright, E. O., 45, 274

Young, J., 3, 6, 219

'Z-Cars', 229